British Trade Unions, the Labour Party, and Israel's Histadrut

Ronnie Fraser

British Trade Unions, the Labour Party, and Israel's Histadrut

palgrave
macmillan

Ronnie Fraser
London, UK

ISBN 978-3-030-86813-0 ISBN 978-3-030-86814-7 (eBook)
https://doi.org/10.1007/978-3-030-86814-7

This Palgrave Macmillan imprint is published by the registered company Springer Nature Switzerland AG.
The registered company address is: Gewerbestrasse 11, 6330 Cham, Switzerland

To the memory of my grandparents, Julius and Sara Frenkel,
who perished in the Holocaust

Acknowledgements

One never knows what life has in store, and no one foresaw that in 1998 when I left a career in engineering to become a mathematics lecturer that I would one day submit a PhD history thesis which has formed the basis for this book.

I first met the late Professor David Cesarani in 2004 at Southampton University, who from then on believed I was capable of this work. His passing in 2015 was for me an immeasurable loss, as I will always be grateful for his support, encouragement, plain talking, understanding and advice.

I also have to acknowledge the help which I received from Emily Russell and her team at Palgrave, especially as this is my first book. I would like to thank all the staff at all the archives I visited for all their help, in particular Darren Treadwell at the Peoples' History Museum, Manchester and the archivists at the National Archives at Kew, and the Modern Records Centre at Warwick University. Finally I have to thank Lotem Kaizer whose enthusiasm and help were unbounded.

I would like to thank my mother, my children and my grandchildren as well as my late father for their love and support as well as giving me the time and space to complete this work.

The one person, however, who has been with me on this life-changing journey over the last 17 years is my best friend, my wife Lola. Without her help, encouragement, support, and for being my editor none of this would have been possible. I will always be indebted to her for suggesting that I undertook this research especially as she is the historian in the family.

July 2021 Ronnie Fraser

Contents

Abbreviations

ACTT	Association of Cinematograph, Television and Allied Technicians
AEEU	Amalgamated Engineering and Electrical Union
AEU	Amalgamated Engineering Union
AFL	American Federation of Labor (USA)
AFL-CIO	American Federation of Labor and Congress of Industrial Organisations
AFPW	Arab Federation of Petroleum Workers
ASLEF	Associated Society of Locomotive Engineers and Firemen
ASTMS	Association of Scientific, Technical and Managerial Staffs
AUCCTU	All-Union Central Council of Trade Unions (Russia)
AUEW	Amalgamated Union of Engineering Workers
AUT	Association of University Teachers
BDS	Boycotts, Divestments and Sanctions movement
BOD	Board of Deputies of British Jews
BUF	British Union of Fascists
CAABU	Council for the Advancement of Arab-British Understanding
CBI	Confederation of British Industry
CGT-FO	Confédération Générale du travail-Force Ouvrière (France)
CIO	Congress of Industrial Organisations (USA)
CO	Colonial Office
COSATU	Congress of South African Trade Unions
CPGB	Communist Party of Great Britain
CPSA	Civil and Public Services Association
CST	Community Security Trust
CTAL	Confederación Inter-Americana de Trabajadores (Mexico)

CWU	Communication Workers Union
DEP	Department of Employment and Productivity
DGB	Deutscher Gewerkschaftsbund (Germany)
EB	Executive Bureau of the ICFTU
EETPU	Electrical, Electronic, Telecommunication and Plumbing Union
EFL	Egyptian Federation of Labour
EHRC	Equality and Human Rights Commission
ETU	Electrical Trades Union
ETUC	European Trade Union Confederation
EUMC	European Monitoring Centre on Racism and Xenophobia
FAU	Federation of Arab Trade Unions
FBU	Fire Brigades Union
FCO	Foreign and Commonwealth Office
FO	Foreign Office
FPTU	Federation of Petroleum Trade Unions (Lebanon)
GFPTU	General Federation of Palestinian Trade Unions
GFTU	General Federation of Trade Unions
GMB	General, Municipal, Boilermakers' and Allied Trade Union
GMWU	General and Municipal Workers Union
Histadrut	Federation of Hebrew Workers in the Land of Israel
ICATU	International Confederation of Arab Trade Unions
ICFTU	International Confederation of Free Trade Unions
IDF	Israel Defence Force
IFTU	International Federation of Trade Unions
IHRA	International Holocaust Remembrance Alliance
ILO	International Labour Organisation
IMG	International Marxist Group
Irgun	Jewish Defence Organisation (Irgun Zvai Leumi)
IS	International Socialists
ISTC	Iron and Steel Trades Confederation
ITF	International Transport Federation
ITS	International Transport Secretariat
ITUC	International Trade Union Confederation
JLM	Jewish Labour Movement
JTA	Jewish Telegraphic Agency
LEHI	Fighters for the Freedom of Israel
LFI	Labour Friends of Israel
LMEC	Labour Middle East Council
LP	British Labour Party
MAB	Muslim Association of Britain
Mapai	Israel Labour Party

Mapam	Mifleget ha-Po'alim ha-Me'uhe det—The United Workers' Party (Israel)
MCF	Movement for Colonial Freedom
MOL	Ministry of Labour
MSF	Manufacturing, Science and Finance Union
NALGO	National Association of Local Government Officers
NATFHE	National Union
NCL	National Council of Labour
NEU	National Education Union
NGA	National Graphical Association
NJC	National Jewish Committee
NUJ	National Union of Journalists
NUM	National Union of Mineworkers
NUPE	National Union of Public Employees
NUR	National Union of Railwaymen
NUT	National Union of Teachers
NVV	Nederlands Verbond van Vakverenigingen (Holland)
OLCC	Overseas Labour Consultative Committee
PACBI	Palestinian Campaign for an Academic and Cultural Boycott of Israel
PAWS	Palestine Arab Workers Society
PCS	Public Commercial Services Union
PGFTU	Palestinian General Confederation of Trade Unions
PLL	Palestine Labour League
PLO	Palestine Liberation Organisation
PLPC	Palestine Labour Political Committee
POEU	Post Office Engineering Union
PSC	Palestine Solidarity Campaign
PSI	Public Services International
PTUF	Palestine Trade Unions Federation
RMT	National Union of Rail, Maritime and Transport Workers
SOGAT82	Society of Graphical and Allied Trades
STUC	Scottish Trades Union Congress
SWP	Socialist Workers Party
TASS	Technical, Administrative and Supervisory Section
TGWU	Transport and General Workers Union
the 35s	British Women's Campaign for Soviet Jewry
TSSA	Transport Salaried Staffs' Association
TUC	Trades Union Congress
TUFI	Trade Union Friends of Israel
TUFP	Trade Union Friends of Palestine
UAR	United Arab Republic

UCATT	Union of Construction, Allied Trades and Technicians
UCU	University and College Lecturers Union
UGTT	Union Générale Tunisienne du Travail (Tunisia)
UKPC	UK Palestine Coordination
UN	United Nations
UNISON	Public Services Union
UNSCOP	UN Special Committee on Palestine
USDAW	Union of Shop, Distributive and Allied Workers
WFTU	World Federation of Trade Unions
WZO	World Zionist Organisation

CHAPTER 1

Introduction

This is the story of the relationship between two international trade union centres, the British Trade Union Congress (TUC) and the Israeli Histadrut, who first made contact with each other in the 1920s. But the narrative also reflects the attitudes of the British labour movement towards the persecution of the Jews, Jewish refugees, antisemitism, Zionism, the right of the Jews to establish their own homeland in Palestine, the State of Israel and the Israel-Palestine conflict. From the 1960s onwards the Israel-Palestine conflict has become an increasingly contentious and divisive issue for the trade unions, and their attitude has changed over the years to become what we see today, strong criticism of Israel and support for the issue of Palestine.

Palestine, which is defined as the land between the Mediterranean Sea and the River Jordan, was the birthplace of Judaism and Christianity. Before the First World War Palestine was part of the Turkish Empire and Britain was granted a mandate for Palestine by the League of Nations at the San Remo Conference in 1920. Jews have lived in Palestine since biblical times and during the British mandate they called themselves Palestinian Jews. For the avoidance of confusion the terms using the word 'Palestine' such as the Palestine labour movement or the Palestine Labour Party refer to Jewish organisations which were in existence during the period of the British mandate for Palestine.

Both the TUC and the Histadrut are key members of their respective national labour movements, but this is where the similarity ends. The

R. Fraser, *British Trade Unions, the Labour Party, and Israel's Histadrut*, https://doi.org/10.1007/978-3-030-86814-7_1

Histadrut was established in 1920 by the Palestine labour movement with the dual role of looking after the interests of the Jewish workers of Palestine and a political role with overall responsibility for the advancement of political Zionism, the establishment of a Jewish homeland in Palestine, with the building of the country to take precedence over all other issues. As a result the Histadrut was never a traditional trade union body in the European sense as it was also an employer providing jobs, homes, education, healthcare, pensions and welfare for its members. During the mandate period the Histadrut was the 'government in waiting' responsible for running the Jewish community, the Yishuv, in Palestine. By the 1970s it was the second largest employer in Israel after the government. It was only in 1990s by, which time it had been divested of its remaining industrial and commercial interests, that the Histadrut was able to concentrate solely on core trade union matters.

The TUC was established in 1868 as the umbrella body to defend and promote the interests of the British trade union movement. The Labour Party was formed in 1900 by the TUC as the political wing of the trade union movement in order to protect the interests of the working class in Parliament. It was the changes in society brought about by the First World War that were responsible for national recognition by the government as the representative body for the labour movement and for transforming it from a purely domestic body to one with an international presence. The TUC has always seen its international role as to support the development of industrial democracy throughout the developed world either by direct contact with trade union centres or through the international trade union movement.

As a member of the Israeli government from 1948 until 1977, political lobbying on behalf of the State of Israel was a key part of the Histadrut's international role especially within the international trade union movement. Another difference between the Histadrut and the TUC was that the TUC rarely issued public statements supporting British government policy relating to the Palestine mandate or the State of Israel, preferring instead to either refer requests for support on political issues to the Labour Party or to adopt the statements and policies of international bodies such as the International Confederation of Trade Unions (ICFTU).

The British labour movement's support for a Jewish homeland in Palestine did not come about because they showed solidarity with the Histadrut, their socialist 'brothers' in Palestine, but because of their backing of Labour's war aims and the Balfour Declaration in 1917, seven years before the TUC's first contact with the Histadrut in 1924.

While there may have been sympathy from the 1880s onwards for Jewish suffering and antisemitism in the pogroms in Russia, the British labour movement was reluctant initially to support the plan for a Jewish homeland in Palestine. The driving forces in the labour movement at this time were the trade unions, and the only domestic Jewish issue that was of interest to them was Jewish immigration to Britain from 1875 onwards and their employment in the 'sweating trades' which the unions frequently claimed put British jobs at risk. It was only towards the end of the First World War that their attitude started to change; consequently the links between the British labour movement and Zionism were based not on socialist ideology but instead on support for Jewish emancipation and nationhood.

The Histadrut's long relationship with the TUC began once Britain's Palestine mandate was in place. Part of the Palestine labour movement's strategy in order to create an independent Jewish state in Palestine was to build a relationship with the Labour Party and the TUC by means of regular visits to London by representatives of the Histadrut and the Palestine Labour Party (Mapai). During the 1920s and 1930s several British Labour Party Members of Parliament and trade union leaders went to Palestine and were impressed with the work of the socialist Kibbutz movement. Dov Hoz came to London initially in 1928 as the Histadrut's representative in order to build relations with the Labour Party, the TUC and the government. His outstanding efforts over the following 12 years promoting the aims of the Palestinian Jews and building a personal relationship with Ernest Bevin are largely unrecognised outside Israel.

The British dominance in the Middle East after the First World War in Egypt, Palestine, Sudan and Iraq has been described as its 'informal empire'. It's authority in the region was not based on formal rule but rather on political influence and military power. There were five essential functions of their 'informal empire': to preserve Britain's prestige and status in the world, to secure its privileged position with regard to the United States, to contain the spread of communism, to protect British assets and to provide stability for sterling.[1] The TUC willingly assisted the Labour government from 1945 onwards in its efforts to maintain and rebuild Britain's prestige and status in the region often at the expense of the Histadrut and the Israelis. As the representative of one of the four great powers and of the mother country in the British Empire, the TUC became by default a key player in the international labour movement, but because it never had the resources to compete 'on the ground' with either their Soviet or American counterparts it was unable to fulfil all its obligations. Nor was it able to match what the Histadrut offered trade unionists in the newly independent countries in Africa and Asia during the 1960s and 1970s.

The Histadrut courted both the American and British labour movements from the 1920s onwards, and the contrast between how the American trade unions and their British counterparts responded is startling. Whereas the Americans played an important role in both the development and establishment of a Jewish state in Palestine, the same cannot be said of the TUC. This was because the TUC regarded the Histadrut as a colonial trade union movement and saw their primary role as one of assisting the Jews of Palestine in improving workers' pay and conditions and not the promotion of political developments in Palestine which they regarded as the role of the Labour Party.

American trade union support for the Histadrut both at home and at the international labour and trade union organisations has been unwavering since the 1920s. This has included issuing statements of support for Israel and the Histadrut at times of crisis, lobbying the American president on behalf of Israel, sending delegations to Israel and providing financial support.

By comparison with the Americans, the TUC can only once be considered an enthusiastic supporter of the Histadrut; this 'golden' period in relations was in the 1960s when George Woodcock was TUC general secretary and lasted until the 1970s. Their relationship changed fundamentally after the creation of the State of Israel in 1948 and was affected by the attitude of the TUC general secretaries towards Israel and the Histadrut, the TUC's relationship with the Foreign Office, the context of the international trade union movement, Cold War politics, Britain's post-war role in the Middle East, and the sometimes surprising approach of individual trade union leaders such as Frank Cousins and Jack Jones. Whereas in 1917 the TUC supported the Jews of Palestine, just over 100 years later the opposite is true, and the TUC now gives outright support to the Palestinian cause with only minimal contact with the Histadrut.

The wars between Israel and the Arab states between 1948 and 1982 also played a part, as well as the influence of the political activists on the Far Left whose support since the 1980s for Palestinian rights and statehood has led to the TUC being a major supporter of the international Boycott, Divestments and Sanctions (BDS) campaign directed at Israel.

The Labour Party by comparison has been one of Israel's staunchest supporters throughout the last 100 years apart from 1945 to 1950 and from 2015 to 2019 when the party was under the leadership of Jeremy Corbyn. Yet the majority of the literature available on the foreign policy of the Attlee Labour government either ignores the trade union movement completely or only mentions it with reference to Bevin because it is assumed that the policies of both the Labour Party and the TUC shared common ground on Palestine. But Bevin's interest in foreign affairs began in the early 1930s, long before he became foreign secretary. In 1929 Dov Hoz persuaded him to intervene with the Labour government on behalf of the Jewish voters in the Whitechapel by-election to reassure them that the government had no intention of altering the terms of the Palestine mandate or stopping Jewish immigration.

As the leading trade unionist of his generation Bevin's opposition to dictatorships whether they were fascist or communist ensured that the trade union movement influenced Labour's foreign policy. As chairman of the TUC General Council from 1936, he along with Hugh Dalton, the chairman of the National Executive of the Labour Party, took control of the National Council of Labour (NCL)[2] in order to change Labour's views on foreign policy and defence in the build-up to the Second World War. In 1937, under his tenure as TUC president, the TUC formed its own Colonial Advisory Committee to lobby government, in order to prevent colonies falling under influence of communism.

As foreign secretary in the post-war Attlee government Bevin put aside his pre-war warm feelings towards the Jews because his priority was the execution of the government's Middle East policy, which was to maintain good relations with the Arab states in order to protect Britain's vital political and economic interests in the region. The Foreign Office was also concerned with the likely effect on Muslims in both the Middle East and India, still a British imperial possession, if Palestine became a Jewish state. It was in support of government policy that Bevin opposed not only the creation of a Jewish state and an Arab state in Palestine but also the unlimited immigration of Jewish refugees into Palestine.

This book is divided into seven chapters, Chap. 2 covers the early years from 1917 to 1948. The British labour movement's public support for Zionism did not begin with the Balfour Declaration but three months earlier with the publication of their *War Aims Memorandum* which set out a Socialist and Labour vision for the future once peace had been achieved, and included a section on the Jews and Palestine. The *War Aims Memorandum* may have been overshadowed by the Balfour Declaration, but it has a unique place in history of the Jews because the Labour Party was the first political party in Britain to declare their backing for the right of the Jewish people to establish a Jewish homeland in Palestine. How Labour was persuaded to embrace Zionism is one of the forgotten stories of World War One. It was achieved by the combined efforts of Chaim Weizmann, his fellow Zionists and the Jewish working classes.

Before the creation of the State of Israel in 1948, the Jewish community in Palestine (Yishuv) was managed by the Jewish Agency which looked after political affairs with the Histadrut responsible for its defence, economic and social development. In the 1920s David Ben-Gurion, then general secretary of the Histadrut, opened an office in London to build links with the Labour Party, the TUC and trade unions which was the beginning of a successful relationship with the Labour Party that has lasted over 100 years. At the same time Walter Citrine, the TUC general secretary decided that unless there was a trade union connection all political matters raised by the Histadrut were to be referred to the Labour Party. The consequence of his decision was that unlike their American counterparts, the TUC leadership were indifferent to the Jewish refugee crisis caused by the rise of Hitler in Germany during the late 1930s.

The Second World War was a key period when relations between the Histadrut and the TUC took on two different personas. The first dealt purely with trade union matters in Palestine and the second with the treatment of the Jews in Europe and in Palestine. The Jewish leadership in Palestine never doubted Labour's backing for a Jewish homeland but were shocked in 1945 when Bevin and the Labour government failed to deliver on their promises. They had trusted Bevin because he was the only trade union leader who had strongly identified himself with the Jews and Palestine. With the intensification of the Jewish insurgency in Palestine in 1946 which continued into 1947 the TUC was forced to defend the actions of the Labour government.

This chapter closes by discussing the lobbying by the Histadrut of the British, American and Soviet trade union movements at the World Federation of Trade Unions (WFTU) from 1945 onwards. This was at a time when the international labour movement was at its most influential in world politics and no more so than in Britain and in Palestine with both the TUC and the Histadrut being unashamedly used by British government and the Yishuv respectively to promote their respective national interests.

Chapter 3 discusses the TUC's years of indifference towards the Histadrut from 1948 to 1960. This chapter explains how TUC-Histadrut relations changed after independence and the Israelis limited success in cultivating new contacts within the British trade union movement. During the immediate post-war period the TUC was a powerful political body both at home and abroad which worked closely with the Labour government. Bevin and the Foreign Office used the TUC to counter Soviet attempts to infiltrate trade unions in the Middle East and Africa at the International Confederation of Trade Unions (ICFTU). The Histadrut continued to lobby the Soviet, American and British unions for support firstly at the WFTU which it left in 1950, and the ICFTU from 1953 onwards. The importance attached to the international labour movement by both the British and Israeli governments resulted in the appointment of a labour attaché to the British legation in Israel in 1949, and London being chosen by the Israeli government as their first embassy to have its own labour attaché.

Even when there was a change of government in Britain with the Conservatives coming to power in 1951, the TUC continued to follow Foreign Office advice and assisted in building British links with the Arab world at the expense of the Israelis. The role of the Histadrut as a member of the Israeli government was to assist in diplomatic efforts to make friends in the Third World to ensure Israel's survival.

The TUC view of the Suez crisis reflected the opposition to events by the unions, whose primary concern was the threat to British shipping and oil supplies with Israel hardly meriting a mention. After Suez, although Israel's relationship with Britain improved, the TUC continued to rebuff the Histadrut's attempts to rebuild links with them. The chapter concludes with an examination of the TUC's continuing support for the Foreign Office, the Histadrut's efforts to cultivate new friendships both with the TUC and the ICFTU, and the TUC's opposition to the Histadrut's international aid and training programmes for trade unionists in Africa.

Chapter 4 covers the 1960s and early 1970s which became the 'golden years' of the TUC's special relationship with the Histadrut. This turnaround was the result of a combination of factors which included the appointment of a new general secretary, George Woodcock, for the TUC, the opening of the Histadrut's European office in London and the interest in foreign affairs shown by Frank Cousins and his fellow union leaders on the political left. Cousins believed there was opportunity immediately after the Six-Day War for the international trade union movement to bring both sides in the conflict closer together with the aim of helping to find a peaceful settlement of the Israeli-Arab conflict. The TUC sent Cousins on fact-finding missions to Israel, Jordan and Egypt. His efforts reinforced relations with the Histadrut which resulted in the British Foreign Office being extremely worried that their closeness with the Histadrut would affect British interests in the Arab world. This chapter investigates how successful these missions were and why the TUC's reaction to the Six-Day War differed from the reactions of European and American trade unionists and the reaction of the ICFTU who were lobbied by both the Histadrut and Arab trade unions.

Once the euphoria of Israel's stunning victory and the reluctance of the Arabs to recognise and talk peace with Israel had passed, there was a re-evaluation of attitudes within the labour movement towards Arab-Israeli relations. This chapter investigates the rise of the Left in the party and the unions who questioned Labour's support for Israel and its effect on TUC policy. It also discusses how the TUC's attitude towards the Histadrut's international aid programme in Africa and how it dealt with the Arab boycott of Israel, the Mancroft affair and their reaction to Arab terrorism directed against Israel.

Chapter 5 covers the period 1973–1983 examining the change in the Labour movements' attitude to Israel, the 1973 Yom Kippur War, the Israeli Labour Party's final years in government, the effect on the TUC of the Helsinki human rights accords and the UN's 'Zionism is racism' resolution.

The decline in support for Israel within the labour movement and the move towards outright criticism of Israel were due to a numbers of factors including the Left's support for anti-colonialism and anti-imperialism policies which questioned Labour's traditional support for Israel and identified Israel with Britain's colonial past, and the retirement of the generation of MPs and activists for whom the establishment of the State of Israel and the plight of the Jews at the time of the Second World War had been important. Their replacements, mainly from the Left, saw support for the Palestinians and the PLO as more important than Labour's historical support of Israel.

The effectiveness of the Histadrut's connections and their lobbying ability with the TUC diminished during the 1970s after the TUC had turned its attention towards Europe and the rebuilding of its connections with the USSR and Eastern Europe. The Histadrut made a conscious decision to spend more time connecting with the European trade unions especially in Germany and Scandinavia rather than the TUC. A feature of this period was the success of the campaign for Jews to be allowed to leave the USSR, which eventually enabled large numbers of Soviet Jews to immigrate to Israel. The TUC's involvement in this campaign is discussed in this chapter.

The Helsinki accords of 1975 allowed the TUC more flexibility in its interpretation of human rights. From then on, the TUC ceased to insist on a trade connection and became much more political which opened the door for them to publicly support non-trade-union political issues which in turn led the successful landmark vote at the 1982 TUC Congress which condemned Israel's invasion of Lebanon and recognised the right of the Palestinian Arabs to self-determination and their own state. Although relations between the TUC and the Histadrut had been cool for long stretches of time, this vote by Congress marked the end of 20 years of support by the TUC for Israel and the Histadrut. It was the turning point for the British trade union movement and its relations with Israel and the Palestinians.

Chapter 6 covers the period from 1982 until 2021 and discusses the TUC's move away from Israel and the Histadrut and the consolidation of its support for the Palestinians. The international BDS campaign directed against Israel has, since 2002, dominated the discussion of the Israel-Palestine conflict within the unions and the TUC. The result has been very divisive as the rhetoric used by the Left has frequently crossed the line into antisemitism and by 2016 relations between the Histadrut and the TUC were almost non-existent. During this period the TUC and its member unions have regularly adopted resolutions containing anti-Israeli rhetoric with only limited disapproval of Palestinian terrorist activities. This has resulted in a generation of British left-wing trade union activists adopting conference motions whose only mention of Israel is in connection with its 'brutality' and 'oppression' of the Palestinian people.

Antisemitism became a major concern when Jeremy Corbyn was elected the leader of the Labour Party in 2015. His election was widely welcomed by left-wing trade union leaders and activists because it provided them with the opportunity to demonise Israel and use rhetoric which often was antisemitic. This chapter discusses the involvement of the unions in Labour's antisemitism crisis concluding with Labour's defeat in the 2019 general election.

Notes

1. Heinlein, *British government policy and decolonisation 1945–63*, p. 1 and pp. 291–294.
2. The NCL, which was established in the 1930s, attempted to coordinate the policies and actions of the TUC and Labour Party. It consisted of representatives from the TUC's General Council and the Executive Committees of the Labour Party and the Parliamentary Labour Party. As time went on, it became less effective, and by the 1960s, the NCL had become moribund.

CHAPTER 2

The Early Years

The Histadrut does not represent the interests of the wage earners in a stabilised country but endeavours to impress the stamp of labour on a country in the process of being built up. It is a colonising agency as well as a trade union alliance and where these two functions clash the building of the country takes precedence.... if any project seems not to be in the interests of Zionism as labour interprets them–it is flatly rejected. In other words the Histadrut is not only an expression of class interests but an instrument of Zionism as well. Its nationalism is just as genuine and strong as its socialist ideals.... The general aims of the Histadrut are clearly formulated in the programme adopted at its first convention in November 1920...[1]

On 2 November, 1917, the British government published the Balfour Declaration which expressed its support for the establishment in Palestine of a national home for the Jewish people. This recognition by a major power of the rights of the Jewish people to re-establish their national homeland was the first step on the road which eventually led to the creation of the State of Israel in 1948.

The British Labour Party as well as the trade union movement, their partners in the British labour movement, are usually both considered as being supportive of Zionism and the establishment of the Jewish national home in Palestine. The Labour Party in particular has on a considerable number of occasions since 1920 voiced its support through conference

R. Fraser, *British Trade Unions, the Labour Party, and Israel's Histadrut*, https://doi.org/10.1007/978-3-030-86814-7_2

resolutions and statements made by senior party leaders. It is often assumed that the British labour movement's support for Zionism began with the Balfour Declaration; however their interest in the Jewish question started earlier, not with the Labour Party, but with the trade union movement. How the British labour movement was persuaded to embrace Zionism is one of the forgotten stories of World War One. It was achieved not only by the efforts of Chaim Weizmann and his fellow Zionists but also by the hard work and determination of the Jewish working classes, the Jewish socialist group, Poale Zion and one Jewish trade union leader in particular, Moses Sclare.

The majority of Jewish immigrants from Russia and Poland who arrived in England from about 1880 onwards settled in major cities such as London, Manchester and Leeds and found employment primarily in certain trades such as the clothing trade, cabinet making, cigar making and boot and shoe manufacture. Many immigrants joined existing trade unions, occasionally forming Jewish branches in order to overcome language difficulties as most of the immigrants spoke Yiddish. However in London, Manchester and Leeds, the preference was for Jewish trade unions especially in the clothing trades.

The use of the 'sweating' system of work in the clothing and boot and shoe trades caused social and economic problems in certain urban areas and the Trades Union Congress (TUC) debates at their annual Congresses from 1875 onwards on this subject frequently targeted Jewish workers which sometimes contained antisemitic comments. The TUC's campaigns against the sweating trades and alien immigration were rewarded in 1905 with the introduction of the Aliens Act which was designed to curb Jewish immigration.

The problems of the 'sweating' trades, alien immigration, the Jewish worker and trade unions were discussed through the columns of newspapers such as the *Jewish Chronicle, Jewish World* and the immigrants' Yiddish newspaper *Der Arbyter Fraynd*. After 1889 the *Jewish Chronicle* had regular reports from the East End on labour matters and by 1901 had a regular column titled Jewish labour news. However the majority of adult first-generation Jewish immigrants were unable to read it as they could not read English.

The golden age for Jewish trade unions in Britain was between 1890 and 1905. In 1896 in London alone there were 13 Jewish unions, and by 1902 there were 32, yet the majority of them remained outside the mainstream labour movement and did not affiliate to the TUC. The *Jewish*

Chronicle commented about the 1902 TUC Congress that '*Jewish unions were not represented in great force and London unions noticeable by their absence*'. It went on to say that the three provincial delegates who attended believed there was no excuse for Jewish members not attending in order to defend their alien brothers and that the London Jewish trade unionists were too absorbed in their own affairs.[2] The only Jewish trade union that had regularly attended TUC Congresses after 1895 was the Leeds Jewish Tailors Union. The 1900 TUC Congress unanimously adopted a motion moved by the Jewish Tailors from Manchester and Leeds calling for the appointment of Yiddish-speaking factory inspectors.[3] Two years later the Manchester Jewish Tailors union submitted a motion on the prohibitive cost of naturalisation which was carried but was moved by the Amalgamated Tailors union '*in order to free delegates of prejudice which may have existed if it was a Jewish question*'.[4]

At the start of the First World War the TUC, which was formed in 1868, was not a national trade union centre in the modern sense; it was then a domestic organisation whose main role was to deal with national industrial matters which affected its affiliated unions and was not yet acknowledged as the national representative of the British trade union movement at either home or abroad. Its relationship with the Labour Party, which the TUC formed in 1901 as the political wing of the trade union movement was at that time ill-defined. International relations with trade unions abroad were dealt with by the General Federation of Trade Unions (GFTU) which had been established by the TUC in 1899 to enable affiliated unions to draw on a strike fund. The First World War was to change both the status and role of the TUC in industrial matters both at home and abroad.

By the outbreak of the First World War the majority of Jewish trade unions had either disbanded or merged with their English counterparts and the only two that attended the 1915 TUC Congress were the London Jewish Bakers Union and the Leeds Amalgamated Jewish Tailors', Machiners' and Pressers' Union. Yet within a year the Leeds Amalgamated Jewish Tailors union had merged with National Union of Tailors and Garment Workers leaving the London Jewish Bakers Union as the only Jewish union to retain its independence continuing to attend TUC Congresses until 1958.

In 1915 Moses Sclare made a unique contribution towards obtaining the Labour Party's support for Zionism and the establishment of Jewish homeland in Palestine. He was born in Russia and in 1899 he emigrated to

Glasgow. In 1906 he moved with his wife and three daughters to Leeds, to become the full-time general secretary of the Leeds Amalgamated Jewish Tailors', Machiners' and Pressers' Trade Union. He represented the Jewish Tailors union at TUC Congresses from 1906 until 1915 and then the National Union of Tailors until 1922. He spoke regularly about improving workers' rights and working conditions in the clothing trade for Jews and non-Jews. Jewish trade unionism was more developed in Leeds than in London or elsewhere as the clothing trade there was concentrated in larger factories which resulted in more contact and cooperation between English and Jewish trade unionists.[5] Leeds was an industrial environment with unionised industries in the engineering, mining and textile trades and Jewish trade unionists like Sclare wanted to be accepted as part of the English labour movement. The Jewish Tailors union had a unique record amongst Jewish trade unions as it was only one which attended every TUC Congress between 1895 and 1915 with one exception in 1898.

As a Jewish trade unionist in Leeds, Sclare was exposed to the ideas of the Poale Zion (the Workers of Zion) movement which the Jewish immigrants from Eastern Europe had brought with them. Poale Zion was a Marxist-Zionist movement which was founded in Eastern Europe at the turn of the twentieth century whose ideology was a blend of socialism and Zionism aimed at persuading Jewish workers to support Palestine as a Jewish homeland as well as campaigning for Jewish equality in all countries. Labour Zionist parties became a powerful force in Russia, Germany, France, and Eastern and Central Europe and there were also groups in Palestine, America, Canada and Britain. Poale Zion was active in Britain from 1905 onwards and established branches in London, Leeds, Manchester and Liverpool. One of Poale Zion's aims was to build links with the British labour movement so that by 1915, Leeds had 40 members, which almost certainly included Sclare and was well established by then as one of the two main Poale Zion centres in Britain.[6] Throughout the First World War Poale Zion, led by J. Pomerantz, the secretary of Poale Zion and Morris Meyer, the editor of the *Jewish Times*, campaigned in Britain within the trade union movement for the granting of political and civil rights for the Jewish people in Galicia and Romania where these common rights were being denied to them.

Since both the TUC and the Labour Party had declared their total support for the war in October 1914, the general feeling at the TUC's Congress in September 1915 in Bristol was one of support for Britain's war effort. It was against this background that Moses Sclare as general secretary of the Leeds Jewish Amalgamated Tailors', Machiners' and Pressers' Trade Union moved his union's motion titled the '*Political and Civil rights for Jewish people*' which stated:

> *That this Congress fervently hopes that civil and political rights will be granted to the Jews of those countries where these common rights are at present denied to them, in recognition of the great sacrifices the best manhood of Jewry is making on the side of the Allies in our common fight for the liberties of the world, and that the Parliamentary Committee shall petition the British Government to use its good offices in that direction when the opportunity will arise.*[7]

Sclare spoke about the plight and maltreatment of the Jews in Russia and Romania as well as the one million Jews who were fighting in the war on the side of the allies. He urged the TUC's parliamentary committee to petition the government to obtain these common rights for these disenfranchised Jews. What had made his 1915 resolution unique was that this was the first time anyone, albeit a Jew, had ever spoken, at a TUC Congress about the civil and political rights of the Jewish people. Sclare was cheered by his fellow delegates when he returned to his seat after finishing his speech with the result that the resolution was adopted unanimously. Within days of Sclare returning home, a Poale Zion backed conference of Jewish labour organisations from all over Britain 'Workers League for Jewish Emancipation' was held in Leeds, which called for '*free immigration and colonisation in Palestine and other lands*'.[8] Shortly afterwards Sclare presided over the first meeting of the Leeds branch of this organisation.[9]

Sclare returned to Congress the following year with a similar motion with the same title which read:

> *That this Congress expresses its emphatic condemnation of the continued oppression and discrimination of the Jewish people, and regrets that in some countries the Jewish people are still deprived of elementary political and civil rights. This Congress, therefore, requests the British Government to urge upon our Allies and the Governments of neutral nations to cease all such discriminations wherever they exist and now practiced against the Jewish people. And further, requests that the British representatives shall endeavour to include in the Peace Treaty, wherever the terms and peace conditions for the conclusion of the present war will be discussed a guarantee for civil and political rights to the Jews and other nationalities who are subjected to such disabilities.*[10]

Once again Sclare called on the British government to ensure that any peace treaty at the conclusion of the war would include a guarantee for the civil and political rights to the Jews. Once again Congress adopted his motion unanimously. Sclare had used his position to promote Jewish rights indicating Poale Zion was the driving force behind the resolutions and were part of their campaign for the acceptance and support of Zionism by the British labour movement.

Sclare also attended both the 1915 and 1916 annual general meetings of the GFTU of which his union was a member, and like the TUC, they sympathetically received telegrams from the federation from the Jewish trade unionists calling for Jewish emancipation.[11] This was another indicator of the acceptance of the Poale Zion campaign for Jewish rights by the trade union movement.

Labour's *War Aims Memorandum*[12]

In August 1917, three months before the publication of the Balfour Declaration, the Labour Party published its draft of the *War Aims Memorandum* which was drawn up for an inter-Allied conference called by the British section of international Socialist Bureau. This conference brought together 68 delegates from eight nationalities who failed to reach a definite agreement relating to war aims.[13]

The memorandum which was drafted by Arthur Henderson, the leader of the Labour Party, and Sidney Webb set out a Socialist and Labour vision for the future once peace had been achieved. It was divided into six sections; making the world safe for democracy, territorial questions, economic relations, the problems of peace, the restoration of the devasted areas and the reparation of wrongdoing, and the holding of an international conference of Labour and Socialist organisations. Foremost in the Labour party's plans was the establishment of the League of Nations. The section on territorial questions proposed solutions for Belgium, Alsace Lorraine, the Balkans, Italy, Poland and the Baltic provinces, the Jews and Palestine, the Turkish Empire, Austria-Hungary and the colonies and dependencies.

The paragraph on the Jews and Palestine stated:

> *The British labour movement demands for the Jews in all countries the same elementary rights of tolerance, freedom of residence and trade, and equal citizenship that ought to be extended to all the inhabitants of every nation. It*

> *furthermore expresses the opinion that Palestine should be set free from the harsh and oppressive government of the Turk, in order that the country may form a Free State, under international guarantee, to which such of the Jewish People as desired to do so may return, and may work out their salvation free from interference by those of alien race or religion.*[14]

Although the call for political and civil rights for Jews was vague and ambiguous as it proposed that Palestine should become a '*Free State*'; as well as a Jewish '*return*' to the country, it did imply an historical connection between the Jews and Palestine. It may not have contained everything the Zionists wanted but this was first official Labour Party declaration relating to the rights of the Jews as well as the first from any political party in Britain. This paragraph was the only one from the memorandum which remained as Labour party policy until 1948 when the State of Israel was established.

In order to be able to present the memorandum to their socialist allies as a British labour movement policy document Henderson obtained the support of the unions at the TUC Congress in September 1917 which adopted a resolution authorising the parliamentary committee to '*assist, arrange and take part*' in an inter-Allied socialist conference. The TUC had not taken part in earlier international socialist conferences as international matters had been the responsibility of the Labour Party and the GFTU. The Labour Party accepted the resolution as the basis for joint action with the TUC and formed a joint committee which produced a memorandum on war aims based on Henderson's draft which was discussed at a special national conference held at the Caxton Hall in Westminster on 28 December 1917. Over 700 delegates from the trade unions and other bodies affiliated to the Labour Party and the TUC voted to adopt as a policy document the *War Aims Memorandum*. The same evening a joint deputation from the Labour Party and the TUC met the prime minister at Downing Street, where they had a frank discussion about the *War Aims Memorandum*. The two groups met again at the Labour Party Conference in Nottingham the following month which adopted a resolution welcoming the statements as to war aims made by the British prime minister and President Wilson, in so far as they were in harmony with the War Aims of the British labour movement.

The influential journal *Zionist Review* wrote that:

> *The special Labour conference approved the Labour Memorandum of Peace terms which includes a demand for Jewish emancipation and for the recognition of Jewish national claims in Palestine. In one form or another these two demands have the sanction of the whole international Labour movement, but English Labour has the credit of having taken the initiative and Jews throughout the world owe it a deep duty of gratitude.*[15]

This reference to the Labour Party's work in the international movement referred to their efforts at a series of conferences held from 1915 onwards by the Labour and Socialist parties of the Allied powers which discussed the socialist attitude to the war. The Inter-Allied Labour and Socialist Conference held in London in February 1918 adopted Labour's *War Aims Memorandum* as its main policy document.

There is little evidence available as to why the authors included in their memorandum the section on the Jews and Palestine. Henderson, as secretary of the Labour Party was known to be sympathetic towards Zionist demands for a Jewish homeland in Palestine as well as being aware of the problems of Jewish labour and the work of the Poale Zion. He was also the first Labour member of the Cabinet when Prime Minister Asquith formed a coalition government in 1915 and continued to serve in the War Cabinet until August 1917. Throughout his time as a member of the Cabinet he would have been aware of the government's discussions with Chaim Weizmann which resulted in the Balfour Declaration. It is not known if his co-author Webb held similar views to Henderson. We can only assume that since he fully supported the aims of the memorandum he was not opposed to the paragraph's inclusion. However Webb later became an opponent of Zionism as the author of the 1930 Passfield White Paper which sought to limit immigration into Palestine. In 1918 Weizmann wrote that Poale Zion had been '*responsible for the favourable declaration of the Labour Party*'.[16]

It is also possible Poale Zion lobbied Henderson and Webb at the international labour and socialist conferences held in London in February 1915 and in Stockholm in 1917 as both men were involved in discussions regarding future peace negotiations at both these conferences. The few Poale Zion records which have survived from the period connecting Moses Sclare to Poale Zion confirm that Poale Zion was the driving force behind the resolutions which he moved at the TUC Congresses and were part of their campaign for the acceptance and support of Zionism by the

British labour movement and that Poale Zion and Moses Sclare both played important roles in bringing the Jewish-Zionist question to the attention of Henderson and his colleagues in the Labour party.

The Jews in Palestine

Although Jews had lived in Palestine since pre-biblical times, large scale settlement only began in the late nineteenth century. The Jewish immigrants who went to Palestine from Russia in the 1880s, in what is known as the first Aliyah, considered themselves pioneers, rather than refugees, who had gone there to make a connection with their ancestors and at the same time build a modern new Hebrew society based on Jewish labour living in agricultural settlements. The next wave of immigrants from the Russian Empire, the second Aliyah, included a small number of socialists known as Labour–Zionists who believed that Jewish settlement in Palestine would allow Jewish workers to play a key role in determining all branches and conditions of production. These Labour-Zionists, who came to Palestine as individuals and not as part of an organised movement were young pioneers, full of revolutionary fervour and dedication to Zionism which they believed would solve the 'Jewish problem'. They were not seeking a better personal life, as many of the first Aliyah did, but instead devoted their lives to the establishment of a socialist Jewish state. Labour-Zionists brought trade unionism and political parties to Palestine, which at the time was a backward and feudal society. Although their European based ideology had to be modified to meet the new conditions that they encountered in Palestine, they built and developed the concept of co-operative farming, the Kibbutz; defence units called Hashomer to protect the Jewish settlements against Bedouin and Arab attacks; and enabled the rebirth of the Hebrew language.

It was in 1920 that the Jewish labour movement in Palestine formed its own trade union body, the General Federation of Jewish Workers in Palestine, known in Hebrew as the Histadrut, to look after the interests of Jewish workers.[17] The Histadrut, with David Ben-Gurion as its first general secretary, was much more than an ordinary trade union in the accepted European sense and set itself up from the beginning as the alternative to existing bourgeois society. It was to become the driving force for the future Jewish state, with its activities always directed towards assisting the absorption of further immigrants and their settlement in the country[18] and described itself '*primarily as serving the cause of Zionism and so makes all of its ramified activists subservient to this supreme aim*'.[19] While European working-class movements sought to defend the workers against the excesses of capitalism, the Histadrut's trade unionism, which was not based on the factory system, created a working class from the immigrants to Palestine.

Initially a contractor on road building programmes for the British mandate, the Histadrut expanded into an organisation with its own labour exchanges, co-operative agricultural settlements, co-operative industry projects and building companies. As well as providing employment it developed a social services programme for the Jewish immigrants which included a network of schools, educational and cultural programmes, a universal sick fund (Kupat Holim), its own newspaper and bank. The Histadrut also controlled the Haganah, a defence force set up in up in 1921 to protect the Jewish community from Arab attacks. In 1920, membership in the Histadrut was approximately 4400. By 1930 it had grown to 25,000 members or 74% of the entire Jewish labour force in Palestine.[20]

The TUC's Move into International Affairs

Before 1915 the British trade union movement had given little thought to the war but as it dragged on they became more sympathetic with those on the Left who had opposed it from the beginning. It was Henderson, as a trade unionist and the leader of the Labour Party who had brought together both sides to work out the movements 'war aims' policy. This ensured that the TUC's parliamentary committee worked closely with the Labour Party executive and also brought the TUC into direct contact with Socialist and Labour groups abroad. The success of the *War Aims Memorandum* resulted in the 1918 TUC Congress approving proposals for the TUC to become the British centre for dealing with international trade union matters, replacing the GFTU which had previously dealt with international issues.[21] Once the decision had been made for the TUC to take on an international role it then followed that the TUC would support all the recommendations in the memorandum including the paragraph about the Jews and Palestine. If there was any opposition to this particular recommendation there is certainly no evidence of it in the limited published sources that have survived.

The 1914–18 war was the catalyst for change in many fields, including the British trade union movement as the British government was now responsible for implementing international conventions relating to working conditions in her colonies and dependencies. This in turn prompted the TUC to begin building links with the trade union movement throughout the British Empire as their prior knowledge of labour problems in the colonies was negligible.[22]

Between 1918 and 1921, the Labour Party's advisory committee on international questions advised the Party's executive on international matters; from 1921 onwards this committee was attached to a new TUC/ Labour Party joint international department. Although all Labour Party international activities were carried out through this new department, the TUC General Council formed, in the same year, its own International Committee specifically to deal with the International Federation of Trade Unions (IFTU) as it wanted to keep these activities under its own control because they felt they had more experience in trade union matters than the Labour Party and that it alone should be responsible for industrial and trade union international matters.

The joint working arrangement with the Labour Party lasted five years by which time the TUC had realised that political and industrial issues should be kept separate, not because the joint committee was not working, but because the Labour Party had dealt mainly with political issues such as the Palestine mandate which was of more interest to them than the TUC. In 1926 with Walter Citrine as TUC general secretary, the joint committee was disbanded and the TUC took control of international industrial matters. As we shall see later this clear division of responsibilities between the Labour Party and the TUC on political and industrial matters was not always recognised by the Jewish leadership in Palestine.

However by 1926, when the TUC formed its own International department, the labour movements in many of Britain's colonies, including Palestine, had already established their own international connections. The Jewish community in Palestine through its political parties and the Histadrut had already made direct contact with the Labour Party, the British government and the local mandate administration but not the TUC.

Poale Zion's Affiliation to the Labour Party

Poale Zion took the lead when in May 1918 it issued a memorandum and invited all Jewish trade unions, Jewish political labour organisations and Jewish workers' societies to a conference to discuss various issues including the formation of a Jewish National Labour Council and the establishment of '*close relations between all trade unions*' and '*intimate relations with the Labour party*' with the aim of attaching themselves '*as a Jewish section to the British Labour Party*'. The conference was held in London in October 1917 and attended by 12 Jewish organisations representing 10,000 Jewish workers, which not only adopted a resolution congratulating the Labour Party for including in its War Aims, a statement on the civil rights of the Jews and Palestine but also formed a Jewish Trade Union Committee.[23] This in turn led to Poale Zion campaigning for the first time for Socialist and Labour Party candidates during the 1918 Parliamentary elections. They also issued a manifesto urging Jewish voters to vote Labour because of its support for the civil and political rights of the Jews.

Poale Zion's aim for affiliation to the Labour Party was achieved in February 1920. This was a significant moment for the future relationship between the Jews of Palestine and the labour movement in Britain as it allowed Poale Zion delegates to submit motions and speak in debates on Palestine at Labour Party conferences. Poale Zion groups in Britain and Palestine were both members of the World Union of Poale Zion and it was this link that provided David Ben-Gurion and his party, Achut ha-Avodah, direct access to the Labour Party.

The San Remo Conference

Before the San Remo Conference of April 1920 which formally recognised Britain as the mandatory authority for Palestine, the Zionists had been worried that the British government might acquiesce to French claims over the division of Palestine and not stand by the Balfour Declaration. As a result of lobbying by Poale Zion and the English Zionist Federation, the Labour Party and the TUC reaffirmed their policy of 'a Jewish Homeland in Palestine' in a telegram to David Lloyd George, the British prime minister at the San Remo Peace Conference which stated:

> *At meetings held in London this week the Parliamentary Labour Party, the Executive Committee of the Labour Party and the Parliamentary Committee of the Trades Union Congress have adopted resolutions to remind the British Government of the Declaration made on November 2nd, 1917 that the Government would endeavour to facilitate the establishment of a Jewish National Home in Palestine, a declaration that was in harmony with the declared War Aims of the British labour movement, and which was cordially welcomed by all sections of the British people, and was reaffirmed by Earl Curzon on November 2nd, 1919.*

> *The National Labour Organisations indicated, now urge upon his Majesty's Government the necessity of redeeming this pledge by the acceptance of a mandate under the League of Nations for the Administration of Palestine with a view of its being reconstituted the National Home of the Jewish People. The National Committee desire to associate themselves with the many similar representations being made to the Government urging the settlement of this question with the utmost despatch both in the interests of Palestine itself as well as in the interest of the Jewish people.*[24]

In August 1920 as a result of the Palestine mandate being awarded to Britain, the World Union of Poale Zion decided, at its conference in Vienna, to send David Ben-Gurion and Sholmo Kaplansky to London to establish a political office to handle international affairs because London was where decisions about the political future of Palestine were going to be made. Part of their mission was also to build a relationship with the Labour Party leadership. However in the autumn of 1920 Kaplansky's application to become a foreign member of the Labour Party's Advisory Committee on International questions as well as Ben-Gurion's paper on the northern borders of Palestine were rejected.

It was then that Ben-Gurion realised that he had '*overestimated the Labour Party's sympathy, failing to realise they were the only ones who regarded the two as sister parties. They had not picked up the subtle difference between the sympathy for Zionism expressed so forthrightly by candidates seeking the Jewish vote and the guarded statements made by the party's ideologists and policymakers*'. He also understood that those members of the Advisory committee who had been sympathetic towards Zionism had serious reservations about how it would be achieved in Palestine and that there were also a few very influential members of the Labour Party who had opposed the Balfour Declaration. Ben-Gurion also recognised that non-representation on this committee would create a problem in the future and that the Labour Party National Executive seemed more sympathetic to the aims of the Zionists than the Advisory committee.[25] In March 1921 the World Union of Poale Zion closed their London office due to lack of funds.

In February 1922, Achut ha-Avodah, led by Ben-Gurion, and the Histadrut hosted a visit to Palestine by Ramsay MacDonald, the leader of the Labour Party. Ben-Gurion asked Dov Hoz to accompany MacDonald who was so impressed with what he saw that wrote a pamphlet about his visit.[26] MacDonald declared that he and his party supported the idea of the '*rebirth of the Jewish people in their land*' promising that his party would assist the Histadrut as much as it could.[27] The trip also marked the start of a long friendship between MacDonald and Hoz which was to prove invaluable in the future.

Palestinian Jewry's priority was to build their own links with the Labour Party and the TUC as well as International organisations such Socialist International and the IFTU. Poale Zion was especially useful as not only was it a member of Socialist International but also the Labour Party. Although Poale Zion had built connections with the British trade unions during the First World War, it never tried to rebuild its relationship with them once it had affiliated to the Labour Party. It was therefore left to the Histadrut, the Jewish Labour council and the Jewish trade unions to build links with the unions and the TUC. By the mid-1920s however there were very few Jewish unions left as most of them had been merged with mainstream unions. The one exception was the London Jewish Bakers Union which kept its independence and was to play an important part in this narrative after the Second World War.

The first mention of the Histadrut in the TUC archives was in the report of the third International Trades' Union Federation (IFTU) Congress held in Vienna in 1924 which noted that: '*An interesting feature of the Vienna congress was the presence of a delegate from the trades unions of Palestine who stated that there were now in Palestine about 20,000 workers, although that number was small, it had to be borne in mind that they were pioneers in a country with a future. The national organisation represented by Mr. Dov Hoz was the only bone fide trade union centre in Palestine and he expressed his hope that the other members of the IFTU would help them in reconstructing his country and especially to introduce socialist legislation which at the present time was entirely lacking in Palestine*'.[28]

The Histadrut's appearance at the IFTU Congress was part of their lobbying campaign for better workplace legislation in Palestine. After the second conference of the Histadrut in 1923 had adopted resolutions dealing with the country's labour legislation the Histadrut approached the British government in 1924 with proposals for workplace legislation which included employers' liability for accidents. The Histadrut also lobbied the joint Labour/TUC advisory committee, the IFTU, and the International Labour Organisation in Geneva for support. The first British Commonwealth Labour Conference in London in July 1925 was used by the Histadrut to lobby and educate a wider audience including the leadership of the TUC and Labour Party about the aims of the Jewish labour movement in Palestine. During the debate on '*Industrial Legislation and Labour Protection in the Mandated Territories*' Ben-Gurion was forced to defend increased Jewish immigration to Palestine as well the right to establish a Jewish homeland there.[29] The Histadrut's efforts were rewarded when in late 1926 the British government published an ordinance modelled on English legislation governing the liability of the employer for accidents.[30]

Once Britain had accepted the Palestine mandate, the future development of Palestine both politically and economically was under the direction of the local mandate government. However the majority of its decisions made by senior officials in Palestine were referred initially to the Colonial Office in London for approval. Even though the Yishuv leadership had established, though the Histadrut a good working relationship with the mandate administration in Jerusalem, by the mid-1920s Ben-Gurion knew that London was where all the important decisions about the future of Palestine were decided. The World Zionist Organisation (WZO) led by Weizmann also based in London, regularly consulted with the British government and the Colonial Office. Ben-Gurion also realised that any major policy decisions made by the Yishuv executive also needed the approval of the WZO. It was therefore clear to him that if the Jewish labour movement wanted to influence the future development of the Yishuv then it needed an envoy based in London with access to the British government who was also involved in the decision-making processes of the WZO.

Since Britain's economy was still in a poor state in 1928, 10 years after the First World War had ended, it was widely thought that support for the Labour Party would increase at the next general election and that the Labour Party might even be able to form the next government. This possibility was of concern to the WZO and its leader Chaim Weizmann as their main political contacts in Parliament were members of the Liberal Party whose popularity was in decline. The WZO did not have the same level of support or connections in the Labour Party as they had with the Liberal Party and Ben-Gurion saw that this was the opportunity for the Yishuv to play a greater part in the work of the WZO, which had been previously denied them, as the Histadrut already had good connections with the Labour Party and the TUC. The Labour Party was also member of the second International, an alliance of social democratic parties in Europe. By strengthening their ties with the social democrats in Europe, Ben-Gurion hoped that it would help the Zionist movement achieve their political aims. Overall there appeared to be many advantages for the Zionists if they were able to build on their existing relationship with the Labour Party.

In 1928, with the WZO's agreement, Ben-Gurion sent Dov Hoz to London as emissary for the Histadrut. Chosen because of his charisma, proven ability in making connections with people in authority, and because he was fluent in both English and Yiddish, Hoz's mission was to promote the establishment of a Jewish state in Palestine with the wider public and especially within the Labour Party and the TUC. He was also tasked with rebuilding the standing of Poale Zion within the Labour Party, which had declined after it had affiliated to the Labour Party in 1920. This was an inspired appointment because fate played its part and Hoz's secondment to London ensured he was the right man in the right place for the Zionists at the general election which took place in the autumn of 1929. Hoz encouraged the local branches of Poale Zion to campaign for the Labour Party, a move which increased his standing with the senior leadership of the party. The result was a hung Parliament; Labour held the largest number of seats, but MacDonald was only able to form a minority Labour government with the support of David Lloyd George and his fellow Liberal MPs.

One of Dov Hoz's first tasks soon after his arrival was to write to the TUC on behalf of the Histadrut about unfair working conditions on the construction of the new harbour at Haifa. The TUC agreed and brought it to the attention of the Colonial Office.[31] This was the first of many letters that both Hoz and the TUC would write on this matter over the next four years before a satisfactory solution was found. It took so long because the Colonial Office had to consult with the High Commissioner for Palestine on every point raised by the TUC. The Haifa Docks project provided Hoz with the opportunity to work closely and build a relationship with the leadership of the TUC, who to their credit wholly supported the concerns of the Histadrut because this was a matter related to wages and conditions and was not a political matter. The TUC made their position quite clear to the colonial secretary, when a TUC deputation met him in May 1929. Before their meeting, Hoz discussed the issues and tactics with the deputation but turned down their request to attend the meeting with them saying that the discussions would have revolved around him if he attended and divert the meeting from its main purpose. However his real reason for saying no was the disagreement between him and the WZO on the matter of the intervention of the TUC in Palestine matters. Hoz had given his word to the WZO that he would not officially meet government officials and in order to keep this commitment he turned down their invitation even though the purpose of the meeting may have justified his attendance. With the benefit of hindsight Hoz wrote that next time he should take part as his '*participation could prevent any mishaps and bring issues up for discussion*' because it warranted his involvement.[32] The opportunity arose two months later when Dov Hoz and Sholmo Kaplansky met with the Secretary of State Lord Passfield. As well as lobbying the TUC, Hoz used his Labour Party connections to ask questions in Parliament of the colonial secretary.

As part of their mission to improve relations and understanding of the development of the Jewish national home in Palestine the Histadrut regularly invited members of the Labour Party to visit Palestine. In 1929 as several socialist and trade union leaders from France, Belgium, Germany and Poland had already agreed to visit Palestine, Hoz decided to invite Citrine to visit Palestine. Citrine declined the invitation on the grounds of his International commitments with the IFTU which did not allow the time.

The 1929 TUC Congress

Ten days before the TUC Congress was due to open in Belfast on 2 September 1929, there was an outbreak of Arab violence in Palestine during which 133 Jews were killed with another 339 wounded. As a result of the violence the TUC received letters from Poale Zion,[33] the Jewish Labour Council[34] and the Rabbi of the Belfast Jewish community[35] all urging that the TUC to pass a resolution deploring the attacks on the Jewish population in Palestine. Telegrams were also received from Sholmo Kaplansky and the Palestine Committee on behalf of Arabs in Palestine urging the intervention of TUC. The 1929 riots were a watershed moment for the TUC in its dealings with the Histadrut and Jews of Palestine. All the correspondence was discussed by the General Council on the eve of the Congress and they decided that no action would be taken regarding the Poale Zion memorandum and the letters from the Jewish Labour Council and the Belfast community but the telegrams from the Palestine committee[36] and Kaplansky[37] were forwarded to the Labour Party. By dealing with the matter in this way, the General Council ensured the riots in Palestine were not discussed at the Belfast Congress. Because it clashed with the Congress, the TUC were not present at a meeting between

Kaplansky, Hoz and William Gilles, the international secretary of the Labour Party which discussed the Poale Zion memorandum which Gilles promised to show to the prime minister.[38]

This was the first time since the TUC had formed its own International department in 1926 that they had been lobbied on a political issue relating to Palestine. Citrine was at the heart of the TUC's decision to do nothing other than pass on the correspondence to the Labour Party. He believed that trade unions were there to raise the standards of the workers and not pursue or become involved in political matters which were the responsibility of the Labour Party, the political wing of the labour movement. Although it may not have been apparent at the time especially to Hoz and the Histadrut, the TUC's inaction and indifference to this horrific incident was to set the standard for the TUC reaction to attacks on Jews and their communities in both Europe and Palestine for the next 50 years.

The Whitechapel By-Election[39]

The Passfield White Paper was the Labour government's response to the Shaw inquiry into the August 1929 disturbances in Palestine. The White Paper stated that while the British government did intend to fulfil its obligations to both Arabs and Jews, treating them both equally in Palestine, the development of a Jewish national home in Palestine was not considered central to the British mandate. It also proposed that in future the Jews would need the approval of the British authorities before purchasing any additional land.

The Arabs saw the White Paper as vindication for their demands to halt Jewish immigration and land sales whilst the Jews viewed it as the British government reversing their support for the Balfour Declaration and the aims of the mandate. There was an immediate international outcry which claimed that the proposals in the White Paper flouted the mandate and demanded its withdrawal. The Zionists considered that the tone of the White Paper was decidedly anti-Jewish as it criticised both the Histadrut and the Jewish Agency for promoting the employment of Jewish-only labour.

The Whitechapel by-election of 1930 was brought about by the death of the constituency's Labour MP Harry Gosling, who was sponsored by Ernest Bevin's Transport and General Workers union. It could not have come at a more inconvenient time for Macdonald's Labour government as the White Paper was published only four days before Gosling's death.

Even though Whitechapel was considered to be a safe Labour seat nearly 40 per cent of the Whitechapel electorate were Jewish, many of whom were Russian immigrants.

However, the publication of the White Paper had changed everything. Poale Zion had to decide whether to support the Labour candidate or Barnett Janner, the Jewish candidate representing Liberal Party, who opposed to the White Paper. Poale Zion however recognised that the by-election gave them the opportunity not only to demand the withdrawal of the White Paper but also to draw the attention of the Labour Party to the unfairness of its proposals. Hoz had been joined in London by Kaplansky and both men were in regular contact with the Labour Party leadership.

Bevin recognised that it was vital for the minority Labour government to hold the seat and that for their candidate to win they would need the Jewish vote and Poale Zion's support. Consequently he had several meetings with Hoz in November to discuss their concerns. Bevin told Hoz that although the government was unwilling to revoke the White Paper he would ensure that all 26 MPs sponsored by his union would vote against the government if it came to a vote on the White Paper, but he was unwilling to force the issue as the government would be defeated. After their second meeting Bevin said he would ask Henderson and Passfield for an agreement to clarify the controversial clauses on Jewish labour and the status of the Histadrut. The offending clauses in the White Paper were eventually amended[40] but only after Hoz had sent Bevin, at his suggestion, a draft paragraph that could be included in any future government statement to repudiate any misunderstanding concerning the Histadrut in the White Paper.[41]

While Hoz was working with Bevin behind the scenes, the government and the Labour Party received many protests including letters and telegrams from Poale Zion,[42] the Jewish Labour Council,[43] Socialist International, Poale Zion International and trade union organisations in Glasgow, New York, Chicago, Boston, Montreal as well as the Palestine Labour Party.

Bevin's efforts resulted in Labour retaining the seat but on a reduced majority of only 1099 votes. He thanked both Hoz and Kaplansky for their support, telling them that '*it was a bitter fight and it looked as if the cross currents would upset us*'[44] and that '*it was great victory … I realise, and the members of this union realise also, that we are indebted to you and your colleagues of the Poale Zion for the invaluable assistance you rendered…*'.[45]

In order to find a way out of the crisis brought on by the Whitechapel result and the international campaign against the Passfield White Paper the British government opened negotiations with the Zionist leadership and two months later Ramsay MacDonald sent Chaim Weizmann a response to the Zionists complaints, which became known as the '*MacDonald letter*'. Although meant as a clarification of future British policy in Palestine the letter was in effect an official withdrawal of the White paper and consigned the Passfield White Paper to a footnote in history. The Zionists and the Jewish voters of Whitechapel had won, as all the promises that Bevin had obtained from the government in return for Poale Zion's support had been honoured. The withdrawal of the White Paper ensured that Jewish immigration to Palestine would be able continue during the 1930s as the threat of antisemitism increased in Europe.

The successful outcome allowed Hoz to build close relationships with the Labour Party leadership over the next decade which ensured continuing Labour support for a Jewish national home in Palestine. The TUC had played no part in the by-election, but one unexpected outcome of the Whitechapel by-election was the friendship and mutual admiration that developed between Bevin and Hoz, which lasted until Hoz's death in 1940. In 1929 Hoz described Bevin as '*one of the most influential forces in the trade unions here. In the TUC and in the Labour Party, he appeared as a leader and as a guide, whose words are heard with admiration and trust*'.[46] Hoz had introduced Zionism to Bevin, which Bevin had acknowledged in an interview in 1932 saying that until the Whitechapel elections he had not known anything about Zionism.[47] Bevin continued to support the Jewish labour movement in Palestine throughout the 1930s. His relationship with Hoz and his fellow Zionists prospered so much that by 1941, they regarded him as one of their friends in the British War Cabinet.[48] The relationship soured once Bevin became foreign secretary in the 1945 Attlee government and Labour's decision to withdraw from Palestine. The Zionists could not forgive Bevin, whom they had thought of as a friend and ally for abandoning the official sympathetic stance of Labour towards Zionism.

The Histadrut continued to lobby the TUC on important political matters because they perceived that the TUC had the same values with regards to the Jewish national home In Palestine as the Labour Party, along with the belief that the TUC was able to influence the Labour Party on political matters. The reality was that there was only one trade unionist that was able to do this, Ernest Bevin. Ben-Gurion and Hoz had realised that political decisions were decided by the politicians, not the trade unions and until he returned to Palestine in 1932 Hoz was in close contact with the Labour Party leadership as well as their International department. Shortly afterwards the Histadrut closed their political office in London as a cost saving measure and left the lobbying of the Labour Party and the TUC to local supporters including Poale Zion, an arrangement which the Histadrut were told was very ineffective.[49] Hoz however continued to write to Citrine about trade union related issues and whenever necessary asked him to contact the government or arrange for their MPs to ask questions of the government.

The TUC and Their Response to the Persecution of the Jews, 1933–39

The key international issues for the TUC during the 1930s were the rise of fascism in Europe and the Spanish civil war because fellow trade unionists and socialists were threatened. Hitler's racial discrimination policies directed at the Jews as well as the building of a national home in Palestine did not have the same sense of urgency or support amongst the trade unions and the TUC. The same applied to the 1936–1939 Arab nationalist uprising in Palestine which demanded Arab independence and the termination of the Jewish immigration, land purchases and the establishment of a Jewish national home in Palestine. The rebellion was brutally crushed by the British Army with more than 2000 Arabs dying in the conflict.

Every TUC Congress from 1933 until the outbreak of war discussed Fascism and the Nazis, yet unlike the Labour Party; the 1936 Congress motion on Palestine was the first discussion about a Jewish homeland in Palestine since the adoption of the *War Aims Memorandum* in 1917. George Isaacs, a non-Jew, moved the motion on the Palestine situation which noted the continuous support given by the British labour movement for a Jewish national home in Palestine and also recognised that the interests of Jewish and Arab workers were threatened by '*the recent outbreak of religious and racial strife which could deprive the Jewish people of developing their own political, social and cultural institutions*'. Isaacs, who had just returned from a visit to Palestine, was the first member of the TUC General Council to go there. He been impressed by the 'Kibbutz' movement and acknowledged that this was an experiment in socialism on the highest possible scale which was an example of cooperation between trade unionism, the labour political movement and the cooperative movement which had been developed to look after every aspect of their lives.[50] The resolution which was adopted unanimously, had Citrine's backing because it was not a 'political' resolution as it addressed the achievements of Jewish workers in Palestine and only mentioned in passing the recent Arab riots.

In January 1937 an American Jewish Labour delegation to Palestine arranged to stop over in London on their return from Palestine in order to discuss their visit with the TUC. The delegation represented the Jewish labour movement in the United States and Canada and had the support of the American Federation of Labor (AFL). On their arrival in London they submitted a report of their visit to the TUC which was very positive regarding what they had seen and described how the Jewish labour movement in Palestine had evolved into a system of cooperative effort in all areas of economic and social enterprise.[51] The delegation stressed that Jewish emigration to Palestine should not be curtailed and called on the TUC to use their influence to support the continued development of Jewish national home. Bearing in mind Citrine's desire that the TUC should not be involved in political matters, Bevin told the General Council that the visitors had been promised '*that if the report of the Royal Commission curtailed facilities for Jewish emigration to Palestine, then the General Council would make representations to the proper quarter*'[52]

When in London Hoz regularly met with Clement Attlee, Herbert Morrison and Hugh Dalton and the members of Labour's Advisory Committee on Imperial Questions. Although Hoz considered Bevin to be one of the most influential forces in the TUC and was the president of the movement he had decided previously that he would only approach Bevin in the Yishuv's hour of need. He wrote '*I want to ask him to consider his personal influence and authority. If I can make him act, then we will have a very valuable device whose influence is unquestionable*'.[53] This was why he arranged to meet with Bevin in 1937. Hoz asked him the same question that he had asked Morrison; if he could arrange a meeting with the government in order to warn them that if the Peel Commission which was investigating the causes of unrest in Palestine, recommended curbing the Jewish people's right for Aliyah, settlement and an independent life which had been promised to the Jews at the end of the war with the full support of the British labour movement, then the Jewish labour movement would see it as treason and would fight against such an attempt with all possible means. Although Hoz felt that Bevin had been very kind to him personally in their meeting, and had showed a positive attitude to the issues as well as promising to see what he could do Hoz did not hold out much hope.[54] The real problem for Hoz was that there was no one else other than Citrine or Bevin in the unions to turn to, especially as Bevin seemed to him to be a lot weaker, more tired and less enthusiastic to take on responsibility and action than he had been in 1930.

Bevin used his presidential address to the TUC Congress in September 1937, to say that

> *Palestine, as it is mandated territory, is one of our responsibilities. One of two great tragedies of the world has been the persecution of the Jews. With the granting of the Palestine Mandate we looked forward with hope to the ending of this persecution, later, when we saw the remarkable response of the Jews in the building of new homes and their co-operative effort, a development which has won the admiration of the world, our expectation ran high. Persecution of the Jews, however, broke out again, particularly under the Nazi regime in Germany. Now a now proposal has emerged to partition Palestine.*
>
> *I make no pronouncement on the merit or demerit of that proposal. It has been the subject of serious discussion at the Zionist Congress. The test which I think will have to be applied by the Labour Movement whether it will contribute towards the ending for all time of the persecution of the Jewish race. Will the fact that they are a State with Ambassadors at the various Chancelleries of the world assist them to a greater extent than the mandate granted by the league.*[55]

Bevin concluded his comments by saying that as the British labour movement had close contacts with the Histadrut and he was sure that that Congress would endorse any consultation that could be arranged between General Council and the Histadrut in order to help solve the problems facing Jewish refugees seeking refuge from Nazi Germany. Bevin was particularly proud of his humanitarian speech and concern for Jewish refugees and made sure the Jews in Palestine knew '*that it was not only Ernest Bevin who said it, all the TUC stands behind it*'.[56]

This was the first time since Moses Sclare had spoken more than 20 years earlier that Congress had heard about the renewed discrimination and persecution that Jews were being subjected to in Europe. What made it much more effective this time was that this was the TUC president urging the League of Nations and governments to find countries willing to take refugees. This was not political rhetoric on his part but another example of his genuine concern for the plight of the Jews which he had previously shown both publicly and behind the scenes. Bevin's comments also ensured that there was no need for the TUC to adopt a resolution on

Palestine to align it with Labour Party policy nor did he commit the TUC to any possible solution of the problem.

The British government published its response to the Peel commission In January 1938, which established the Woodhead Commission to draw up a detailed scheme for the partition of Palestine and related arrangements. Hoz sent a telegram to the TUC and the Labour Party urging them to issue a '*clear unequivocal statement concerning the new government proposals*'.[57] Two days later a special meeting of the National Executive of the Labour Party, the TUC General Council and the Executive Committee of the Parliamentary Labour Party considered the situation in Palestine and expressed their '*profound regret that the British Government had failed to arrive at a decision on a question of such vital policy. It declared that the Government's vacillation had put a premium on disturbance and terrorism. It called upon the Government to make an early and clear declaration of its policy for submission to Parliament*'.[58] In February Weizmann urged Ben-Gurion to send Hoz back to London as it was essential to have a representative there who had '*intimate*' knowledge of our activities *as* '*there is no such individual in London*'.[59] As Hoz was unavailable, another member of the Mapai[60] executive, Berl Locker, a veteran Poale Zion and Histadrut member was sent to London as the permanent representative of the Jewish Agency and the Histadrut. Although his posting was originally only for a year he served in that role until 1948.

The TUC made two decisions in February and May 1938 which set the standard for their future dealings with the Histadrut and Palestine. The first was an invitation from Hoz for Citrine to attend the 4th Conference of the Palestine Labour Party, Citrine said he was unable to accept because the General Council had previously decided that they would be represented at meetings of National centres by the IFTU to which the Histadrut was affiliated.[61] Although Citrine's refusal seemed perfectly acceptable, it was the first of many excuses over the next three decades used by TUC general secretaries not to attend Histadrut conferences. As president of the IFTU, Citrine could have cited more pressing international issues instead of a General Council ruling. His refusal to lobby the government on political matters set the standard for the next 30 years and confirmed for the first time that the TUC were only Zionists by their association with the Labour Party. Their second decision was in response to a request from Hoz asking that the TUC make an appeal to the government against the White Paper on Palestine. The General Council decided that in the light of the Labour Party's Parliamentary amendment that this matter was best dealt with by the Labour Party.[62]

The 1938 TUC Congress was dominated by the international situation and the government's indecisive policies towards Germany and Italy. The president, Herbert Elvin, in his opening address said that '*the expelling of Jews from Germany was an outrage and we must render all possible assistance to these unfortunate people*'.[63] The General Council followed up with a statement on the problems of German and Austrian refugees which referred to the setting up of a Coordinating Committee for Refugees. They also felt that '*some practical expression should be given to the sympathy which is generally accepted*' by these proposals which should be '*subject to a yearly limit on the number of refugees entering Britain*.'[64] While the TUC was ambivalent towards the influx of German Jews into Britain which they saw as a threat to their members jobs, both they and the Labour Party agreed that the refugees should be allowed to go to Palestine regardless of whether it was beneficial to the Arabs, or the impact the refugees made on the country.

As tensions mounted in Europe and during the summer of 1938 it was clear to Palestinian Jewry that the government was contemplating abandoning partition and continuing with the mandate even though the Woodhead Commission had yet to present its report. The Yishuv needed a favourable response from the British labour movement but as there was no Labour Party conference planned for that year Locker wrote to Citrine on 19 August, asking to meet with him to discuss the current situation in Palestine as the Jewish labour movement in Palestine needed as much encouragement as possible from its friends outside Palestine, and especially from Great Britain.[65]

The following week Locker met with the Head of the International department, Mr W. Bolton, who told Citrine that Locker had asked if the forthcoming Congress could make a declaration in agreement with the Histadrut demanding from the government a restoration of the full quota of Jewish immigration into Palestine and Locker had left with him a draft copy of their declaration. Citrine then sent Locker a copy of the TUC's proposed statement which was based on Locker's draft. He added that there was no need for a resolution or declaration, as whatever was decided could be submitted to Congress as a statement.[66] When Hoz heard what had happened he immediately wrote to Citrine urging him to speak with Locker. Citrine replied saying that arrangements had been made to bring the matter before the General Council in order to see if it was possible to have it referred to at the Congress and was it possible to speak to Locker at Congress.[67]

On the eve of the debate Hoz sent the best wishes of the Histadrut to Congress, adding that the Jewish people trusted that British labour would stand by them in their efforts to re-establish a Jewish homeland.[68] Citrine reported to the General Council that he had met with Locker who had hoped the Council would make a statement to the Congress and he had explained to him the difficulty of raising this on the Congress but said that some reference might be made to the matter in the international debate.

Although there was no mention of Palestine in the International debate, the TUC Standing Orders Committee published a joint TUC-Labour Party declaration on Jewish refugees which was based on Locker's draft. The declaration expressed their abhorrence of the continuance of Jewish repressions in Fascist states and that this repressive policy assisted by Arab opposition in Palestine had made Britain's obligations under the Palestine mandate more urgent than ever. It urged that more opportunities should now be given for Jewish refugees to be admitted to Palestine.[69] Hoz was happy because he had got the declaration he wanted and by focusing the joint statement with Labour on humanitarian issues surrounding Jewish refugees Citrine had ensured that the TUC did not have to make a political statement or a commitment on any future Jewish homeland. It also confirmed that the British labour movement preferred Palestine as a refuge for Jews as an alternative to admitting them into Britain which would increase pressure on jobs. In the wake of their declaration over the next few weeks, the TUC received telegrams and letters from various American and Canadian trade unions including the AFL, the United Hebrew trades union and the Trades and Labor Congress of Canada calling on the TUC to protest about any future government restrictions on Jewish immigration to Palestine.[70]

The 1938 TUC Congress had met two weeks before the Czech crisis reached its peak and made a number of decisions about it, yet immediately after Congress had ended Citrine travelled to the West Indies as a member of a Royal Commission to investigate labour problems there. The question was why was it more important for Citrine to be away from England for six months and not stay in London in order to work with the Labour Party and the government to ensure that Britain would be ready for war? Citrine knew the crisis would continue because he met Prime Minister Chamberlain the day after his return from Munich and that he would also have to implement Congress policy. He felt he could go because his priority was wages and working conditions for the working man and not politics and had left the TUC in what he believed were Tewson's capable hands. Hoz however could not understand how Citrine could leave the TUC and ignore the politics of Europe as well as the Jewish refugee crisis.[71]

In November 1938, the British government announced their intention to invite representatives of the Arabs of Palestine, certain neighbouring countries and the Jewish Agency to London to consult with them regarding future policy. Hoz was so concerned about this development that he sent copies of his telegram calling on the Labour Party Executive to issue a clear unequivocal statement of support for the Jews of Palestine in response to this statement to Bevin, Citrine and Elvin as well as Attlee and Morrison.[72] The pressure was on the government because in addition to campaigning for a Jewish homeland in Palestine, Jewish communities in Britain, Palestine and the diaspora were also campaigning for British government help for the Jewish refugees fleeing the Nazis to be allowed to settle either in Palestine or Britain.

Knowing that the British government's long-awaited White Paper was to be issued at the end of May 1939 Hoz arrived in London at the beginning of the month and fearing the worst his immediate priority was to plan a campaign to oppose government's proposals. Within days he had met with the leaders of the Labour Party that took place with the knowledge and agreement of Attlee. Hoz was told that the Parliamentary leadership were united and were willing to fight this battle on behalf of the Jews of Palestine.[73] The British government's White Paper which was issued on 21 May and approved by Parliament six days later rejected the Peel Commission's partition plan and proposed that Palestine would not be either a Jewish or Arab state, but an independent state to be established within 10 years. Jewish immigration to Palestine was to be limited to 75,000 for the first five years, which was dependant on 'economic absorptive capacity' of the country, and would afterwards depend on Arab consent. Severe restrictions were also to be imposed on land acquisition by Jews. The Jewish Agency accused the British of denying the Jewish people their rights to a Jewish homeland in the '*darkest hour of Jewish history*'.

The next day Hoz phoned the TUC asking for a meeting with Citrine to discuss the White Paper. He left a message for Citrine reminding him that since 1917; the TUC and Labour Party had intervened several times on behalf of the Jews of Palestine and he would like the TUC to make an appeal to the government not to abrogate their responsibilities and that even if the TUC had no influence on government, he was asking them to protest because of the possible bearing it would have on League of Nations Mandates Commission. He added that in the following week's Parliamentary debate the Labour Party would tell the prime minister that they would reverse the policy when in office.[74] Hoz phoned again a few days later and was told that as Citrine was again unavailable, his request would be placed before the General Purposes Committee and that the TUC was aware that the AFL had issued a statement against the proposals and had also asked the American government to use their influence with the British government on the matter. Citrine however would not be drawn into discussing the matter with Hoz and wrote to him saying that the view of the General Council was that the matter was best dealt with by the Labour Party.[75]

It must have been clear by now to Hoz that Citrine was never going to commit the TUC to independently supporting their fellow trade unionists in Palestine but Hoz never gave up, even though all Citrine was ever prepared to do was to pass the matter on to the Labour Party or the National Council of Labour (NCL) or even the IFTU of which he was the president.

How Labour's relations with the Histadrut differed to those of the TUC is vividly illustrated by the party's reaction to the memorandum on the political situation in Palestine it received in June 1939 from the Palestine Arab Workers Society (PAWS) in Haifa. The first thing Gilles, the Labour Party international secretary did was to send a copy to Locker asking for his observations. Locker told Gilles that the true character of the group emerged in the last few pages of the memorandum where the '*Jews were accused of trying to overrule the world*' and that the signatories of the letter declared that unless the British and international labour movement accepted their demands, they would '*embrace National Socialism, because we shall then become disciples of and missionaries to these new ideas*', making it quite clear that they were supporters of the Grand Mufti of Jerusalem who supported the aims of Hitler and the Nazi Party.[76]

As a measure of Citrine's standing within the British labour movement in June 1939 he was appointed along with Dalton and Morrison by the NCL to consult with the prime minister on various matters of international importance. While strongly opposing the Nazi government and its persecution of Jews, the TUC supported the government's policy of drastically limiting the flow of Jewish refugees into Britain as it did not feel that the country could accommodate large numbers of refugees into the workforce at a time of economic hardship. The TUC may have been strong on words but failed to publicly support the refugees to be allowed to enter either Britain or Palestine. His American colleagues took opposite view as they vigorously lobbied for the Jewish refugees to enter Palestine.

Citrine may have kept the TUC out of debate over the White Paper which abandoned partition while making concessions to the Arabs at the expense of Jews but for the Labour Party, it was the start of a pro-Zionist campaign which stepped up at the start of the war. Labour then used every possible opportunity support the Jews and attack the government either in Parliament, or at their annual conference or in the pages of *the Daily Herald*. The NCL argued in February 1940 that the government was treating Palestine as a colonial possession and not as a mandated territory.[77]

The next month Hoz asked for a meeting with Citrine but met instead with his Deputy, Vincent Tewson. He told him that he needed to see Citrine in order to explain the critical position which had been reached on the Palestine question and that the Histadrut needed the British labour movement's support. He had hoped that Citrine, as president of the IFTU would be able to intervene with the prime minister before the forthcoming parliamentary debate on Palestine to explain TUC's opposition to the White Paper. Hoz argued that the primary concern of the Histadrut was that the government was in effect, saying '*you have enough Jews in the country and enough land for their settlement*', which meant that Palestine was no longer the Jewish national home. Tewson replied saying that Congress had made declarations on Palestine in the past at the request of the Histadrut, but this was purely political question.[78] He made it clear to Hoz that the TUC would not become involved in what they considered to be political matters which directly involved the government and was following the policy laid down by Citrine.

The Labour Party continued to support its Jewish comrades in Palestine and at its 1940 Party conference unanimously adopted a resolution written by Poale Zion critical of the British government's restrictions and the problem of antisemitic persecution. Once again Berl Locker wrote to Citrine on the eve of TUC Congress in September 1940 outlining the Histadrut's war aims, the problems facing the Jewish people in Palestine and the basis of any future peace settlement. In response to his request for the adoption of a motion of support for the rights of the Jewish people and their national home, Tewson wrote to Locker saying the General Council had considered his request and decided to take no action[79] and that it was '*not possible to submit an emergency resolution as conference lasts only three days*', *adding that as the subject had been discussed by unions at the Labour Party conference in May, it was 'felt to be adequate in the circumstances*'.[80]

The reality was that none of the speakers at the Labour conference were from the unions. Locker's alternative suggestion was that the chairman insert a sentence or two in his presidential address to Congress, expressing '*sympathy with the Jewish Trade Union Movement in Palestine whose achievements are endangered by the Axis aggression in the Middle East. Our Jewish comrades take a foremost part in mobilising the manpower and resources of Palestine in our common struggle, and we wish to express to them our determination to continue our policy of support towards the Jewish National home and the rights of the Jewish people in all countries*'. This proposal was dismissed by saying that the speech was already in the printer's hands.[81] So much for Citrine saying that '*the fate of the Jews was always on their minds*',[82] inaction was the TUC's keyword as they used every possible reason and tactic to dismiss the Histadrut's requests to do nothing. In response to a Histadrut telegram to the Congress which stated that '*we are working together in fight against Nazism and fascism*'. Citrine replied that they appreciated the sentiments expressed and assured the Histadrut that they would do all '*they can to secure for the Jews civil, political and economic equality and their national rights*'.[83] Locker told the Mapai Central Committee in 1943 that the lack of public support by the TUC for the Histadrut was not unusual as the leadership (*Citrine*) had refused on principle and had consistently declined to adopt an independent stand on Zionism and Jewish affairs. All their appeals had been rejected and passed onto the Labour Party.[84] He linked Citrine with a group of Labour cabinet ministers who thought it advisable to '*water down*' any pro-Zionist statements.[85] Citrine had made it clear where he stood on political issues and would willingly support the Histadrut labour matters. Poale Zion assisted the Histadrut in its lobbying activities by individuals such as MPs who were members of Poale Zion, the Labour Party and the Zionist Federation. Although Locker had taken over from Hoz as the Histadrut's London representative, Hoz was sent back on more than one occasion to London by Ben-Gurion to talk to Ministers and the Labour Party leadership before his untimely death in December 1940. So great was the impression that Hoz had made on the Labour leadership that the memorial meeting for Hoz's death in London was attended by Middleton and the Labour MP's Janner and Creech Jones, with Bevin, and Morrison sending messages.[86]

The American Trade Union Movement and Palestine

IN 1917 both the TUC and the American Federation of Labor (AFL) supported the creation of a Jewish homeland in Palestine, but the AFL's attitude to the establishment of a Jewish national home and their relationship with the Histadrut differed widely from that of the TUC. The Jewish labour movement in America had developed in a similar manner to Britain because of the large influx of Jewish immigrants during the late nineteenth and early twentieth centuries. Whereas in Britain the Jewish trade union movement never played a significant role in the wider movement once Poale Zion had affiliated to the Labour Party, the American Jewish trade unions and their leaders had, by the early 1920s, gained the respect and support of the AFL, which in turn led to them backing the Jewish unions fund raising campaigns to support the work of the Histadrut in Palestine.

In the 1930s the American unions began to use their political connections to gain American government support for a Jewish state in Palestine as well asking them to use their influence with Britain with regard to the Palestine mandate and their treatment of the Jews. Both Dov Hoz and Berl Locker had spent time in the USA and when the Passfield White Paper was issued in 1929, the two men ensured that both the TUC and the Labour Party received letters and telegrams from the American unions urging them to protest against the government's proposals. In 1939 not only did William Green, president of the AFL, write to President Roosevelt urging him to use his influence with the British government against the proposals but he also sent a telegram to the British prime minister. As a measure of Green's standing, Roosevelt sent him a two-page reply which expressed his sympathy for the idea of a national home for the Jews in Palestine but he did not take the matter any further with the British government. This was the big difference between the standings of the unions in their respective countries.[87] Citrine's responses to the many letters and telegrams from the American unions often gave the impression that the TUC, along with the Labour Party was actively lobbying the government, which of course it wasn't. He even told Green that '*the Jewish problems were constantly on their minds*'.[88] It is very likely that the Americans understood that the TUC played a supporting role to the Labour Party and that Citrine was not as influential as he made out but nevertheless they continued to lobby Citrine because he was very supportive of the Histadrut and also because he was president of the IFTU.

The Spanish Civil War

July 1936 saw the start of the Spanish Civil War between the Spanish Republic and the Nationalists led by General Franco who wanted to establish a fascist dictatorship in Spain. The British government, along with France and several other European countries supported a policy of non-intervention including an arms embargo which they believed would restrict the spread of hostilities across Europe. Nazi Germany and fascist Italy ignored the pact and sent weapons and men to support Franco. The reaction of the Left throughout Europe was to oppose Franco and urged volunteers to go to Spain to fight alongside the Republicans.

The TUC's international agenda between 1936 and the outbreak of the Second World War was dominated by discussions about German aggression in Europe including the Spanish Civil War, Czechoslovakia, the persecution of the Jews of Germany and the admission Austrian and German Jewish refugees into Britain and Palestine.

In the autumn of 1936 Bevin became chairman of the TUC General Council as well as joint-chairman of the NCL with Hugh Dalton, the chairman of the National Executive of the Labour Party, Along with Citrine, all three men realised that fascist aggression in Europe could lead to war.

When the war in Spain started the Labour Party was still embroiled in an internal dispute over the party's support for pacifism and its opposition to rearmament which had led to George Landsbury resigning as Party leader over his support for pacifism just weeks before the 1935 General Election when Labour suffered its worst defeat unrivalled until 2019. The failure of the League of Nations to defend democracy against the threat of fascism had shocked the Labour Party. That they had supported the League as a vehicle for world peace only added to its turmoil. The predicament which Labour found itself in mirrored the wider debate in Britain on foreign and defence policy.

The 1936 Labour Party and TUC conferences both approved policies of non-intervention in the conflict which they believed if supported by Britain and her allies, as well as Germany and Italy, the threat of war in Europe would be reduced. They also called for an immediate enquiry into any alleged breaches of the embargo. While Bevin and Citrine defended the policy of non-intervention as the best way of avoiding war in Europe, the Left condemned Labour for not backing the call for volunteers to join the International Brigades as well as not calling on the British government to supply arms to the Republicans. An additional complication for the

TUC was that although sympathetic to the Republicans both Bevin and Citrine opposed Communist influence in the unions and did not want to work alongside the Soviet Union which backed the Spanish Communist Party and supplied arms to the Republicans.

Both Bevin and Citrine realised that fascist aggression in Europe could lead to war and they supported an arms embargo because they were concerned about the state of the British armed forces. They argued that weapons could be sent to Spain, provided they were not British weapons or needed by the British armed forces as Britain would need to rearm rapidly if there was a war against Germany.

The suffering of the Spanish people led many in the labour movement to question the party's previous policy of disarmament and non-intervention which in 1937 resulted in Labour abstaining in the debate about the government's defence estimates rather than opposing them as they had done in the past. This move enabled both the TUC and Labour Party conferences to approve a new NCL report '*International policy and defence*' which although ambiguous in parts, argued that the party could not call on the government to stand up to dictators whilst at the same time opposing rearmament. The Spanish Civil War changed Labour Party's stance on the use of force and rearmament which allowed Winston Churchill to include the Labour Party in his coalition government in 1940.

Thousands of volunteers from around the world went to Spain between 1936 and 1939 to join the International Brigades fighting alongside the Republicans in the civil war against the Nationalists. Neither the TUC nor the Labour Party publicly supported the International Brigade. Approximately 2400 Britons served in the British Battalion; the majority of whom were either members of the Communist Party or active in the trade union movement.[89]

It is estimated that, approximately 8000 of the volunteers were Jewish including around 350 from Great Britain and 300–500 Palestinian Jews. Proportionally the Palestine contingent was the largest Jewish contingent from any country. The percentage of Jews who served in the British Battalion was 15% which was highly disproportionate given that Jews counted for only 0.5% of the general population. Of the 526 British volunteers who died in the conflict, 89 were Jewish or 17% of the total. This again was a disproportionate figure especially as it represented 36% of those British Jews who had volunteered.[90] The reason why Jews were so disproportionately represented in the British Battalion is because many young Jews in Britain, especially in London's East End, were attracted to the Communist Party because of its militant stand against fascism and as it was the only political Party advocating intervention against the nationalists to challenge the threat of fascism and antisemitism it provided the motivation to travel to Spain and fight alongside the Republicans.

The situation in Palestine was more conflicted than in Britain. As the majority of Palestinian Jews supported the Republicans, Mapai called on its members to aid Spain, calling the war '*a war of the working class against reaction, against antisemitic fascism, against the danger of world slaughter*' and the Histadrut, like the TUC, supported the international campaign to help the Spanish workers. The Histadrut's newspaper *Davar* condemned the British government's policy of non-intervention towards the war and described the nationalists as fascists and Franco an ally of Hitler.[91]

However the leadership of the Yishuv were against their young people serving in Spain; firstly because their number one priority was to reinforce the Jewish presence in Palestine during Arab rebellion rather than international solidarity or fighting fascism and secondly they did not want to enter into another conflict with the British as the government could have responded by withdrawing their support for a Jewish homeland in favour of the Arabs. While some Arabs did fight together with Palestinian Jews, the Mufti of Jerusalem, who was the Arab leader in Palestine, was forging links with both Germany and Italy.

The result was that most of the Palestinian Jews who went to Spain belonged to the Palestine Communist Party. Whilst it was legal to be a member of the Communist Party in Britain, active support for the communists in most parts of the British Empire usually resulted in imprisonment or fines. However in Palestine, the British deported any communists who did not have Palestinian citizenship and used the civil war to 'encourage' communists to leave for Spain as an alternative to prison.

The memory of General Franco's close ties to Nazi Germany in World War Two lingered on in Israel for many years. In 1948, shortly after the State of Israel had been established, Prime Minister David Ben-Gurion rejected Franco's proposal for establishing diplomatic relations between the two states because of his close ties with the Nazis.[92] The Palestinian Jews who went to Spain fared no better as they were snubbed by their fellow Israelis until the early 1970s when their efforts in fighting fascism eventually began to be acknowledged.

The Communist Party of Great Britain and the Jews

The Communist Party of Great Britain (CPGB) was founded in 1920. Although the party failed to be a major force in the general strike of 1926, by the 1930s it could count on the support of the miners' union and the engineering and textile trades. It was very strong in both Glasgow and the East End of London which both had large Jewish populations, many of whom were attracted to socialism and joined either the Labour Party or the CPGB. The attraction of communism for Jews on the political Left was not only its ideology, but also its opposition to antisemitism. Britain during the 1930s saw growing support within the Left for the Zionist project in Palestine but not amongst the young working-class Jews of the East End for whom Zionism '*made no headway*'. They preferred instead to join the CPGB which offered them the best solution to their problems.[93] The party opposed the rise of fascism and was against the Conservative government's policy of appeasement towards Nazi Germany. The CPGB played a leading role in the fight against the British Union of Fascists (BUF) and in 1936; Jewish Socialists and left-wing Zionists came together with the CPGB to oppose the BUF in a series of clashes known as the 'Battle of Cable Street'.

Membership of the CPGB rose steadily throughout the 1930s and by 1939 it had nearly 18,000 members. Communists were excluded from membership of the Labour Party and were restricted by the TUC's 1934 'black circular' which forbade communists to stand as delegates for local trade councils. As a member of Comintern, the Communist International, it was the duty of the CPGB to support Soviet actions and explain Stalin's policies to its members. While the CPGB denied Jewish claims to be a political nation, from the mid-1930s onwards it allowed the Jews to be designated as a people or nationality, but always stopped short of support for Zionism. In 1936 the CPGB founded a Jewish Bureau to advise on policy issues such as the 'Jewish question' and the Arab-Jewish violence in Palestine. The Middle East conflict was viewed both as a class struggle and as a liberation struggle by the Palestinian Arabs against British imperialism. Jews were called upon to support the Arab revolt and oppose Zionism—which the CPGB said served the interests of Jewish capitalists and British colonialists. The signing of the Soviet-German non-aggression pact on 23rd August 1939 obliged the CPGB to reverse its pre-war policy of standing up to Hitler. The *Daily Worker* described the agreement as a '*dramatic peace move to halt aggressors*'.[94] After Hitler invaded Poland on 1 September, and Britain declared war on Germany two days later, the

Daily Worker wrote that this was '*a war that can and must be won*'. Within weeks, however, the CPGB had received instructions from Moscow and reversed its policy and opposed the war.

The British labour movement was shocked by the signing of the Molotov-Ribbentrop non-aggression pact because it destroyed Labour's foreign policy which had been based on British cooperation with France and Russia in order to deter German aggression. On 3 September as delegates gathered in Bridlington for the TUC annual Congress, war was declared. The next day Citrine told Congress that he had been staggered to learn of the non-aggression pact and that '*one of our three partners upon whom we had rested our hopes for a united resistance to Nazi aggression has concluded this agreement with the Nazi aggressor*'.[95] Congress approved the General Council's declaration which affirmed their solidarity with the British government to resist Nazi aggression so that '*liberty and order*' could be '*re-established in the world*'.[96] Many Jews left the CPGB in protest at the Soviet alliance with Hitler, because for them their opposition to antisemitism undermined their loyalty Stalin and communism. Only people such as Ivor Montagu and Eric Hobsbawm remained.

The Second World War, 1939–45

Once war had been declared, Bevin and Citrine made it clear to the government that they wanted the TUC to be directly involved in consultation and decision making with all government departments and not just Ministry of Labour and National Service. The following month instructions were issued to all governmental departments to cooperate and consult with the TUC and its affiliate unions. The effect of this decision along with the appointment of Bevin as Minister for Labour in 1940 was that the TUC was able to play a key role in the British industrial war effort so that by 1945 the TUC had become a respected and influential organisation.

The attitude of the Jewish community in Palestine to the outbreak of war was summed up by Ben-Gurion as: '*We shall fight with Great Britain in the war as if there were no White Paper and we shall fight the White Paper as if there were no war*'.[97] Consequently Ben-Gurion placed the resources of the Jewish community in Palestine at the disposal of the British war effort whilst continuing to oppose restrictions on immigration by supporting 'illegal' Jewish immigration. Ben-Gurion believed that the only way forward was the establishment of a Jewish state and all the efforts of the Zionist movement should work towards that one aim. In 1942, a conference in New York of Zionist leaders from America and 17 other countries adopted Ben-Gurion's plans which became known as the 'Biltmore Program' whose aim was the establishment of Palestine 'as a Jewish commonwealth integrated into the structure of the new democratic world'. It also agreed that the Jewish Agency should have control of immigration and the development of the Jewish economy to allow it to absorb large numbers of Jews after the war.[98] The Histadrut, which controlled the Jewish economy in Palestine, played a key role in Ben-Gurion's plans and worked with the British administration in Palestine to ensure industrial output for the war effort was maintained. At the same time it pursued a political role by lobbying Labour politicians and the TUC throughout the war. The Colonial Office described the power and influence of the Histadrut in Palestine as formidable.[99] The TUC's relationship with the Histadrut during wartime with regard to labour issues can be described as that of branch office and head office.

The TUC was asked to intervene with the British government on the Histadrut's behalf in July 1941 when the Palestine government published draft labour legislation to ensure the continuous output of supplies essential to the war effort. Citrine immediately wrote to Lord Moyne, the Minister of State in Cairo, asking for safeguards as it was important to keep the Palestinian workers on the British side. Moyne replied saying that the Palestinian legislation would follow the British model as closely as possible and would include the reasonable claims of the Histadrut.[100] By 1942, 21,000 Palestinian Jewish men and women had enlisted in the British armed forces. Once reports of the Hitler's plan to exterminate the Jews had started to appear, there were calls in Palestine as well as in Parliament for the creation of a Jewish fighting force and home defence in Palestine. The Histadrut responded by calling on the TUC to lobby the government for a Jewish fighting force and home defence in Palestine '*in this fateful hour*'.[101] Tewson told the NCL meeting on 21 July 1942 that the TUC had considered the Histadrut's telegrams from the Histadrut and had decided that the matter was entirely a political question and had therefore referred the correspondence to the NCL. After a long discussion the NCL resolved that the matter should be left in the hands of the government.[102] Two weeks later the government announced their plans to defend Palestine which included the creation of a Palestine Regiment of the British Army consisting of separate Jewish and Arab infantry battalions and a Palestine Volunteer Force.

The Mass Murder of the Jews

The mass murder of the Jews in Europe during the war by the Germans was first brought to the attention of the TUC and the Labour Party in July 1942. The Labour Party NEC had been so appalled by the horror of the news from Poland and Czechoslovakia that they immediately passed a resolution on behalf of the British labour movement calling for the perpetrators to be brought to justice after the war. Once the TUC had signed up to the motion, a deputation then delivered it to both the Foreign Office and the American ambassador.[103]

The Labour Party then launched a campaign among British workers to win support for measures proposed by the United Nations[104] which they hoped would bring a halt to these atrocities. On 2 September 1942 they organised the only public meeting to be held during the war to protest at the German atrocities. At the beginning of December copies of Histadrut resolutions relating to the extermination of Jews in Poland as well calling for Jews including children be allowed to enter Palestine were sent to the Labour Party which were passed onto the Foreign Office who replied saying that that children from Romania were already being admitted to Palestine.[105] This was followed by a meeting between a joint Labour Party/TUC deputation and the foreign secretary to discuss the steps being taken by the British government "to secure a United Nations policy on this matter". Then on 15 December the TUC International Committee discussed the latest communications they had received from the Histadrut; the World Jewish Congress and the Jewish Labour Committee of New York, all of which asked the TUC to take all possible steps to stop the mass slaughter of Jews in occupied countries. The Committee passed a strong resolution of protest embodying an appeal to the former trade unionists in Germany as well as endorsing the action of the IFTU which had met on 11 December 1942.[106] The following day the TUC and the Labour adopted another resolution which acknowledged that '*There is ample evidence that this crime has been methodically organised, and is being carried out with such persistence and thoroughness that within a short time the Jewish people, within the frontiers of the New German Order in Europe, will have been exterminated*' and that '*this unparalleled and stupendous act of barbarism will always be associated in history with the name of modern Germany*'.[107] Because so much evidence of the Nazi plan to exterminate the Jews had come into the public domain the Allies were forced to break their veto on all publicity about the atrocities so that on 17 December

1942 the governments of Britain and the United States issued a public condemnation of these Nazi war crimes.

The NCL meeting in January 1943 were told that an all-party deputation was to meet with the deputy prime minister, the foreign secretary, the home secretary and the colonial secretary in order to press for action by the government on the persecution of the Jews. Tewson told the meeting that Locker had made a series of suggestions to save the Jewish population in occupied Europe from extermination. His proposals included that subject to security safeguards, the British government, her colonies and all territories under her control offer asylum to Jewish refugees and they attempted to persuade the United States, the Allied Nations, the British Dominions and neutral countries to make similar offers. Locker had also pointed out that there were still some 37,000 immigration certificates available under the 1939 White Paper and that Palestine was suffering from shortage of labour which meant that 50,000 able bodied men and women could readily be absorbed in agriculture, industry and Palestine's war effort. The cost of absorption could be met in part by funds from Jewish sources. The meeting resolved to give its '*general support for any practical proposals for providing asylum for members of the oppressed Jewish community who it may be possible to rescue from their present dangers*'[108] which was no more than they could have done.

The following month the Histadrut sent an emotive telegram to the TUC: '*Our members were deeply impressed by the IFTU announcement to the workers of the Nazi dominated countries on the wholesale slaughter of the Jews. Many of us have relatives in those countries, for all of us it is a question of extermination of half our nation. Unfortunately it seems that the measures taken until now did not stop this process*'.[109] It must have been a surreal situation for the Histadrut especially in autumn 1942, to be writing to the TUC on trade union matters knowing not only that events in the North Africa could bring war closer to Palestine but also that the Nazis had exterminated hundreds of thousands of Polish Jews.[110] From then on the Histadrut used every opportunity to impress upon both the TUC and the Labour Party of the maltreatment of the Jews by the Nazis.[111] In September 1943 they urged the TUC to consider that '*Jewish labour in Palestine participating wholeheartedly in war effort looks to your help and understanding in its anxiety that Jewish people does not remain losers in a democratic victorious world. We are certain you will not fail us*'.[112] The following month the TUC International Committee as a mark of respect, decided to minute the 1943 TUC Congress resolution which condemned the inhumane crimes '*against the peoples in all the occupied countries and against the Jewish race in particular*'.[113]

The 1943 TUC Congress adopted a resolution moved by the Transport and General Workers Union (TGWU) which demanded punishment for war criminals, and those responsible for the persecution and massacre of hundreds of thousands of European Jews, The resolution read that '*The Congress, after four years of the most terrible war the world has ever seen, a war in which the Nazis have perpetrated inhuman crimes against the peoples of all the occupied countries and particularly against the Jewish race, pledges itself to continue the struggle until the unconditional surrender*' of the Axis powers and demanded that '*after victory is achieved, all those responsible for atrocities, whatever their rank or position, be brought to justice before an Allied tribunal and punished according to the extent of their responsibility. The German people cannot escape the responsibility for starting the war and for the crimes committed…*'.[114] There were no further discussions about the killing of the Jews for the remainder of the war.

Jewish Labour groups in Britain including Poale Zion, the Jewish Bakers union, the Jewish Furnishing Trades Union, sections of the National Union of Tailors and the Workers Circle came together In November 1943 to form the United Jewish Labour Committee in order to raise funds for the Histadrut Rescue fund which had been established to take Jews out of Nazi-occupied territories. The campaign gained the support of the Labour Party and the unions and over the next 12 months raised £2000 for the fund.[115]

Throughout the rest of the war when the Histadrut protested to the TUC about the Palestine government's actions against the Jewish population such as the raiding of settlements looking for illegal immigrants and deserters; the TUC would often ask the Colonial Office for advice before replying. This did not however affect the TUC's lobbying of the Colonial office on behalf of Histadrut on work related issues.

In October 1943 Locker wrote to his colleagues in Palestine about his dealings with the politicians in Parliament and the TUC. He believed that that Churchill was their best friend in the government along with Lord Cranbourne and Leo Amery but Anthony Eden, the foreign secretary, was opposed to the Zionists. With regard to the Labour Party Ministers he only occasionally saw the people who were close to them. Bevin, who as Minister of Labour was popular and thought to be doing a good job was inaccessible and even Arthur Creech Jones, '*one of our closest and most loyal friends*' had told Locker that he that rarely spoke to Bevin.

Locker said that Bevin, Attlee and Morrison all knew that there was a Jewish question and could not say '*oh well, after the war, everything will go back to the way it was*'. But they all said that '*maybe perhaps we should go find another land?*' whilst adding that it does not mean that Palestine is out of the question. When Morrison had raised the matter, Harold Laski told him: '*I am not an extreme Zionist, but I will tell you that no Jew will even fathom such thing, that bringing up such question is an insult*'. Locker wrote that he was also worried about the future as one their key people James Middleton, the general secretary of the Labour Party was due to retire and that his replacement might not continue to look after the Yishuv's interests.

The atmosphere in the trade unions, Locker said was different to Labour as they were a less interested in the big political questions, which was the big difference between the general secretaries of TUC and the Labour Party. Citrine, he wrote, "will never say anything against us (the Zionists), but in his heart there are reservations". When Locker asked him for their support two years previously Citrine answered "we are not a political body, we are a trade union. The most important trade unionists are part of the Labour Party, they voted for your decision. Why do you want to put in another resolution? What more do you want? Of course we are interested in politics, we are represented by the Labour Party".[116]

The Situation in Summer 1945

From 1917 the British labour movement had, given their complete support for a Jewish homeland in Palestine but after winning the 1945 general election it found itself divided both individually and politically over Palestine. This conflict of interest between support for the Jews and Britain's need to maintain the friendship of the Arab nations was further deepened by the guilt they felt for the suffering of the Jews during the Holocaust. Moreover, British post-war immigration policy deliberately excluded Jews who had survived the war and were now living in displaced persons camps. Now leading the government, Attlee and Bevin soon realised that the problems in Palestine would have to be dealt with and they would have to balance the reality of Britain's post-war situation against what the Labour Party had said in the past. The question of how much was political posturing and how much was true conviction would now be tested. Once they became aware of the realities of government Labour abandoned their pro-Zionist policies in favour of a continuation the pre-war Conservative government's policies. This was not a problem for the TUC as they would automatically support whatever policy their colleagues in the Labour Party decided because Citrine had always declined to make political statements relating to the Histadrut or a Jewish national home in Palestine.

When in November 1945 Bevin announced that the Labour government would continue with the 1939 White Paper policy on Jewish immigration to Palestine it came as a surprise to the Yishuv. Labour had first pledged their support for a Jewish national home in 1917 and had renewed that promise a further 10 times including at their last conference in May 1945. The Jews were outraged and decided to openly challenge British rule by attacking and sabotaging British property and installations throughout Palestine. The moderate Haganah the national defence force for all the settlements, joined with the extremist organisations, the Irgun and LEHI to force the British to withdraw. The British brought in an extra 80,000 troops in order to put down the opposition but to no avail. The violent Jewish campaign continued and on 22 July 1946 the Irgun blew up the British military headquarters in the King David Hotel in Jerusalem killing 91 civilians. The impact of the attack shocked the British both in Palestine and Britain. At the same time as the military campaign, Jewish emissaries in Europe were actively bringing thousands of illegal Jewish immigrants by ship to Palestine every month. The result was a British naval blockade of Palestine to try and stem the flow illegal immigrants.

British Labour's Position

The Labour Party's approach to Zionism had evolved from their recognition of the right of Jews to return to Palestine in 1917 into their 1944 Conference declaration that Palestine was the Jewish national home. All previous resolutions had been based on pre-war party policy and the 1944 statement was the first to take into account the plight and suffering of the Jews in the Holocaust. The declaration stated that '*there is surely neither hope nor meaning in a 'Jewish National Home', unless we are prepared to let Jews, if they wish, enter this tiny land in such numbers as to become a majority. There was a strong case for this before the War. There is an irresistible case now, after the unspeakable atrocities of the cold and calculated German Nazi plan to kill all Jews in Europe*'.[117] Although the Labour Party knew that conference motions and policy statements were not binding on any future Labour government, the Zionists understood this latest pledge to be a binding commitment on their behalf by the Labour Party, which was why they were so upset when Bevin ignored the resolution. The declaration was also controversial not because it stated that Palestine was the Jewish national home, but because it called for the '*Arabs to be encouraged to move out as the Jews move in*'. The text had been written by Dalton, a committed Zionist who was in favour of partition. The Palestine Arab Workers Society (PAWS) wrote to the IFTU about the transfer of Arabs out of Palestine. The letter was passed onto to the TUC who explained that it only referred to the voluntary evacuation of Palestine territory by the Arabs and that no compulsion of any kind was intended.[118] The 1944 declaration was the high point in Labour's sympathy and identification with the suffering of the Jewish people and the Zionists aspiration for a Jewish homeland in Palestine.

Even though the TUC Executive had discussed the extermination of the Jews in Europe in 1942 and were associated with the Labour Party subsequent actions the only time during the war that the murder of millions of Jews by the Nazis was ever mentioned at the TUC Congress was in 1943, in an address by Isidore Nagler, the AFL fraternal delegate.[119] His statement reflected the fact that the American trade union movement was much more openly supportive of the Histadrut and sympathetic to the problems facing the Jews than was the TUC. Another example of the TUC's ambivalence regarding the fate of the Jews which had started in the 1930s was that Congress never discussed the 1944 Labour Party resolution on Palestine or the Holocaust.

Although sympathetic to the plight of the Jews before the war as well as the issues, Bevin, believed that Jews were a religious group and not a nation. As a matter of policy he took the view that the Jewish refugees should be returned to their country of origin regardless of whether they wanted to go there or not. He also opposed the relaxation of restrictions on the numbers of Jews entering Britain, believing that they would be accused of using the horrors of the Holocaust to go to the head of the queue. Upon entering office Bevin realised that the Labour Party now had to take responsibility for British policy in Palestine and the Middle East. Although often thought of as an antisemite for his actions and remarks as foreign secretary, his primary aim was to look after British interests as the governing power in Palestine, which he did to the best of his ability. Bevin was confident that having been a successful trade union leader he could solve the Palestinian problem by negotiation. However neither he nor his advisors fully appreciated that the Holocaust had united the Jews more than ever before around the creation of a Jewish state in Palestine, an ideal which they were prepared to fight for. He also deeply resented American pressure to change his policy.[120] The worsening conflict in Palestine deepened the rift between the Labour government and its pro-Zionist MPs. Most of the criticism of the government came from the Tribune group of Left-wing MP's, who accused the government of trying to placate the Arabs and forced moderate Zionists, who wanted to cooperate with Britain into the extremist camp.[121]

The Role of Histadrut Lobbying TUC

The Jewish economy and industrial output in Palestine expanded greatly during the war because of the demands of the British war effort. Ben-Gurion and his colleagues hoped that recognition of the Jewish war effort would in 1945, as it had in 1918, produce support for their claims for a Jewish state. The British however saw the Palestine problem and the plight of the Jews in Europe as two separate issues.

Immediately after Labour's general election in July 1945 the Histadrut sent a telegram saying '*Hope you will act without delay to help save the remnants of our brethren and enable us to rebuild our free Jewish homeland*'.[122] When rumours began to circulate that the 1939 White Paper was about to be maintained, they lobbied both the TUC and the Labour Party asking them to support their demands for the White Paper to be abolished and that Jews be brought to Palestine by all available means.[123] They were unsuccessful as in November 1945 Bevin announced that the immigration restrictions in the White Paper were to be implemented. Locker immediately asked for meeting with the Sub-committee of the National Executive Committee to discuss Bevin's statement only to be told that the Committee were generally in agreement with the foreign secretary's statement and that no useful purpose could be served by any further discussion before the Anglo-American Joint Committee of Inquiry had an opportunity to start its work.[124] The Labour Party also wrote to the Histadrut saying that they understood and deeply sympathised with their disappointment, but believed it would be possible to find a fair and just solution for both the Jews and Arabs.[125]

As well as the violence directed at British troops and property, there were continual attempts to break the British blockade directed at restricting Jewish immigration into Palestine. As part of their political campaign, throughout 1946 the Histadrut regularly protested to the TUC and the

Labour Party over the Palestine government's actions against the Jewish population and controls on immigration. The TUC General Council always discussed these communications and often asked the Colonial Office for advice before replying to the Histadrut. In July, Tewson told the General Council that the NCL had discussed the latest arrests in Palestine and had decided that the matter should be discussed unofficially with the government. The NCL also discussed telegrams received from Histadrut and the American Jewish Trade Union committee for Palestine protesting against the government's action in Palestine.[126] The TUC was also lobbied by trade unionists from home and abroad to intervene with the government over restrictions on Jewish immigration into Palestine.[127] Tewson's reply to the AFL displayed both his and the TUC's support for the Labour government '*the matter is one of great complexity which British Government is anxious to secure a solution but obviously cannot do so on the basis of unrestricted immigration*'.[128]

Britain was fighting an insurgency in Palestine with British soldiers and police dying in a foreign land and the TUC, which was a key partner of the Labour government, was being asked to lobby the same Labour government on behalf of the Histadrut, to stop the violence, even though they themselves were a part of the Jewish insurgency. The TUC leadership never saw themselves as having conflicting loyalties, loyalty towards the Labour government and loyalty to their colleagues in the international labour movement, as their priority was to give unwavering support to the Labour government and defend its actions in Palestine. The Histadrut as well as Mapai continued to lobby the Labour Party, the TUC and the international labour movement for support for an independent Jewish state in Palestine. They found allies in the Labour Party who would speak on their behalf such as Richard Crossman MP and Harold Laski,[129] but after 1945 there was no one in the TUC or the unions that was willing to challenge Bevin or Arthur Deakin, Bevin's successor as general secretary of the TGWU on the General Council. This situation had come about because their lobbying of the British labour movement which started in the 1930s, had concentrated mainly on the Labour Party and not the unions or the TUC. Consequently they had failed to recruit any trade unionists who would speak on their behalf at the General Council and most of the post-war contact between the Histadrut and the TUC was by either telegram or letter.

The Emergence of the WFTU

The World Federation of Trade Unions (WFTU) was the brainchild of Citrine, the TUC general secretary, who in October 1943 set out his ideas for a new world conference of trade unions which he hoped would play a substantive role in international affairs. He envisaged that by building on the cooperation and links that had been forged during the war the new organisation which would include all the unions in Europe, America and the USSR.[130]

The Soviet Union had realised early on that the WFTU would be an ideal organisation for promoting Communist values within the international workers' movement and as a result took the WFTU more seriously than the TUC. Palestine was just one of many East–West flashpoints during this period. As a member of the international labour movement, the Histadrut lobbied the WFTU to put pressure on the TUC. This provided the USSR with an opportunity to support the Histadrut and thwart British influence in the Middle East. The WFTU's involvement in Palestine affairs lasted from 1946 to the beginning of 1948.

In order to challenge the Soviet Union for the leadership and counter their dominance of the WFTU, Deakin became the organisation's president in 1946, ignoring Bevin's advice that the WFTU would gradually fall under Soviet control and that a non-communist president would give a false impression of unity.[131] Deakin remained president until 1949 when as a result of disputes over support for the American government's Marshall Plan the non-Communist unions led by the TUC left the WFTU to form the International Confederation of Trade Unions (ICFTU). Their withdrawal allowed the Soviet Union complete control the WFTU.

The Histadrut leadership was extremely concerned about the inaugural WFTU conference which was to be held in London in February 1945, firstly because the Soviet Union would be there and secondly that the TUC had approved the participation of the Histadrut as well as the Arab trade unions in Palestine. Locker had warned his colleagues that their delegates needed to be well prepared for a serious offensive. Ben-Gurion's priority however was not the speeches to the Congress but meetings with people, because he said that '*We first have to maintain the relationship with our friends, and not take them for granted. It is not the Labour Party, where Middleton is no longer the head, it is Citrine. They will all meet Arabs, and the atmosphere will not be convenient for us. That is why these conversations are very important*'.[132]

The founding WFTU conference was the most representative labour gathering ever held and was attended by delegates from 63 trade union movements, representing 50 million workers from all parts of the world. All the major powers were represented, including the Soviet Union, Britain and the USA. The CIO represented the United States because the AFL, which had taken an anti-communist position, refused to join the WFTU. Palestine was represented by the Histadrut, which included Arab members of the Palestine Labour League in their delegation as well as two organisations representing Arab workers—the Palestine Arab Workers Society (PAWS) and the Federation of Arab Trade Unions (FAU).[133]

When the conference discussed the situation in Palestine the most significant feature was the sympathy and support shown by the Soviet delegation for article 26 of the declaration '*The Union Attitude to the Peace Settlement*', which was adopted by the Conference and supported the idea of a Jewish national home in Palestine.[134] The statement on Palestine was based on the declaration made by the allies at the Yalta Conference. Article 26 which was written by committee chaired by the CIO, who supported the Histadrut and a Jewish state in Palestine stated:

> *This World Conference is of opinion too that after the war, thorough going remedies must be found, through international action, for the wrongs inflicted on the Jewish people. Their protection against oppression, discrimination and spoliation in any country must be the responsibility of the new International Authority. The Jewish people must be enabled to continue the rebuilding of Palestine as their National Home, so successfully begun by immigration, agricultural resettlement and industrial development; respecting the legitimate interests of other national groups and giving equality of rights and opportunities to all its inhabitants.*

Locker was very satisfied with the outcome, writing that the Balfour Declaration '*spoke about establishing a national home for the Jews in the land of Israel*', and the Conference had used even more binding wording: '*To allow the Jewish people to continue the successful reconstruction of the Land of Israel as its national home*'.[135]

However the Histadrut suffered set back when at the WFTU meeting in Paris in October 1945 it assigned a seat on the executive to the Arab delegate from the Lebanon, rather than the Histadrut as the sole representative of all Middle East countries in the Federation. This was the result of Arab workers' organisations in Palestine lobbying unions in neighbouring

Arab countries after the London meeting urging them to send delegations to Paris, in order to present a unified 'Arab front' to oppose the WFTU's support for a Jewish homeland in Palestine. According to the *Jewish Chronicle*, '*Sir Walter Citrine, who was elected President to the federation, strongly supported the Histadrut emphasising that it was the strongest and oldest trade union body in the Middle East. When delegates refused to vote by a show of hands Sir Walter forced a secret ballot which resulted in 36 votes in favour of the Arab delegate and 18 against*'.[136]

Palestine and the WFTU

The Histadrut wrote to the WFTU in October 1945 saying that they had called a general strike in order to warn Britain about continuing to restrict the rights of the Jews in Palestine and appealed to WFTU to stand by its conference declaration calling for immediate Jewish immigration to Palestine. The WFTU Executive Board decided not to support the strike action but confirmed the decision taken in London. They stood by the declaration while 'scrupulously' acting as a conciliator to both the Palestinian Arab and Jewish labour organisations. The TUC representative told the WFTU Board that the WFTU could give moral support to the Histadrut but they should not approve strike action as it could create difficulties with for the British government.[137]

Throughout 1946 and 1947, the Jews waged a bloody and violent insurgency to try and persuade the British to withdraw from Palestine. As well as the violence, the British authorities had to deal the arrival of thousands of illegal Jewish immigrants who were brought to Palestine each month, many of whom were survivors of the Nazi concentration camps. In April 1946, the Anglo-American Committee of Inquiry which had been set up by the American and British governments to investigate the fate of the displaced persons and the Palestine question recommended that 100,000 certificates be issued immediately for the admission of Jews into Palestine. The Attlee government refused to accept the committee's recommendations as they believed the immediate admission of 100,000 Jews would almost certainly have provoked an Arab uprising.

Louis Salliant, the WFTU general secretary, was in regular contact with the TUC from 1946 onwards over the Palestine question and Tewson's responses reflected his support for the British government's policies. The TUC were suspicious of Salliant because of his strong connections with the Soviets. Salliant was entitled to write to Tewson because the WFTU had adopted a resolution at their founding conference supporting the establishment of a Jewish home in Palestine. It is not known whether his interventions on behalf of the Histadrut were made genuinely in support of the Histadrut or if, as a Communist he was following orders from Moscow to try and weaken British influence in the Middle East.[138] Whatever the reason, Tewson always replied, as was expected because the WFTU was the TUC's brainchild.

Salliant wrote to Tewson in August 1946 asking for his opinion on the request from the Dutch unions, the NVV, that the WFTU should investigate the latest incidents in Palestine and intervene with the British government if necessary.[139] Tewson replied saying that the Palestine issue was a very complex problem and that it was impossible to allow unrestricted immigration into Palestine. He told Salliant that as this was a political problem and not an industrial matter he doubted whether anything would be achieved by discussing the matter unless '*you want to see the contentions of the Arabs and the Jews being fought out within our Federation on a matter which has no direct industrial implication*'.[140] Tewson's efforts were successful because Salliant told the NVV that as the WFTU had not been notified directly by either the Arab or Jewish trade union centres in Palestine of the problem '*they must be happy to observe these events without calling for outside intervention*'.[141] A few days later, after receiving another telegram from the Histadrut regarding action by British troops against the Jewish population, Salliant wrote again to Tewson who replied that this request also fell into the same category as previously but added that he was hopeful that the conference currently meeting in London may reach an agreement. Tewson then told Salliant that the London conference was held up due to absence of Jewish representatives but was hopeful that negotiations be able to proceed soon but although the British government were anxious for a settlement they could not ignore the Arab point of view.[142]

In November 1946 the Histadrut requested TUC intervention in order to stop the deportation of 4000 'uncertificated' Jewish immigrants to Cyprus. Their request was quickly followed by a note from Walter Schevenels, deputy general secretary of the WFTU who wrote to Tewson that he had received a personal appeal from the Histadrut, '*which, as you know, has been for many years and still is one of our most faithful trade union movements, to intervene in a personal capacity with the TUC in favour of the Jewish refugees threatened with deportation to Cyprus*'. Schevenels asked if would be possible for the TUC to intervene either '*officially or otherwise*' with the government on the matter of these Jewish refugees? He stated that he thought '*that at this juncture the TUC, better than any other organisation in the world, could exert a conciliatory influence in the solution of this thorny problem, in which the labour forces constitute on both sides the main element*'.[143] Tewson wrote back saying that the TUC would discuss the matter but pointed out that the Histadrut claimed to have '*no contact with any organisation for illegal immigration*'. He went on to say that the Histadrut had also stated that although they would obviously prefer immigrants to enter Palestine in a normal way they would help the immigrants to reach their '*homeland*' in whatever way they could. Tewson added that a conciliatory attitude towards the Jews was likely to result in strong Arab protests and also be regarded '*as a climb-down to the terrorist tactics used in Palestine*'.[144] After the International committee had discussed the Histadrut's telegram, the TUC cabled the Histadrut asking '*if they were asking the TUC endorse the policy of illegal immigration?*'[145] That the TUC should try to overturn the ban on illegal immigration was exactly what the Histadrut wanted. However it is not clear why or how the committee arrived at this decision.

The Histadrut's reply made it clear that the situation had arisen because of the '*absolute inadequacy of authorised immigration*' and urged the TUC to make representations for the implementation Anglo-American committee recommendations including the admission of 100,000 refugees into Palestine.[146] The relentless stream of telegrams that the Histadrut sent to the WFTU and the TUC, along with Deakin's Presidency of the WFTU, ensured that the TUC took on the role of defending the government's political decisions and actions in Palestine. It was a role that it had not previously undertaken, but was now necessary and the TUC International Department, with help from the Foreign Office, regularly updated both Deakin and the General Council on the latest developments. At its December meeting the General Council[147] discussed the Histadrut's telegram and agreed that the TUC would not intervene on the Histadrut's behalf. The minutes of the meeting record that Andrew Naesmith, from the Amalgamated Weavers Association, felt that '*responsibility for the situation in Palestine should be thrown on to the Palestinian Jews and the Histadrut should be informed that the British TUC was not prepared to take any action on the lines suggested by them*'. The TUC's reply to the Histadrut noted that they had considered the Histadrut telegrams and whilst sympathetic to the position of the '*displaced persons*' they strongly urged the Palestinian Jews to accept the British government's invitation to a joint conference with the Arabs.[148] Throughout the exchange of letters the TUC had continued to express their support for the government whilst using every opportunity to point out the problems and pitfalls of the situation.

The Palestine conference met in London at the end of January 1947 and Bevin soon realised that it would be impossible to arrive at a peaceful settlement in Palestine on any basis whatsoever, except with the support of the Americans and the UN. Without an agreement in sight, Britain's commitment to Palestine seemed pointless as British lives were being lost, it was costing too much money which Britain could ill afford and above all there seemed no benefit, strategic or otherwise to Britain. The following month, the government announced that they would refer the mandate back to the UN in April 1947. By this time over 100,000 British soldiers were stationed in Palestine.

The Colonial Office regularly updated both Tewson and Deakin on the security situation in Palestine.[149] Deakin, as chairman of the International Committee and an influential member on the General Council, ensured that the TUC defended Bevin and the Labour government policy. When the government proposed imposing martial law in Palestine in February 1947, the Histadrut cabled both the TUC and the WFTU. Salliant responded immediately by asking the TUC to arrange a meeting with the British government in order to secure postponement of the proposal.[150] Tewson and Deakin met with Salliant in London and it was decided that Deakin should informally approach the foreign secretary in order to safeguard the position of the Histadrut. It is not known if Deakin did talk to Bevin but they had managed to satisfy Salliant.[151]

The Histadrut lobbies the WFTU Prague Conference for a Jewish State in Palestine

As a result of Britain's renunciation of the mandate in early 1947, the UN established a special committee, the United Nations Special Committee on Palestine (UNSCOP), to investigate and make recommendations regarding the future of Palestine. In June representatives from unions from all over the world, including the Histadrut, and the Palestine Arab TUC assembled in Prague for the WFTU General Council meeting. The conference took on extra significance as it took place just before the UNSCOP committee arrived in Palestine. The implications of this coincidence were understood by the Foreign Office who briefed both Tewson and Deakin before they left for Prague. The Foreign Office commented that it was probable that Deakin was concerned that the WFTU had become an '*an instrument for purely political ends in the international field*' and that '*in the past eighteen months there have been several occasions when it looked as though an open rupture might come, but both sides have been anxious to avoid this and have found ways of "papering the cracks"*'. The future of Palestine, although of major importance to the Jews, was just one of many issues discussed and the Foreign Office was satisfied that the two men would be able to defend British interests.[152]

The Histadrut wrote the motion on Palestine which was proposed by the American trade union, the CIO[153] It was first discussed by the Executive Bureau[154] where Deakin made it clear that he found the draft motion unacceptable because it attacked British government policy.[155] After the removal of the wording attacking British policy, the motion was approved for discussion by the General Council. The motion also expressed the hope that the Jewish and Arab workers in Palestine, could through their respective trade unions, find a basis for '*rapprochement*'.[156] The General Council debate was an acrimonious affair, which Deakin said illustrated the difficulties that the British government had faced before they had returned the Palestine mandate to the UN. Significantly the American, British and Soviet delegates all voted for the motion which was carried by a large majority. However after complaints by the Lebanese delegation, a compromise text was produced which was unanimously accepted by all the delegations including the Histadrut.[157]

The Foreign Office was highly satisfied with how both Tewson and Deakin had firmly defended British interests and noted that the resolution appeared '*to have been intentionally ambiguous to avoid antagonising the Arab delegates*' The Histadrut, who had made it a priority to build relations with the WFTU, must have felt enthused that their motion had been unanimously adopted even though Deakin had told the Histadrut that as chairman it was his international duty to demand that the Palestine issue should not be brought to the Council and would not reflect badly on his government.[158] Uniquely, it was one the few times that Great Britain, France, the USSR and America all agreed to support a resolution calling for a Jewish homeland in Palestine. What is not clear is if the Histadrut realised that they were being used as a pawn in the confrontation between East and West, however membership of the WFTU had enabled the Histadrut to put pressure on Britain and the TUC.

Another potential East-West confrontation that the TUC had to contend with was the WFTU plan to send a delegation to Palestine during the autumn of 1947. The British government clearly did not want the mission to go ahead, and along with the TUC put several difficulties in the way of the mission during its preparation phase. As a result, in January 1948, Salliant and the WFTU were left with no alternative but to cancel the trip.[159] The WFTU's Palestine mission was the last opportunity for the WFTU and the Soviet Union to put pressure on the British over Palestine. At Prague, Deakin did everything he could to stop a resolution being adopted which criticised his government's actions. Even if the mission to Palestine had gone ahead it is unlikely that it would have achieved anything and by the time it was cancelled its usefulness had been overtaken by events on the ground.

The WFTU failed because of the Cold War and was used by the TUC, the Histadrut and the Soviets to promote their own political agendas. The TUC was always on the defensive whenever Palestine was discussed by the WFTU and the outcome of the Prague congress allowed each party to claim some success. Between 1945 and 1949, the WFTU passed two motions on Palestine, yet the organisation had very little impact on the politics of the Middle East.

The Impact of Antisemitism and Fascism on British Attitudes and Activities

Jewish insurgency in Palestine which had intensified in 1946 continued into 1947. One of the most serious incidents that took place was in July 1947, when the radical Zionist group, the Irgun, hanged two British Army sergeants in retaliation for the execution of three Jewish terrorists. The British press and population were horrified by the hangings and anti-Jewish riots over the August Bank holiday broke out in Liverpool, Manchester, London, Cardiff, Halifax and Glasgow. Fortunately the violence disappeared almost as quickly as it had started.[160] Two local Trade Councils passed motions on the situation and sent copies to the TUC. One condemned the outrage in Palestine and called on the government to punish those responsible for series of antisemitic outrages in Britain while the other demanded the recall of British troops from Palestine.[161] A draft statement was prepared for the General Council which stated that '*the General Council's sense of outrage is shared by the British people and responsible Jewish organisations and individuals.... Believing they speak the mind of all the people of Britain the General Council denounces any attempt to put the responsibility for the activities of minority criminal elements upon the shoulders of the Jewish community in Britain which has declared it to have no sympathy with or part in such activity*'. The statement was not used possibly as the TUC wanted to 'cool' the situation in the run up to the TUC Congress at the beginning of September.[162]

The General Council, at their pre-Congress meeting, discussed the trouble in various parts of the country caused by anti-Jewish activities, including an unofficial strike by members of the Union of Shop, Distributive and Allied Workers (USDAW) at Birkenhead who had refused to handle kosher meat. The General Council was concerned that this strike action could be seen as antisemitic and sent a message to USDAW saying that the spread of antisemitism should be discouraged. Even so the USDAW strike continued until the end of August.[163] Nor did the General Council want the matter discussed at Congress as it would raise the '*Jewish problem*'. If necessary, delegates would be told that the only effective way of getting the '*Jewish problem*' examined was through the United Nations (UN).[164] What the TUC leadership had done was to conflate anti-Jewish activities in Britain with the problems in Palestine.

To the relief of the General Council, Congress was more concerned about the rise of fascist activities in Britain than the problems in Palestine. The TUC report to Congress noted that the TUC had received a letter dated 14 February 1947, from the Amalgamated Engineering Union '*asking the TUC jointly with the Labour Party use their influence to secure immediate legislation outlawing fascist and pro-fascist activities*'. It was left to Solomon Lever of the London Jewish Bakers Union to tell Congress that the fascists' activities had nothing to do with the campaign in Palestine. The *Jewish Chronicle* reported that delegates had cheered his speech and that '*strong demands were voiced for taking more positive and energetic measures and the General Council were left in no doubt that they were expected to initiate definite action for stopping fascism*'. The *Daily Herald* wrote that '*the anger and alarm expressed by various speakers at the Congress about the growth of fascist activities in London and other cities was widely shared and appealed to the Government that a way must be found to prohibit antisemitic provocation*'. Even though Tewson told delegates that the General Council could '*handle the matter*' delegates voted by a large majority to refer back to the General Council, for further action, the section dealing with the NCL report on fascism. The NCL, which had issued a declaration against fascism in 1946 considered this letter along with others and pledged to continue to closely monitor the fascist activities in Britain.[165]

The Illegal Immigrants on Board the 'Exodus'

As a reaction to the hanging of the two British army sergeants and the outrage that it had caused in Britain, the British government decided to return the 4500 Jewish illegal immigrants aboard the ship the '*Exodus*' to Germany. It was a public relations catastrophe for Britain and a disaster for their relations with the Jews in Palestine.

Shortly before Salliant contacted Tewson about the '*Exodus*', Salliant had sent him a copy of a telegram from the American Jewish Labor Council referring to martial law and conditions in Palestine.[166] Tewson replied that the letter's '*content is a travesty of the fact*' and the fact that there was an Arab problem as well as a Jewish problem in Palestine.[167] Salliant then cabled Tewson urging '*the TUC to agree that an allied neutral country be found to receive the emigrants on the "Exodus"*'. The General Council considered his request along with one from the World Jewish Congress and decided to take no action.[168] Tewson's long reply not only gives an insight into his thinking at the time but also shows his irritation with Salliant. He explained that the matter of the '*Exodus*' could not be dealt with in isolation from the whole problem of Jewish immigration into Palestine and blamed the instigators of the action responsible for sending the illegal immigrants on the ships, saying that the immigrants had declined to go to France and could not come to Britain as there was no suitable accommodation for them. There was a serious health risk if the Jews remained on the ship, but the only place '*where they could be accommodated under reasonable conditions*' was the British Zone in Germany.[169]

Tewson also described as '*sheer nonsense*' a message they had received from a Soviet organisation which claimed that following the hanging of the two sergeants in Palestine, pogroms were taking place in Britain but admitted that there had been trouble in one or two centres. He said that the General Council had not intervened because of delicate nature of the situation and pointed out that all foreign criticism had been directed at the British government, rather than at the instigators of the problem. Tewson reminded Salliant that no solution could be found in Palestine without considering the wishes of the Arabs and although they were waiting for a UN recommendation he was not personally satisfied '*that a solution will be found upon which both Jews and Arabs will be agreed*'. Tewson concluded with a warning that the letter '*contains my personal comments for you on a problem which will be as big headache to the WFTU if they become embroiled in it as it is to the British Government and the UN*'.[170]

The Position of the CPGB

The prime concern of the CPGB after Germany's invasion of Russia in 1941 was the survival of the Soviet Union. Support for the CPGB amongst Britain's working classes gradually increased and they opposed any strike that affected the war effort. Once the USSR had entered the war the Party dropped its support for Arab nationalism but still remained opposed to Zionism. The CPGB backed the policies of the Moscow-based Soviet Jewish Anti-fascist Committee and wooed Britain's Jews to support the USSR's struggle against Nazi Germany.[171] The CPGB's Jewish Bureau, which had been dissolved at the outbreak of the war, was reformed in 1943 as the National Jewish Committee (NJC). At its first meeting, the NJC '*came out in favour of the Yishuv, espousing positions that were difficult to distinguish from mainstream Zionist positions*'. In March 1945, the NJC argued that since Palestinian Jewry was 'the most progressive force in the Middle East', Palestine should be open to Jewish immigration on a mass scale and the White Paper should be denounced '*by all sections of Jewry as wrong policy*'.[172] The monthly magazine of the NJC, the *Jewish Clarion*, which was first published in 1945, provided leading Jewish members of the CPGB with the opportunity to put forward the Jewish communist point of view especially on Palestine.

The CPGB won two seats in the 1945 general election, one in Scotland and one in Mile End in London's East End where the Jewish vote contributed to the party's success. Although Jews were not prominent within the top leadership of the CPGB, they held 7% of the full-time posts in the party hierarchy and administration. This was a disproportionate involvement as Jews formed less than 1% of the British population.[173] However, it was not unusual when compared to the relationship between Jews and communism in other countries nor did the majority of Jewish communists have a problem with openly embracing their Jewishness while at the same time opposing Zionism.

The CPGB's post-war plans to work closely with the Labour government came to nothing because of Britain's economic problems, her dependence on American financial support and the onset of the Cold War. Both the Labour Party and the TUC mounted a campaign to isolate the CPGB, with the Labour Party rejecting the communists request for affiliation. In October 1948 the TUC General Council accused the CPGB of pursuing a strategy of industrial disruption on orders from Moscow. The following year the TUC Congress overwhelmingly backed the TUCs anti-communist position and withdrew from the WFTU.

The Labour government believed that the Middle East was critical for Britain's economic and strategic needs and saw the Soviet Union's support for Israel as a threat to its interests in this region. Bevin thought that Jewish emigration from Eastern Europe could turn Israel into a Soviet ally. The CPGB, however, thought that a pro-Soviet Jewish state would undermine Britain's 'imperialist' interests in the region. Soviet support for partition brought the CPGB into direct conflict with the Labour Party. The Soviet Union's unexpected backing for an independent Jewish state resulted in the CPGB describing that decision as an act of last resort, the outcome of the West's failure to clamp down on antisemitism and the inability to provide equality for everyone. The establishment of the State of Israel was portrayed as '*a big step toward fulfilment of self-determination of the peoples of Palestine*' and '*a great sign of the times*'.[174] The CPGB joined with the Labour Left in protesting against Bevin's Palestine policy accusing him of having committed a '*shameful betrayal*' of the Jews and claiming that '*Bevinism leads to antisemitism and all that follows*'.[175] Both groups were disappointed with the government's approach as they both believed that the government had put at risk its commitment to a socialist foreign policy. The *Jewish Chronicle's* claim in 1949 that the *Jewish Clarion* had reversed its position in 1948 in line with the new Soviet position was vehemently denied. Nevertheless the CPGB's opposition to Zionism continued after 1948, with the *Jewish Clarion* continuing back to the official Party position.

Relations between the Arab Labour Movement and the TUC

The Arab trade unions in Palestine, although not as well organised, received encouragement from both the Palestine administration and the TUC. After 1945, the Arabs, like the Histadrut, lobbied the British government and attended international labour movement conferences.

In 1944 the IFTU asked the Histadrut, their largest affiliate in the Middle East, to produce a survey of the labour movements in Palestine, Egypt, Syria, Iraq and Iran. Their survey of Arab labour organisations in Palestine criticised the Palestine government for giving considerable assistance to the Arab workers organisations regardless of their quality and '*ultimate*' aims as well as encouraging them to amalgamate into one organisation. The Histadrut believed that their organisation was only tolerated by the authorities and not encouraged to find an Arab partner. In August 1945 The TUC were told of the formation of an Arab TUC by the government of Palestine who hoped this move would result in all the Arab trade unions agreeing to affiliate to one central body.[176]

The Arab workers organisations mentioned in the report were the Communist controlled Palestine Arab Workers Society (PAWS), the Federation of Arab Unions (FAU) and the Palestine Labour League (PLL) which was part of the Histadrut. The survey found that the FAU had shown no sign of genuine trade union activity but published a weekly newspaper containing violent anti-Jewish propaganda and that the PLL, was not supported by the Arab public or the other Arab workers organisations. The report concluded that the social status of the Arab workers had changed radically changed since the 1920s and working conditions and wages were far higher than those in neighbouring Arab countries.[177]

By 1943 PAWS, which had substantial support amongst Arab workers, '*Lacked the bargaining power with the British civil and military authorities nor did it have anything approaching the Histadrut's close and long standing connections*' with the Palestine government or the Colonial Office or the TUC.[178] The TUC received a copy of PAWS letter to the IFTU asking about the 1944 Labour Party comment that the Arabs should be encouraged to move out as the Jews move in. The IFTU replied to PAWS that they were not prepared to discuss the issues in writing, but hoped that PAWS would be able to present their views to the world for a just solution safeguarding the social and economic rights of Jewish and Arab populations. The TUC explained to PAWS that Labour Party comment only referred to the voluntary evacuation of Palestine territory by the Arabs and that no compulsion of any kind was intended.[179] Throughout the final years of the mandate the TUC was frequently approached by both the Arab unions and the Histadrut for their help regarding wages and conditions and the recognition of Arab unions in military workshops. During 1946–47 the PLL was not involved in Arab-Jewish workers disputes and by 1947; the Histadrut's Arab department knew that the PLL was ineffective and '*discredited amongst Arab workers in Palestine*'.[180]

The TUC continued to support the Palestine administration's efforts to build up the Arab unions and noted that the Histadrut had been good for raising the wages and working conditions for Arabs workers.[181] The industrialisation of Palestine was a consequence of the war effort also raised awareness amongst the Arab population of trade unions. The Palestine government committee to consider employment problems in Palestine estimated in 1944 that out of a total labour force of 285,000 in industry, some 110,000 workers were employed in war work. The Histadrut estimated that the Army employed 45,000 workers, 15,000 Jews and 30,000 Arabs. The majority of Arabs were villagers for whom their employment as hired labourers was only on a temporary basis.[182] These links with Palestine stood the TUC in good stead for its role after 1948 which we will see involved continuing to monitor the progress of the Arab workers in Israel.

The United Nations and Palestine

The United Nations Special Committee on Palestine (UNSCOP),, which went to Palestine in June 1947, met with Jewish representatives but was boycotted by the Arab community in Palestine. UNSCOP presented its report on 31 August 1947 with the proposal that the mandate should be terminated and the land partitioned between Jews and Arabs. On 29 November 1947, the UN General Assembly with the support of both the USSR and the United States, adopted UNSCOP's partition recommendation. This was due to an effective Jewish diplomatic lobbying campaign and widespread sympathy for the Jewish people, following the death of six million Jews in the Holocaust.

The British understood that partition would likely result in civil war and thought that the Arabs would have the upper hand. The British government announced early in 1948 that the mandate in Palestine would end on 14 May by which time all remaining British forces would have been withdrawn.

Ben Gurion and his colleagues, who had been planning for independence, realised well before the UN decision that the Arab states would not accept the partition and planned accordingly for a military conflict with the neighbouring Arab states. The civil war in Palestine between the Arabs and the Jews started in December 1947 with the Arabs initially gaining the upper hand. Following the Haganah offensive called 'Plan D' in March 1948, however, the Jews soon gained control of most of the areas assigned to them with the exception of the Negev. It was during the civil war that the 'Palestinian refugee problem' first emerged. It started when the Palestinian leadership and middle classes left for what they believed to be temporary refuge in neighbouring Arab states. The killing of approximately 100 Arabs by the Irgun in the battle to capture the Arab village of Deir Yassin in April 1948 convinced many Arabs to leave and it is estimated that 750,000 in total left at this time. This radically altered the strengths of the two communities in Palestine.[183]

In December 1947, as the situation in Palestine worsened, the Histadrut sent copies of their telegrams to the TUC to the WFTU and the American and Soviet unions in order to put pressure on the TUC. They asked the TUC to intervene with the government in order to avoid further bloodshed and chaos and support the UN decision to establish a Jewish state in Palestine. The TUC, which received similar letters from the AFL and the WFTU, replied saying the matter was now in the hands of the UN. The TUC also asked the Histadrut who else they had written to, which the Histadrut ignored as they knew the TUC already knew the answer.[184] Tewson wrote the NCL statement regarding the British withdrawal from Palestine which followed British government policy saying that '*Britain could not accept responsibility for imposing by force a solution of the Palestine problem which is unacceptable to either Jews or Arabs*' *and also called upon both parties to enter into negotiations for a peaceful resolution of the conflict.*[185]

The British mandate ended on Friday 14th May 1948 and at the same time, Ben-Gurion, as leader of the Jewish community in Palestine, declared Israel's independence. Within 24 hours armed forces from Egypt, Trans-Jordan, Syria, Iraq and Lebanon had invaded the country and Israel was at war with her neighbours. The Arabs who had refused to accept the UN plan promised that the aim of the invasion was 'the elimination of the Jewish state'. In terms of numbers, by mid-July, the Haganah which was now incorporated into the Israel Defence force (IDF) had 65,000 troops against 40,000 in the Arab armies. The numbers had increased by early 1949 to 115,000 in the IDF and 55,000 in the Arab armies, which gave the IDF a huge advantage. The war of independence was over by January 1949 and Ben-Gurion's strategy of creating facts on the ground had paid off, because, after several UN-called truces, Israel now controlled an area one third larger than that envisaged by the UN partition plan. Separate armistice agreements to end the fighting were signed in 1949 with Egypt, Lebanon, Trans-Jordan and Syria. The UN did try to bring a lasting peace to region when in 1949, at Lausanne, it convened a peace conference, but no agreement was reached as the differences between the parties over refugees and borders were too wide. The result of the war left the Arab nations humiliated in defeat and Palestinian Arab society shattered. Israel although surrounded by hostile nations had survived and was now an independent nation that was internationally recognised and in 1949 became a member of the UN. It did, however, have an Arab minority of 150,000 out of a total population of 900,000 which were regarded by many Israelis as either an unknown quantity or potential fifth column. The areas in which they lived were controlled and supervised by the military government, and although it was not official policy, they were treated as second-class citizens. It was not until 1966 that these military government controls were abolished. The proposed Palestinian state envisaged by UN plan did not materialise either, as the West Bank was taken over by Trans-Jordan and the Gaza Strip by Egypt.

Conclusion

When Labour came to power in 1945 the experience gained by Attlee and Bevin concerning Britain's foreign policy and security in the wartime coalition government resulted in them ignoring the socialist foreign policy advocated by the left wing of the party. Bevin's standing within the party, along with support from the unions and the TUC allowed him to stand up to his critics and pursue a foreign policy which had the support of the Conservatives. Even though Labour lost the 1951 election, Bevin's legacy to the TUC was that they continued to support the Conservatives' Middle East policy. Labour's decisions over the future of Palestine were seen by many Zionists as a betrayal of Zionism and party policy which overshadowed the British labour movement's exceptional pre-war support for the Zionism and the Jews of Palestine.

The Histadrut sent dozens of telegrams after 1945 to both the TUC and the Labour Party on various issues in the hope that they might lobby the Labour government on their behalf. As a strategy it was partially successful. Within the Labour Party, Harold Laski, the Labour Party chair man and Richard Crossman MP frequently raised matters on their behalf. This approach failed completely with the TUC, unlike the Labour Party there was nobody on the General Council who was prepared to support the Histadrut. Although the Histadrut and the WFTU had tried to provoke a reaction from the TUC over Palestine, they failed because the TUC was totally loyal to Bevin and the Labour government.

Bevin may have worked behind the scenes with both Hoz and Locker when it came to a Jewish homeland but he was the only union leader who spoke out on behalf of the Jews in 1930 at the time of the Passfield White

Paper and when he was TUC president in 1937. As a result of his willingness to intervene with the government on the Zionists behalf Bevin was considered by the Yishuv leadership to be a powerful political friend.[186] It was only in 1942 after he became aware of the complexities of the Palestine issue that his attitude towards the Yishuv began to change.

On the eve of 1945 General Election, *the Zionist Review* published a guide for Jewish voters of supportive statements made by MPs and others on behalf of the Jews of Palestine; there were no current quotes from the TUC or the unions, and even Bevin's quote came from one of his speeches made in the 1930s. Unlike the Labour Party, the TUC did not send a message of condolence to the memorial meeting commemorating the death of Dov Hoz. In addition Poale Zion was affiliated to the Labour Party rather than the TUC and the party's MPs enthusiastically supported Poale Zion's pro-Zionist conference motions unlike the unions who rarely spoke in favour of the motions. Whereas many Labour MPs had visited Palestine in the 1930s, only one union leader, George Isaacs, who was also an MP, visited Palestine in 1936.

The TUC's post-war priority was to oppose the spread of communism in Europe, and Palestine was never an important issue for them; their indifference towards the Jews of Palestine was there for all to see. As we shall see later, the Histadrut was fundamentally pro-British and saw it as a priority after independence to rebuild links with the British labour movement.

Notes

1. A. Revusky, *Jews in Palestine* (New York: Vanguard Press, 1945), p. 253.
2. *Jewish Chronicle*, 5th September 1902, p. 7.
3. The TUC archives at the Modern Records Centre, University of Warwick, MSS.480/4/1/12, p. 17 (Hereafter cited as MRC) and MRC, TUC Congress proceedings 1900, p. 85.
4. MRC, TUC Congress proceedings 1902, pp. 75–76, and *Jewish Chronicle*, 5 September 1902, p. 24.
5. A. Kershen, *Trade Unionism amongst the Jewish Tailoring workers of London and Leeds 1872–1915*, in D. Cesarani, ed., The making of Modern Anglo-Jewry (Oxford: Basil Blackwell, 1990), p. 47.
6. G. Shimoni, '*Poale Zion: A Zionist Transplant in Britain (1905–1945)*', in *Studies in Contemporary Jewry* Vol. 2, ed. P.Y. Medding (Bloomington: Indiana University Press, 1986), p. 231.

7. TUC Congress motion '*Political and Civil rights for Jewish people*', MRC, TUC Congress proceedings 1915, pp. 306–307.
8. G. Shimoni, *Poale Zion*, pp. 230–231.
9. *Jewish Chronicle* 24 September 1915.
10. TUC Congress motion '*Political and Civil rights for Jewish people*', MRC, TUC Congress proceedings 1916, pp. 405–406.
11. The General Federation of Trade Unions AGM, 2 July 1915, and 6 July 1916, MRC, MSS.480/4/1/13, p. 23.
12. An abridged version of the author's essay '*Before Balfour, The Labour Party's War Aims Memorandum*', was published by www.fathomjournal.org.uk, Summer 2017.
13. P. Kellogg, A. Gleason, *British Labor and the War: Reconstructors for a New World* (New York: Boni & Liveright, 1919), p. 16.
14. Labour Peace Aims, *The Times*, 11 August 1917 and S. Levenberg, '*The Jews and Palestine*' (London: Poale Zion, 1945), pp. 204–205.
15. *Zionist Review*, January 1918, Vol. 1, No. 9, p. 169.
16. Weizmann to Brandeis, Weizmann archive, 5 March 1918.
17. The General Federation of Jewish Workers in Palestine did not officially adopt the name Histadrut until after the Second World War. For continuity, the General Federation of Jewish Workers in Palestine will be referred to throughout as the Histadrut.
18. The Histadrut's written submission to the Anglo-American of Inquiry, March 1946, The TUC Library Collection at the London Metropolitan University (Hereafter cited as LMU), HD8759, p. 9.
19. A report prepared for the security services on political parties in Palestine, 23 November 1945, The National Archives of the UK (TNA): Public Record Office (PRO), KV5/16 (Hereafter cited as TNA: PRO).
20. S. Levenberg, *The Jews and Palestine*, p. 56.
21. MRC, TUC Congress 1918 International Trade Union Bureau, pp. 64–65.
22. M. Nicholson, *The TUC Overseas, the Roots of Policy* (London: Allen and Unwin, 1986), pp. 41 and 46.
23. Poale Zion Conference report, Weizmann archive, 28 October 1917.
24. S. Levenberg, *The Jews and Palestine*, pp. 206–207.
25. S. Teveth, *Ben Gurion: The Burning Ground 1886–1948* (London: Robert Hale, 1987), pp. 175–176.
26. J. MacDonald, *Socialist in Palestine* (London: Jewish Socialist Labour Confederation Poale-Zion, 1922).
27. S. Teveth, *Ben-Gurion: The Burning Ground 1886–1948*, p. 203.
28. MRC, TUC Congress proceedings 1924, p. 224.
29. The report of the First British Commonwealth Labour Conference, 1925 (London: Trades Union Congress and the Labour Party, 1925).

30. TUC International Committee, 13 April 1926, MRC, MSS.292/901/1.
31. TUC International Committee, 11 December 1928, MRC MSS.292/901/1.
32. The Histadrut archives at the Pinchas Lavon Institute for Labour Movement Research, Tel Aviv (Hereafter cited as PLILMR), Hoz letter to the TUC, Histadrut Executive, IV-104-49-2-44, May 3, 1929.
33. Poale Zion memorandum to the TUC, 2nd September 1929, PLILMR, IV-104-49-2-41.
34. Item 294, General Council meeting minutes, 2nd September 1929, MRC, MSS.292/20/13.
35. Item 292, General Council meeting minutes, 31 August 1929, MRC, MSS.292/20/13.
36. Item 34, General Council meeting minutes, 4th September 1929, MRC, MSS.292/20/13.
37. Item 305, General Council meeting minutes, 5th September 1929, MRC, MSS.292/20/13.
38. Labour Party to the Histadrut 3rd September 1929, PLILMR, IV-104-49-2-44.
39. An abridged version of the author's essay '*British Foreign policy: the 1930 Whitechapel By-election*', was published by www.fathomjournal.org.uk, January 2018.
40. J. Gorny, *The British labour movement and Zionism 1917–1948* (London: Frank Cass, 1983), pp. 92–94.
41. Hoz to Bevin, 26 January 1931, PLILMR, IV-104-49-2-41.
42. Peoples History Museum Manchester (Hereafter cited as PHM), Poale Zion to Labour Party, 7 October 1930, JSM/ZIO/47, Poale Zion to Henderson, 28 October 1930, JSM/ZIO/41, Labour Party to Poale Zion, 29 October 1930, JSM/ZIO/42 and Deputation to the Prime Minister, 30 October 1930, JSM/ZIO/45.
43. National Jewish Labour Council to Labour Party, 10 October 1930, PHM, JSM/ZIO/48.
44. Bevin to Hoz, 8 December 1930, PLILMR, IV-104-49-2-41.
45. Hoz to Bevin, 8 December 1930, PLILMR, IV-104-49-2-41.
46. Z. Goren, *Dov Hos – A Pre-State Statesman* (Ramat Efal: Yad Tabenkin, 1999), p. 280.
47. Elsie Gluck interview with E. Bevin, 8 December 1932, PLILMR, IV-104-49-1-40.
48. A. Bullock, *Ernest Bevin, Foreign Secretary, 1945–1951* (London: Heinemann, 1983), p. 165.
49. Bar Shira to Remez, 24 May 1934, PLILMR, IV-209-4-42.
50. MRC, TUC Congress proceedings 1936, pp. 393–396.

51. The American Labour delegation report on Palestine, 23 February 1937, MRC, MSS.292/956.9/2.
52. TUC General Council minutes, 24 February 1937, MRC, MSS.292/20/21.
53. Dov Hoz to Locker, 21 March 1937, the Moshe Sharett Israel Labor Party Archive, Israel (hereafter cited MSILP), (Hebrew original), 2-003-1936-63.
54. Dov Hoz to Ben-Gurion, March 1937, PLILMR, IV-104-49-1-44 LA.
55. MRC, TUC Congress proceedings 1937, p. 75.
56. Bevin asked Ari Ankorion, the London correspondent for the Histadrut newspaper *Davar*, to convey the message to his comrades in Palestine, J. Gorny, *The British labour movement and Zionism*, p. 141.
57. Hoz to Citrine, 7 October 1938, MRC, MSS.292/956.9/2.
58. Labour Party press release, 7 October 1938, MRC, MSS.292/956.9/2.
59. Weizmann to Mapai executive, 22 August 1938, PLILMR, IV-104-71-2-20A.
60. The Labour Zionist Party, Mapai led by David Ben-Gurion was established in 1930 as a result of the merger of Ahdut HaAvoda and HaPoel HaTzair. Mapai was the dominant political Party during the mandate as it controlled both the Zionist Congress and the Histadrut.
61. Citrine to Hoz, 19 February 1938, MRC MSS.292/956.9/2.
62. Finance and General Purposes Committee, 22 May 1938, MRC, MSS.292/24.1/9.
63. MRC, TUC Congress proceedings 1938, p. 78.
64. Ibid, pp. 207–208.
65. Locker to Citrine, 19 August 1938, MRC, MSS.292/956.9/2.
66. Citrine to Locker, 26 August 1938, MRC, MSS.292/956.9/2.
67. Hoz to Citrine, 26 August 1938, MRC, MSS.292/956.9/2 and Citrine to Hoz, 30 August 1938, PLILMR, IV-209-4-405.
68. Hoz to the TUC, 6 September 1938, MRC, MSS.292/956.9/2.
69. TUC Labour Party declaration, PHM, JSM/ZIO/149, 7 September 1938.
70. TUC correspondence with the American Federation of Labor, the United Hebrew trades union, the Amalgamated Clothing workers, New York and the Trades and Labor Congress of Canada, MRC, MSS.292/956.9/2.
71. Citrine met with Chamberlain the day after Chamberlain had returned from meeting Hitler, yet still went to the West Indies, Lord Citrine, *Men and Work* (London: Hutchinson, 1964), p. 329 and p. 361 also Dov Hoz notes, 14 February 1939, PLILMR, IV-104-49-1-28.
72. Hoz to the Labour Party, 7 December 1938, PLILMR, IV-104-49-1-43.
73. Hoz diary notes, 7 May 1939, PLILMR, IV-104-39-3-8.

74. TUC memos of telephone conversations between Miss McDonald and Dov Hoz, 18 May and 22 May 1939, MRC, MSS.292/956.9/2.
75. Minutes of the Finance and General Purposes committee, 22 May1939 and Citrine to Hoz, 24 May 1939, both MRC, MSS.292/956.9/2.
76. Palestine Arab Workers Society to Labour Party, 27 June 1939, PHM, WG/PAL/193 and Locker to Gillies, the Labour Party, PHM, WG/PAL/195, 31 June 1939.
77. Item 112, NCL minutes, 27 February 1940, MRC, MSS.292/956.9/3.
78. Memo of meeting between Hoz and Tewson, 4 March 1940, MRC, MSS.292/956.9/3.
79. PLPC to the TUC, 16 September 1940, MRC, MSS292/956.9/3.
80. Tewson to Locker, 29 September 1940, MRC, MSS292/956.9/3.
81. Locker to Tewson, 25 September 1940, and Tewson to Locker, 26 September 1940, both MRC, MSS.292/956.9/3.
82. Citrine to AFL, 30 May 1940, MRC, MSS.292/956.9/3.
83. TUC to the Histadrut, 15 October 1940, MRC, MSS292/956.9/3.
84. J. Gorny, *The British labour movement and Zionism 1917–1948*, p. 190.
85. Ibid. p. 178.
86. 'Memorial for Dov Hoz in London', *Jewish Telegraph Agency*, 14 January 1941.
87. On 20 May the AFL and CIO leadership along with others sent a telegram to the prime minister noting their deep concern about the new policy in Palestine. Adam Howard, *Sewing the Fabric of Statehood* (Urbana: University of Illinois, 2017), p. 40.

    The TUC memo of telephone conversation with Hoz noted that Mr. Green of the AFL had issued a statement and interviewed the American Government asking them to use influence with the British Government against the proposals, MRC, TUC memo, 22 May 1939, MSS.292/956.9/2.
88. AFL to the TUC, 25 April 1940, TUC reply to AFL, 30 May 1940, MRC, MSS.292/956.9/3.
89. M. Sugarman, 'Jews in the Spanish Civil War', https://www.jewishvirtuallibrary.org/jews-who-served-in-the-international-brigade-in-the-spanish-civil-war.
90. Ibid.
91. R Rein, 'Echoes of the Spanish Civil War in Palestine: Zionists, Communists and the Contemporary Press', *Journal of Contemporary History*, Vol. 43, No. 1 (2008), p. 13.
92. Spain and Israel only established diplomatic relations in January 1986.
93. G. Alderman, *The Jewish Community in British Politics* (Oxford: Oxford University Press, 1983), p. 271.
94. *The Daily Worker*, 23 August 1939.

95. 'The international situation', MRC, TUC Congress report 1939, p. 290.
96. General Council declaration, 4 September 1939, MRC, TUC Congress report 1939, p. 337.
97. A. Bregman, *A History of Israel* (Basingstoke: Palgrave Books, 2002), p. 33.
98. H. Sachar, *A History of Israel: from the Rise of Zionism to our time* (New York: Knopf, 2008), pp. 244–245.
99. SIS security file on the Histadrut and other Jewish organisations, 27 March 1942, TNA: PRO, KV5/16.
100. Histadrut to the TUC, 23 July and 4 August 1941, TUC to Lord Moyne, 28 July 1941, Lord Moyne to the TUC, 22 August 1941 and the TUC's reply to the Histadrut, 29 September 1941, all MRC, MSS.292/956.9/3. TUC report of the activities of the Colonial Advisory Committee, 18 November 1941, MRC, MSS.292/932.9/1.
101. Histadrut to the TUC, 4 July 1942 and 18 July 1942. The report of the NCL meeting on 21 July 1942 noted that Berl Locker had addressed a meeting of members of Parliament. The FGPC meeting on 20 July 1942 turned down the request for TUC to be represented on a committee to further the cause for a Jewish fighting force and home defence in Palestine. All MRC, MSS.292/956.9/3.
102. NCL minutes, 21 July 1942, MRC, MSS292/956.9/3.
103. Labour Party letter to the TUC with copy of motion, 22 July 1942, TUC reply, 24 July 1942, PHM, 1935–45 Box LP Foreign/defence policy.
104. 'The United Nations' in this context refers to the allied powers fighting against the Germans in WW2.
105. Histadrut to Labour Party, 1 December 1942, TNA: PRO, CO733/438/11.
106. It was reported that the Socialist International had taken similar action and proposed an inter-Allied conference that would issue a warning to Germany. TUC International Committee minutes, 15 December 1942, MRC, MSS.292/901/5.
107. MRC, Labour Party annual report, 1943.
108. 'Jewish persecutions', 28 January 1943, PHM, NCL Minutes Jan 40–Dec 43 (Box 4 136).
109. Histadrut to the TUC, 29 January 1943, MRC, MSS.292/956.9/3.
110. The Histadrut had asked to be put on the TUC mailing list for publications, Histadrut to TUC, 22 July 1942 and the Histadrut to the TUC, querying changes in Palestine Labour Bill, 3 February 1942, all MRC, MSS.292/956.9/3.
111. Histadrut to the Labour Party, 10 June 1943, PLILMR, IV-208-1-3313 and General Council minutes, 21 April 1943, MRC, MSS.292/20/27.
112. Histadrut to the TUC, 5 September 1943, MRC, MSS.292/956.9/3.

113. TUC International committee minutes, 19 October 1943, MRC, MSS.292/901/6.
114. MRC, Report of the 1943 TUC Congress, pp. 329–333.
115. Patrons of the committee included J. Middleton, the Secretary of the Labour Party, Laski and Deakin, Acting Secretary of the TGWU, the United Jewish Labour Committee letters to the Histadrut 1 November, 15 November 1943 and 7 November 1944, PLILMR, IV-208-1-3309.
116. The Moshe Sharett Israel Labor Party Archive, Israel, Locker statement to Mapai committee, Minutes of meeting 6 October 1943 (Hebrew original), MSILP, 2-024-1943-6.
117. "The international Post-war settlement", Labour Party declaration, PHM, boxes 10/11, Middleton papers.
118. Ben-Gurion explained that in advocating the transfer of Arabs out of Palestine there was no intention to force the Arabs to leave Palestine against their will. J. Gorny, *The British labour movement and Zionism 1917–1948*, p. 182 and TUC to IFTU, 14 August 1944, MRC, MSS292/956.9/3.
119. MRC, TUC annual report for 1943, p. 271.
120. Bevin received many letters protesting about British policy in Palestine, examples include the National Union of Miners (Scottish Area) Rankington No. 19 Branch sent him in July 1947 a copy of their motion deploring the British Government policy in Palestine. He also received letters from the Jewish communities in Panama, Venezuela, Geneva, Newcastle, and Manchester. TNA: PRO, FO371/52540.
121. The MP's included Richard Crossman, Jennie Lee, Michael Foot, Sidney Silverman, and Woodrow Wyatt.

    P. Kelemen, *The British Left and Zionism History of a Divorce* (Manchester: Manchester University, 2012), pp. 121–122.
122. Histadrut to the Labour Party, 27 July 1945, PLILMR, IV–208-1-3313.
123. The Labour Party replied saying that the prime minister would soon make a statement. Histadrut to the TUC and Labour Party, 28 September 1945 and 20 October 1945, MRC, MSS.292/956.9/4 and Histadrut to the TUC and the Labour Party, 4 October 1945, and the Labour Party's reply to the Histadrut, 27 October 1945, PLILMR, IV-208-1-3313.
124. International sub-committee of the National executive, 20 November 1945, PHM, LP-1-110815.
125. Labour Party to the Histadrut, 30 November 1945, PLILMR, IV-209-4-359.
126. TUC General Council minutes, 3 July 1946, MRC, MSS.292/20/30, the Histadrut to the TUC and the Labour Party, 2 July 1946, and the American Jewish Trade Union committee for Palestine to the TUC, 9 June 1946, MRC, MSS.292/956.9/4.

127. See the AFL's telegram to the TUC, 13 August 1946, and the TUC's reply, 23 August 1946. Also see the National Union of Tailors and Garment Workers, London No 2 branch to the TUC, 3 July 1946 and the Leeds Trade Council to the TUC, 29 Sept 1946, all MRC, MSS.292/956.9/4. The Leeds District committee of the National Union of Tailors & Garment Workers sent their resolution to Bevin, 19 July 1946, TNA: PRO, FO371/52541.
128. AFL president Green told the 1946 AFL annual convention that "*our great labour movement has been tremendously disappointed over the attitude of the party in power in Great Britain towards the open door in Palestine....*" Report of the fraternal delegates to the annual convention of the AFL, MRC, TUC Annual Report 1947, pp. 214–215.
129. When Parliament debated the withdrawal from Palestine in March 1948, 32 Labour MPs voted against their Government's policy. Several ministers who had doubts about this policy included Bevan, Creech Jones, Dalton, Shinwell, Strachey, Strauss and Williams.
130. TUC memorandum, I/C1, 1943–44, 19 October 1943, MRC, MSS.292/901/6.
131. V. Allen, *Trade Union Leadership* (London: Longmans 1957), p. 290.
132. Planning for the WFTU conference in London, Protocols, January 1945, (Hebrew original), MSILP, 2-024-1945-11.
133. For the background to the issuing of invitations to the Histadrut and the Arab trade unions see: MRC, TUC International committee minutes, 17 February and 28 November 1944, MSS.292/901/6.
134. Appendix D (ii) Clause 26 of the Declaration on the Attitude to the Peace Settlement, the World Trade Union Conference, 6–17 February 1945, MRC, MSS.159/5/2/124.
135. E. Manor, *Berl Locker: A Zionist Diplomat, Socialist and Optimist* (Jerusalem: Hasifria Hatzionit, 2010) (Hebrew original), p. 163.
136. 'World trade union body, Lebanese to represent Middle East', *Jewish Chronicle* 12 October 1945, p. 15.
137. WFTU Executive Board meeting minutes, 6 October 1945, the WFTU Collection at the International Institute of Social History Archives, Amsterdam (hereafter cited as ISSH), WFTU series, file 38.
138. Peter Brod, 'Soviet-Israeli Relations 1948–56', in *The Left against Zion*, ed. Robert Wistrich (London: Valentine Mitchell, 1979), pp. 58–59.
139. Salliant to Tewson, 5 August 1946, MRC, MSS.292C/918.23/2.
140. Tewson to Salliant, 22 August 1946, MRC, MSS.292/956.9/4.
141. Salliant to Tewson, 27 August 1946, MRC, MSS.292/956.9/4.
142. Histadrut to the WFTU, 7 September 1946, and Tewson to Salliant, 12 September and 30 September 1946, all MRC, MSS.292/956.9/4.

143. Schevenels was a loyal supporter of the TUC and their choice for WFTU general secretary but he lost to Salliant. Histadrut to the TUC, 27 November 1946 and Schevenels to Tewson, 28 November 1946, MRC, MSS.292/956.9/4.
144. Tewson to Schevenels, 2 December 1946, MRC, MSS.292/956.9/4.
145. The TUC telegram to the Histadrut asked for a reply not later than Monday 16 December 1946, when the matter was to be considered by the General Council. TUC International committee minutes, MRC, 10 December 1946, MSS.292/956.9/4.
146. Histadrut to the TUC, 15 December 1946, MRC, MSS.292/956.9/4.
147. The International Department had provided the General Council with a six-page briefing document on the Government's decisions regarding the recommendations of the Anglo-American Inquiry. MRC, TUC International Department briefing on Palestine, 16 December 1946, MSS292C/918.23/2.
148. TUC General Council minutes, 18 December 1946 and the telegram from the TUC to the Histadrut, 24 December 1946, both MRC, MSS.292C/20/31.
149. The briefing prepared by the International department in February 1947 included details of unpublished British government proposals for a five-year trusteeship agreement. Bell to Deakin, 11 February 1947, MRC, MSS.292C/918.23/2.
150. WFTU to the TUC, 12 February 1947 and the Histadrut to the TUC, 12 February 1947, MRC, MSS.292/956.9/4.
151. The memorandum of the meeting at TUC between Salliant, Tewson and Deakin, 13 February 1947, MRC, MSS.292C/918.2/3.
152. Briefing document for Prague Embassy, 2 June 1947, TNA: PRO, LAB13/597. Also see P. Mason, file comment, 7 May 1947, TNA: PRO, FO371/64485B, and D.J. McCarthy, file comment, 10 May 1947, TNA: PRO, FO371/67613.
153. Report on the WFTU conference in Prague, PLILMR, Histadrut Executive Committee minutes, 25 June 1947.
154. The Executive Bureau, which was the inner circle of the Executive Committee consisted of nine members—one each from the USSR, Britain, America, France, China, Holland, Italy, South America and the WFTU General Secretary. Deakin was the TUC representative as well as the WFTU president.
155. Minutes of the WFTU Executive Bureau meeting in Prague, 7 June 1947, ISSH, WFTU series, file 66, and Histadrut Executive Committee minutes, report of the WFTU conference, 25 June 1947, PLILMR.
156. Histadrut Executive Committee minutes, report of the WFTU conference, 25 June 1947, PLILMR, and the minutes of the WFTU Executive Bureau meeting, 14 June 1947, ISSH, file 66.

157. N. Jackson's report on the Palestine debate at the WFTU, 1 July 1947, the Levenberg Collection at the London School of Economics Archive, University of London, file G/1/2 (Hereafter cited as LSE), TUC memorandum on WFTU conference, TNA: PRO, FO371/67613 and the report of the WFTU conference, the Histadrut's Executive committee minutes, 25 June 1947 PLILMR.
158. The Foreign Office memorandum on WFTU conference, 17 June 1947, TNA: PRO, FO371/67613. The report of the delegation to WFTU conference, PLILMR, the Histadrut Executive Committee meeting minutes, 13 August 1947.
159. TUC report IC2/1, for the International committee, 21 January 1948 which includes the minutes of the WFTU Executive Bureau meeting, 19–24 November 1947, MRC, MSS.292/901/8, the TUC report of the WFTU delegation to Palestine, IC3/2, 17 February 1948, MRC, MSS.292/956.9/7 and the TUC report on the WFTU, IC/5/3, 30 April 1948, MRC, MSS.292C/918.2/9, WFTU correspondence includes; WFTU to the TUC, 22 January 1948, MRC, MSS.292C/918.23/2, Salliant to Tewson, 2 February 1948, Tewson to Salliant, 11 February 1948, TUC General Council minutes, 28 January 1948, MRC, MSS.292/956.9/7 and WFTU Executive Bureau meeting minutes Rome, 4 May 1948, ISSH, file 75.
160. "No trace of kidnapped sergeants", *The Manchester Guardian*, 31 July, 1947, "New outbursts against Jews: Manchester scenes, fire and looting in Liverpool", *The Manchester Guardian*, 4 August 1947, *The Jewish Chronicle*, 8 August, 15 August and 22 August 1947 and Tony Kushner, 'Antisemitism and Austerity; the August riots in Britain', ed. Panayi Panikos, *Racial Violence in Britain 1840–1950* (Leicester: Leicester University Press, 1993), pp. 149–168.
161. The Beckenham Trade Council to the TUC, 9 August 1947 and the Holborn and City Trades Council to the TUC, 9 August 1947, MRC, MSS.292/956.9/4.
162. Draft statement on events in Palestine statement, undated, MRC, MSS.292/956.9/4.
163. TUC General Council Minutes, 30 August 1947, MRC, MSS.292/20/32.
164. Ibid.
165. "Menace to democracy" and "TUC condemn fascism, Jewish speakers cheered", *Jewish Chronicle*, 12 September 1947, *The Daily Herald*, 6 September 1947, p. 2, and paragraph 244, MRC, TUC Congress proceedings 1947, p. 213, and pp. 516–519.
166. Salliant to Tewson, 14 August 1947, MRC, MSS.292/956.9/4.
167. Tewson to Salliant, 20 August 1947 and the TUC memo to Tewson, 26 August 1947, MRC, MSS.292/956.9/4.

168. Salliant to Tewson WFTU to the TUC, 27 August 1947, World Jewish Congress to the TUC, 25 August 1947, MRC, MSS.292/956.9/4 and TUC General Council minutes, 30 August 1947, MRC, MSS.292/20/31.
169. The letter from the Foreign Office to the TUC stated that "Immigrants were given opportunity to disembark in France," 28 August 1947, MRC, MSS.292/956.9/4.
170. Tewson to Salliant, 16 September 1947, MRC, MSS.292/956.9/4.
171. Rubinstein, W.D., *The Left the Right and the Jews* (Beckenham: Croom Helm, 1982), pp. 100–102.
172. Johan Franzén, "Communism versus Zionism: The Comintern, Yishuvism, and the Palestine Communist Party", *Journal of Palestine Studies*, Vol. 36, No. 2 (Winter 2007), p. 17.
173. Jason Heppell, "A Question of 'Jewish Politics'? The Jewish Section of the Communist Party of Great Britain, 1936–45," in *Jews, Labour and the Left, 1918–48,* eds. Christine Collette and Stephen Bird (London: Ashgate, 2000), p. 95.
174. *The Daily Worker*, 15 May 1948.
175. Tony Kushner, 'Jewish Communists in Twentieth-century Britain: the Zaidman collection,' *Labour History Review*, Vol. 55 (1989), pp. 70–71, and June Edmunds, The *Left and Israel, party policy change and internal democracy* (London: Macmillan, 2000), p. 112.
176. Histadrut survey of Arab labour organisations in Palestine, Jan 1945, MRC, MSS.292/956.9/4, Histadrut to the IFTU, 3 December 1944, MRC, MSS.292/956.9/3 and The Government of Palestine to the TUC, 22 August 1945, MRC, MSS.292/956.9/4.
177. The status of the Arab trade unions was confirmed in a letter the TUC received from a British Army officer, Captain Filsan, who wrote that PAWS and FAU were as steeped in Arab nationalism as the Histadrut was in Jewish nationalism but the PLL has no real standing in the Arab world. MRC, Filsan to the TUC, undated, MSS.292/956.9/4.
178. Z. Lockman, *Comrades and Enemies Arab and Jewish workers in Palestine 1906–1948* (London: University of California, 1996), pp. 278–279.
179. TUC to the IFTU, 14 August 1944 and IFTU to PAWS, 22 August 1944, MRC, MSS.292/956.9/3.
180. Z. Lockman, *Comrades and Enemies Arab and Jewish workers in Palestine 1906–1948*, pp. 344–345.
181. The TUC wrote to the Colonial Office on 13 March 1947 saying that the Arab trade unions in Palestine still do not have the legal right of collective bargaining. TUC to Colonial Office, 13 March 1947, MRC, MSS.292/956.9/4.

182. Membership of the Histadrut at the end of 1944 was 143,311 (223,651 if one included children and dependants) which was 35% of the Jewish population in Palestine, *The Zionist Review*, 23 November 1945, TNA: PRO, KV5/16, the report of the Palestine Government committee to consider employment problems in Palestine, 7 July 1944, TNA: PRO, FO921/312, p. 3 and the Histadrut survey of Arab labour organisations in Palestine, January 1945, MRC, MSS.292/956.9/4.
183. B. Morris, *Righteous Victims a History of the Zionist-Arab Conflict 1881–2000* (New York: Vintage Books, 2001), pp. 205–209.
184. Histadrut to the TUC, 26 December 1947, MRC, MSS.292/956.9/4, Histadrut to the WFTU, 3 January 1948, MRC, MSS.292C/918.23/2, the TUC to the Histadrut, 3 January 1948, MRC, MSS.292/956.9/4 and the TUC International committee minutes, 21 January 1948, MRC, MSS.292/901/8.
185. The NCL statement on Palestine, 15 April 1948, MRC, MSS.292/956.9/3 and the Labour Party to Tewson, 24 February 1948, MRC, MSS.292/956.9/4.
186. Bevin intervened with the colonial secretary and the prime minister over the establishment of Jewish fighting units. J. Gorny, *The British labour movement and Zionism 1917–1948*, p. 171.

CHAPTER 3

The Years of Indifference

Rebuilding Relations, 1948–51

As the second most important Jewish organisation in Palestine after the Jewish Agency, the Histadrut's immediate priority after independence had been declared in 1948 was to build support within the international labour movement for a Jewish state. This would be the Histadrut's contribution to Ben-Gurion's foreign policy objectives to find friendship and understanding for their cause anywhere in the world. Almost immediately after declaring independence the Histadrut received telegrams of support from both the Soviet and American trade union movements, but not from the TUC who backed Bevin's Middle East policy to rebuild links with the Arabs nations.[1]

Once the State of Israel had been declared the connection between the Histadrut and the TUC immediately changed to a relationship between two national centres rather than that of head office and branch office. Both still had similar political roles as they both supported a Labour government and each promoted their government's policies to the international labour movement. However during the final years of the mandate there had been a noticeable tension between the two organisations and relations with the Histadrut were by then at their lowest point since 1920.

The Histadrut's first action was to thank the American and Soviet trade unions for their support, but not the TUC. In June 1948 the Histadrut, announced in an attempt to rebuild links that they intended to send

R. Fraser, *British Trade Unions, the Labour Party, and Israel's Histadrut*, https://doi.org/10.1007/978-3-030-86814-7_3

goodwill delegations to several European countries including Britain and the USSR, to explain the Histadrut's work and its part in the struggle for Jewish independence. Whereas the Soviets responded immediately by thanking the Histadrut for their desire to strengthen relations, Tewson replied saying that their request would be discussed at the next General Council meeting. The Histadrut's telegram to the TUC spoke of strained relations between the organisations in recent years and the British government's attitude towards Israel but they hoped that the visit would improve relations and asked if TUC would be interested in meeting with them. Further pressure was applied on the TUC when a few days later the *Daily Worker* printed an interview with the Histadrut general secretary, Yosef Sprinzak, stating that the Histadrut intended to send a special mission to TUC. The TUC again told the Histadrut that their '*request will be considered by the General Council*',[2] and following the Labour government's lead of not having officially recognised Israel told the Histadrut that as the situation in '*Palestine*' was unclear, no action should be taken.[3]

The Histadrut Attends the 1948 TUC Congress

The Histadrut's second action was to send Reuven Barkatt, the Histadrut political secretary, to Europe in summer of 1948 in order to try and rebuild links with the European labour movement. When the Home Office refused Barkatt an entry visa, the Jewish Agency in London phoned the TUC, saying they were ringing on Locker's behalf and asked for the TUC's help to obtain a visa, claiming that Barkatt was a personal friend of Tewson. The caller was told that '*Tewson has no knowledge of Barkatt and resents him using his name in this connection*'. The TUC, however, did check with the Home Office and in order to cover themselves the TUC told the Home Office that they would have no objection to a visa being granted. Barkatt was duly given his visa and arrived in time to attend the TUC Congress at the beginning of September.[4]

Barkatt told his colleagues on his return that he now had a better understanding of the current state of affairs in the WFTU, which he blamed on the Western Federations and the TUC in particular. The TUC had objected to any cooperation with the USSR by the trade unions from the smaller countries and he thought that Deakin's TUC Congress speech was a worrying sign for the future of the WFTU. The TUC withdrew from the WFTU the following year. Barkatt described relations with

Britain as the hardest and also the most important because they needed to find a way to rebuild and reconnect with the British labour movement.

He was disgusted with the way the TUC had behaved towards Solomon Lever, of the London Jewish Bakers Union, who had submitted a motion to Congress calling on the government to recognise the State of Israel.[5] There was no way that Deakin would allow Congress to either discuss or vote on such a motion as Britain had not yet recognised Israel and was still recovering from a bloody campaign in Palestine. Barkatt was told that the TUC president had asked that Lever's pro-Zionist motion be withdrawn as Congress would not approve the motion and the Zionist cause would suffer a '*prominent defeat*'. Barkatt, who was politically astute enough to know the real reason, described the subsequent negotiations with Lever as a '*scandalous fiasco*' because Lever agreed to withdraw the motion in return for permission to address Congress.[6] The *Guardian* newspaper reported that Lever had made a challenging speech protesting that it was a tragedy that Britain had not recognised Israel and It was all the more deplorable because Britain had a Labour government in power.[7]

Barkatt noted that Lever's speech was made to a half-empty hall on the last day of Congress passed without '*any impression or reaction*' and concluded that '*our issue was presented there in a very poor way, unprepared and undignified*'. Deakin had told Barkatt that he had opposed the discussion of the Lever's motion by Congress because people had not forgotten '*the Sergeants' affair*' and he urged Barkatt not to raise the issue again. Once again Deakin had protected the Labour government from any embarrassment or criticism.[8]

Barkatt's trip to Europe took two months and he left England a few days after the assassination of the UN mediator, Count Bernadotte, by the militant Zionist group LEHI. He reported to the Histadrut Executive committee that the murder of Count Bernadotte which had already been forgotten about in Israel was still talked about in Europe and that the British public had reacted more strongly to the killing of Bernadotte than had the British press, but they still talk about the hanging of the two Sergeants a year after the event. Barkatt noted that to the British, Bernadotte had been a symbol of peace, who had been murdered by the Jews, and that his death might affect Israel's relations with both Britain and Europe for some time to come.

From 1948 onwards, the maintenance and monitoring of links with the Histadrut became a priority for the Foreign Office because Mapai dominated both the Histadrut and the coalition Israeli government. The importance of this close alliance was due to half the population being members of the Histadrut, as well as the Histadrut owning the biggest industrial conglomerate in Israel and being the biggest employer after the government. The Foreign Office, who were keen to rebuild links with the Arab states needed stability in the region to ensure that oil supplies would not be interrupted and that any unrest in Palestine would not inflame the Muslims in India who were about to gain their independence. They were also determined to curb increasing Soviet interest in the region as they feared that Israel might become a Communist or a Soviet satellite state because they believed that the majority of new Jewish immigrants who came from behind the Iron Curtain were communists. Once Israel had supported the UN over Korea, the Foreign Office gradually realised that Israel was moving towards the West, which was confirmed by the British ambassador in Israel after the Slansky trial who reported that '*the Soviet Government and her allies had now given up hope of bringing Israel into the communist orbit*'.[9]

The British government's post-war Middle East policy was to rebuild its relations with the Arab states in order to protect its vital political and economic interests in the region which resulted in Bevin withholding recognition of the State of Israel until 1949. However soon after independence had been declared, the TUC received letters from several American unions urging them to lobby for the reversal of British policy towards Israel and stop aiding the Arabs. Tewson, who had been fully briefed on the situation, was told that recognition of the State of Israel could not be given until the '*usual conditions have been fulfilled, a functioning Government, known frontiers and the ability to carry out international obligations*'. He therefore saw no wrong in talking about the situation in "Palestine" rather than "Israel".[10]

Reciprocal Visits and Improving Histadrut Relations with Britain

While Barkatt was in Britain he sounded out both the TUC and the Labour Party about sending a delegation to Israel. Deakin told him that it was too soon but it was the government, not the unions, who would make the final decision. With regard to the WFTU, Deakin said that it was too soon for them to send a delegation, this would be seen as a communist action which he would '*vigorously*' oppose. Before meeting Tewson,

Barkatt talked to the secretary of the parliamentary faction of the Fabian society, who was very keen on the idea of a delegation and raised the matter with the Executive committee of the Parliamentary Labour Party, which approved of the idea of sending a delegation to Israel. Barkatt's meeting with Tewson was difficult and like Deakin, Tewson thought the suggestion was premature and that contacts could be made without a delegation. Tewson offered to give Barkatt all the information he wanted without the need for a visit but changed his mind when Barkatt told him it had the approval of the Labour parliamentary group, saying, that maybe the trade unions should initiate a delegation. Barkatt then met with the chairman and secretary of the Labour Party who told him that as this was a significant political issue they would need to talk with Attlee and Bevin. The answer Barkatt received revealed the state of mind in the party regarding Israel; that if asked for its opinion they thought that it was too early and that a delegation wouldn't serve any useful purpose at this time. Barkatt concluded after meeting with Michael Foot and other Labour MPs, that whoever he met from the British labour movement had been happy to talk to him and were ready for a new approach towards Israel. He also made sure that his meetings with Labour Party officials and MP's were on an unofficial basis.[11] Although there was enthusiasm for a visit, it was clear that any official trip would have to wait until after Britain had officially recognised Israel. This took place in January 1949.

Barkatt concluded his report to the Histadrut Executive Committee saying that it was now up to them to decide whether to pursue the visit or '*to wait for greater changes in England*'. He advised that he didn't '*want to make general conclusions, as anyone going to Europe today feels himself treading a very narrow wire, stretched above a great chasm. Many things we thought to be firm are found to be illusionary; there are sympathies that are built on sand. On the other hand, there is interest we didn't see from here and this is real interest. We are now, politically speaking, in a very fluid position, and many possibilities and many mishaps rest on the doorstep of our future. I have the feeling that by this trip a large opening for political action was opened for the Histadrut, which can be valuable if we persist in it, both to the state and to the Histadrut*'.[12]

Barkatt's report to the Histadrut executive is one of the few documents that has survived that outline his views and thoughts on the TUC and their relationship with the Histadrut. He indicated that Deakin made all the decisions relating to the TUC's international policy and that Tewson was unimpressive. One thing was clear from his visit that there was support from within the unions and the Labour Party for the rebuilding of links with Israel.

Before independence, the Jewish Agency, the Histadrut and Mapai all had their own representatives in Britain, often sharing offices and personnel. By 1949, Dr Schneier Levenberg, a lifelong Zionist and Labour Party member was the London representative of the Jewish Agency, the Histadrut, and chairman of both the Palestine Labour Political Committee (PLPC) and Poale Zion. He also worked closely with the Israeli legation in London. In August 1949, Levenberg, on Barkatt's instructions, issued a joint invitation to Labour Party, the TUC and the Co-operative Union to send a joint labour movement delegation to Israel which was accepted and organised for late December.[13] The delegation was to be led by the Labour Party chairman and Durham miners' leader Sam Watson. Although this visit was intended to rebuild relations nine months after Britain had recognised Israel, the NCL called the trip a '*goodwill mission to Palestine*'.[14] Levenberg advised Barkatt that other than Alice Bacon MP, none of the party had any prior connection or knowledge of Israel. He also suggested various strategies for the visit including political points that would need explaining including; Israel was a democracy, Arab citizens enjoy full equality and that Israel intended to live in friendship and peace with Britain.[15]

The delegation was received with the highest protocol; they met with the president of Israel, the prime minister, members of his Cabinet and leaders of the Histadrut. As well as visiting schools, kibbutzim and factories they met with the Palestine Labour League. Even Sir Alexander Knox Helm, the Head of the British legation who was not known for his positive views on Israel, reported that he was glad the visit had taken place and that the delegation had realised how little was known in Britain about Israel.[16] Watson made it clear he would, in future try to correct some of the misapprehensions that existed about Israel; saying '*I came as a friend but somewhat ignorant of what that State was trying to accomplish and left as a friend, much better informed, much clearer in their conception of Israel's hopes and desires*'.[17]

The official report of the visit noted it had been inspired by political reasons because of the deteriorating relations during the mandate. The delegation was deeply impressed with the spirit and determination to build the country on a democratic and socialist basis which they hoped would prove a most valuable development in the Middle East. They also noted a real fear of a second round of war, and were reminded many times that Britain was supplying arms to Egypt and Trans-Jordan. The delegation discovered an admiration for the British labour movement and a desire for friendship with Britain which they hoped would be reciprocated and recommended that relations between the two countries be urgently improved.[18] However the Foreign Office advised Attlee not to attend the reception Levenberg had organised for the delegation on their return on the grounds of not wanting to upset the Arabs countries.[19]

In March 1950 the Labour Party decided to invite a Histadrut delegation to pay a return visit Britain. This time it was the Labour Party general secretary, Morgan Phillips, who in his letter to the TUC described the mission as the '*delegation to Palestine*'.[20] The invitation was issued in spite of objections from the Foreign Office who were concerned that any Histadrut delegation would also include members of the pro-Moscow Mapam Party.[21] The visit eventually took place in December 1950 with Barkatt leading the delegation.[22] The Israelis met with leading politicians and trade union leaders impressing upon them Israel's wish for peace in the Middle East and the Histadrut's desire for good relations with the British labour movement with Attlee declaring the visit had done much to promote friendly relations between Britain and Israel.[23] On many levels both visits were successful, with the Labour Party being the main beneficiary during the next few years as many senior members of the Labour Party went to Israel, but neither Tewson or Deakin ever visited Israel. It did not help that the Histadrut had remained in the WFTU after the TUC had resigned. Sadly, until the Histadrut joined the ICFTU in 1953, Tewson made sure that he never contacted Barkatt directly.

The Role of British Labour Attaché in Israel

Because of the importance the Foreign Office accorded to events in Israel, Ivor Thomas was appointed the first labour attaché to the British legation in Tel Aviv in January 1950 shortly after Britain had recognised Israel.[24] Previously, the British labour attaché based in Cairo had covered labour issues in Palestine, but after 1948, he was no longer allowed to travel to Israel or directly contact his opposite number in Tel Aviv in case he jeopardised his credibility with the other seven Arab countries he covered in his work.

The Ministry of Labour (MOL) sent copies of Thomas's reports to the Foreign Office, who before sending them onto the TUC, edited them in order that the TUC would not be sent material on '*hot political subjects*'. This decision only compounded the TUC's lack of knowledge and understanding of the politics of the region.[25] The Foreign Office were also monitoring the status of the Arab population in Israel at this time as they wanted to know if the Arabs would become a '*fifth column*' in any future wars and their attitude to the possibility of Israel aligning with the Soviet Union.[26]

Was Bevin's International Labour Policy Successful?

In 1946 Bevin, who understood the importance of the international workers' movements, suggested to the Foreign Office that there should be an exchange of information between the Labour Party, the TUC and the Foreign Office. Consequently Hubert Gee became the first Foreign Office labour advisor in April 1949.[27] His main duties were public relations work with the TUC, unions and employers organisations and to provide a link with British labour attachés abroad in order to counter Communist influence in international federations and conferences. Bevin then recruited the TUC to work closely with the labour attachés and by 1952 it was a government priority to encourage the development of bona fide trade unions in the Middle East.[28] With their own advisor on international labour questions and their network of labour attachés the Foreign Office was often better informed on events in Israel than the TUC.

Bevin's Middle East policy was dictated by the need for Britain to regain its position of influence in the Arab world as well as securing oil supplies for Britain and a military base in the region; whilst actively opposing the spread of communism and Soviet efforts to gain a foothold in the region. The emergence of a Jewish state which was opposed by the Arabs complicated matters. His choice of the international labour movement as one of several avenues open to him to implement these aims was very successful, and successive British governments continued to support the movement long after his death. On his instructions the Foreign Office worked closely with the TUC and both were well supported by the labour attachés based in Tel Aviv and Cairo. His plan was for the labour attachés and the TUC to establish and build pro-British links with trade unionists internationally rather than just in the British Empire, which had been the TUC's pre-war policy. The TUC was unable to fulfil this role because, although they were highly influential at the WFTU and subsequently at the ICFTU, they were unable to compete with the American unions who were backed financially by the CIA and could afford to develop contacts in Africa and Asia.[29] The TUC lacked the necessary resources for this work because of the poor economic conditions in post-war Britain, and had to depend on the labour attachés who were civil servants and not trade unionists. Tewson rarely went on foreign visits and when he did it was frequently only on international labour movement business. As a result of the TUC's wartime involvement with the government and their loyalty to Bevin they continued to align their Middle East policies with those of the subsequent Conservative governments. Without Bevin none of this would have happened.

The Histadrut Leaves WFTU

As was evident at Prague, not only was the WFTU being used by both sides as a weapon in the Cold War, but the TUC were also fighting the Soviets for control of the WFTU. Matters came to a head in early 1949 when the TUC, along with the American and European trade unions, resigned to form the anti-Communist, International Confederation of Trade Unions [ICFTU]. When it was clear that the TUC was about to leave the WFTU, Barkatt asked Levenberg to monitor the attitude of the TUC towards the WFTU. It was important for the Histadrut at that time to maintain contact with and follow the developments both inside and outside the WFTU, but it had to balance this against the stance taken by the TUC.[30] The break-up of the WFTU coincided with the Israeli government's negotiations with the Soviet Union, Romania and Hungary about Jewish emigration to Israel and presented the government with the problem as to whether the Histadrut should remain a member of the WFTU. The subsequent discussions highlighted the political and ideological differences between Mapai and Mapam which was first discussed at the Histadrut's conference in 1949.[31] Although the conference agreed to the Histadrut remaining part of the WFTU, they also decided to send observers to both the forthcoming WFTU conference in Milan and the preliminary conference of the ICFTU in Geneva. Their decision followed the Israeli government's policy of neutrality between West and East. On the eve of the Geneva conference Tewson wrote that the Histadrut was a special case.[32] The British legation reported to Bevin that there was a strong divergence of views between Mapai who wanted the Histadrut to leave the WFTU immediately and declare its neutrality and Mapam and the communists who argued that the Histadrut should remain a member and condemned those who had left the WFTU.[33]

Barkatt attended both conferences as a neutral observer and reported that at Geneva there was not just an ideological battle but also a tactical one between Britain and America for the future leadership of the ICFTU. The attitude towards Israel, he noted, had changed since they were '*no longer the world's focus of attention*' nor had '*to beg for the help of our friends and sympathisers*', but overall '*we were treated with coolness and lack of knowledge*'. He also reported that the Lebanese delegation had queried the Histadrut's right to be present at Geneva. As a neutral observer, all Barkatt could do was to work behind the scenes to ensure that question of the Histadrut's status did not receive official approval. He warned his colleagues that once the many unions in Asia and Africa had become members of the ICFTU, the Histadrut had to expect to find serious problems caused by the increase of these unions' disproportionate voting power in the new organisation.

Barkatt described the atmosphere in Milan as a show of power, with the atmosphere as one of '*unanimous voices of all the speakers*' with applause after every speech. Whereas in Geneva the Histadrut was not allowed to address the conference, Histadrut delegates spoke twice in Milan. Although their speeches were accepted coolly because they were so different they were given a disproportionate importance because the Soviets wanted to impress the non-communist members of WFTU and wanted the Histadrut to remain as members of the WFTU and not join the ICFTU.

The main aim of their delegation was however to try and negotiate with the Soviets, Romanians and Hungarians about the right of Jews to emigrate to Israel. Barkatt revealed that that the Soviets had made it clear that leaving the WFTU would seriously damage Israel's relations with the USSR and end their discussions about Jewish emigration.[34]

These two meetings were very important for the Histadrut which was coming to terms with its newly gained status as a minor but independent member of the international labour movement. Many Israelis, including the Histadrut, saw themselves as natural allies of Britain and since their priority was the rebuilding of relations with the TUC they were concerned that by going to Milan their invitation to attend the forthcoming founding conference of the ICFTU as observers in London would be withdrawn. They need not have worried, because Tewson regarded the Histadrut as a special case and the British were keen for the Israel to stay out of the Soviet Union's sphere of influence.

Because the TUC had left the WFTU, Barkatt no longer had any direct contact with the TUC and depended on Levenberg to act as a go-between.

The British legation closely observed these developments reporting that the Histadrut was thinking hard about its international policy but their government's concern for the Jews in the USSR and satellite countries as well as the strength of the left-wing minority in their organisation would prevent any change of course for some time.[35]

In March 1950, Thomas, the labour attaché, reported that in the light of their continued membership of the WFTU the Histadrut had become '*very cagey*' when discussing their '*international position*' which was in sharp '*contrast to their former readiness*'.[36] He noted that Barkatt had said that the TUC had wanted the Histadrut to leave the WFTU but in his opinion Bevin's recent comments in Parliament had undone all the work they had done to improve Israel-UK relations and there was no way that they could now leave the WFTU. Thomas commented that Barkatt had used the opportunity to air his views on Bevin, partly in the hope that his views would be passed on to the TUC and to justify the Histadrut's continued membership of the WFTU. Thomas concluded that he was also most anxious to remain on good terms with the TUC.[37]

It soon became clear to the Israeli government that the Histadrut could no longer remain in the WFTU as the three issues that had applied to their 'neutral' stance were no longer relevant; Jewish emigration was no longer conditional on the Histadrut remaining a member of the WFTU,[38] Mapai had been unable to form a government coalition with Mapam and the split between the ICFTU and WFTU had become irreversible. After extensive discussions between the Mapai executive, Mapai Knesset members and the executive committee of the Histadrut on 11 May 1950 the Histadrut Executive Committee decided, to leave the WFTU.[39] Barkatt had argued that the realignment of the international labour movement was an extension of the Cold War and both the WFTU and the ICFTU were political in character and purpose. Whilst membership of either organisation conflicted with Israel's policy of strict neutrality he denied that the decision to leave the WFTU was the result of pressure from the West and said that the British labour delegation which had visited Israel understood the Histadrut's position. The Histadrut also decided to maintain friendly relations with labour organisations irrespective of their affiliation and not align itself at that time with either the ICFTU or the WFTU.[40] In order to maintain its neutrality the Histadrut turned down the WFTU's request to discuss their withdrawal.[41]

Leaving the WFTU was an important decision for the Israelis, but persuading the Histadrut to join the ICFTU as Israel was moving towards the

West was not a priority for either the Foreign Office who continued to monitor the Histadrut or the TUC. There is very little evidence of direct contact between them. Barkatt had received updates about the TUC and the ICFTU's plans for the Middle East from the British labour attaché.[42] Tewson did not deal with the Israelis directly for possible fear of offending the Arabs in his role as president of the ICFTU and his connection with the Foreign Office. Although there had been no direct contact with the TUC or the ICFTU since 1949, he gave an assurance as ICFTU president that no pressure would be put on the Histadrut to join the Federation.[43]

The Histadrut Joins the ICFTU

The question as to whether the Histadrut should join the ICFTU was part of a much wider debate in Israel which focused on whether Israel should be aligned with the West or the Third World. By 1952, the Israeli government had realised that it could no longer remain neutral and the country's survival depended on friendship with other powers but postponed making a decision to join the ICFTU as they did not want to cause a domestic crisis with their coalition partners, the pro-Communist Mapam party, and split the Israeli labour movement.[44]

In June 1952, Barkatt travelled to Brussels, Helsinki and London in order to ascertain the ICFTU's plans for the Middle East. Tewson only agreed to meet him after being told that the discussions would be about the Histadrut's future relationship with the ICFTU.[45] Their meeting was reported to have been very friendly and the Histadrut indicated that they would have sent observers to the next meeting of the ICFTU General Council if it had been held anywhere other than Berlin. Tewson told Barkatt that it would improve matters if the Histadrut became an affiliate in order to help build up the ICFTU's Middle East regional organisation and he did not believe that the Arab-Israel conflict presented any '*insuperable obstacles*' to the development of the regional grouping.[46]

The Slansky show trial which took place in Prague in November 1952 caused alarm in Israel because the prosecution not only emphasised the Jewish origins of the majority of the accused but also denounced Zionism and the Israeli government. An emissary of Mapam, Mordechai Oren who was visiting Prague was also arrested and testified at the trial that he had helped Slansky and his co-defendants. The defendants, who were accused of being 'Zionists' were, devoted Communists. They all were found guilty and the majority of them were executed. Then in January 1953 the Soviet

Union announced a conspiracy by a group of mostly Jewish doctors from Moscow who were accused of 'poisoning' the leaders of the Kremlin. Like the Slansky defendants they were accused of being part of a Zionist plot to undermine communism. Many leading Jews were arrested and there were rumours that there would be a wholescale deportation of Jews from major cities. A few weeks after Stalin died on 5 March the case against the doctors was dropped.

The Jewish Agency responded to these events by arranging for an emergency conference to be held in Zurich on 10 March to consider the plight of Eastern European Jewry in the light of the ongoing antisemitic propaganda campaign in the Soviet Union and Eastern Europe. The American office of the ICFTU wrote to the TUC advising them that the American Jewish Labor Committee[47] would be attending the conference and taking with them statements of support from the leaders of the AFL and CIO. Tewson declined an invitation to send a statement of support saying that it was not the TUC's practice to send messages to conferences outside the trade union movement. Tewson's carefully worded reply, which was true to form did not include the words 'antisemitism' or 'Jews', concluded by saying that the General Council had issued an official statement '*expressing the revulsion of the British workers at the new wave of purges which had occurred in the Soviet Union and the satellites*'.[48]

Mapam were Marxist-Zionists who were pro-Soviet at that time, were seriously weakened by the events in Prague and Moscow. Mapai, who had previously clashed with Mapam at the Histadrut Council meeting in October 1952 over compliance with the decisions of the Histadrut elected bodies, used the opportunity to move against Mapam by banning Communists from holding office in the Histadrut.[49] Then in May, Mapai decided that the Histadrut should join the ICFTU a move which was approved by the Council of the Histadrut. Barkatt told the Council that affiliation was necessary for Israel in order to fight the political battle for her survival and the Histadrut, he had argued, could no longer remain neutral as it was now time to join the ICFTU in order to strengthen their friendships with trade unions especially in Europe and the free world. Barkatt hoped that membership of the ICFTU would provide the opportunity for closer cooperation with the TUC.[50] This decision to join allowed the Histadrut to attend the ICFTU Congress in Stockholm at the end of July.[51] Their presence in Stockholm justified their participation and served the interests of the State of Israel because they had returned with a seat on the Executive Board and had prevented Congress discussing the report on the Arab refugees which contained several unfriendly statements towards Israel.

The Histadrut's participation in the Stockholm Congress led to their involvement in the wrangling between the TUC and the AFL-CIO for the leadership of the organisation. The Americans made it known that they would not accept Tewson's re-election as ICFTU president and the Histadrut subsequently became an integral part of American plans to enlarge the Executive in order to extend American influence between trade unions in the Americas and Asia. The expansion of the Executive was '*in part precipitated and certainly aggravated*' by the affiliation of the Histadrut, the largest and most successful trade union in the Middle East.[52]

In his post-Congress report Barkatt said that he only found out about the expansion plans for the Executive after he had arrived in Stockholm which seems unlikely bearing in mind the Histadrut's excellent relations with the Americans. However once the delegation learnt of ICFTU report on Arab refugees and plans for a regional office in Beirut, they changed their minds dropping plans to wait two or three years before standing for the Executive because membership of the Executive was no longer about '*representation and prestige*', but an issue of '*political realism*' which was essential for the Histadrut and Israel. Barkatt described the two days spent discussing the enlargement of the executive as a dramatic struggle which he believed was a fight for Israel. He felt there were four reasons why delegates opposed the changes; a divided Executive, the maintenance of the status quo, the feeling that the Histadrut's presence on the Executive would affect ICFTU activity amongst the Arabs and a small amount of an anti-Israeli feeling.[53] The British embassy in Stockholm reported that Barkatt was disappointed by the TUC's opposition to the enlargement of the executive because they had in the past strongly advised them to join the ICFTU and had hoped for a more sympathetic attitude from the TUC. Their report suggested that the TUC should be advised that next time '*it would be worth showing the Histadrut a little extra consideration*'.[54]

The Appointment of an Israeli Labour Attaché in London

The building of bridges between Britain and the new Jewish state was slow and it was only after the Labour/TUC and Histadrut visits that the British Labour Party began to return to its previous pro-Zionist stance. Moshe Bar Tal was appointed labour attaché in December 1952.[55] His appointment reflected the importance Israel placed on its relationship with the TUC, as London was the first Israeli Embassy to have its own labour attaché. Bar Tal made a huge impact building relationships with the TUC and the unions. Unlike British labour attachés who were civil servants, Bar Tal's membership of the Histadrut enabled him to relate to his fellow trade unionists.

After his return from Israel in 1949, Sam Watson, was true to his word and went on to become a leading supporter of Israel in Britain during the 1950s. Bar Tal reported that his '*influence, importance and respect that he gets from all circles were readily apparent*'.[56] The TUC's growing cooperation[57] with the Histadrut included official invitations for them to attend the TUC Congress in 1953 and 1955.[58] With the build-up of arms in the Arab states from the autumn of 1954 onwards the Histadrut contacted the TUC[59] and the Labour Party asking them to oppose arms deals which threatened peace and stability in the region.[60] They thanked the TUC and the Seaman's union in December 1955 for their opposition to the British arms deal with Egypt.[61]

The Israeli embassy in London adopted the strategy of inviting politicians and trade unionists to Israel in the early 1950s as this was the best way to gain support. They divided Israel's parliamentary supporters into two groups; those who were loyal supporters and helped on every issue which included MPs Janner and Greenwood and those who didn't want to be characterised as pro-Israeli, but would help of most of the time which included Sam Watson.[62] The Israeli ambassador repeatedly complained to Barkatt that the trade unions were being neglected once Bar Tal had finished his tour and not been replaced as the embassy did not have the time or anyone with the necessary experience to do the work.[63] Bar Tal was never replaced and another five years would pass before the Histadrut posted a permanent representative to London.

The Foreign Office Uses the TUC-ICFTU Link to Promote British Interests in the Middle East

The Foreign Office played a major role in the 1950s influencing the TUC's international work and also worked behind the scenes to bring to fruition the ICFTU proposal for a regional office in Beirut. The Foreign Office labour advisor produced a report on trade unionism in the Middle East which described the Histadrut as the most powerful trade union organisation in the Middle East and the most influential organisation in Israel.[64] The ICFTU mission in April 1952 to Lebanon, Syria, Iraq and Jordan to investigate trade union activity recommended opening an information centre in Beirut.[65]

Barkatt, who was aware of both the ICFTU mission and the Beirut office proposal, asked Thomas, the British labour attaché if Audsley, the British labour attaché in Cairo, could come to Israel to discuss the issues with him. Sir Francis Evans, the British ambassador, supported Barkatt's request warning that if an ICFTU office was opened and operated only in Arab states, Israel would become more isolated and as the Histadrut was moving cautiously towards the ICFTU and it was important that the ICFTU should not make further progress impossible.[66] The Foreign Office, which did not officially consult the TUC, vehemently opposed the visit, arguing that if it became public knowledge it might seriously prejudice Audsley's standing in Arab countries and there was also a risk that the Israelis might use his visit for propaganda purposes.[67]

Undeterred Evans then wrote that although it seemed almost impossible to realise British policy to integrate Israel into a secure Middle East, Britain should try to encourage better relations between the ICFTU and Jewish and Arab trade union leaders. He warned that if the ICFTU recognised the much smaller Arab unions and established an office in the region without making an approach to the Histadrut, such a move would be regarded by them as blatant discrimination. The Foreign Office view prevailed and the meeting never took place.[68]

The British embassy in Israel were advised in August 1953 that the Lebanese unions supported the ICFU's choice of Beirut for a regional office and that the TUC hoped that trade union leaders in Israel and the Arab states could rise above national political feelings and be prepared to work together wherever the office was located. The Foreign Office wrote that '*this may be utopian*' but asked for advice on how the Histadrut could be persuaded to work along these lines. The labour attaché's reply which was seen by TUC stated that as it was impossible for an Israeli to enter an Arab country, the Histadrut felt that a neutral country should be chosen such as Cyprus, even though they knew that the TUC did not support this idea.[69]

Barkatt wrote to Jacobus Oldenbroek, the ICFTU general secretary, after the Stockholm Congress warning that the principles of international labour cooperation would be breached if the Histadrut was not allowed to enter the country where the regional office was established. Oldenbroek replied saying that it would be an information centre not an office.[70] In October 1953, the British Embassy reported that the Histadrut's opposition was obvious as they would not be able to attend meetings in Beirut and that it seemed unwise for the ICFTU where Israelis and Arabs would sit together that they should promote an arrangement which would aggravate the differences between them.[71] The following month a TUC delegation visited Lebanon to show support for a Beirut office.[72] The Histadrut's pressure however finally paid off; when in May 1955 the TUC told the Foreign Office that the ICFTU had agreed a compromise with the Histadrut which would allow their Middle East representative to have a roving commission in the region.[73]

In May 1955 the Lebanese and the Tunisian trade unions presented to the fourth ICFTU Congress in Vienna the Arab side of the conflict with Israel. The Lebanese delegate told Congress that there were more than 100,000 Palestinian refugees in Lebanon and the ICFTU had accepted Israeli affiliation before the problem has been solved. Barkatt's response was that the Histadrut's aim was to integrate the Arab community in Israel and to give them full and equal opportunity. He blamed the Arab states for this tragic situation as they had invaded Israel in 1948.[74] Barkatt thought this attack on Israel had done Israel more good than harm and was pleased that the Histadrut had the freedom to consult with delegates without being seen by the Europeans as '*hostages of the USA*'. Although Barkatt's meetings with Tewson had a '*cordial and lively attitude*', the TUC had seemed to him to be rather aloof as they had not been conspicuous in the main Congress.[75] According to the MOL, the TUC had been anxious not to put a foot wrong by appearing to be friendlier with one delegation than another and that the TUC's attitude had not been not connected to their relationship with the Histadrut which had '*always been sound and is likely to remain so*'. The TUC was told of their reserved behaviour at the time, but had not taken the hint.[76] Barkatt was pleased however that this time, the Histadrut had been allowed to manoeuvre at Congress without being seen by the Europeans as '*hostages of the USA*'.[77]

At the end of 1955, Oldenbroek presented new proposals for future ICFTU work in the Middle East which concluded that the ICFTU's programme for peace and social progress in the region was handicapped by Arab political demands and Israel's desire for recognition by its neighbours. His new plan divided the region into two fields of action, one for the Arab countries and the other for Turkey, Iran, Cyprus and Israel.[78]

Barkatt realised that they would have to continue to monitor future ICFTU events.[79]

Audsley reported that Egypt was considering forming an Arab Confederation of Labour, which would be an independent labour bloc of Arab nations free from foreign influence.[80] He was told that Egypt would not join the ICFTU whilst Israel was a member and '*in the eyes of the Egyptian people America was responsible for the Palestine war and the State of Israel. The American government was under the control of the Jews and was pro-Jew in policy and had financed the State of Israel heavily*'.[81] The Foreign Office who were trying to improve relations with Egypt did not pass this information on to the TUC.[82]

Suez and Beyond 1956–60

While the establishment of the State of Israel in 1948 was an important event for the labour movement, the Labour Party and the Left, subsequent events in the Middle East involving Israel were ignored as other issues such as the Cold War between The Soviet Union and the West assumed greater importance.

Even though the TUC had given unquestioning support to British government post-war policies towards Palestine and after the emergence of the state of Israel, the difference between the TUC and the Histadrut was that whilst the Histadrut knew that its international role both before and after independence was to support the State of Israel, the TUC, which had previously operated independently of the British government, found itself in partnership with the Attlee government after having been asked to expand its international work, a role for which it was ill-prepared and under resourced. Given Britain's post–war financial problems it is highly unlikely that the British government gave the TUC any funding for its expanded international role. While Bevin had a vision of what he wanted the TUC to do, its international work was implemented not by him but by his two close allies; Deakin, who had told the Histadrut in Prague in 1947 that his masters were Bevin and the Labour government, and Tewson, who was hesitant and over-cautious, had made sure there was no direct contact with the Histadrut until after they had joined the ICFTU. Tewson then regarded the Histadrut as allies of the Americans, because the Histadrut had been elected to the ICFTU executive.

The British government's Middle East policy was to maintain good relations with the Arab states in order to protect Britain's vital political and economic interests in the region often at the expense of Israel. Tewson always wanted to do the right thing for his country and regardless of any personal feelings towards Jews and the Holocaust; he believed that if he openly gave his support to the Histadrut and Israel it would antagonise the Arab world and damage British interests, which was why the TUC continued to support the Middle East policies of the Conservative government which took office in 1951; The Foreign Office used the TUC and the ICFTU to help rebuild British interests in the Arab world but unlike Bevin, they did not totally trust the TUC and as we have seen often held back information about Israel and the Histadrut.

The Histadrut's priority after 1948 was to rebuild relations with the British labour movement, they were successful when it came to trade union issues but there is no evidence to suggest that they fully understood the TUC's position on political matters.

Throughout the 1950s and 1960s the TUC, which was well respected in international trade unions affairs vied with the American unions for the leadership of the ICFTU. The TUC's delegations to the ICFTU were led by Tewson, who actively supported British government Middle East policy. While Tewson was in charge, the TUC was indifferent to the Histadrut and for most of the 1950s; relations mirrored Anglo-Israel relations. Whereas Anglo-Israel relations improved after 1958, TUC-Histadrut relations did not.

Unlike Gaitskell and his Labour Party colleagues who understood the Arab-Israel conflict and also recieved regular briefings from the Israelis, the Suez conflict demonstrated the TUC's lack of understanding of the politics of the Middle East. Although the TUC was in regular contact with the Foreign Office, they did not collaborate with the Labour Party on international issues and had no first-hand knowledge of either Israel or Egypt. The result was that the British government described the TUC as 'ill informed'.[83]

From 1953 onwards the Israeli government along with the Histadrut pursued, a very active international policy with two main aims; firstly, they sought to demonstrate Israel's achievements to the world and, secondly, to win friends and influence people in countries outside the Arab World. The Histadrut made a fundamental change of direction in international affairs in 1953 when it joined the ICFTU; as the Histadrut's international activity previously had been limited to America and Europe. Confirmation that the ICFTU was important to Israel came from Barkatt, who told the Histadrut Convention in March 1956, that at a time when Israel had few friends in the world, the friendly attitude of the labour movements in Western countries was due to Israel's active membership of the ICFTU.[84]

The Build-Up to Suez

Israel's chief concern after 1948 was her survival and maintaining military equivalence with her Arab neighbours so Israel's collusion with the UK and France in the 1956 Suez conflict was totally unexpected considering how poor Anglo-Israel relations were at the time.

Even though Labour had lost the 1951 general election, the TUC's relations with the new Conservative government remained unchanged because the General Council led by Deakin was not prepared to abandon over ten years of consultation and cooperation with the government and the Foreign Office. Deakin and his General Council colleagues dictated TUC policy and were solidly behind the Labour Party being openly hostile to the Communists. This status quo continued until Deakin died in May 1955, only a few weeks after Churchill had resigned from the government. The new prime minister Anthony Eden adopted a harder line towards the TUC and with Deakin's death the consensus within the General Council disappeared once Frank Cousins, the new general secretary of the TGWU had joined the General Council as his left-wing views were consistently at odds with the other members of the Council.

By 1956 Britain was beginning to enjoy the benefits of the welfare state, full employment, the general recognition of the trade unions and British involvement in the Cold War. The Parliamentary Labour Party had also changed and was now a mixture of working-class trade unionists and middle-class intellectuals. Although the majority of trade unions were still led by colleagues of Bevin and Deakin, new leaders on the left such as Frank Cousins had emerged with new radical ideas. The primary concern of the trade unions throughout the fifties was domestic economic issues apart from support for nuclear disarmament, with little involvement in international issues.

Throughout this period the Foreign Office were concerned about the rapid industrialisation of the Middle East and any possible inroads the communists could make within the Arab labour movements. It was to their advantage that the TUC continued to back Britain's need for good relations with the Arab world. The government's awareness of Israel's political and economic problems were heightened by Marsh, the British labour attaché in Tel Aviv who wrote a series of reports including one on the growth of the Histadrut which was labelled as a very valuable aid to understanding the position and influence of this organisation. In August 1956, after Egypt's nationalisation of the Suez Canal, Marsh commented that '*Israel believes herself at present to be in greater danger than at any time since 1948*'.[85]

The Foreign Office which had a reputation for being strongly pro-Arab, enthusiastically supported the ICFTU's plans for a regional office in Lebanon because their plans for the Middle East were broadly similar those of the ICFTU. They were unhappy with the Histadrut's continued opposition to ICFTU's plans. A Foreign Office official noted that the prospects for the ICFTU in the region were not bright because of the hold '*the American Jews and the Israelis had over the foreign policies of the American labour movement*' which effectively antagonised the Arabs, preventing any ICFTU action which might have been regarded as deferring to Arab opinion.[86] Barber, the British labour attaché in Brussels who knew more than the TUC about ICFTU's intentions in the Middle East, was often reluctant, like the Foreign Office to share information with the TUC.[87] It is also clear that the Foreign Office used the TUC for their own ends.

The rising tension in the Middle East during the first half of 1956 caused by the Egypt's alignment with the Soviet Union was at the centre of all contacts and correspondence between the British labour movement and the Israeli embassy in London, the Israeli Labour Party, Mapai, and the Histadrut. Elath, the Israeli ambassador met regularly with Hugh Gaitskell, the Labour leader, throughout the year and sent to Jerusalem over 20 reports of meetings with Gaitskell and other members of the Shadow cabinet.[88] The relationship was so good that before sending a deputation to see the foreign secretary in May 1956, Labour asked Mapai if they had any special points that should be made at the meeting.[89] The Foreign Office was aware of the close relationship that existed between the embassy and the Labour party.[90] Apart from Sam Watson, the Durham miners' leader, a key figure in the Labour Party and close confidant of Gaitskell, the only union leader that the Histadrut could count on was Solomon Lever, the general secretary of the London Jewish Bakers Union. All the efforts that Bar Tal, the Israeli labour attaché, who had returned to Israel in 1954, had put into building relationships with the unions had not been followed up as the TUC was now very reticent towards the Histadrut.

At the same time the ICFTU were worried that Egypt's moves to link the Arab labour movements of North Africa were another anti-Israel move, as they was also trying to forge links in the region. Despite the Histadrut's success in thwarting Oldenbroek's plans for a Middle East office the Israelis now faced a new problem; Oldenbroek and the Americans were '*running*' after the Arab trade unions. Barkatt discussed with

Mordechai Namir, the Histadrut general secretary, on how best to deal with the '*Arab issue*' at future ICFTU Executive meetings. They anticipated that the developments over Suez might cool or even postpone discussions but as a precaution they decided to activate their friends in the American workers' movement.[91]

The ICFTU received an urgent request from its, in late August after Egypt's nationalisation of the Suez Canal from its Tunisian affiliate to issue a statement of solidarity with Egypt and Arab aspirations.[92] Conscious of the ICFTU's desire for links with the Arab unions and with the knowledge that the WFTU had already issued a statement supporting Egypt, Oldenbroek proposed in a draft statement, that the ICFTU should take a position which emphasised the need to find a solution for freedom of passage through the Suez Canal but he ignored the fact that Egypt had not allowed Israeli ships to use the canal. He then sent out the statement asking for comments.[93] Although Tewson broadly agreed with the statement it was not issued as there were considerable differences of opinion between the other affiliates.[94] Schneier Levenberg, who was Mapai's UK representative, was also the Embassy's link with the Labour Party and with Socialist International, the worldwide organisation of social democratic, socialist and labour parties which was based in London. Although the Socialist International had very little real influence in world affairs it was one of the few international bodies at Israel's disposal for strengthening their position internationally, in Europe, America, Asia and Africa.[95] Both Mapai and the British Labour Party supported the Socialist International, but for different reasons. In February 1956, Socialist International adopted, with Levenberg and Watson's support, the British and Norwegian Labour Parties resolution on the growing tension in the Middle East which asked all socialist Parties to urge their governments to allow Israel to recieve the necessary arms for self-defence.[96]

The TUC and Suez

Two weeks after the Suez canal had been nationalised in July 1956, the British government felt it neccessary to consult with the TUC, not only because of the unions immense power base within the Labour Party but because of the possibility of industrial action as part of their opposition to government plans to retake control of the canal by force. Tewson told Ian Macleod, the Minister of Labour, that the TUC Congress in September was likely to follow Labour Party policy and pass an emergency resolution on the Suez situation calling on the government to refer the matter to the UN and not use force to retake the canal.[97] Macleod recommended to the Cabinet that the position of the TGWU and Frank Cousins, was crucial if the Left wing unions united to oppose the use of force in any circumstances and recommended that the TUC be properly briefed as he thought that Tewson was '*very feeble and ill-informed about Suez*'.[98] In order to ensure that both the resolution and debate would not embarrass the government it was arranged for the prime minister to meet a TUC delegation on 20 August.[99] Shortly afterwards Eden received a message from the TUC that saying that they had reached agreement on the need for a firm and positive General Council statement and requested that the government not say anything that could undermine the TUC's statement.[100]

The International department prepared a report on the Suez crisis for the General Council which dealt with the political and trade implications for the United Kingdom. The only mention of Israel referred to the 1950 Egyptian decision to impose a blockade on Israeli shipping to stop Israel receiving oil though the canal.[101] The TUC General Council however was split between the older members on the Right, led by TUC president Charles Geddes, who preferred not to have a motion and the younger members on the left, led by Alan Birch of USDAW, the shopworkers union, who said that Britain must refer the dispute to the UN Security Council. Birch threatened to put down a hostile amendment if the General Council sponsored a motion which supported the government's actions.[102] Eventually after hours of discussion a compromise emergency motion was agreed which stated that '*force should not be used until the question has been referred to the United Nations and with its consent*'.[103] The Congress debate lasted over an hour and delegates voted unanimously in favour of the resolution. The case for Israel was put by Solomon Lever from the Jewish Bakers union, who said that Nasser had sworn to wipe Israel off the map and called on the General Council to do their utmost not to permit it. Other speakers told Congress that Israel was worthy of the TUC's support and that peace depended on the Arab states recognising Israel.[104]

Although Congress had been united over Suez and their opposition to the government's economic policies, *the Times* wrote that neither the General Council nor the general secretary had shown any signs of leadership over the last twelve months.[105] Tewson sent the government a copy of the resolution who asked Macleod to discover the likelihood of serious industrial trouble if Britain invaded Egypt.[106]

The government's Suez invasion plans united the Labour Party behind Gaitskell's anti-war campaign. The Labour Party with the TUC jointly organised a series of nationwide anti-war protests.[107] They were also aware that a high proportion of the Labour Party's working-class supporters approved of the Suez intervention and that no resolutions were adopted either in the Party or the unions which directly supported the Eden government's actions.[108]

Labour's strong support for Israel was due to its links with the Israeli leadership and an awareness of the potentially damaging political effect of adopting an anti-Israel policy given the long relationship that existed between Jews and the Party. Nor did they have comparable links with Arab nationalists. Once military action began, the NCL issued a statement which not only condemned the invasion but also urged workers not to take industrial action.[109] The government's concerns about industrial action were justified, but protests were confined to local and regional levels. They included the call from the AEU in Sheffield for a total stoppage of the engineering industry and the Fire Brigades union which called for a national strike, whilst the South Wales area of the Mineworkers union rejected a call for industrial action.[110] The only strike action that took place was at Crawley when 1200 workers attended a protest meeting to urge for an immediate ceasefire.[111]

The ICFTU and Suez

The Hungarian revolution, which took place in the same month as the Suez war was more important for the ICFTU, because it had took place in Europe and involved working class freedom, trade union rights and democracy. The Suez crisis was seen by the ICFTU partly as Israel's fight for survival and for recognition by her neighbours. The ICFTU urged its affiliates to make representations to their governments to support UN resolutions; action for stopping Soviet armed intervention in Hungary and for the immediate end to hostilities in Middle East.[112]

In November 1956 the ICFTU Executive committee discussed the ICFTU's reaction to events in Hungary and the Middle East and unequivocally condemned the Soviet intervention in Hungary, yet their discussions on the Middle East were muted by comparison.[113] The Arab and Muslim states were understandably more interested in the Middle East than Hungary and viewed Israel's involvement as secondary to the imperialist military action by Britain and France. The Histadrut felt that Israel's actions attracted a great deal of sympathy and understanding from all sides and that the British had been more sympathetic towards them than previously as they had asked that every effort be made to achieve peace between Israel and Arabs and that a way should be found to guarantee Israel's continued existence.[114] The challenge for the Histadrut was how to use their position on the ICFTU executive to make new connections and support for Israel throughout the world.

The Histadrut recognised that the ICFTU's problem was how it was going to balance the Histadrut's needs in future with their plans for growth in the Middle East which would have to take into account the emergence of the Egyptian-led Arab Confederation of Labour and the USSR's links with Egypt. Two weeks later the ICFTU issued a statement on the Middle East crisis which recognised Egypt's right to nationalise the canal with the hope that the UN would find the basis for a just and durable peace, which included the recognition of Israel and her borders.[115]

The CPGB, the Jews and Suez

Many Jewish members left the CPGB after the Slansky show trial in Prague in November 1952 and the doctor's plot in Moscow three months later, because they had realised that the Soviet Union was now promoting a policy of anti-Jewish incitement. There was also some internal dissent within the CPGB from leading figures such as Professor Hyman Levy.

The revelations in April 1956 of Stalinist purges against the Jews resulted in Levy and Chimen Abramsky publicly challenging the CPGB's position on Israel and Zionism. These disclosures disappointed many Jewish communists in the CPGB because they realised that the Soviet Union was not a society free of antisemitism, and that there had been a cover-up of the truth about Stalin's anti-Jewish moves; while Abramsky and many others resigned from the Party, Levy was forced out. This was the beginning of the end for Jewish communism in Britain which by the end of the 1950s ceased to have any significance in Jewish life.

As a result of its close relations with the USSR, the CPGB adopted a pro-Arab position on Suez and saw the nationalisation as of the canal as '*Egyptian defiance of western imperialism*' and the Anglo-French invasion as evidence of the West's intention to undermine national liberation movements in the Middle East and North Africa.[116]

Although the Labour Party and the CPGB were both opposed to the Suez invasion, Labour clearly indicated that its anti-war stance was not anti-Israel and that its opposition to the war did not mean support for Nasser's nationalist aims. The CPGB who regarded Israel as an imperialist state and an ally of the West joined Labour's anti-war demonstration in Trafalgar Square, but explicitly identified itself with Arab nationalism and anti-Zionism.

The Lessons of Suez

Although Suez had reunited the Labour Party, the Soviet invasion of Hungary led to the formation of the New Left which brought together those members of the labour movement who saw the Suez invasion as an example of imperialism and the supporters of the Communist party, which included many trade unionists, who had disapproved of the Soviet actions. Israel's relations with the Labour Party remained unchanged as ambassador Elath continued to lobby Gaitskell and his shadow cabinet.[117] However their inability to lobby the TUC during the crisis was recognised as a serious problem that needed their attention.

Up until 1955 Bevin and Deakin had provided strong and decisive leadership for the TUC until 1955, but with their departure, no one person emerged to replace them especially as Tewson was clearly not capable of strong leadership. The TUC may have had close ties with the Labour Party on domestic issues but were ill-informed when it came to Israel and had little real contact with the Histadrut. The international role of the TUC was unchanged with their continued support for strong and independent trade unions throughout the free world as key members of the ICFTU and the ILO. However their international work was severely hampered by a lack of resources and manpower as it depended on government and the ICFTU support.[118] Tewson continued to be guided by the Foreign Office with regard to Israel and the Middle East, and despite the efforts of the Histadrut, kept contact with the Israelis to a minimum. Even though Israel had joined with Britain in the battle for the canal, nothing had changed as the TUC had remained silent but had received the backing of the American unions along with limited support from the ICFTU.

Barkatt knew that relations with the British unions were problematic and the Histadrut's failure to build a network of supporters became immediately obvious to him once Egypt had nationalised the Suez Canal. He concluded that fresh efforts had to be made with the unions, who still held an important and influential role in British society, in order to counter the pro-Arab inclinations of the Foreign Office and the ICFTU. Barkatt immediately raised his concerns with Elath, saying that the situation was far from satisfactory and that the TUC was being overwhelmingly cautious towards Israel. Their problem was that Sam Watson was the only trade union leader who publicly supported Israel and he was a member of Labour Executive and not the TUC General Council.[119] Both men continued to lobby for another labour attaché as after Bar-Tal had returned to Israel, relations with the TUC and the unions had been left to Elath and Levenberg.[120] It appears that they both had assumed that as the Labour Party and the TUC were part of the same labour movement, the TUC would automatically support the Labour Party in a similar manner to the way the Histadrut would support Mapai but neither had previously flagged up the obvious difference between the support for Israel by the leaders of the Labour Party and that of the TUC leadership. The lessons of the TUC's resolve not to be involved in political lobbying in the 1930's and 1940s had been forgotten, if they had ever been learnt.

Barkatt suggested to Elath that they try and recreate his successful lobbying of the Labour Party within the TUC and the trade unions and that they should invite people who could influence attitudes on Israel, if not the view of the TUC.[121] As a first step, Levenberg was asked to make contact with the TUC and in January 1957 he met with Vic Feather, TUC deputy general secretary, who told him that although politically the TUC backed Labour Party policy, there was a certain amount of internal criticism. Feather assured Levenberg that the TUC was '*fully appreciative of Israel's point of view*' and their friendly feelings towards the Histadrut were unchanged.[122] Although Feather was known to be sympathetic to Israel, he appears to have been saying what he thought Levenberg wanted to hear. Levenberg also floated the idea of a visit to Israel by a NCL delegation with Gaitskell, Bevan and Frank Cousins all showing interest in the suggestion.[123]

As part of the same strategy, the Histadrut contacted Marsh, the labour attaché, who told Greenhough his contact at the Ministry Of Labour that the Histadrut had said that they did not have a regular channel of contact with the TUC and that Tewson had blocked the opportunity to build informal relations at ICFTU Executive meetings. Marsh pointed out that although the Histadrut had more in common with the TUC than they had with the American unions; relations with the TUC were poor compared with the Americans which had been strengthened with exchange visits and declarations of support for Israel. He suggested that Greenhough make enquiries with the TUC about establishing a direct contact.[124] Although he arranged for the Histadrut to contact the TUC directly nothing changed as relations remained cool for the rest of the 1950s.[125]

Repairing the Damage of Suez

In February 1957 the TUC General Council discussed the freedom of passage through the Suez Canal. Although Britain was the biggest user of the canal it is not clear who was responsible for putting this on the agenda. Concerns were raised that the earlier blockade by Egypt of Israeli ships and the ships from other nations trading with Israel including Britain, should not be renewed in the event of Israel complying with the UN resolutions calling for her withdrawal from Sinai. Tewson reported that he had been visited by a representative of Histadrut (probably Barkatt) who was touring Europe, who asked that he write to the UN. He discussed their request with the chairman, but since it was within the '*established policy of the Council*', he wrote to the UN strongly urging that the Suez Canal and the Gulf of Aqaba as international waterways should be open to the shipping of all nations without discrimination.[126] This was an important moment in TUC-Histadrut relations because, at long last the TUC had responded positively to a Histadrut request concerning a political matter rather than a straightforward labour issue. The Israeli withdrawal from the Sinai was completed in March after receiving international reassurances that the Straits of Tiran would be open to Israeli shipping. The Egyptians, however, refused to open the Suez Canal to Israeli ships.

During the summer of 1958, the General Council endorsed a NCL statement on threats to peace in the Middle East a move which was out of character with their previous pro-Arab sentiments.[127] This pledge gave Levenberg the opportunity to discuss with the international departments of both the Labour Party and the TUC the possibility of a debate on the Middle East at their annual conferences. Levenberg drafted a motion for the TUC Congress which reiterated Labour Party policy whilst taking into account both TUC caution relating to problems affecting Israel and ICFTU plans to obtain support in Arab countries. The resolution, which was adopted by Congress, was proposed by Solomon Lever from the London Jewish Bakers Union who used the opportunity to promote Israel's desire for peace and her economic progress after independence.[128] The Israelis were extremely pleased when the Labour Party conference in October adopted a similar resolution.[129] Levenberg also raised the possibility with the TUC of sending a delegation to Israel in the light of improving Anglo-Israel relations. He was rebuffed with the excuse that although Tewson and Sir Alfred Roberts, the chairman of the international committee, would like to visit Israel it was unlikely as they were extremely busy and there were also concerns about the political implications such a visit would have on ICFTU aims in the region of the visit.[130]

After Suez, Israel's search for diplomatic support became increasingly important and the Histadrut reassessed its role in Europe Although they had always assumed that they could count on the friendship of the European labour movement they recognised that Europe was becoming more important as a political force in the world, and that they would have to become more active in Europe as a new generation of leaders emerged.[131] In September 1958, Hugo Morratt was appointed as the labour attaché at the Israeli Embassy in Brussels. Parker, the British labour attaché in Tel Aviv reported that Ambassador Elath would continue to cover the British labour movement as the Israelis had yet to decide whether or not to appoint a labour attaché in London.[132]

Whilst the TUC had yet to visit Israel, arrangements were made with Foreign Office agreement, for Roberts to visit the Lebanon in November 1957. The aim of the visit was to help reverse any anti-British feeling which had occurred after Suez as well and build support for the TUC and the ICFTU.[133] Eighteen months later, Roberts again showed his pro-Arab side, when he supported the ICFTU's plans to invite the Egyptian Confederation of Labour (EFL) as observers to the next ICFTU Congress. The Histadrut and the AFL-CIO opposed this proposal on the grounds that the ICFTU should not compromise its principles by inviting a government controlled organisation like the EFL.[134] Barkatt, who did not believe that the Egyptians wanted to join the ICFTU, interpreted the ICFTU's move as an attempt to weaken the Histadrut's position on the executive and that the TUC's support for the ICFTU's overtures towards the Arab unions indicated that their relations with the British labour movement were still poor.[135] Whereas the Foreign Office was trying to reduce Nasser's influence in the Arab world and to improve relations with Israel, the TUC was still trying to develop Britain's relations with the Arab trade unions. Tewson and his colleagues were either ignoring government advice or too set in their ways.

In order to counter TUC interest in the Arab world, Barkatt asked Elath in August 1959 to encourage the TUC to send a delegation to Israel or arrange visits for Roberts or Frank Cousins. He warned Elath against '*running after*' Roberts as they had made many unsuccessful attempts in the past.[136] The following year, Morratt was told that a visit by either man was unlikely and that he should concentrate on other members of the General Council.[137]

The Histadrut in Africa—The New Beginning for Relations with the TUC

Africa was targeted by both the ICFTU and the WFTU between 1956 and 1966 as a key area in their expansion plans for the international labour movement with both organisations offering aid and training packages to local trade union movements. The British and American governments worked closely with the TUC and the AFL-CIO respectively to further these aims using their labour attachés to monitor, the ICFTU, the rise of Arab nationalism, the Arab trade unions and the Histadrut. Throughout this period the TUC liaised with the trade unions in Britain's colonies and helped them prepare for independence.

When the ICFTU was established in 1949, it was decided that all affiliates would support agreed programmes and not work independently. However the rivalry and mistrust that existed between the two dominant affiliates, the AFL-CIO and the TUC, was at the root of the ICFTU's failure to develop and support trade unionism which was at the heart of African independence movements in both the British and French colonies as well as dealing with pan-Africanism and the threat of communist infiltration.

The TUC, which had worked closely with the British colonial administrations since the 1930s believed that the African trade union movement should be encouraged to build from its grassroots upwards in a similar manner to the way British trade unions had developed. This strategy was threatened in 1957 by the AFL-CIO who encouraged the ICFTU to adopt a more forceful approach in Africa by supporting those emerging labour movements, even if they lacked an organisational structure. By actively giving their support to the leadership they hoped that the African trade unions would affiliate to the ICFTU rather than the WFTU or an independent African trade union federation. The TUC, although concerned about African nationalism did not believe that communism posed a threat whereas the Americans did.

From 1953 onwards Israel pursued a very active international policy by demonstrating to the world Israel's achievements in order to win friends and influence people in countries outside the Arab world, which they hoped would bring them both diplomatic and political support. Membership of the ICFTU allowed the Histadrut to aggressively support this policy. These plans received a setback in 1955, when the Arab nations succeeded in blocking Israel's participation in the Bandung conference, the first Afro-Asian meeting of ex-colonial states. Israel's leaders were shocked as they had believed they were members of this group. In order to challenge the isolation that the Arabs wanted to impose on Israel, the Israeli government with the Histadrut's help targeted Africa because they believed Israel was in a unique position to offer her nation building experience in the form of development and technical programmes to the newly independent counties. The Histadrut, with its numerous enterprises and institutions became the cornerstone of Israel's plans for technical assistance programmes in the Third World.[138] The first countries in Africa to benefit from their programmes were Ghana and Liberia. Four African trade unionists from Ghana, Nigeria, Zambia and Upper Volta contacted the Histadrut in the winter of 1956 and were invited to visit Israel as guests of the Histadrut.[139] The visit had a tremendous impact on John Tettegah, from Ghana, who announced in August 1957 that the Ghana TUC was to remodel itself on the Histadrut,[140] a decision which upset the TUC, who had jealously guarded their own interests in Africa and not only felt let down by the Ghanaians, but were also worried about their future relations with them.[141] Although the TUC was initially wary of the Histadrut's activities, their development programmes would eventually prove to be a significant factor in the improvement of relations between the TUC and the Histadrut.

In November 1957, after more than four years of vehemently opposing plans for an ICFTU regional office in Beirut, Barkatt announced that the Histadrut had withdrawn its objections, provided that the representative's main role would be to assist the development of trade union movements in Arab countries and they would be given a clear undertaking that their representative would maintain regular contact with all the affiliated trade union movements in the area, including the Histadrut. He also emphasised that the Histadrut welcomed the emergence of a genuine free and democratic trade union movements in Arab countries, which could help to establish relations and mutual respect between Israel and the Arab countries.[142] Since the ICFTU had maintained a presence in Beirut for several years Barkatt's gesture led to the ICFTU discussing the Histadrut's aid programmes in Africa and Asia.[143]

In February 1958 Marsh, the labour attaché in his report 'the Histadrut and the Ghana TUC' noted that the free trade union movement could benefit from contact between Israel and underdeveloped countries[144] and that Israel had a good deal to offer as an alternative advisor to the ex-colonialist powers of the West and communist countries. He pointed out that by using their trade union connections the Histadrut could make contact with countries that might otherwise be blocked to Israel such as the Muslim States.[145] In response to the ICFTU's concerns about their activities in Africa which they felt should be under their auspices, Barkatt justified the Histadrut's actions by saying that their growing links promoted international labour solidarity, the growth of free trade unions and acted as a buffer against Soviet penetration.[146]

As Israel's aid programmes became more popular the Histadrut organised a three-month study seminar for workers from Asian and African countries in November 1958. Rundall, the British ambassador wrote to the foreign secretary that '*Not only has Israel a rich fund of technological know-how and experience which the Afro-Asians badly need for their development, but it is a store untainted by suspicion of imperialist ambition*' and that '*there would not seem to be any real conflict between Israeli policies or tactics in Africa and Asia and our own*'.[147] The government were also advised that the Israeli government fully supported the seminar and that '*The Israelis are still sometimes nervous that we may resent their efforts to take an interest in Africa and I imagine we should want to disabuse them of this idea in as far as we can. At the same time it might be no bad thing to mitigate the stigma of "colonisation" by a display of our own knowledge and experience, as well as our good intentions, on these occasions. This is in addition to taking the chance of channelling Israeli efforts in this field in an acceptable direction*'.[148]

Whilst agreeing that African co-operative movements could benefit from Israel's knowledge, Tewson queried what exactly the Histadrut seminar had to do with the unions.[149] Barkatt then asked Elath to discuss the Histadrut's African development programme with the TUC. In order to minimise TUC objections, he told Elath that the Histadrut would be willing to share information about their activities and coordinate in the areas in which they overlapped.[150] There is no record of this meeting taking place and it is probable that the TUC refused the offer as they backed the ICFTU stance on the Histadrut. Nor is it known if the Foreign Office shared the regular updates they received on the Histadrut's African activities with the TUC. The Foreign Office was greatly impressed by these reports as they were written at a time when the Anglo-Israel relations were just starting to improve unlike TUC-Histadrut relations which remained unchanged.[151]

Relations with Israel Improve

The coup in Iraq in 1958 as well as the need to support Jordan brought about changes to Britain's Middle East policies which allowed Britain to sell military hardware to Israel. It was the start of new era of Anglo-Israeli relations.

During the late 1950s Britain was under pressure during the late 1950s to grant independence to her colonies, especially in Africa. The Foreign Office wrote to the Colonial Office in January 1959, suggesting that it would be in Britain's interests to help the Israelis in British territories in Africa in order to counter the spread of Arab nationalism and Nasser's activities and as way of demolishing Israel's suspicion of Britain's hostility towards them. They asked that all of Britain's Governors, High Commissioners and representatives in Africa help the Israelis as a general rule.[152] This Foreign Office request was endorsed by Britain's ambassador to Israel[153] and Parker, the labour attaché in Israel reported that as large numbers of labour and political activists from Britain's African territories were visiting Israel, it provided an ideal opportunity for Britain to assess their thoughts on future political developments in Africa. This was further evidence of the improvement in Anglo-Israel relations and the transformation of Israel's image post-Suez. Unfortunately Tewson either ignored or was unaware of these changes in British policy towards Israel and continued to oppose the Histadrut's work. He believed it was the TUC's role to train the trade unions in Britain's African colonies and also regarded the Histadrut as a close ally of the AFL-CIO.

In March 1959 the Histadrut announced, that it was to establish an information centre in Africa to maintain contact with local labour movements. Parker reported that the centre would probably be active in those areas where Israel had no diplomatic representation.[154] The ICFTU was concerned that this development could provide the Americans or the British with the justification they needed for their own independent activity[155] and that the Histadrut would, by being directly involved with the local trade unions be undercutting the work of the ICFTU.[156]

The differences between the TUC and the AFL-CIO over the Africa resulted in open conflict between them at the ICFTU Congress in December 1959. Tewson had his own agenda regarding Britain's African colonies which he regarded as his domain. His position on African trade unionism was that trade unions should be built up from the ground upwards along the lines of the British model, whereas the Americans believed that the way forward was to support national trade union centres. Although the TUC did not have the necessary resources to run its own programmes Tewson was concerned that the AFL-CIO might start their own independent activities, which would directly affect the ICFTU's work.[157] The Americans thought that Tewson was being unrealistic as existing conditions showed that the communists could gain a foothold in Africa as a result of the widespread anti-colonial outlook. Despite the TUC's opposition the ICFTU agreed to establish an African regional organisation to support the new unions in Africa.[158] Six months later, the Histadrut announced that as a development of their existing training schemes, the Afro-Asian Institute of Labour Studies would be established in Israel to run two five-month courses a year each for around 60 trade unionists from Asian and African countries.[159] Financial support for the project was provided by the AFL-CIO and the Israeli government.[160] The ICFTU, who were initially unhappy with the proposed college reluctantly agreed to support the plans as they knew that the Histadrut would go ahead with the scheme with or without their approval.[161]

Britain was now interested in the progress of the Afro-Asian Institute as the Colonial Office thought that it could make a significant impact on the trade unions in Britain's African colonies as they moved towards independence and asked for more information as they were looking at training schemes in Britain for trade unions from overseas.[162] Both the TUC and the Foreign Office asked the Histadrut for the names and countries of the course participants but they only received a list of the countries.[163]

By 1964 the Histadrut was beginning to think that the ICFTU was finished in Africa unless it became more flexible and more realistic in its attitude towards African trade unionism as the unions were beginning to have less in common with the ICFTU and were turning more towards association with other African unions. Although there was evidence of Soviet influence in the unions, none were communist and both the Soviets and the Chinese understood as little about the Africans as everyone else. The Histadrut now proposed that African trade unions should be encouraged to ask for the services of Israeli trade union experts, rather than send their officials to the Afro-Asian Institute.[164]

The result of the ever increasing expansion of Israel's assistance to the Third World meant that by 1966, 28 countries in Africa, Latin America, and Asia had signed technical aid and co-operation agreements with Israel and Israeli experts were working in 62 countries and students from 80 countries studying in Israel.[165] The British labour attaché in Dakar had reported that since the Togolese trade unions request for a British trade unionist to run seminars in Togo was unlikely to be fulfilled, it should be passed onto the Histadrut who, unlike the TUC, had their own French speakers.[166] Israel's success in Africa was summed up by a British Foreign Office official who wrote '*Israel has either given some form of aid to, or opened negotiations on aid with, most newly independent countries in Africa. Israeli assistance has attractions for African countries since she has no colonial associations, has won her independence very recently, and has successfully created a modern state and an impressive defence force by methods applicable to Africa*'.[167]

Notes

1. AFL to the Histadrut, AUCCTU to the Histadrut, both 28 May 1948, TNA: PRO, KV5/16.
2. TUC International Committee minutes, 16 June 1948, MRC, MSS.292/901/8 and TUC to the Histadrut, 7 June 1948, MSS.292/956.9/4. The Histadrut also sent a copy of their telegram to Berl Locker, the Head of the London office of Mapai, 10 June 1948 and Berl Locker to the Histadrut, 6 June 1948, TNA: PRO, KV5/16.
3. See the TUC International Committee minutes, 16 June 1948, MRC, MSS.292/901/8 and the TUC to the Histadrut, 24 June 1948, MRC, MSS.292/956.9/4.
4. TUC to the Histadrut, 24 June 1948. See also the TUC memorandum to Tewson, 18 August 1948, the PLPC to the TUC, 26 August 1948 and the TUC's reply, 30 August 1948, all MRC, MSS.292/956.9/4.
5. The London Jewish Bakers Union resolution read: "*This Congress, having in mind the many promises given by the Labour movement to the Jewish people, in support of their struggle to establish a home in Palestine calls upon the Government to recognise the State of Israel as set up in accordance with the decision of the United Nations. Congress also calls on the Government to support the application of Israel for admission into the United Nations organisation.*" "Recognition of Israel demanded", *Jewish Chronicle*, 13 August 1948.
6. Barkatt's report on his visit to Europe. PLILMR, Histadrut Executive Committee minutes (Hebrew original), 29 September 1948.
7. "TUC critics of purge policy", *The Manchester Guardian*, 11 September 1948. Lever withdrew his motion on Palestine and spoke instead on paragraph 400 "Palestine" of the TUC report to Congress which only contained the NCL statement. MRC, TUC Congress 1948, p. 299 and pp. 527–529.

8. Barkatt's report on his visit to Europe when he visited Britain, France, Belgium, Holland and Czechoslovakia Europe, PLILMR, Histadrut Executive Committee minutes (Hebrew original), 29 September 1948.
9. The Slansky trial in Prague in November 1952 emphasised the Jewish origins of the accused and denounced Zionism and the Israeli government, The British Ambassador to the Foreign Secretary, 13 February 1953, TNA: PRO, FO371/104733.
10. AFL to the TUC, 25 May 1948 and the TUC's reply, 10 June 1948. The TUC also received seven other similar letters from American unions between 22 May and 30 August 1948, all MRC, MSS.292/956.9/4. TUC briefing document on Palestine, 31 August 1948, MRC, MSS.292/956.9/5.
11. Barkatt's report on his visit to Europe, PLILMR, Histadrut Executive Committee minutes (Hebrew original), 29 September 1948.
12. Ibid.
13. Levenberg to the TUC, 9 August 1949, MRC, MSS.292/956.9/5 and Barkatt to Levenberg, 22 August 1949, PLILMR, IV-208-1-5217.
14. The NCL minutes, 22 November 1949, PHM, 25 Jan–22 Nov 49 (Box 5).
15. Levenberg to Barkatt, 25 November 1949, PLILMR, IV-208-1-5213.
16. Legation report to the Foreign Office, 2 January 1950, TNA: PRO, FO371/82526. The Histadrut file of the delegation's visit includes minutes of the meetings with delegation, press conference details, speeches and radio broadcasts by Watson and an article in the *Daily Herald*, PLILMR, IV-219A-7-352.
17. British legation report to the Foreign Office, 13 January 1950, TNA: PRO, FO371/82526. Sherringham, an official in the Foreign Office wrote that "*the visit may have led to increased understanding but may increase the pressure when the Israelis want to get something from us e.g. arms*", 11 January 1950, TNA: PRO, FO371/82526.
18. The report of the Joint NCL Delegation to Israel, MRC, MSS.292/956.9/5.
19. Attlee apologised for his absence citing pressure of work and instead sent the meeting a message. Foreign Office to Prime Minister's Office, 19 January 1950 and Attlee to Levenberg, 23 January 1950, both TNA: PRO, FO371/82526. Levenberg to the Histadrut, 25 January 1950, PLILMR, IV-208-1-5213.
20. Morgan Phillips to the TUC, 23 March 1950, MRC, MSS.292/156.9.8. The TUC International Committee gave its approval for the visit on 14 April 1950, MRC, MSS.292/901/9.
21. Mapam (United Workers' Party) a Marxist-Zionist party, was the second largest political party in the early years of the State.

Foreign Office to Morgan Phillips, 2 May 1950, MRC, MSS.292/156.9.8. Philips then wrote to the Histadrut general secretary, Pinchas Lubianker saying he was looking forward to the visit which he hoped would "*put our problems in their proper perspective*", 28 July 1950, IV-208-1-5220. Levenberg wrote to Barkatt; "the delay in issuing the invitation was caused by procedural rather than political reasons" 16 August 1950, PLILMR, IV-208-1-5212.

22. Levenberg's letter to Barkatt included the Labour Party National Executive Committee report which was presented to the 1951 Labour Party Conference, 25 September 1951, PLILMR, IV-208-1-6063. For details of the activities of the Histadrut delegation to Britain, see Liff to letter to Bar-Tal, 17 January 1951, PLILMR, IV-208-6061 and the Israeli legation in London to the Foreign Office in Israel, 8 December 1950, the Israel State Archives, Jerusalem HZ36/7 (Hereafter cited as ISA).
23. Attlee sent a message to the farewell reception for the delegation. Levenberg to Barkatt, 25 September 1951, PLILMR, IV-208-1-6063.
24. MOL to TUC, 19 January 1950, MRC, MSS.292/900/5.
25. The Foreign Office also decided that they should keep a record of what documents that were sent to the TUC File note, 28 January 1948, TNA: PRO, LAB13/280.
26. Knox Helm to Bevin, 9 July 1949, TNA: PRO, FO371/67613.
27. Gee was seconded to the Foreign Office in 1947 and officially appointed labour advisor two years later. See the discussion of the proposal for an interchange of information between the TUC, Labour Party and Foreign Office and the appointment of a Labour Relations Officer, 30 October 1946, TNA: PRO, FO371/67613.
28. In April 1949, the MOL organised a conference in London for labour attachés which was addressed by the FO labour advisor and the TUC. By 1952 there were 22 labour attachés covering 47 countries whose role was to establish relationships with workers and employers organisations in the country or region in which they were operating. The Conference of labour attachés in London organised by the MOL, 25 April 1949 and TUC memorandum, 30 October 1952, both MRC, MSS.292/900/5.
29. Anthony Carew, 'The American Labor Movement in Fizzland: The Free Trade Union Committee and the CIA', *Labor History*, Vol. 39, No. 1 (1998), pp. 25–32.
30. Barkatt to Levenberg, 22 August 1949, PLILMR, IV-208-1-5217, 11 October 1949 and 8 November 1949, both PLILMR, IV-208-1-5213, and 5 December 1948, PLILMR, IV-208-1-5218.
31. For a full report of conference see *Israel Labour News*, 29 June 1949, ISSH: ICFTU, 3501 and PLILMR, the minutes of the Histadrut's 7th conference, 28 May 1949 (Hebrew original).

32. Tewson wrote a paper for the conference 'Free Trade Unions Plan For Unity' ISSH: ICFTU, 392a.
33. Report on the 7th conference of the Histadrut, Knox Helm to Bevin, 8 June 1949, TNA: PRO, FO/371/67613.
34. To add to Barkatt's problems some Mapam members of the Histadrut's delegation gave an interview in which they attacked the ICFTU and opposed the Histadrut's neutrality. Barkatt reported on both conferences to both the Histadrut's executive committee and the Mapai Secretariat, PLILMR, the minutes of the Histadrut's executive committee, 11 August 1949 (Hebrew original).
35. Thomas to the MOL, 23 February 1950, TNA: PRO, LAB13/554.
36. Thomas to the MOL, 24 March 1950, TNA: PRO, FO371/82513.
37. Thomas to the MOL, 1 April 1950, TNA: PRO, LAB13/554.
38. Gabriel Sheffer, *Moshe Sharett: biography of a political moderate* (Oxford: Clarendon Press, 1996), p. 527 and Bailer, *Between East and West: Israel's foreign policy orientation 1948–1956*, p. 25.
39. For a full report of the Mapai meetings see Bailer, *Between East and West: Israel's foreign policy orientation 1948–1956*, pp. 25–29 and PLILMR, the Histadrut debate [82 pages], the Histadrut's executive committee minutes 11 May 1950 (Hebrew original).
40. Knox Helm to Bevin, 15 May 1950, TNA: PRO, FO371/82637 and PLILMR, Histadrut Executive Committee minutes, 11 May 1950. Unsigned comment in FO file "This is excellent" but "the strong Mapam minority vote must be noted".
41. The British legation to the foreign secretary, 26 February and 16 April 1951, both TNA: PRO, LAB13/554.
42. The MOL to the TUC, 15 June 1953, 17 June 1953, MRC, MSS.292/956.9/5.
43. The ICFTU wanted the Histadrut to affiliate earlier to their organisation but did not pressurise them to do so. ICFTU to the NVV, 14 February 1951, ISSH: ICFTU, 3501. "American Trade Unionists visit," *Jewish Chronicle*, 27 July 1951.
44. Thomas to Greenhough, 3 March 1952, TNA: PRO, LAB13/554.
45. TUC memo to Tewson, 10 June 1952, and TUC to Levenberg, 19 June 1952, both MRC, MSS.292/956.9/5.
46. Diack's comments on Barkatt's visit in Foreign Office file, 21 June 1952, TNA: PRO, FO371/98819.
47. The American Jewish Labor Committee, which was founded in 1934, consisted of trade unionists of the Jewish faith in the AFL and CIO unions and was officially recognised by both organisations.
48. MRC, ICFTU letter to TUC, 26 February 1953, TUC letter to ICFTU, 5 March 1953, MRC, MSS.292/956.9/5.

49. The decision by the Histadrut executive was formally approved by 68th Council of the Histadrut. Labour News from Israel, Bar Tal to the TUC, 12 March 1953, MRC, MSS.292/956.9/5.
50. Barkatt to Tewson, 1 June 1953, MRC, MSS.292/956.9/5.
51. Poulsom, the labour attaché wrote to Greenhough four weeks before saying that the Histadrut had decided to join the ICFTU. Poulsom to Greenhough, 15 May and 1 July 1953, which was copied to the TUC, both TNA: PRO, LAB13/1079, the minutes of ICFTU Executive Board meeting at Stockholm, 9EB/18, ISSH: ICFTU, 24, 1 July 1953 and PLILMR, the minutes of the meeting of the Council of the Histadrut, 21 June 1953 and Barkatt to Tewson, 1 June 1953, MRC, MSS.292/956.9/5.
52. John Windmuller, *American Labor and the International Labor Movement 1940 to 1953* (Ithaca, New York: Cornell University, 1954), pp. 208–217.
53. PLILMR, Histadrut Executive Committee minutes (Hebrew original), 17 September 1953.
54. Tel Aviv Embassy to Foreign Office, Poulsom to MOL, both 14 August 1953, TNA: PRO, FO371/104849.
55. Barkatt to Tewson, 4 December 1952, MRC, MSS.292/956.9/5.
56. Bar Tal to the Labour Office Israel, 6 August 1953, ISA, "labour attachés England" (Hebrew original), G2776/9.
57. The MOL and the British Council supported three or four official visits a year by Histadrut officials and Israeli workers. The TUC wrote to unions asking for help in organising the visits. Barkatt to Tewson, 13 December 1951, MRC, MSS.292/956.9/5.
58. TUC International Committee minutes, 19 April 1955, MRC, MSS.292/901/11.
59. The Histadrut also contacted the ICFTU which passed on the information to all its affiliates. Histadrut to the TUC, 5 September 1954, MRC, MSS.292/956.9/6.
60. The Histadrut open letter to the ICFTU included discussion of recent political developments in Middle East including the Egyptian attitude to towards Israel and the Czechoslovak-Egyptian arms deal, 4 November 1955, ISSH: ICFTU, 3503, the Histadrut open letter to the TUC, 5 December 1955, MRC, MSS.292/956.9/6.
61. Histadrut to the TUC, 1 December 1955 and the Histadrut to the Seamen's Union, 3 January 1956, both IV-208-1-8593.
62. The Israel Embassy in London to the Foreign Office Jerusalem, 29 January 1954 (Hebrew original), ISA, HZ43/14.
63. Elath to Barkatt, 5 July 1955 and 18 Aug 1955 (Hebrew original), PLILMR, IV-219A-1-14A.
64. The Foreign Office labour advisor wrote, the Histadrut can "*hardly fail to impress neighbouring countries in spite of the* "*political differences between*

Arabs and Jews." It is not clear if this conclusion was based on information received or just wishful thinking on his part. Foreign Office report "Trade Unionism in the Middle East", brief prepared for Sir Roger Makins visit to the Persian Gulf", 13 January 1952, TNA: PRO, FO371/98785.

65. The TUC advised the Foreign Office of the ICFTU mission, which arranged for the delegation to meet with Audsley, the labour attaché in Damascus The ICFTU Executive Board meeting minutes, 13EB/21, 9 November 1950, ISSH: ICFTU, 3289 and Foreign Office file, "ICFTU plan to send delegation to Middle East" 5 May 1952, TNA: PRO, FO371/98318.
66. Thomas to Greenhough, 25 August 1952, TNA: PRO, FO371/98318 and British Embassy to the British Middle East Office, 29 September 1952, TNA: PRO, FO371/98318.
67. Audsley's brief covered not only Egypt, but the Lebanon, Ethiopia, Jordan, Iraq, Saudi Arabia and Syria Foreign Office file comment, 8 September 1952, TNA: PRO, FO371/98318.
68. See unidentified Foreign Office file comment, 1 September 1952, the British Middle East Office to the Foreign Office, the British Embassy Cairo to the Foreign Office, both 13 September 1952, the MOL to the Labour Attachés in Tel Aviv and Cairo, 15 September 1952, The British Middle East Office to the Foreign Office 17 September 1952, the British Embassy to the British Middle East Office, 29 September 1952, Richmond, file comment, 13 October 1952, all TNA: PRO, FO371/98318.
69. Poulsom to Greenhough, 11 August 1953, Mason to Bell, 17 August 1953, Poulsom to Greenhough, 20 August and 27 August 1953 and Greenhough to Bell, 4 September 1953, all TNA: PRO, LAB13/1080.
70. See the correspondence between Oldenbroek and Barkatt, 3 August, 30 September and 12 November 1953, all ISSH: ICFTU, 3501.
71. The British Embassy to the Foreign Office, 20 October 1953, FO371/104849, Poulsom to Greenhough, 21 September 1953, TNA: PRO, LAB13/1080.
72. The Foreign Office to the British Embassy Beirut, 24 October 1953. Also unsigned file comment, "*We have since heard from Brussels that the ICFTU is not to open a regional office in Beirut but something much smaller and less controversial*," 19 November 1953, all TNA: PRO, FO371/104849.
73. The minutes of ICFTU Executive Board meeting, 16 May 1955, ISSH: ICFTU, 44, the British Embassy Brussels to the British Embassy Beirut, 16 June 1955, and Barnes to the labour attaché Brussels, 22 September 1955, both TNA: PRO, FO371/115610.

74. The Report of the 4th ICFTU World Congress Vienna, 20 May 1955, ISSH: ICFTU, ZO474496.
75. Marsh to Greenhough, 21 June 1955, TNA: PRO, LAB13/1111.
76. Greenhough to Marsh, 13 July 1955, TNA: PRO, LAB/13/1111.
77. Barkatt to Elath, 22 June 1955 (Hebrew original), PLILMR, IV-219A-1-14A.
78. The plan was accepted on the understanding that discussions would be held with the ICFTU affiliates in the area The ICFTU Executive Board meeting agenda 16EB/26 and the ICFTU Executive meeting minutes, 16EB/43, 12–16 December 1955, ISSH: ICFTU, 46.
79. Barkatt later remarked that "*the intrigues which are formed against us are also in the field of the workers movement.*" Barkatt to the Foreign Office in Jerusalem, 29 December 1955 (Hebrew original), PLILMR, IV-104-1296-5.
80. The TUC were allowed to pass on this information to the ICFTU as long they did not reveal the source. Barnes to Bowers, 18 May 1955, TNA: PRO, FO371/115610.
81. Audsley to Barnes, 14 May 1955, TNA: PRO, FO371/115610. See also the minutes of the meeting of the founding Inter-Arab Confederation of Trade Unions, held in Cairo, 8 October 1955, ISSH: ICFTU, 3289.
82. Unidentified comments in the Foreign Office file, 24 May and 24 June 1955, TNA: PRO, FO371/115610.
83. Macleod to Eden, 14 August 1956, TNA: PRO, FO371/82526.
84. Marsh to Greenhough, "The eighth convention of the Histadrut (7/56)", 27 March 1956, TNA: PRO LAB13/449.
85. The British Embassy Tel Aviv to the foreign secretary Selwyn Lloyd, 17 July 1956 and 'The Growth of the Histadrut, its relations with Mapai and the Israel State (9/56)', Marsh to Greenhough, 13 July 1956. A great deal of praise was given to Marsh by the Foreign Office for his excellent reports on the economic situation, wages policy and the strikes In Israel. Undated file comment, all TNA: PRO, LAB13/1181. Marsh to Greenhough, "Problems of Policy and leadership in the Israel Labour Party (10/56)", 23 August 1956, TNA: PRO, LAB13/1181.
86. Bulpitt file note, 7 February1956. Barber, the labour attaché in Brussels wrote that the ICFTU had attempted to pacify the Histadrut's suspicions about ICFTU activities in the Middle East by asking it to carry out a mission for the ICFTU in Iran. Barber to Greenhough, 30 January 1956, both TNA: PRO, LAB13/1149.
87. Barber asked that the contents of the letter are not shared with the TUC. Barber to Greenhough, 13 February 1956, TNA: PRO, LAB13/1149.

88. These reports included a personal message from Gaitskell to Ben-Gurion who assured him of Labour's support for Israel and help with buying arms. But Gaitskell asked that Israel stop the reprisal actions that "*lead to our condemnation in the UN and increase the tension in the area,*" 24 January 1956, ISA, HZ 329/8.
89. Ericsson, the Labour Party international secretary, to Morrat, 4 May 1956, PHM, LP/ID 1956 ME, Palestine, Israel.
90. Memo of meeting between Sir Ian Kirkpatrick, Foreign Office and the Israeli Ambassador, 15 August 1956, TNA: PRO, FO371/8252.
91. Namir to Barkatt, 15 September 1956 and Barkatt to Namir, 30 September 1956 (both Hebrew original), both PLILMR, IV-104-1296-5.
92. Barber to Greenhough, 20 August 1956, TNA: PRO, LAB13/1149.
93. ICFTU Circular ES/25(1956), 20 August 1956, ISSH: ICFTU, 476.
94. Tewson agreed with the statement since it did not criticise British actions over the canal and suggested only a slight change in the wording, that in the sentence demanding that any agreement on the Suez Canal should be under the auspices and guidance of the United Nations, the words "*under the auspices*" should be replaced by the phrase "*associated with*". For full details of the replies received see point 12, agenda Item 1(a): Trade Union Action on Hungary and the Middle East, ICFTU Executive Board, Brussels, 26–30 November 1956, 18EB/12(i), ISSH: ICFTU, 63.
95. Elath to Sharett, Israel Minister of Foreign Affairs, 1 February 1956 (Hebrew original), IV-219A-1-14A.
96. Resolution adopted by the Council of the Socialist International, Zurich, 2–4 March 1956, LSE, Levenberg G/5/2. Marsh to Greenhough, 14 March 1956, TNA: PRO, LAB13/1181.
97. Rhiannon Vickers, *The Labour Party and the world Vol. 2 Labour's foreign policy since 1951* (Manchester: Manchester University Press, 2011), pp. 34–38.
98. Macleod to Eden, 14 August 1956, TNA: PRO, FO371/82526.
99. Suez Canal, Cabinet Secretaries' notebooks, 14 August 1956, TNA: PRO, CAB195/15.
100. TUC president Geddes to prime minister Eden, 28 August 1956, TNA: PRO, PREM11/1172.
101. TUC report No11/1 30, 'The Suez Crisis', 30 August 1956, MRC, MSS292/901/12.
102. 'Labour's complicated position', *The Observer*, 2 September 1956, and 'Congress Commentary', *Tribune*, 14 September 1956.
103. TUC emergency motion on Suez, MRC, TUC annual report 1956, p. 433.
104. MRC, TUC annual report 1956, pp. 433–441 and p. 451.
105. "*During the last 12 months the General Council of the TUC appear to have abdicated from the leadership of the trade union movement. On the major*

issues of the day they have remained silent...the truth is the old General Council died with Deakin....there has perhaps been a greater dependence than before on initiative from the staff but Sir Vincent Tewson, the General Secretary has not the qualities of a leader...." "Lack of guidance from the TUC General Council", *The Times*, 30 July 1956.

106. Cabinet minutes 11 September 1956, TNA: PRO, PREM11/1172.
107. These included a rally in Trafalgar Square as well as sixty local meetings. 'Law, Not War', The *Manchester Guardian*, 5 November 1956.
108. Martin Harrison, *Trade unions and the Labour Party since 1945*, p. 122.
109. NCL statement, *1 November 1956*, PHM, uncatalogued papers, Box 6 file 5, NCL Minutes and Papers, 20 October 1954–November 1956.
110. 'Sign Protest', *The Manchester Guardian*, 5 November 1956, p. 9.
111. 'Work stopped for protest over Suez policy', *The Manchester Guardian*, 7 November 1956, p. 4.
112. ICFTU press release, 5 November 1956, TNA: PRO, FO371/122384. Following the lead of the Austrian and Italian trade unions, Oldenbroek sent telegrams to all affiliates urging them to join in a worldwide workers' protest against war and foreign intervention by calling upon all workers to stop work if possible on 8 November for five minutes before noon. ICFTU circular No17 (1956), 6 November 1956, ISSH: ICFTU, 359a.
113. The committee was advised that its affiliates, especially those in Europe, had either supported its day of action or held mass meetings to protest against military action in Hungary and the Middle East. Agenda Item1(a): Trade Union Action on Hungary and the Middle East, ICFTU Executive Board, 26–30 November 1956, 18EB/12(i), 63 ICFTU. Minutes of the ICFTU Executive Board meeting, 26–30 November 1956, 18EB/18 ISSH: ICFTU, 65, pp. 26–28.
114. Mark Yarblum's report to the Histadrut of the ICFTU Executive Board meeting (Hebrew original), PLILMR, IV-219A-1 44A.
115. ICFTU statement on the crisis in the Middle East, 12 December 1956, ISSH: ICFTU, 65.
116. June Edmunds, *The Left and Israel, party policy change and internal democracy* (London: Macmillan, 2000), p. 113.
117. See the report of meetings with Labour MP's Crossman, Greenwood, Wilson, Robens, Griffith, Strauss and Gordon Walker. Israel Embassy to Prime Minister Ben-Gurion, 15 November 1956 and instructions for the meeting with Gaitskell and Bevan. A Labour Party delegation, briefed by the Israelis, met with Prime Minister Macmillan to discuss Israel's problems including the supply of arms to Egypt and Israel. Israel Foreign Ministry to Elath, 4 December 1956, and Elath's undated reply to Israel Foreign Ministry, December 1956 (all Hebrew original), all ISA, HZ329/8.

118. TUC notes for Sir Alfred Roberts, chairman of the International committee who attended the labour attachés' conference in London, 3 April 1959, MRC, MSS292/900/5.
119. There were a large number of union leaders on the TUC General Council including Tewson who were in favour of Bevin's Middle East pro-Arab policies.
120. Barkatt to Elath, 21 September 1956 (Hebrew original), PLILMR, IV-219A-1-14A and Elath to the Israel Foreign Ministry, 22 November 1956 (Hebrew original), ISA, HZ329/8.
121. Barkatt to Elath, 12 August 1956 (Hebrew original), PLILMR, IV-219A-1-14A. Tom O'Brien MP, who was also the general secretary of the National Association of Theatre Employees and a member of the TUC International Committee, accepted an invitation to visit Israel but only in a personal capacity in the autumn of 1956. O'Brien to Tewson, 9 August 1956, MRC, MSS292/956.9/6.
122. Levenberg to Barkatt, 1 January 1957, PLILMR, IV-208-1-10089.
123. Levenberg to Barkatt, 23 January 1957, PLILMR, IV-208-1-10089.
124. Ezra Hayut, Director of the Histadrut's International Department, discussed with Marsh the lack of contact between the Histadrut and the TUC. Marsh to Greenhough, 29 January 1957, TNA: PRO, LAB13/450.
125. Wilson, file note, 22 February 1957, TNA: PRO, LAB13/1255.
126. Minutes of the International Committee for 22 February 1957, MRC, MSS292/901/13 and the International Committee report, MRC, TUC Congress 1957 report, pp. 200–201.
127. TUC International Committee report on the Middle East, MRC, TUC Congress report 1958, p 219.
128. Levenberg to Barkatt, 28 August 1958, PLILMR, IV-208-1-10089. Also see TUC to London Jewish Bakers Union, 21 August 1958. ISA, HZ336/8 and the debate on the Middle East, MRC, TUC Congress report 1958, pp. 403–406.
129. Israel embassy to Israel Foreign Ministry, 25 September 1958 (Hebrew original), PLILMR, IV-219A-1-16B.
130. Levenberg to Barkatt, 28 August 1958, PLILMR, IV-208-1-10089.
131. R Barkatt address to the Histadrut's executive committee, PLILMR, Histadrut's executive committee minutes, 4 March 1958 (Hebrew original).
132. Parker to Marsh at the Brussels Embassy, 23 September 1958, TNA: PRO, LAB13/450.
133. See letters from the MOL to the labour attaché in Lebanon, 28 October 1957, the TUC to the Labour Attaché in Lebanon, 29 October 1957, the Foreign Office briefing note for Sir Guildhaume Myrddin-Evans, 6 November 1957 and the labour attaché in Lebanon to the MOL, 30 November 1957, all TNA: PRO, LAB13/1149.

134. Parker to MOL, 31 July 1959, TNA: PRO, LAB13/1353 and ICFTU Executive Board Minutes, 24EB/19, 29 June-3 July 1959, ISSH: ICFTU, 93.
135. Marsh letter to MOL, 14 July 1959, LAB13/1353. Barkatt letter to Morrat, 7 August 1959 (Hebrew original), and Morrat reply to Barkatt, 18 August 1959 (Hebrew original), both PLILMR, IV-219A-1-32A.
136. Barkatt to Elath, 3 August 1959 (Hebrew original), PLILMR, IV-219A-1-29C.
137. Morrat to Hayut, 29 April 1960, and Hayut to Morrat, 6 June 1960 (both Hebrew original), both PLILMR, IV-219A-1-32B.
138. Notes for Barkatt's report about the International department's work to the Histadrut's 8th conference in March 1956 (Hebrew original), PLILMR, 4-11-1950-28.
139. The four trade unionists contacted the Histadrut because they were curious why the Arab states, with no free trade union movements themselves, should be so biased against the one country in the region with a model trade union movement. Mordechai E. Kreinin, 'Israel and Africa: the Early Years, in *Israel in the Third World*, pp. 54–68 and Akiva Eger, 'Histadrut: Pioneer and Pilot Plant for Israel's Cooperation with the Third World', in *Israel in the Third World*, pp. 75–80.
140. John Tettegah made his decision after studying two different forms of centralised trade union structure, the Histadrut and the West German DGB, as well as discussing the matter with the ICFTU. He decided that he would recommend not to send students any longer to Britain for training and that he had learnt more in eight days in Israel, than he would have done in two years studying trade unionism in any British University. He did not know of any country in which the dignity of labour was so highly respected as in Israel, where "*the Prime Minister continues to hold a trade union membership card.*" 'Union leaders to train in Israel', *Ghana Daily Graphic*, 13 August 1957, p. 3.
141. Shortly after Tettegah made his statement about the Histadrut, Magnus George, Tettegah's assistant general secretary, came to London as guest of the TUC and published some highly complementary remarks about the British movement. As a result he was immediately recalled by Tettegah and was not allowed to complete his visit. The TUC were surprised and resentful, not to say insulted. Lucatz to Barkatt, 7 November 1957 (Hebrew original), PLILMR, IV-219A-1-18.
142. Barkatt to Millard ICFTU, 25 November 1957, ISSH: ICFTU 3503. Boudali was ICFTU Special Representative in the Middle East from 1955–57. In 1959, the ICFTU appointed Victor Defalle, as their Special Representative in the Middle East. ICFTU Executive Board minutes, 24EB/8(d) (v), 29 June 1959, ISSH: ICFTU, 90.

143. Barkatt report to Histadrut executive committee about the ICFTU Congress, 5–13 July 1957 (Hebrew original), PLILMR, 4-11-1947-9A and ICFTU Executive Board minutes, 24EB/16, 10 January 1958, ISSH: ICFTU, 3501.
144. Report "Labour in Israel", Marsh to the MOL, 7 February 1958, TNA: PRO, LAB13/1182. "The Histadrut and the Ghana TUC", Marsh report to the MOL, 16th April 1958, TNA: PRO, LAB13/450.
145. Barkatt asked Marsh for information about the trade union movements in India and Pakistan, as Israel was trying to foster relationships with those countries and did not have diplomatic relations with either country. Marsh to the labour attaché at the British embassy in Delhi, 13 March 1958, TNA: PRO, LAB13/2291.
146. Barkatt to ICFTU, 15 January 1958, ISSH: ICFTU, 3503.
147. Ambassador Rundall to the foreign secretary 20 February 1959, TNA: PRO, Lab13/1353.
148. Tel Aviv embassy to Foreign Office, 16 March 1959, TNA: PRO, LAB13/1352.
149. Barkatt to Tewson, 16 April 1959, Tewson to Barkatt 18 June 1959, all MRC, MSS292/956.9/6.
150. Barkatt to Elath, 3 August 1959 (Hebrew original), PLILMR, IV-219A-1-29C.
151. Unsigned and undated file note, TNA: PRO, LAB13/1420.
152. Foreign Office to the Colonial Office, 27 January 1959, TNA: PRO, LAB13/1353.
153. Parker to MOL and the Foreign Office, 4 September 1959, TNA: PRO, LAB13/1309.
154. Parker to Wallis, 26 March 1959, TNA: PRO, LAB13/1353.
155. Morratt, Histadrut Brussels, to Barkatt, 15 April 1959 (Hebrew original), PLILMR, 4-11-1952-10B.
156. Millard ICFTU to Barkatt 8 June 1959 and Barkatt's reply, 19 June1959, ISSH: ICFTU, 3504.
157. Bar Yaakov to Barkatt, 27 August 1959 (Hebrew original), PLILMR, 4-11-1947-9A.
158. For ICFTU efforts in Africa see, Anthony Carew, A False Dawn; The WFTU 1945–1949 and Towards a Free Trade Centre: the ICFTU (1949–72) in *The International Confederation of Free Trade Unions* (Berlin: Peter Lang, 2000), pp. 258–270.
159. Parker to MOL, 4 March 1960, TNA: PRO, LAB13/1371. The Histadrut's plans were the subject of articles in the *Washington Daily News* on 15 and 17 March 1960 and the *Economist*, 19 March 1960, TNA: PRO, LAB13/1420.

160. AFL-CIO financial support was initially set at $175,000, *AFL-CIO news*, 26 March 1960, MRC, MSS292-956.96.
161. British labour attaché in Washington to the MOL, 10 March 1960, TNA: PRO, LAB13/1420.
162. Colonial Office to MOL, 10 May 1960, TNA: PRO, LAB13/1420. MOL to Parker, 6 July 1961, TNA: PRO, LAB13/1503.

    Parker noted that the establishment of an institute which was independent of the ICFTU, might achieve more for Western trade unionism than if it were associated directly with an ICFTU scheme, as not all students supported the ICFTU in Africa. Parker to MOL, 14 August 1961, TNA: PRO, LAB13/1503.
163. Morrat to Hayut, 26 December 1960 (Hebrew original), IV-219A-1-32B, Hayut reply to Morrat, 11 January 1961 (Hebrew original), IV-219A-1-32C.
164. Marshall to MOL, 29 December 1964, LAB13/2006.
165. Marshall report "Israeli Technical assistance" to MOL, 28 March 1966, TNA: PRO, LAB13/2445.
166. Marshall to MOL, 29 December 1964, TNA: PRO, LAB13/2006. British labour attaché Dakar to MOL, 14 January 1965, TNA: PRO, LAB13/2006.
167. Briefing notes for the Minister of State's visit to Israel October 1965, 17 September 1965, TNA: PRO, FO371/180866.

CHAPTER 4

The 1960s, the Golden Era in the TUC's Relations with the Histadrut

Two significant decisions were made in 1960, both of which were instrumental in improving TUC-Histadrut relations over the next decade. The first, in March 1960; was when the Histadrut decided to open a European office in London in order to strengthen contacts with the British and European labour movements. The Histadrut had decided to present Israel's case themselves rather than continue to depend on the Israeli embassy, as recent developments at the ICFTU with their overtures towards the Arab unions, had proved once again to them that they should not neglect Europe. London was chosen because the majority of the leaders of the international organisations and trade federations were Europeans and based there.[1] Secondly in September 1960, George Woodcock was appointed TUC general secretary. Woodcock, who had no previous experience of international affairs decided that in future the TUC would only deal with issues directly related to the TUC and would work on other issues such as foreign affairs by supporting organisations such as the ICFTU rather than direct action by the TUC.[2]

Gideon Ne'eman, the new Histadrut representative in London, worked hard trying to build bridges and the first step towards a better relationship was taken when a Histadrut delegation of trade unionists came to Britain in November 1961. This was followed, in January 1962, by a visit to Israel by Frank Cousins who had previously admitted that he knew very little about the Arab-Israeli problem. Yehudit Simchoni, the Head of the Histadrut International department, wrote that '*Cousins will be helpful for*

R. Fraser, *British Trade Unions, the Labour Party, and Israel's Histadrut*, https://doi.org/10.1007/978-3-030-86814-7_4

us regarding constructive action"[3] His visit, although not the first by a British trade unionist to Israel, was extremely successful and caused a positive change in Cousins opinions. Marshall, the British labour attaché, noted that the visit showed the importance of visits by leading British trade unionists. Although no practical benefit had resulted from the visit, the opportunity to discuss problems with a leading trade union figure was worthwhile in terms of the goodwill created towards Britain and its trade union movement. Five months later, a delegation from the General and Municipal Workers Union (GMWU), led by Fred Hayday, became the first ever British trade union delegation to visit Israel. The visitors remarked, after visiting the Afro-Asian Institute that the Histadrut had contributed much more to the underdeveloped states than their British colleagues. The aim of all these visits was to provide the visitors with a good understanding of the Histadrut and Israel's problems and the Histadrut soon realised that they urgently needed to educate members of the British labour movement who knew very little about the subject.[4]

Eighteen months after arriving in London, Ne'eman persuaded George Woodcock to visit Israel. Forty years after the Histadrut had first made contact with the TUC; Woodcock became the first TUC general secretary to go there. Marshall wrote to Woodcock saying that his visit along with those by Cousins and Hayday had finally dispelled any suspicions the Israelis had, that their own warm feelings towards the British trade union movement had not always been reciprocated.[5] The Histadrut noted that Woodcock had said frequently that he was deeply impressed with Israel and with the Histadrut's achievements, including its aid programmes.[6]

British Unions Investments in Israel

One unexpected outcome of the improvement in relations was the announcement in the *Daily Herald* of April 1963 that the TGWU and GMWU were to invest £250,000 in Histadrut enterprises and that other unions were thinking of following suit.[7] The investments would be in the form of loans to be used for whatever purposes the Histadrut thought fit, but would be subject to conditions as to how they were to be used.[8] The Arab embassies in London were shocked that two British unions were to invest in the Histadrut and attempted to put pressure on the TUC and the unions to reverse the decision.[9]

The British ambassador observed that the increased interest in the Histadrut by British trade unions and the TUC would benefit the British labour movement and Britain. The reason for this increased interest was the '*enthusiasm for Israel brought back*" by the various British trade union visitors to Israel. Both Hayday and Woodcock had praised the Histadrut's work in Africa and said that the Histadrut could do much for the trade union movements of Africa that Western trade union movements could not do.[10]

However negotiations over terms and conditions of the loan were long and convoluted and, by August 1966, the conditions for investing in Histadrut US dollar bonds were no longer financially attractive and the Histadrut investment managers decided to reject the deal.[11] However as both unions, especially the TGWU, were still willing to make the loans, discussions continued for another two years when the deal was finally cancelled.[12]

TUC Support for the Afro-Asian Institute

On his return to London from Israel, Woodcock asked the International department to write a paper on the Afro-Asian Institute. They contacted Walter Treganowan, the Foreign Office labour advisor who helped them by collecting evidence of Israeli influence on labour movements from labour attachés in West Africa and Asia.[13] In April 1963, a report on the Afro-Asian Institute was presented to the TUC International committee along with the proposal that the TUC should finance a number of scholarships at the Institute, which since its establishment in 1960, had trained more than 300 students and the courses included students from Latin America and the Caribbean.[14] In its deliberations the committee raised concerns about the special relationship between the Histadrut and the state, and were apprehensive that after attending courses in Israel students might be inclined to model their own particular institution too closely on the Israeli model, as had happened in Ghana and Niger.[15] After an extensive discussion the committee agreed to provide £2000 for four scholarships at the Afro-Asian Institute[16] which the Histadrut agreed would be reserved for trade unionists from either Africa or the West Indies.[17]

This gesture by the TUC, following on as it did so quickly after the announcement to invest in the Histadrut, showed a positive appreciation of the Histadrut's work in the third world as well as the limitations of the TUC's own efforts. As a measure of how much they valued this work they continued to fund scholarships at the Institute for the rest of the decade. The ICFTU soon dropped their objections to the Institute having accepted that useful lessons could be learnt.[18] Although in 1960 the British Government had realised the value of the Histadrut's work, it had taken the TUC another three years to reach the same conclusion; TUC-Histadrut relations had finally caught up with Anglo-Israel relations. It was also clear that the Foreign Office, who had wanted the TUC to become more involved in similar training programmes, had yet to persuade them to do so.

In December 1963, with Britain facing a General Election the following year and with the possibility of a Labour win, the Histadrut decided to relocate Eli Marx to London to work alongside Ne'eman to reinforce their connections with the unions and the TUC.[19] Although nobody knew at the time, this move was to have an enormous influence on future relations.

The Arab Boycott of Israel and the Mancroft Affair

The Arab boycott of Israel was adopted by the Arab League and its member states in 1948 to prohibit all commercial and financial transactions between the Arab States and Israel. Although the British government made it clear that the boycott was illegal and unjustified, they left it to individual companies to decide whether to comply with the boycott or not.[20] The result was that Britain was one of the most cooperative countries in complying with the Arab boycott. Many of the British companies which found themselves on the Arab League's boycott list took the commercial decision to comply with the request.

In December 1963, Lord Mancroft, a British Jew, was forced to resign as a result of Arab pressure from the Board of Directors of the Norwich Union insurance company. Once they admitted they had complied to the boycott request, the incident became a public scandal and was widely covered in the media and Parliament. The British government acted immediately saying that it opposed outside interference in British domestic affairs and strongly resented pressure on British firms to discriminate against their staff.[21]

On hearing the news, Ne'eman met with twelve members of the TUC International committee to express the Histadrut's serious concern about the issues surrounding the incident including racial discrimination, anti-semitism and the boycott of Israel.[22] He reported that they had unanimously agreed that the TUC should speak publicly about this issue. As this was an 'internal" British affair, Cyril Plant, the leader of the Inland Revenue Staff Federation, who had previously visited Israel, wrote to the

TUC calling for a discussion of the affair and suggested that the General Council issue a statement.[23] Woodcock told Ne'eman that the boycott was a political issue and that if the boycott was causing serious damage to the Israeli economy and the livelihood of Israelis, which it was not, then it served as an expression of the animosity between the Arab states and Israel, he therefore saw no reason to take a stand. Woodcock thought that the TUC would be unable appeal to the Government since they were about to announce a TUC boycott against South Africa.[24]

The International department prepared a report for the General Council which stated that General Council policy on international trade which had been formulated to support the defence of the West did not have guidelines on trade with Israel.[25] The view of the General Council was that it was impossible for the TUC to remain silent because the affair not only related to racial discrimination, but the Arab boycott might also affect British jobs. Woodcock found no backing for his belief that the TUC did not have to take a stand as it was a political dispute. In order to allow the TUC to support the proposed boycott against South Africa, while at the same time condemning the Arab boycott,[26] a press statement was issued which called on British companies not to surrender to any pressure aimed at discrimination '*by either side*" in a political dispute to which Britain was not a party.[27] That Ne'eman had been able to engineer a response from the TUC highlighted the good relations that he had built with the unions. The Histadrut was pleased with the outcome, especially as the TUC had taken a decision that so far every other non-Jewish body had refused to take. In order to build on their success, the Israeli embassy and the Histadrut tried unsuccessfully to get the Arab boycott discussed at the 1965 TUC Congress. Their plans which included asking the American unions to encourage the TUC to take immediate public action against the boycott failed because Marx contacted the TUC only one month before the Congress and was told it was far too late for the topic to be included.[28] Twelve years would pass before the TUC and the Histadrut would next discuss the Arab boycott of Israel.

Woodcock's Special Relationship with Becker

Aharon Becker's successful visit to London in May 1963, his first as Histadrut general secretary, was seen in Israel as a turning point for the improvement in TUC-Histadrut relations.[29] Becker, who also represented Mapai in the Knesset, met several politicians in London including Harold

Wilson, the Labour Party leader. His visit consolidated the understanding and friendship between the two organisations as well as between Becker and Woodcock. Hayday assured Ne'eman that '*You can trust even in troubled times your many friends and their enormous empathy towards the Histadrut and Israel*'. Woodcock described Israel as indestructible and emphasised that the free world would support Israel against the Arabs. When asked if the TUC would issue a statement supporting Israel, Woodcock said that he understood the Histadrut's need for supportive statements, like those from the American unions, but he preferred not to do so unless a special development took place in the region. Any decision, he said, would be made in consultation with the Labour party, as had happened during the Cuba crisis. There is further evidence of the close relationship between the two men when in November 1963, Becker, went at short notice to London prior to the meeting of the governing body of the ILO and the ICFTU Executive committee in order to discuss with Woodcock several issues including the TUC's attitude towards South African membership of the ILO.[30]

British trade union delegations now started to visit Israel on a regular basis. Cousins returned to Israel in November 1963 with a TGWU delegation and a TUC General Council delegation in April 1964. In the autumn of 1964 two Histadrut delegations came to Britain both receiving warm and friendly receptions, one was hosted by the AEU and the GMWU and the second by TGWU which was seen as a return visit by friends which went ahead even though Cousins was now a Minister in the new Labour Government. Marx noted that there was still plenty of work to do with the British unions, who knew very little about the Histadrut and Israel, especially as the Labour Party was now in government and the trade unions were a powerful group within the Party.[31] The close relationship between Becker and Woodcock was also reflected in the access Woodcock gave to Marx, who regularly discussed ICFTU business and the Afro-Asian Institute with him.

The importance that the Israelis placed on relations with the labour movement was emphasised when Israeli prime minister Levi Eshkol came to London in March 1965, a meeting was also arranged for him to meet with the TUC.[32] Their discussions were described as lively and friendly and focused not on foreign affairs, but on employment and economic issues. Zev Levin, the Head of the Histadrut International department, who met separately with TUC, the Labour Party and the MOL, reported that the TUC was now taking even less interest in international issues than before. The MOL, which had confirmed his view, blamed Woodcock's passive approach as a serious obstacle to providing British aid to the unions in underdeveloped states. Levin noted that although the people he met were sympathetic and understood Israel's political and security problems there was a lack of interest and willingness to get involved in new international crises. He concluded that direct contact with the unions and the TUC would strengthen support within the Labour Party and that the visits to Israel by union leaders were very valuable as they were the best ambassadors for Israel.[33]

Becker's comments to the Histadrut Convention in December 1965 reflected the improved state of TUC-Histadrut relations when he said that with a Labour government in Britain, the Histadrut was entitled to a more truthful view of the Middle East situation and demanded that British workers stop supporting calls for the destruction of Israel.[34] The TUC did not attend the convention, but Victor Feather, TUC deputy general secretary, who had visited Israel for the first time earlier that month, met senior members of the Histadrut and the government. Even though he described himself as an old friend of the Histadrut, it was apparent that he knew very little about Israel or the Histadrut.[35]

Problems at the ICFTU

In November 1964 Marx approached Woodcock to discuss Histadrut's concerns that the ICFTU had remained silent whilst threats to Israel were voiced by its neighbours and that the ICFTU had never issued a clear and positive statement concerning Israeli-Arab relations even though it regularly expressed its views on other international issues. Woodcock advised Marx that the Histadrut should table a motion calling for the differences between Israel and various Arab countries to be settled by peaceful means which was then adopted by the next ICFTU Executive Board meeting.[36] When the Lebanese unions submitted a motion regarding Palestinian refugees to the 1965 ICFTU Congress in Amsterdam, the Histadrut briefed its friends on the ICFTU including Fred Hayday, chairman of the TUC International committee which ensured the motion was removed from the Congress agenda.[37]

By now the TUC was on very good terms with the Histadrut and helped the Histadrut whenever it could. In May 1965, the Histadrut asked both the ICFTU and the TUC to write to the Syrian president asking for clemency for Eli Cohen, an Egyptian-born Israeli agent living in

Damascus who had been sentenced to death for spying. The TUC responded positively whereas ICFTU refused to help.[38] The following year, Becker successfully lobbied both the ICFTU and the TUC for help in gaining Israel's admission as an associate member of European Community.[39]

1967–1972: The Golden Period in TUC—Histadrut Relations

The golden period in TUC Histadrut relations was due to the work and hopes of two men, Frank Cousins and Fred Hayday who realised there was an opportunity for the British labour movement to play its part in breaking the deadlock between Israel and Egypt and Arab states in the immediate aftermath of the 1967 Six-Day War. Although their brave attempt to persuade their fellow trade unionists in the Arab world to talk directly to the Israelis failed, they never gave up, but found it difficult playing the role of honest broker as the TUC was perceived by the Arabs as a pro-Israel organisation. Along with the ICFTU who in October 1967 arranged a face-to-face meeting with both parties, their efforts have gone unnoticed and have never been given the credit they deserve. The driving force behind the TUC missions to the Middle East was Cousins despite Hayday being the chairman of the TUC international committee. While Hayday represented the Right wing of the Labour Party, Cousins represented the Left and was close to Harold Wilson, the prime minister, who was supportive and looked upon him in the way that Attlee had depended upon Bevin. Cousins, who was strong on international affairs had serious conversations with Israeli prime minister Golda Meir and President Nasser, very much wanted there to be cooperation between the Israelis and the Arabs.[40]

Although Woodcock's priority as general secretary was to safeguard the interests of the TUC, support the UN and the Labour Government's Middle East policy, he played an important supporting role to Cousins and Hayday.[41] Even though he considered Becker to be a personal friend, Woodcock always did his best to appear supportive of the Histadrut and Israel but was always reluctant to make any written or public commitment on any international political issue, let alone towards Israel, nevertheless Woodcock was more than happy to work on their behalf behind the scenes, especially at the ICFTU.

The 1967 Six-Day War and the Labour Movement

Tension in the Middle East increased when in May 1967 Egypt moved her military forces into the Sinai and blockaded the Straits of Tiran. These actions were seen by Israel as a threat to her security and almost immediately the Histadrut's regular work was set side and replaced by intense lobbying of the international labour movement. They contacted twenty-four unions worldwide including the TUC.[42] The responses received from the international labour movement were overwhelmingly sympathetic and supportive of both Israel and the Histadrut.[43]

The TUC General Council issued a statement on 25 May, which expressed their concern at the recent developments in the Middle East and called on the British Government to bring the matter before the UN Security Council.[44] It was a carefully constructed non-committal statement with no direct mention of Israel or even solidarity with the Histadrut which was the TUC's only public declaration on the war. This was not totally unexpected as the TUC had never previously issued a statement in support of Israel or on the Arab-Israeli conflict. The only British union which issued their own statement was the TGWU whose declaration followed the TUC and failed to mention either of the participants in the conflict.[45]

Throughout the Six-Day War the Labour Party produced a series of private and confidential internal briefing papers and daily updates, it is unlikely however that they shared this information with the TUC.[46] Once again Israel used the Socialist International as a means of gaining international support by adopting a resolution on the crisis.[47] The German trade union federation, the DGB, unlike the TUC, condemned the Arab threat to destroy Israel, and as an expression of solidarity with the Histadrut had agreed to invest DM 3 million in Israeli bonds.[48] The war led to another spate of anti-Zionism from the CPGB which had throughout the 1950s consistently reflected the Soviet Union's anti Zionism. They declared their solidarity with the Arabs and accused the Labour Government of colluding with the United States by supporting Israeli aggression.[49]

Even though the friendship between the Histadrut and the TUC was at an all-time high, the Israelis were disappointed by the TUC's response. On 31 May, the TUC received a letter from the Histadrut asking '*the General Council to express as a matter of urgency, open solidarity with the Histadrut in supporting Israel's right to unchallenged peace for the continuation of its social and economic development*'.[50]

By following the Labour Government's policy of remaining neutral in the dispute, the TUC International committee waited until the war was over before meeting to discuss their response to the Histadrut letter as well as those received from Arab trade unions accusing Israel of aggression.[51] The International department had prepared a briefing note, which pointed out that in the light of the friendly relations between them the Histadrut could reasonably expect an expression of TUC solidarity on the basis of Israel's right to exist. Three options were offered; the first stated that it would be impossible to satisfy the Histadrut completely without losing the goodwill of the unions in the Arab states for many years to come. The second suggested that the Histadrut might accept a truthful explanation from the General Council that it was really hard for them to issue a statement which was satisfactory to them mainly because of Britain's special position in relation to a number of Muslim Commonwealth countries. Their third suggestion was that as hostilities had ended it they could issue a non-committal statement on general lines calling on all parties to observe the cease-fire and negotiations on a peace treaty which recognised Israel's right to exist.[52]

No reasons were given as to why only Hayday, Cousins, Douglass, and Woodcock attended the special meeting of the International committee on 12 June, but it is clear that Woodcock had been in no hurry to reply to the letter. The minutes state that the General Council took the view that it '*should avoid formally taking sides in the conflict even though their sympathies may lie in a certain direction*'. After the committee had been told that '*the General Council might wish to indicate their views informally to the Histadrut as it would be unwise for the General Council to make public pronouncements that might add to present difficulties*', it was agreed to a draft reply to the Histadrut along the lines of a non-committal statement for the committee's next meeting.[53] No record exists of this letter and it is unlikely that it was ever drafted.

The Histadrut Has Concerns About the TUC and ICFTU

The Histadrut did not wait long to thank their friends for their support. Shortly after the war had finished, they embarked on a worldwide information campaign to explain Israel's case to the labour movements in order to retain their support for Israel's cause. Over the next few months delegations were sent to the USA, Europe and several Latin American countries with reciprocal visits occuring in many cases.[54]

Skinner, the British labour attaché in Tel Aviv, reported that the Histadrut was very concerned that the TUC '*the one prominent labour movement in the free world (which) had not yet taken a positive stand on the current Middle East situation*'. Nor were the Histadrut totally happy with the '*non-committal and disappointing*' policy of the ICFTU. They had made it their first priority '*to obtain a clear expression of solidarity and support from the TUC, both in its own right and as a member of the ICFTU*'.[55]

Becker's first move was to speak to Woodcock at the ILO conference in Geneva who told him of '*Labour's warm support for Israel's cause in her just fight*'. Woodcock accepted Becker's invitation to visit Israel and indicated that he might be able to make a short visit in August 1967.[56] However after meeting Woodcock, Becker decided that the best course of action would be for him to go to London to discuss the issue face to face with the TUC.[57]

Once the International committee heard that Becker was coming to London they delayed their discussion on the Middle East situation until after his meeting with the General Council on the 10 August. The committee were told that any future TUC statement which stressed the need for a negotiated settlement, freedom of passage through the Straits of Tiran, and the settlement of the refugee problem would not satisfy the Histadrut who wanted the TUC to openly express support for Israel. They also heard that recognition of Israel by the Arab states was a basic requirement for Israel's future security and that the Wilson Government was concerned that Arab hostility towards Britain could affect sterling balances[58] Woodcock later told Marx, that as he would not be able to go to Israel before the TUC Congress in September, Cousins and Hayday should go in his place as it was important that there was a statement about Israel in the General Council's report to Congress.[59]

Before Becker's meeting with the General Council he had a private discussion with Woodcock who made it clear to Becker that he was personally dissatisfied with the TUC's position regarding the Arab-Israel conflict and blamed some senior members of the Council for preventing the TUC from taking a clear position on the subject. He explained to Becker that in the past he had always tried to postpone discussions on political problems in the General Council, especially those which related directly to British government foreign policy. On the question of Israel, however, Woodcock said that he would like to see a clear declaration from the TUC, because, in his opinion, the TUC could not avoid this problem and must therefore make its opinion heard. He urged Becker to stand by his demands and not shy away from criticising the TUC's inaction. Woodcock also explained to Becker that although the TUC rulebook did allow an emergency resolution to be submitted to the TUC Congress in September, Congress would be able to debate the war without any official TUC policy in place which could either restrain any future TUC action or embarrass the Labour Government. Becker made it clear to Woodcock that the TUC needed to make a clear declaration of policy at the beginning of the meeting without the need for questions or comments from him.[60]

At his meeting with the General Council Becker called on the TUC to issue a constructive declaration of sympathy with Israel's requirements for negotiations and peace in the Middle East. Woodcock then told his colleagues that Becker had not expressed strongly enough the Histadrut's unhappiness with the TUC's neutral stance and that apart from wanting to send a delegation, the TUC had not yet said anything regarding the Middle East. Woodcock '*praised the victors for talking about peace, whilst the defeated Arabs still talked of their plans to destroy Israel, and denied any attempts at negotiation*', adding that '*the most important thing to do was to bring the Arabs to the negotiating table, thus making them recognise the existence of the State of Israel*', and that this should be agreed as the official policy of the TUC. Cousins said that Israel's friends should use their influence directly on the Arabs, to convince them that Israel existed and that the TUC should use its international position to bring both sides together. The General Council decided that Hayday and Cousins should to go to Israel to report on the country's economic and political situation, which would be presented to Congress.[61] Becker said on his return to Israel that '*he had been delighted by the unanimous support of Israel's position by members of the TUC General Council*'. '[62]

Why did Woodcock, normally so cautious, make a positive intervention and demand that the Arabs be brought to the negotiating table and that the TUC make a stand? He may have seen this as an opportunity to allow him to make a positive contribution behind the scenes and we know that he deeply cared about Israel and felt that the time had come for the Arabs to recognise Israel.[63] He said later that without his intervention the visit might not have taken place. Friendship and support for Israel may have helped but it is not the complete answer especially as Woodcock had previously said that the TUC would not embarrass the Government by issuing a statement in support of Israel.

Was the suggestion for the visit a purely Israeli proposal or had it been planned beforehand between Israel and Britain as Harold Wilson was known to have close personal and political ties with Israel? Firstly we know that in June the MOL and therefore the Foreign Office knew of the invitation and whilst the official British position was to be neutral, it is possible that the Foreign Office saw this as an opportunity for the TUC to assist the Government who were trying to take a leading role in Arab-Israeli peace efforts.[64] Goodman suggests that the Foreign Office, as they had in past, saw an opportunity for the TUC to assist the British government and help bring about a peaceful solution in the Middle East.[65] Secondly the Histadrut would not have embarked on such a mission without the prior agreement and support of the Israeli government of which they were an integral part.

Cousins and Hayday's Fact Finding Trip to Israel

The visit provided Cousins and Hayday with the opportunity of mediating in the Arab-Israeli conflict, a role which lasted several years. The TUC's message to both sides was that peace and a permanent settlement could not be reached unless the Arab States recognised the State of Israel. This visit had the approval of the Foreign Office and it was only when their mission was extended to visiting Arab states that a rift developed between them and the TUC.

Cousins and Hayday left London on 17 August for a hectic three-day fact-finding trip which included meetings with the Israeli prime minister, Foreign Minister, the Minister of Labour and the British ambassador. They also attended of the opening of the Histadrut branch in East Jerusalem. Cousins and Hayday's speeches were non-controversial and called on Arab workers to work together with Jewish workers.

Skinner reported that the Israelis were well satisfied with the outcome of the visit and in an interview with the *Jerusalem Post* Cousins and Hayday had said that their report would include a recommendation to the TUC to support direct negotiations between Israel and the Arab states and direct Arab-Israel peace negotiations.[66] Skinner, however, told the MOL that his impression of the visit was that it was '*friends meeting with friends*'', and it '*provided welcome confirmation for the Israelis that the events of June 1967 have not altered the strong bonds which exist between the TUC and the Histadrut'*. He was left '*in no doubt of their sympathy and support for Israel'*. The pair told Hadow, the British ambassador that their primary international objective was to strengthen trades union cooperation, but the political situation was bound to impose on their views and actions. Hadow concluded that the Israelis have been both skilful and successful in putting across their point of view and the political solution they would like to see as the outcome of the war.[67]

Woodcock told the General Council at their pre-Congress meeting on 31 August, that it was essential for the Council to make a statement to Congress, but it should be limited to supporting direct negotiations between Israel and the Arab states and that there should be no mention of Israel's occupation of Jerusalem or the territories that had recently been gained. He added that although it was preferable for the TUC not to get involved in international politics, it was important that the recognition of Israel was necessary in order to avoid further conflict in the Middle East. The Council generally agreed with this sentiment and decided that Hayday would make a short statement on the report to Congress.[68]

Such was the interest in the Six-Day War in Britain that the Congress debate was shown live on television. Hayday began with a report of their visit to Israel, the view of the General Council, he said, was that the Arab nations should recognise the existence of the State of Israel and that direct negotiations should take place between the two sides over the problems arising out of the war which the Council hoped would lead to a general settlement of the Middle East situation. Israel, he said, desired to live in peace, secure from future attacks, but the war aims of the Arab states were very simple; to drive the Israelis out of Israel and to destroy them as a people. Cousins told Congress that the greatest disservice they could do was to divide into pro-Jew and pro-Arab. The Arab workers that they had met in Jerusalem had been told that the TUC would be happy to meet workers representatives in the Arab states. He then asked Congress for their approval to let the TUC try and convince the Jordanians, the Egyptians, the Lebanese that their workers' interests will best be served by sitting down and discussing how the two sides could work together, a situation from which everyone could benefit.[69]

Although it had taken the Histadrut three months to accomplish, the TUC's public call for Arab recognition of Israel and direct peace negotiations between Israel and the Arab states was exactly the outcome that they had sought. Woodcock told Marx afterwards, that he was very pleased with the outcome and that without Becker's presence at the meeting he doubted if the General Council would have agreed to send Cousins and Hayday to Israel.[70] The fact that the TUC Congress had not formally adopted a statement of intent did not dim the Histadrut's enthusiasm for the TUC's support, which they hoped would have a big impact on public opinion in Britain and elsewhere. Both the General Council and Congress, who were broadly pro-Israel, had also given Cousins and Hayday a mandate to talk to the Arab trade unions. This had a twofold advantage for Britain, not only it would enhance Britain's role in the peace process but also would help to rebuild her image in the Arab world by building links with the Arab trade union movement.

Three weeks later, Marx met separately with both Woodcock and Cousins to discuss the TUC's next move. Woodcock told him that there was a strong possibility that a letter outlining their position would be sent to the Foreign Office. He was however apprehensive about Cousins plans to visit various Arab states and speak with not only the unions, but also with their governments and political parties. The TUC, he said, should only interact with trade unions in countries like Jordan and Lebanon and he was opposed to the TUC having contact with governments, especially those who were members of the Arab League. Woodcock asked Marx to tell Becker that he was always ready to discuss matters with him and that Becker should contact him whenever necessary.

Cousins told Marx, when they met a few days later, that it was important that the TUC take an active role in furthering peace in the Middle East, and therefore must be in contact with the Arabs, adding that he already had received requests for visits from Lebanon,[71] Jordan, Kuwait, and the Secretary of the Arab League. He said that he was not concerned that the TUC might be seen as a tool of Israeli propaganda, as he saw the TUC's role as trying to influence the Arabs into taking a realistic view by recognising Israel and entering into peace talks with them. Cousin's emphasised that the Histadrut could count on his friendship and sympathy and that he was glad that he '*had not inherited the opinion of his predecessor Bevin*'. The scope of his visits and contacts, he said, would be decided by the General Council but would not include the Arab League and he would not hesitate to meet government representatives, as he had in Israel. Marx concluded that Cousins understood Israel's position, Woodcock's personal approach, TUC policy and the wider context. He realised that there was only so much pressure that the Histadrut could put on the TUC as they were not going to make any more pro-Israel statements until they had seen if their policy would work.[72]

The ICFTU Executive Board meeting at the beginning of October 1967 which was the first since the war provided Woodcock with the opportunity to ensure a positive outcome to discussions about the Middle East conflict. The Board established an ad-hoc committee which produced two draft statements, one supported by the DGB, Histadrut and the AFL-CIO, which called for bilateral Arab-Israel peace talks and the other supported by the Tunisian and the Lebanese trade unions, which called for the Arab refugee problem to be part of a general settlement. Both statements were then composited into a final resolution which was unanimously approved by the Executive Board. Although not an agreed statement, as the ICFTU had originally hoped for, this declaration called for direct negotiations between Israelis and Arabs on all issues including the refugee problem. This was a truly important initiative not only for the international labour movement but also for international politics, as the ICFTU had achieved a successful outcome to direct talks between the Arabs and Israelis, a feat which had not yet been equalled by any other forum in the world.

The Histadrut Central Committee were told that the worldwide information campaign had played an important part in securing support for the ICFTU resolution and gave special mention to the friendship shown by the American and German unions.[73] Woodcock was praised by the Histadrut delegate for his role in the behind the scene discussions.[74] The ad-hoc committee was given permanent status in the hope that the might help further in bridge-building between the two parties. The continually changing political landscape in the Israel-Arab conflict resulted in the working group not reconvening until November 1968 when it decided not to discuss the conflict as it appeared at the time that the exisiting UN mediation process would yield positive results.[75]

In October 1968 the ICFTU closed its Beirut office for financial reasons.[76] From then on, mainly due to pressure from the TUC and the AFL-CIO who wanted to run their own aid programmes, the ICFTU only offered advice and the coordination of activities on behalf of affiliates rather than run their own programmes.[77] The ICFTU representative, who had been based in Beirut, never travelled to Israel or met with the Histadrut outside ICFTU meetings, probably because the ICFTU felt that his credibility with the Arab trade unions would have been compromised if he been in regular contact with the Israelis. For the same reason, the British labour attaché in Israel was never allowed to travel to neighbouring Arab States, yet the ability of the TUC to meet with both Arab and Israeli trade unionists was never questioned. The ICFTU had been unable to get both sides together, primarily, because it had been used as a political battleground by both the Arabs and Israelis whose trade union movements were also part of their political infrastructures.

TUC Missions to Jordan, Lebanon and Egypt

The Foreign Office saw TUC's missions to Jordan, Lebanon and Egypt as an opportunity to restore Britain's position in the Arab world and re-engage with Arab trade unionists that had been previously ignored and were now under Egyptian influence and might turn to Moscow for help.[78] The visits were also regarded as an opportunity to counter the strong influence of the Histadrut within the TUC General Council, which in their view had taken a one-sided view of Arab-Israel affairs. Cousins was also a concern for them, because as a former government minister his views and opinions were respected and he had in the past, been critical of the Government's Middle East policy on the grounds that it was too pro-Arab. Foggon, the Foreign Office labour advisor, welcomed the reopening of relations with the Arab world as he saw this as an opportunity for further visits by the TUC to other countries in the region. But he recommended that the TUC should follow the British Government's example of attempting to be scrupulously neutral in the Arab-Israel dispute.[79] However the visits created an unprecedented difference of opinion between the TUC and the Foreign Office because Cousins and Hayday saw their primary role as trying to bring peace to the Middle East through the international labour movement and not as part of an effort to rebuild British relations with the Arab States.

Before the visit to Jordan and Lebanon in December 1967, Hayday was briefed by the Foreign Office and also met with Goronwy Roberts, a Government Minister.[80] The meeting with Roberts had been arranged because the Government considered that one of their most loyal supporters (*Cousins*) had '*changed sides*" and they needed TUC support for British diplomatic efforts attempting to bring the Arabs to the negotiating table. The Israeli Government viewed these efforts as further appeasement of the Arabs. Hayday had previously told the Foreign Office that the TUC was only interested in non-political contacts because of Woodcock's '*very rigid views on this subject*" and they would '*not want to get too close to the British diplomatic network'*.[81] As the British Government were concerned about the status of Jerusalem which had already been noted as a possible sticking point in any future peace negotiations, the two men were made aware of the political implications of the Histadrut's trade union activities in East Jerusalem and were asked to take them into account if they made any public comments on the matter.[82] Roberts asked Hayday if he would advise the Histadrut of the political difficulties and dangers of pre-judging the future of Jerusalem. Hayday replied saying that '*neither he nor Mr. Cousins would be able to say to the Histadrut that they would not like to see Jerusalem unified. Divided cities produced nothing but bitterness and misery and the Jews should have access to their historical holy buildings*'. Hayday was told that '*the Arabs would be bound to resent this pre-judging of the final solution and the consequences could be dangerous*" and he was '*unmoved*" by their request to adopt a more pro-Arab line. The Foreign Office concluded that Cousins and Hayday were not going to help them.[83] The Foreign Office were left in no doubt that Cousins and Hayday's priority was to use the international trade union movement as a force for good in the Middle East and that they were not going to take a more pro-Arab line.[84]

The Foreign Office warned the TUC, that in order to avoid any embarrassment when travelling to Lebanon and Jordan, Cousins needed a new passport as his current one contained an Israeli visa. Cousins declined their request and told the Lebanese ambassador in London that he saw no reason why he should travel to Lebanon on the basis of a lie and that since everyone knew he had been to Israel, it was not neccesary for him to have a new one in order to go there. His refusal was seen as a setback which could cancel the whole initiative. However, after an intervention by the Foreign Office, the Lebanese and Jordanian ambassadors, to everyone's surprise issued the necessary visas on his existing passport.[85]

On their return Cousins and Hayday reported that they had had meetings with trade union leaders, ministers and officials, and had also visited factories as well as refugee camps. Neither country had pursued, in their opinion, effective measures of settlement with refugees being encouraged to look towards a return to the Palestinian territories with no regard to the human problem that they presented. They gained the impression that the Lebanese saw the Palestinian refugees as foreigners and a burden on society. The conditions in the camps in Jordan illustrated clearly for them that there was very little social conscience in the Arab world.

In all of their meetings with trade union and Government officials, the pair explained Congress policy and the need for them to enter into a dialogue with the Israelis. All they heard in return, especially in Jordan, was '*a recital of all the political arguments dating back to the time of the Turks*' for it was never accepted that talks could commence with the Israelis other than on the basis of a restoration of the pre-1948 situation. In their opinion, the human problems involved were not a priority and were secondary to the political arguments, that Israel was the aggressor and the enemy. Hayday noted that the Jordanian trade unionists in particular laid too much emphasis on well-known Arab political points of principle with too little on the social welfare of their members or their fellow countrymen. Both men were worried by the Jordanians willingness to accept the inevitability of further war if they were unable to achieve Arab rights through negotiations. The trade unions in both countries had originally been established to serve political ends, rather than the interests of the workers. The political views that were presented to them were dominated by the Israel question; the Jordanian trade unionists tended to support President Nasser which isolated and reduced the influence in the Arab world of the Lebanese and Tunisian ICFTU affiliates.[86]

Their remarkable report not only concisely and clearly revealed what the Jordanians thought of the refugees and how they treated them but also that the Palestinians were being used as political pawns in the long running Arab-Israeli conflict. Both men were distressed by what they had witnessed in the camps and that the Arab-Israeli conflict dominated both political life and trade union activities as well as the inevitability of another war. Although they never gave up, they must have realised that they would be unlikely to achieve the task they had set themselves. The MOL were extremely upbeat about their trip and future relations with the Arab unions[87] especially as the TUC had received an invitation to send a delegation to visit Egypt which Cousins wanted to accept, but Woodcock felt that this was not the right time.[88]

Cousins and Hayday went to Egypt in March 1968 where they had extensive discussions with union and government officials and President Nasser. They were told that there would be no negotiations as long as Israel occupied the Sinai and that their hosts '*constantly referred to Zionists and the choice of Palestine for the Jewish state*' as well as questioning '*the Balfour declaration which they declared allowed the Jews to have dual loyalties*'. Nasser told them that a settlement could not be achieved by direct talks and that the UN and the great powers would need to underwrite any agreement. He added that he would only recognise Israel provided the borders were based on the original UN boundaries along with an agreed solution to the refugee problem. Nasser also denied ever saying that his aim '*was to drive the Israelis into the sea'*. The Egyptians saw Cousins and Hayday's reference to direct talks with Israel as '*a constant irritant*;" which resulted in them realising that they needed an alternative to direct negotiations. On their return Cousins and Hayday recommended that in future the General Council consider UN initiatives.[89]

Although the two men had succeeded in establishing contact with the trade union movements in Egypt, Jordan and Lebanon which pleased the Foreign Office, their mission had failed not only because of the Arabs deep-rooted opposition to direct negotiations but also because of their refusal to recognise and accept the existence of the State of Israel. The pair were perceived as friends of the Histadrut because they were promoting the Israeli point of view for direct talks. Two years later, Hayday said that it had not been easy for them to play an impartial role in the Arab-Israel dispute as many of his colleagues were sympathetic towards Israel and had also visited Israel as guests of the Histadrut. He added that the TUC had not only followed Government policy but also had tried to steer a middle course in order to build bridges between the two sides. Hayday revealed that the Israelis knew of TUC's contacts with the Arabs and had not been opposed to their initiative.[90]

The Six-Day War had provided the TUC with the opportunity to play its part on the world stage to try and bring peace to the Middle East. Ironically if it had not played safe by not issuing a statement in support of Israel at the beginning of June, it is unlikely that any of their missions to Israel and the Arab States would have taken place. Cousins and Hayday had serious conversations with both the Israelis and the Egyptians in order to bring about cooperation between them, even though their efforts were certainly genuine, they have not been given the recognition they deserve.

The TUC's efforts failed partly because both the Arab and Israeli trade unions movements were closely allied to their respective governments and were unable to deviate from their government's decisions and policies. But the initiative ultimately failed because the Foreign Office took control in order to help restore British links with the Arab world.

Anglo-Israel Relations

The Labour Party had continued to be pro-Israel but the big difference between 1967 and 1956 was that both the British Labour Party and the Israeli Labour Alignment were in government in 1967 with broadly similar ideological and political policies. The Israelis also believed that this time they had friends in high place and their close links with the Parliamentary Labour Party ensured that there was very little dissention over their support for Israel even from the Left.[91] Israel's victory in the Six-Day War not only totally changed the dynamics of the region but also affected Anglo-Israel relations.

Before the war, Britain's Middle East policy was one of disengagement from the region whilst attempting to achieve a balance and even-handedness towards the Arabs and Israelis. The war provided Harold Wilson with the opportunity to deflect attention away from Britain's economic problems, whilst heightening expectations of Britain's influence in world affairs. He wanted to be seen as working with Washington and the UN, in order to avoid any charges of imperialism being levelled against Britain. Even though the UK had tried to remain neutral it was accused of involvement by Egypt in the war, which resulted in an Arab oil embargo on the West as well as the withdrawal of funds from British banks by the Arab states.

The war transformed Britain's Middle East policy as the government adopted a more active foreign policy in the hope of securing an Arab-Israeli peace agreement. The initial upsurge of pro-British sentiment in Israel disappeared once Britain publicly disagreed with Israel on how best to achieve a political settlement to the Arab-Israeli conflict and over contentious issues including Jerusalem, refugees, and the Suez Canal. Britain did, however, sponsor UN Security Council resolution 242 which was accepted by Egypt, Jordan, and Israel.

Once the euphoria of Israel's stunning victory had passed and it was clear that the Arab states were unwilling to talk peace and recognise Israel, there was a re-evaluation of attitudes within the Labour Party towards the conflict between Israel and her Arab neighbours. Dissent against Labour's support for Israel came from MP's on both the Right and the Left in the party. The priority for those on the Right was the promotion of British interests in Arab States, whilst those on the Left began to question Labour's traditional support for Israel.

From 1969 onwards Anglo-Israel relations deteriorated due to Israeli concerns about Britain's intentions which included criticism of Israel's policy on Jerusalem and delays in the sale of British tanks to Israel. Britain's view was that her diplomatic efforts were an attempt to ensure that hostilities were not resumed which could jeopardise Britain's oil supplies.[92] With a change of government in 1970 relations appeared to be friendly but the Israelis felt that British efforts at the UN to secure a settlement were motivated by their interests in the Arab world at the direct expense of Israel.

The Foreign Office Forms the Overseas Labour Consultative Committee (OLCC)

In 1965, the Foreign Office instituted a review of British influence and organised labour overseas because the Government was concerned that British influence abroad was falling behind that of Germany and America. Organised labour was also being targeted by the Communists because of their influential role in political decision making in many of the newly independent states in Africa and Asia. The review revealed that despite the TUC's influential position within the international labour movement it was not really interested in international affairs or building links with their foreign counterparts. Woodcock was blamed for the TUC's indifference, because his priority was domestic affairs. He considered the ICFTU to be wasteful and dominated by the Americans.[93]

The outcome was the establishment of the Overseas Labour Consultative Committee (OLCC) in 1967 on which both the TUC and the CBI were represented.[94] One of its aims was to encourage the TUC to become more actively involved in international affairs. The committee regularly discussed the Arab-Israeli conflict with Hayday and Cousins initially reporting on their visits to Jordan, Lebanon and Egypt. Foggon, the labour advisor believed that the ICFTU had lost ground in the Arab world to the Egyptian led International Confederation of Arab Trade Unions (ICATU), and that was unlikely to change as long as the Histadrut, with AFL-CIO support, continued to be a leading ICFTU affiliate. Hayday thought he had over-estimated the influence of Histadrut.[95] In May 1968 Foggon told the Foreign and Commonwealth Office (FCO) that the OLCC had already helped '*lever the TUC out of its self-imposed isolation*'.[96]

Over the next few years the TUC supported the work of the OLCC whilst cooperating with the Government whenever possible on a wide range of issues overseas aid, the work of the ILO and the development of TUC contacts in the Middle East. They notified the OLCC of all the TUC's overseas visits as well as visits by trade union delegations to Britain. In September 1969, Foggon explained to Lehmann, the Histadrut European representative that relations with the Arab unions were now under Foreign Office supervision. Their policy was to try to improve relations with those unions as well as preventing the Arabs moving closer to the WFTU. He told Lehmann that an Egyptian delegation had visited the UK and Cousins future plans included visits to Egypt, Sudan and maybe Libya. Lehmann warned that these visits might be exploited by the Arabs for anti-Israel propaganda which Foggon admitted was possible; he added that the Foreign Office had issued advice to the trade unions not to intervene in the Israeli-Arab conflict'.[97]

By 1970, the TUC's links with Egypt had expanded, even though not all the major British unions were as keen as the TUC to build links with their Arab counterparts. They had even tried to involve their European colleagues, but had made little progress as support for Israel was very strong both in Germany and Scandinavia.[98] The TUC's efforts paid off, when in September 1970, they contacted the Egyptians regarding the hijacking of a British airliner by Palestinian terrorists, as their request received a more positive response than similar appeals made by others.[99]

The success of the pro-Israel lobby at the TUC during this period had caused alarm at the Foreign Office, who openly admitted that they wanted to reduce the influence of the Histadrut on the TUC General Council. The OLCC was successful as it helped change the TUC's attitude to international affairs by giving Hayday's and Cousins visits to the Middle East credibility and support. It was an honest attempt by the Foreign Office to rectify the mistakes of the past. The committee did not directly input into the TUC's involvement in Arab-Israeli affairs, but allowed the Foreign Office to influence their international work. The main thrust of the transformation in remodelling the TUC's international presence in the Middle East only came after Woodcock's retirement as well as from within the TUC itself with the energy, enthusiasm and vision of Feather, Cousins, Hayday and Jones. But the reality was that a lack of resources did not allow the TUC to run its own aid programmes in developing countries or send specialists abroad, which meant that its international work was limited to making contacts and the ICFTU.

Whether the Labour Party was in Government or not during the 1960s and 1970s they made it clear that their friendship and support for Israel would not stop them making statements critical of the actions of the Arab States. The TUC on the other hand were still very careful not to take sides unlike their American or German counterparts who made it quite clear that they supported Israel. In the late 1960s this reluctance led the TUC to endorse the ICFTU's actions and statements rather than issue their own.

Building on Improved TUC-Histadrut Relations

Israel's stunning victory in the Six-Day War had an immediate effect on all parts of Israeli society. Not only had victory reunited Jerusalem but the newly Israeli—occupied territories[100] provided a buffer zone for her security along with the promise of recognition by her enemies as well as an agreement on peace and security. However Israelis were divided over how to deal with the territories, the 'Land for Israel' movement called for Israel to retain the territories not only for security reasons but also on religious and historical grounds. They were opposed by the Israeli Left who feared that holding onto the territories would be too much of a financial and political burden as well a demographic problem. As time went on more and more Israeli settlements were built in these areas resulting in this debate becoming a major issue and dividing Israeli society but initially Israel's priority was, with the help of her allies, to try and reach a peace agreement with her enemies. The Arab leaders however decided at their summit meeting in Khartoum in August 1967 there should be no peace, no recognition and no negotiation with Israel. The following year saw the start of the Palestinian terror campaign directed at Israel based on the hijacking of passenger aircraft.

The Movement for Colonial Freedom (MCF) which was formed in 1954 successfully lobbied both the Labour Party and the TUC for their support for campaigns to end British colonial rule in Africa, Asia and the Caribbean as well as for national liberation movements elsewhere. From the early 1960s the MCF built a relationship with the Left in Israel through the Israeli journal *New Outlook*. The Israeli Left's opposition to the drive to build settlements on the lands captured by Israel in 1967 coincided with a period of independence for Britain's colonies as well as the rise of the Palestine Liberation Organisation (PLO), which was formed in 1964 as a third world independence movement. The PLO fitted ideally into the MCF's world outlook as well as that of a new generation on the Labour Left for whom the Holocaust was a distant memory and who were becoming aware of the Israel-Palestine conflict. The MCF, which was renamed

'Liberation' in 1970, sent to the TUC in February 1983 a copy of their conference resolution which condemned Israel's invasion of Lebanon the previous year as well as declaring their support for the establishment of a Palestinian homeland.[101]

The first of many trade union delegations to visit Israel over the few next years was made in November 1967 by the Inland Revenue Staff Federation led by Cyril Plant, a member of the TUC General Council. Plant was seen by the Israelis as an important visitor and throughout his visit he frequently urged the need for direct negotiation. He said that when Frank Cousins met with the Jordanian and Lebanese trade unions they would be urged to press their governments for direct talks with Israel[102] In November 1968, Cousins, who paid a return visit refused to discuss Arab-Israeli relationships or any matters arising from his visit to Egypt, emphasising instead that this was not a political mission as he had come as a trade union leader to maintain the friendship and co-operation.[103] The unions' unique relationship with Israel was signified by Becker, the Histadrut general secretary, who told the 1968 TUC Congress, that '*we yearn for peace and want to start negotiations today rather than tomorrow*'.[104] Becker also used the opportunity to talk with other fraternal delegates including those from Lebanon, Tunisia, Cyprus and Turkey.[105] In October 1968 a Histadrut delegation that visited Britain recommended that relations with the British unions could be strengthened further by the appointment of a labour attaché as well as sending more delegations to meet with the unions. They realised that the problems of the Middle East were only a minor topic in their talks and felt that the TUC and the majority of unions had a positive attitude towards Israel but noted that people like Hayday, insisted on taking an 'objective" stand in order to be a capable mediator between the Arabs and the Israelis.[106]

Although there was no debate on the Middle East at the 1968 TUC Congress, the International committee published a report about the visits to Jordan, Lebanon and Egypt, which they hoped would eventually lead towards an improvement of relations between Israel and the Arabs. The TUC expected that these initial contacts with the Arab trade unions would eventually build into relationships similar to those which existed with the Histadrut. The report warned that the delegation had discovered that in all three Arab countries there was a general and deep-rooted opposition to direct negotiations with Israel, although the suggestion that they should recognise and accept the existence of the State of Israel was not totally rejected.[107]

The Histadrut Moves Its European Office to Brussels

The ruling party in Israel, Mapai and the Histadrut shared a common ideology and history as well as the same loyalty to State of Israel and a mutual desire for Mapai to remain in government. But the relationship between the Histadrut and the Israeli government remained a complex one. Before 1948 the Histadrut played a major role in the organisation and economic expansion of the Yishuv in addition to its role as a trade union movement. After independence their relationship was widely discussed before the Government took control of the Histadrut's institutions with all the Histadrut's major political decisions and policy being decided by the Mapai leadership who were also the Government. Although the Histadrut retained the right to act independently on domestic economic matters there was no such conflict when it came to the Histadrut's international role, which was to support the interests of the State and its policies. Its function in international affairs '*was to aid it to the extent of its power and relations, strengthen the State's position, as well as to support the state in its struggles and to make friends, sympathisers and supporters amongst the workers movements of the world*'.[108]

Marx, the Histadrut's European representative reported to Jerusalem that six years after the Histadrut's had opened their London office their initial objective of building good relations with the TUC and the unions had been achieved and he was now spending 70% of his time in Europe rather than in London. Britain, he said, needed its own fulltime representative and suggested that Histadrut needed separate representatives in France, West Germany, Italy, and Scandinavia rather than a single European representative who could not work efficiently. He urged them not to undervalue an independent European Histadrut representative, who he wrote, could go places and talk to people without restrictions unlike diplomats.[109]

In April 1968, the Histadrut decided to relocate the office to Brussels because they realised that the EEC would become increasingly important to Israel and the Histadrut in the future. They chose Brussels, as it was centrally located and many of the organisations such as the ICFTU and the ILO were already based there. Hanan Lehmann, Marx's replacement was given the responsibility for not only maintaining relations with the UK unions but also for building relationships with the German, French, and Scandinavian unions. Woodcock said he understood the motives for the move and the Foreign Office regretted that they would no longer be in regular contact with the Histadrut's representative.[110]

Becker told Lehman in 1968 that the leadership of the TUC, the unions and the Labour Party was changing because the incumbents were getting older and he had warned his colleagues that the Histadrut needed to build relationships with the younger generation who would eventually replace them.[111] Despite his admonition, the building of long term relationships with the next generation of leaders suffered because in future their European representative could only meet with them once a month.

The Histadrut's move to Brussels, whilst making perfect sense in terms of their relations with the international labour movement, did not initially affect their relations with the TUC. Even though Jack Jones had replaced Hayday as chairman of the International committee, the Histadrut failed to realise that it made no sense to close their London office when relations with the TUC were at an all-time high and attitudes towards Israel were starting to change for the worse. What happened was very similar to what had taken place in the early 1950s after Bar Tal, the Israeli labour attaché had returned to Israel; connections were no longer as strong, with greater reliance, once again being placed on the Israeli embassy. The consequence by 1972 was that the excellent relationship between the Histadrut, the TUC and the unions that had taken years to achieve started to breakdown. For the time being however, relations between the British trade union movement and the Histadrut continued to be close and friendly.[112] In December 1971, while praising the advantages of exchange visits between Histadrut and the British unions, the Israeli embassy commented that without a permanent Histadrut mission in London, the effectiveness of the embassy in the labour field was limited and could only be fundamentally improved in future by appointing a labour attaché.[113] A similar plea had been made fifteen years earlier with the same message; if you want to keep the British unions on your side then you need a permanent representative based in Britain.

Afro-Asian Institute

During the 1970s when Israel was denied diplomatic recognition in large parts of the world, the Histadrut played a significant international role because its trade union credentials ensured an Israeli presence in third world especially in Africa. With greater diplomatic recognition in the 1980s, an Israeli presence through the Histadrut became less and less important, but for a time it was the face of Israel in many countries with the Histadrut's Afro-Asian Institute playing a key role.

By 1967 the Histadrut's Afro-Asian Institute had become very successful in training manpower for the labour movement in Africa and Asia with 70% of participants coming from Africa. The Histadrut provided 60% of the funding with the rest coming from the Israeli government, the AFL-CIO, European trade unions, UN agencies and foundations dealing with Africa. Between 1959 and 1967 nearly 700 students from African and Asia countries had taken part in thirteen international courses and thirteen special courses for French speaking African countries.[114] The Histadrut had also provided experts for Israeli government aid programmes, which in 1970 were running in 27 African States which included 10 Commonwealth counties and 15 former French colonies.[115]

The TUC which had provided an annual grant of £2000 between 1964 and 1967 for four scholarships for students from the Commonwealth continued to support the Institute and in 1967 funded students from Grenada, Ghana, Uganda and Zambia.[116] The British government received regular updates from their labour attaché on the Afro-Asian Institute and the Histadrut's overseas aid programmes which noted that there was no evidence of any permanent representation of the Histadrut in developing countries, even though the Histadrut's, Soleh Boneh construction arm, had been awarded $30m of contracts in Asian and African countries in 1965.

In March 1972, the TUC ended its association with the Afro-Asian Institute when the General Council approved its final scholarship grant. The General Council said they withdrew their support because their original reason for sponsoring courses, the need to build a relationship with the Histadrut, was no longer valid since the TUC now had a very strong relationship with them.[117] The General Council was also told that the Institute itself now had access to more sources of funding than previously.[118] These were excuses as no payments had been made after 1969 because Hargreaves, the Head of the TUC International department had taken it upon himself not to bring the matter to the International Committee until the Afro-Asian Institute wrote to the TUC in December 1971.[119] The real reason for the change was that by 1972, the General Council was now controlled by the Left as many of the original supporters of the Institute had been replaced by people who had other priorities. Although the TUC was still working with the Foreign Office on overseas aid programmes, its main focus was now on Europe. Yagol, the new Histadrut European representative, on his next visit to London asked the TUC to reconsider the matter, but by then it was too late.[120] If the Histadrut had still been based in London then Yagol may have been able to intervene before the decision had been taken. This episode was a perfect example of how the Histadrut's relationship with the TUC and unions had suffered because of the move to Brussels. Another measure of the loosening of ties was that Yagol wrote fewer reports about Britain compared to his predecessors.

The TUC, the Histadrut and Terrorism

Arab terrorism towards Israel had a global impact in 1968, when Palestinian groups launched a terror campaign based on the hijacking of passenger aircraft. Between 1968 and 1977 twenty-nine aircraft were hijacked or suffered attempted hijacks. Their campaign, affected the TUC and the ICFTU as they came under pressure to ensure the safety of aviation workers.

The policy of the Histadrut whenever the security of State of Israel or any of its population comes under threat is to immediately appeal to its friends for help and support. One such threat was the hijacking of an El Al Boeing 707 in July 1968, by Arab terrorists, which was flown to Algeria.[121] The Histadrut immediately sent telegrams to the ICFTU and the International Transport Secretariat (ITS) asking them urgently to do everything they could to obtain the immediate release of the aircraft, its crew and passengers by Algerian authorities.[122] Both organisations responded straightaway because hijacking was a civil aviation industry problem and not directly related to the politics of the Middle East.[123] Although the Algerian government had released all the non-Israeli passengers they refused to release the Israeli passengers, crew and the aeroplane. The Histadrut was concerned that apart from the German DGB, all their 'friends" in Europe including the TUC had remained silent over the matter.[124]

The reason for the TUC's inaction, were revealed in a memo to Woodcock which presented him with two alternatives. The TUC could either send telegrams to the Algerian Government and the Algerian transport union demanding the release of the plane and the passengers as the Histadrut had asked them to do or make a formal approach to the government asking them to intervene. Woodcock, who also discussed the matter with the British Airline Pilots Association, the Civil Aviation Authority and the Government, was advised to take some action in anticipation of questions being asked at the forthcoming TUC Congress.[125] Two weeks later the TUC decided to write to the Algerian trade union centre rather than Algerian government as the International Committee saw little value in protesting to the government since it might lead in future to the TUC being asked to protest to foreign governments on other matters.[126] Woodcock's letter which was weak and said very little and failed to ask the Algerians to take action to obtain the release the hostages and the plane.[127] It seems that although Woodcock and several members of the committee were friends of Israel, their main concern was for those working in the civil aviation industry. When the Israeli hostages were released in exchange for sixteen convicted Arab terrorists, the Histadrut only thanked the ICFTU for their support and prompt action.[128]

How seriously the TUC now took its role as potential peacemaker in the Middle East was illustrated by their reaction to the next Palestinian terrorist attack on an Israeli airliner in Athens on 26 December 1968.[129] The outcome may not have been to the Histadrut's satisfaction, but the TUC certainly did what they thought was best for the TUC. Israel's response to the Athens attack was to destroy thirteen airliners at Beirut airport two days later,[130] which was condemned by the UN Security Council.[131] Vic Feather, who had just succeeded Woodcock as TUC general secretary, discussed developments at a meeting with Lehmann including the Israeli operation at Beirut Airport. Lehmann explained to Feather the Histadrut's concerns, including their fears about an enforced Middle East settlement and asked for a TUC statement or letter expressing solidarity which would reiterate their statement regarding a direct settlement between both sides in the conflict. Feather explained that despite their friendship, support for the UN was a key part of their international policy,[132] adding that the atmosphere in the General Council was hostile towards the Histadrut following the Beirut action, and suggested a decision at that moment would "*bring undesirable results*". He also said that a pro-Israel statement from the TUC would damage their ability to put pressure on the Arabs. Their two hour 'robust" discussion ended with Lehmann refusing to accept the TUC's position.[133] Feather's reaction was not totally unexpected as Lehmann already knew that Israel's Beirut action had produced a negative response from other European unions.[134]

At the beginning of February 1969, nine Jews were publicly hanged in Baghdad after being convicted of espionage.[135] The immediate reaction of the Histadrut was to ask the TUC, the ICFTU and other affiliates, to protest at the hangings and demand that the remaining Jews in Iraq be allowed to leave.[136] Hargreaves prepared a summary of the situation in the Middle East and advised Feather that the General Council would back his judgment if he took immediate action on the Histadrut's request.[137] Feather decided not to take any action and waited three weeks until the next International committee meeting, by which time the need for a public condemnation had passed. The International committee were informed of the Histadrut's request and telegrams received from the International Confederation of Arab Trade Unions (ICATU) and the Arab Federation of Petroleum Workers (AFPW) asking the TUC to protest to the British Government against the supply of arms to Israel. They were also advised that the International Transport Federation (ITF) had condemned a terrorist attack in February 1969 at Zurich airport.[138] The committee minutes do not show if there was any discussion of the Histadrut's request and once again no action was taken to avoid being seen as taking sides. The Committee decided instead to advise to General Council to ask for a meeting with the foreign secretary to discuss the issues. Briefing notes prepared for the delegation included questions to ask about the supply of arms, the imposition of an interim settlement, and the refugee problem.[139] The delegation were told that Government policy on the Israeli-Arab conflict was based on support for UN resolution 242 and that the foreign secretary had broadly agreed with the TUC's views. They were also told that representations had been made to the Iraqi Government about the hanging of Jews in Iraq.[140] The TUC sent identical letters to the Histadrut, ICATU and the AFPW informing them of their meeting with the foreign secretary.[141]

In September 1972 the Government, the Labour Party and the TUC, along with the majority of the British population were horrified by the attack on Israeli athletes at the Munich Olympics. News of the kidnapping was received whilst the TUC Congress was in session and Yagol, the Histadrut representative, put pressure on the leadership to condemn the attack whilst the hostages were still alive. Initially the TUC was reluctant to agree to his request, but eventually agreed to send a telegram to the Foreign Office, which condemned the '*horror at Arab banditry and murder in Munich*" and called on the government to make representations to all Arab governments to immediately bring these activities to an end.[142] The foreign secretary replied saying that the Government had repeatedly condemned such acts.[143] When the news of the deaths arrived, the next morning's session opened with a minute of silence followed by an emotional statement from the TUC president.[144] Harold Wilson, the prime minister, condemned the murderous attack on the Israeli team and the Labour Party sent telegrams to the Israeli prime minister and the Israel Labour Party expressing '*deepest sympathy*" and that the crime would be condemned '*by the whole civilised world*'.[145]

Notes

1. 'Histadrut Political Bureau for London", *Jerusalem Post*, 25 May 1960, p. 3, TNA: PRO, LAB13/1420, Hayut to Morrat, 6 June 1960 (Hebrew original), PLILMR, IV-219A-1-32B and the British Embassy in Israel to the Foreign Office, 3 March 1961, TNA: PRO, LAB13/1503.
2. Morrat to Hayut, 15 November 1960 (Hebrew original), PLILMR, IV-219A-1-32B.
3. Lehmann to the Histadrut, January 1962 (Hebrew original), PLILMR, IV-21 9A-2-18B.
4. Ibid.
5. Marshall to Woodcock, 24 September 1962, MRC, MSS.292B/956.9/2.
6. Ne'eman to Simchoni, 29 April 1963 (Hebrew original), PLILMR, IV-104-286-1-320.
7. 'Unions invest abroad', *Daily Herald*, 16 April 1963.
8. Marshall to Treganowan, 1 May 1963, TNA: PRO, LAB13/1764.
9. Ne'eman to Simchoni, 3 April 1963, PLILMR, IV-104-286-1-320 and 27 October 1963 (all Hebrew original), PLILMR, IV-219A-1-106.
10. Ambassador Beith to R A. Butler, foreign secretary, 29 November 1963, TNA: PRO, LAB13/1764.
11. Marx to Ne'eman, the department for economic cooperation, 23 May 1965 (Hebrew original), PLILMR, IV-219A-1-142C, Marx to Levinson, the workers cooperative, Tel Aviv, 24 January 1966 (Hebrew original), PLILMR, IV-219A-1-160C and Levinson to Marx, 7 August 1966 (Hebrew original), PLILMR, IV-219A-3-19A.
12. The Histadrut investment fund issued a prospectus to issue two-million-dollar bonds, listed on the Tel Aviv stock market. The bonds were made available for purchase in mid-December 1965 for 6 months. They had a 6% interest rate. However there was a problem in paying the dollar premium; after negotiating with both unions, the Histadrut agreed with the TGWU that both unions will share the premium equally. The GMWU did not agree and offered to pay the entire premium on its own and later deduct the sum from the whole investment. Marx to Israel Embassy London, 3 May 1968 (Hebrew original), PLILMR, IV-219A-3-19A.
13. Report on trade union developments in West Africa by the labour attaché based in Dakar, 31 December 1962, TNA: PRO, LAB13/1852.
14. TUC report, IC7/5, "Scholarships at the Afro–Asian Institute in Israel," 23 April 1963, MRC, MSS 292B/901/3.
15. Treganowan to the labour attaché in Dakar, 5 February 1963, TNA: PRO, LAB13/1764.
16. TUC International Committee minutes, 23 April 1963, MRC, MSS 292B/901/3.

17. Vincent-Smith, MOL to Barclay, FO, 13 June 1963, TNA: PRO, LAB13/2006.
18. Labour attaché Brussels to MOL, 27 March 1963, TNA: PRO, LAB13/1764.
19. Minutes of the Histadrut's International department meeting, 15 December 1963 (Hebrew original), PLILMR, IV-219A-1-87B, Ne'eman to Simchoni, 16 December 1963 (Hebrew original), PLILMR, IV-219A-1-106.
20. Foreign Office to the Crown Agents, 7 February 1961, TNA: PRO, FO371/158745.
21. After the Norwich Union had issued their statement, the Arab League information centre in London published a press release which boasted of their achievement. The League of Arab States press release, 4 December 1963, BT58/1243. For full details of the British government's response see the press cuttings from the Times, Financial Times and the Guardian in the file TNA: PRO, BT58/1243.
22. Ne'eman to Simchoni, 5 December, 14 December, 15 December 1963 (all Hebrew original), PLILMR, IV-219A-1-106.
23. Inland Revenue Staff Federation to the TUC, 13 December 1963, MRC, MSS.292B/901/4.
24. Ne'eman to Simchoni, 5 December, 14 December, 15 December 1963 (all Hebrew original), PLILMR, IV-219A-1-106.
25. TUC report IC3/3 "Activities of the Arab boycott office", 17 December 1963, MRC, MSS.292B/901/4.
26. The TUC were considering supporting the ICFTU call for a boycott South Africa. Ne'eman to Simchoni, 24 December 1963 (Hebrew original), PLILMR, IV-219A-1-106 and TUC International committee minutes, 17 December 1963, MRC, MSS.292B/901/4.
27. TUC press statement, 18 December 1963, ISSH: ICFTU, 2887D.
28. Israel ambassador to Marx, 11 August 1965 and Marx reply, 6 September 1965 (both Hebrew original), PLILMR, IV-219A-7-254.
29. Levin to Ne'eman, 30 April 1963, PLILMR, IV-219A-1-123C and Simchoni to Becker, 5 June 1963 (both Hebrew original), PLILMR, IV-219A-1-97B.
30. Ne'eman to Simchoni, 5 May 1963 (Hebrew original), PLILMR, IV-104-286-1-320 and Marshall to MOL, 7 November 1963, TNA: PRO, LAB13/1764.
31. Marx to Simchoni, 12 October 1964, PLILMR, IV-219A-1-129A and 24 November 1964 (both Hebrew original), PLILMR, IV-219A-1-142B.
32. 'Britain's views on Arab-Israel issues outlined to Eshkol in London', Jewish Telegraph Agency, 28 March 1965 and Marx to Simchoni, 30 March 1965 (Hebrew original), PLILMR, IV-219A-1-142C.

33. Levin to Simchoni, 30 March 1965, Marx to Simchoni, 30 March 1965 (both Hebrew original), both IV-219A-1-142C.
34. Ambassador Beith to the foreign secretary, 13 January 1966, TNA: PRO, LAB13/2445.
35. Perdo to Levin, 21 December 1965 (Hebrew original), PLILMR, IV-219A-1-129B.
36. Minutes of the ICFTU Executive Board, 30 November 1964, TUC International Committee minutes, 19 February 1965, MRC, MSS.292B/901/5.
37. ICFTU to Levin, 16 June 1965, ISSH: ICFTU, 3505 and Marx to Simchoni, 23 June 1965 (Hebrew original), PLILMR, IV-219A-1-160A.
38. The ICFTU contacted the Lawyers International organisation in Geneva and the TUC protested to Syrian embassy in London. Marx to Levin, 18 May 1965 (Hebrew original), PLILMR, IV-219A-1-142C, Woodcock to Aldouby, 1 December 1969, MRC, MSS.292B/956.9/1.
39. The TUC reported that the General Assembly of European Free Trade Unions had adopted a resolution urging that Israel's request should be urgently expedited. TUC International Committee minutes, 25 November 1966, MRC, MSS.292B/901/7 and Becker to Buiter, 16 October 1966, ISA, HZ1389/28.
40. Author's interview with Geoffrey Goodman, biographer of Frank Cousins, London, 11 November 2007.
41. Author's interview with Mike Walsh, Head of TUC International Department, 1980–99, London, 29 November 2012.
42. The Histadrut telegram to the 24 unions, 24 May 1967, PLILMR, IV-219A-6-29.
43. Alfred Braunthal, ICFTU deputy general secretary to Becker, 31 May 1967. Messages of support were received by the Histadrut and the ICFTU from labour organisations in Germany, France, Austria, Luxemburg, Norway, Sweden, Denmark, Peru, Holland and 13 other international labour and trade federations, all ISSH:ICFTU, 3509 and the NVV Holland, ISA, HZ1389/28.
44. The minutes of the TUC's International committee and the General Council which met on the 23 May, do not show that there was any discussion of events and the speed at which the TUC issued a statement the next day indicates that Woodcock, Hayday and Cousins must have previously discussed and agreed the TUC's rapid response. Copies of the statement were sent to the British Government, the UN, the Israeli and Egyptian Governments, the Labour Party, the ICFTU, the Histadrut and the Federation of Labour of the United Arab Republic. TUC General Council minutes, 23 May 1967, MRC, MSS.292B/901/8.
45. TGWU to the Israeli embassy London, 6 June 1967, ISA, HZ1389/28.

46. PHM, LP/ID 1967 Middle East, Palestine, Israel.
47. Resolution on the Middle East, the Bureau of the Socialist International, 26 May 1967, LSE, Levenberg G/5/2.
48. TUC briefing note, 11 June 1967, MRC, MSS292B/956/3.
49. Leading the party's attacks on Israel was Bert Ramelson, a fervent anti-Zionist Jew who believed that Jewishness was defined only by religion and not nationality. Ramelson wrote that '*Zionism as an ideology is based on false premises*" which was '*incapable of solving the real problems of the Jews.*" He maintained that Israel's '*military, financial, strategic*" force depended on '*imperialist arms and general support in exchange for acting as the West's watchdog in the Middle East.*" Bert Ramelson, "The Middle East, crisis causes, solution", Communist Party pamphlet, 1967.
50. The letter is not in the files but is mentioned in the TUC International Committee minutes, 12 June 1967, MRC, MSS.292B/901/8.
51. The International Confederation of Arab Trade Unions to the ICFTU, 17 May 1967, The UAR Federation of Labour to the ICFTU, 27 May 1967 and The Arab Federation of Petroleum Workers to ICFTU, 30 May 1967, all ISSH:ICFTU, 3509. Also TUC International Committee minutes, 12 June 1967, MRC, MSS.292B/901/8.
52. Briefing note for the TUC International Committee, 11 June 1967, MRC, MSS.292B-956-3.
53. TUC International Committee minutes, 12 June 1967, MRC, MSS.292B/901/8.
54. Skinner to the MOL, 1 January 1968, TNA: PRO, LAB13/2180.
55. Skinner to the MOL, 22 August 1967, TNA: PRO, LAB13/2445.
56. Skinner to the MOL, 23 June 1967, TNA: PRO, LAB13/2440 and 22 August 1967, TNA: PRO, LAB13/2445.
57. Author's interview with Hanan Lehman, the Histadrut European representative 1968–71, Tel Aviv, 30 September 2005.
58. TUC International Committee minutes, 27 June 1967, MRC, MSS.292B/901/8.
59. Marx letter to Becker, 14 July 1967 (Hebrew original), PLILMR, IV-219A-3-32.
60. Marx report to Haring of Becker's meeting with the TUC, 10 August 1967 (Hebrew original), PLILMR, IV-219A-3-32.
61. Ibid.
62. 'Cousins to visit Israel', *The Guardian*, 13 August 1967.
63. Woodcock made this point to the pre-Congress General Council discussion. TUC General Council minutes, 31 August 1967, MRC, MSS.292B/956.9.3.
64. John W. Young, *The Labour Governments 1964–70, Vol. 2: International Policy* (Manchester: Manchester University Press, 2003), p. 109.

65. When Bevin was foreign secretary he sent Feather to Greece on a similar mission. Geoffrey Goodman, '*The Awkward Warrior; Frank Cousins: His Life and Times*', pp. 536–537.
66. Skinner to MOL, 22 August 1967, TNA: PRO, LAB13/2445.
67. British ambassador to Israel to the foreign secretary, 24 August 1967, TNA: PRO, LAB13/2440.
68. TUC General Council minutes, 31 August 1967, MRC, MSS.292B/956.9.3.
69. TUC Congress 1967 report, The Middle East debate, pp. 489–492.
70. Marx to Becker, 8 September 1967 (Hebrew original), PLILMR, IV-219A-3-33.
71. Lebanon Federation of Trade Unions letter to the TUC, 15 September 1967, ISSH: ICFTU, 3510.
72. Marx to Haring, 27 September 1967 (Hebrew original), PLILMR, IV-219A-3-32.
73. Barritt to MOL, 12 October 1967, TNA: PRO, LAB13/2599, the ICFTU Executive Board meeting, 4–6 October 1967, Item 8, 43EB/8e(i), ISSH: ICFTU, 3506, The ICFTU Press release, PRS/41, 12 October 1967, TNA: PRO, LAB13/2599 and the TUC International Committee minutes, 24 October 1967, MRC, MSS.292B/901/9.
74. "Arabs and Israelis sit on same labour committee", *The Jerusalem Post*, 13 October 1967.
75. The minutes of the ICFTU ad hoc Committee on the Middle East, 20 November 1968, 44EB/8[b], ISSH: ICFTU, 3513, TUC International Committee minutes, 23 July 1968, MRC, MSS.292B/956.9.3.
76. Notes of a discussion on the ICFTU between the British and American labour attachés based in Beirut. The British labour attaché in Beirut to Foggon, MOL, 24 January 1968, TNA: PRO, LAB13/2599. By 1968 the TUC no longer considered political propaganda, such as preventing a communist takeover as an important or primary justification to keep the Beirut office open. Marx to Haring, 28 February 1968 (Hebrew original), PLILMR, IV-219A-3-30.
77. Anthony Carew, *The International Confederation of Free Trade Unions* (Berlin: Peter Lang 2000), pp. 311–312.
78. Foggon to Moore FCO, 27 September 1967, Foggon to the Secretary of State for Foreign Affairs, 28 November 1967, briefing notes for Sir R. Beaumont, 1 December 1967 and the Eastern Department briefing notes, 5 December, 1967, all TNA: PRO, FCO17/42.
79. Foggon recommended visits to Libya, Sudan, Morocco and Tunisia but not Algeria, Syria, Iraq, Kuwait, Aden. He did not totally reject a visit to Egypt. Foggon to FCO North and East African Dept, 5 October 1967, TNA: PRO, FCO17/42.

80. Foggon to Fred Mulley, Secretary of State for Foreign Affairs, 28 November 1967, TNA: PRO, FCO17/42.
81. Haighton, FCO to Moore, Eastern Dept, 10 October 1967, TNA: PRO, FCO17/42.
82. Foggon to Maitland FCO 27 November 1967, TNA: PRO, FCO17/42.
83. Arbuthnott, FCO to Eastern Dept, 7 December 1967, TNA: PRO, FCO17/42.
84. Moore, file note, 8 December 1967, TNA: PRO, FCO17/42.
85. Moore, FCO, to Benchley and Maitland, FCO, 27 November 1967, TNA: PRO, FCO17/42.
86. Report of visit to Jordan and the Lebanon, IC4/3, TUC International Committee minutes, 19 and 23 December 1967, MRC, MSS.292B/901/9.
87. Foggon to Barritt, 11 January1968, TNA: PRO, LAB13/2599.
88. TUC International Committee minutes, 21 November 1967, MRC, MSS.292B/901/9.
89. Draft report of the TUC visit to Egypt, 4–9 March 1968, TUC International Committee minutes, 26 March and 23 April 1968, TUC General Council minutes, 27 March 1968, all MRC, MSS.292B/9.56.9.3.
90. Note of a discussion on Arab Labour affairs with representatives of the British trade union movement, Morris, the British labour attaché in Beirut to the Foreign Office, 9 September 1969, TNA: PRO, LAB13/2680.
91. Just over 300 Labour MPs were members of the Labour Friends of Israel and 105 Labour MPs were signatories to a 1967 pro-Israel Parliamentary Early Day Motion compared with 19 Labour MPs who signed a pro-Arab Early Day Motion. Edmunds, *The Left and Israel: Party Policy Change and internal Democracy*, pp. 64–71.
92. Michael Stewart, *Life and Labour: an autobiography* (London: Sidgwick & Jackson, 1980), p. 213.
93. Foreign Office review "British influence and organised labour overseas", February 1965, TNA: PRO, FO1110/199.
94. The TUC and the CBI issued a press release welcoming the establishment of the OLCC, 5 September 1967, TNA: PRO, LAB13/2474.
95. "Labour and trade unions in the Arab Countries of the Middle East" Paper prepared by the OLCC, TNA: PRO, LAB13/2625. Minutes of the 2nd Meeting of the OLCC, 2 February 1968, TNA: PRO, FCO59/493.
96. Foggon to Johnson FCO, 1 May1968, TNA: PRO, FCO77/20.
97. Lehmann to Haring, 29 September 1969 (Hebrew original), PLILMR, IV-219A-3-15.
98. TUC International Committee minutes, 24 March 1970, MSS.292B/901/12 and the Meeting of the OLCC, 15 May 1970, TNA: PRO, LAB13/2625.

99. TUC International Committee minutes, 30 October 1970, MRC, MSS.292D/901/1.
100. The territories occupied by Israel in the Six-Day War in 1967 were the West Bank which had been formally annexed by Jordan in 1950, the Gaza strip which was occupied by Egypt in 1949, the Egyptian Sinai peninsula and the Syrian Golan Heights. Israel returned the Sinai Peninsula to Egypt after signing the 1979 Israel-Egypt peace treaty.

    When the Israeli government and its supporters refer to the 'occupied territories' they mean the Israeli-occupied West Bank which some Israelis call Judea and Samaria. They do not consider the Gaza Strip to be occupied as Israel unilaterally withdrew from the Gaza Strip in 2005 and which is now controlled by Hamas.

    When the Palestinian National Authority and it supporters use the term 'occupied territories' they mean the West Bank, East Jerusalem, and the Gaza Strip.

    The West Bank, East Jerusalem, and the Gaza Strip are subject to the jurisdiction of Israel and the Palestinian National Authority, with the division of responsibilities overlapping in much of the territory.
101. Liberation letter to TUC, 8 April 1983, MRC, MSS292D/956/511/3.
102. Skinner letter to MOL, 16 November 1967, TNA: PRO, LAB13/2440 and Hagai to Haring (Hebrew original), November 1967, PLILMR, IV-219A-3-47.
103. Skinner letter to Oates, MOL, 27 November 1968, TNA: PRO, LAB13/2590.
104. Address by Becker to the TUC Congress, 2 September 1968, MRC, TUC Congress report 1968, and pp. 82–83.
105. 'Becker reports on TUC Conference', *The Jerusalem Post*, 13 September 1968.
106. Report of the visit of Histadrut delegation to Britain, 27 October 1968 (Hebrew original), PLILMR, IV-208-1-14407 and Lehman to Haring, 5 November 1968 (Hebrew original), PLILMR, IV-219A-3-14.
107. 'Middle East', MRC, TUC Congress report 1968, pp. 288–289.
108. Reuven Barkatt presented a 10-year review of the Histadrut's international activity to the Histadrut Executive Committee, Histadrut Executive Committee meeting minutes, 4 March 1958 (Hebrew original), pp. 161–174.
109. Marx letter to Haring, 6 March 1968 (Hebrew original), PLILMR, IV-219A-3-30.
110. Marx to Morratt, 25 April 1968, PLILMR, IV-219A-3-41 and Oates File note MOL, 2 May 1968, TNA: PRO, LAB13/2673.
111. Author's interview with Hanan Lehman, Histadrut European representative 1968–71, Tel Aviv, 22 October 2004.

112. In September 1969, the 12th Congress of the International Federation of Building and Woodworkers was held in Tel Aviv which was the first time it had met outside Europe. Delegates came from seventeen different countries including Britain. Skinner report for 1969 to the DEP, 3 February 1970, TNA: PRO, LAB13/2180.
113. Letter from the Israel embassy in London to Israeli Foreign Ministry, 10 December 1971 (Hebrew original), PLILMR, IV-219A-4-7A.
114. Draft report on Afro-Asian Institute, 23 November 1967, LAB13/2006.
115. Michael Curtiss (Ed.), *Israel in the Third World* (New Jersey: Transaction Books, 1976), pp. 393–397.
116. Skinner letter to MOL, 14 April 1967, LAB13/2440 and TUC General Council minutes, 23 May 1967, MSS.292B/901/8.
117. Feather to Eger Afro-Asian Institute, 18 April 1972, MRC, MSS292D/956.9/508/1.
118. TUC International Committee minutes, 21 March 1972, MRC, MSS.292D/901/3.
119. TUC memo Kolarz to Hargreaves, 8 March 1972, MRC, MSS292D/956.9/508/1, Afro-Asian Institute to Feather, 11 January 1972, MRC, MSS292D/956.9/508/1.
120. Yagol to Ben Aharon, 12 June 1972 (Hebrew original), PLILMR, IV-219A-5-17.
121. "France puts Israeli plea for El Al passengers", *The Guardian*, 26 July 1968.
122. Haring to Buiter, 24 July 1968, ISSH: ICFTU, 3520.
123. ICFTU press release, 30 July 1968 and ITF Congress resolution meeting, Wiesbaden, 28 July–3 August 1968. Affiliates who responded included the AFL-CIO, the Canadian unions, the Swiss Federation of Trade Unions and the Colombian trade unions, all ISSH: ICFTU, 3520.
124. Haring to Lehmann, 9 August 1968 (Hebrew original), PLILMR, IV-219A-3-14.
125. Kolarz to Woodcock, 7 August 1968, MRC, MSS.292B/956.9/2.
126. TUC International Committee minutes, 20 August 1968, MRC, MSS.292B/901/9.
127. Woodcock to the Union Generale des Travailleurs Algeriens, 27 August 1968, MRC, MSS.292B/956.9/1.
128. Histadrut to ICFTU, 1 September 1968, ISSH: ICFTU, 3520.
129. '2 Arab Terrorists Attack Israeli Jetliner in Athens; Arab Terrorists Attack an Israeli Jet in Athens', *New York Times*, 26 December 1968.
130. 'Israelis attack Beirut airport; wreck 13 planes,' *New York Times*, 29 December 1968.
131. 'Israelis attack censured by UN, vote unanimous,' *New York Times*, 1 January 1969.

132. Author's interview with Mike Walsh, TUC International Department 1966–99, London, 29 November 2012.
133. Lehmann to Haring, 20 January 1969 (Hebrew original), PLILMR, IV-219A-3-15.
134. Lehmann to Haring, 4 February1969 (Hebrew original), PLILMR, IV-219A-3-15.
135. "Iraq Hangs 16, Including 10 Jews, as Israeli spies," *New York Times*, 27 January 1969, p. 1.
136. Histadrut to TUC, 4 February 1969, MRC, MSS.292B/956.9.3 and Histadrut to ICFTU 28 January 1969 ISSH: ICFTU, 3522.
137. Hargreaves to Feather, 6 February 1969, MRC, MSS.292B/956.9.3.
138. TUC General Council minutes, 25 February 1969, MRC, MSS.292B/956.9.3 and MSS.292B/901/10.
139. TUC briefing notes, 17 March 1969, MRC, MSS.292B/956.9.3.
140. TUC General Council minutes, 25 February 1969, MRC, MSS.292B/956.9.3 and MSS.292B/901/10.
141. The report of the meeting with the foreign secretary, 18 March 1969, TUC Press release IC6/3, 19 March 1969, TUC International Committee minutes, 25 March 1969, all MRC, MSS.292B/956.9.3.
142. Feather to Foreign Office, 5 September 1972, MRC, MSS.292D/956/511/1.
143. MRC, TUC Congress proceedings 1972, pp. 505–506.
144. Yagol to Ben Aharon, 14 September 1972 (Hebrew original), PLILMR, IV-219A-5-17.
145. "Wilson: Labour outraged", *The Guardian*, 6 September1972.

CHAPTER 5

The Move to Outright Criticism of Israel

If the 1960s were the golden years for TUC-Histadrut cooperation, then the 1970s signified a move towards increased support for the Palestinians matched by a falling away in support for Israel. Not only was the TUC moving towards the Left but the younger members of the Labour Party and the unions especially those on the Far left both at grassroots and leadership level were beginning to show an active interest in foreign affairs and the Arab-Israeli conflict by questioning Labour's previous, traditional support for Israel at the expense of the Palestinian Arabs. Other factors included the renewed interest in the Arab world by both the British Government and the TUC and the Arab unions which had started to lobby the TUC and the ICFTU to specifically counter Histadrut and Israeli influence.

Anglo-Israel Relations

Throughout this period, Britain continued its gradual move away from Israeli positions and towards support for the Arab and Palestinian view even though two of Britain's three prime ministers, Wilson and Thatcher were seen as pro-Israel. The Foreign Office began to reappraise its relationship with Israel in 1976 when Callaghan replaced Wilson, the result of which was that Britain took a much more critical line with Israel. The British government viewed the settlements in the West Bank and Gaza as a serious threat to the peace process.

R. Fraser, *British Trade Unions, the Labour Party, and Israel's Histadrut*, https://doi.org/10.1007/978-3-030-86814-7_5

Although Britain continued to support Israeli interests which included the blocking of the 'Zionism is racism' issue at the UN and opposition to both the creeping legitimisation of the PLO and the Arab boycott; the Foreign Office had unofficial contacts with the PLO. Both Mrs. Thatcher and the Foreign Office believed that pressure had to be put on Israel to make concessions using the 'land for peace' formula and were irritated by the lack of progress in the peace process. She also used her position as a friend of Israel to criticise actions of the Begin government, such as Israel's bombing of Iraq's nuclear reactor in 1981 and the Knesset vote to annex the Golan Heights which were seen as having the potential to lead to renewed fighting. Israel's invasion of Lebanon in 1982 only added to British concerns and frustration.

The Left and the TUC

The final two years of the 1960s were momentous years both in Britain and abroad. In 1968 there was the anti-war movement protests against the Vietnam war and the worldwide student revolution, while in Britain in 1969, the government issued its white paper 'In Place of Strife' aimed at curbing trade union 'power' which had dominated the industrial scene for most of the decade. There was a direct link between the Far Left's involvement in the 1968 student revolution and the change in the attitude of the Labour Party and the unions towards Israel during the following decade.

Although the media portrayed this period as the age of student revolution, the British student movement protests compared to those in France and the United States were much less radical and less violent. Nevertheless a minority of revolutionary students and far Left Trotskyist groups used the opportunity to influence the majority of British students, who were not politically motivated, encouraging them to join them in demonstrations against the authorities. The result was that Trotskyist groups such as the International Marxist Group (IMG) and International Socialists (IS) were very active in the protests and played a central role in organising many of the demonstrations and sit-ins.

By 1969 the leadership of the TUC was controlled by left-wing trade union leaders who led the confrontation with the Wilson government's White Paper which attempted to use the law to reduce the power of the unions. These proposals never passed into law and were replaced in the 1970s by a voluntary agreement brokered by the TUC. During the 1970s the TUC's priorities also changed, focusing on closer cooperation with their European colleagues. The two most influential left-wingers were Hugh Scanlon, president of the AEU, and Jack Jones who, in 1969 had succeeded Frank Cousins as General Secretary of the TGWU were behind the move towards a closer relationship with the Soviet Union and Eastern bloc. On international human rights, Jones took a 'trade union point of view' by supporting protests and sanctions against government policy on trade unions in Bolivia, Chile, South Africa and Spain. He considered that trade union rights were the proper concern of trade union leaders but not human rights, which were a matter for Amnesty International.[1]

Jones who had fought with the International Brigade in Spain was a lifelong supporter of the Left and the Soviet Union. Although he always gave the impression that he had never been a member of the CPGB it is believed he was a member from 1932 onwards and was reported to have left the party in 1949. Jones resumed contact with the CPGB 15 years later and during the 1960s passed confidential Labour Party documents to the Russians.[2] He was someone with whom the Communists felt comfortable and with their help was elected TGWU General Secretary. However because of his long-term connections and his desire for the TUC to normalise relations with the Soviet Union, Jones opposed all moves for the TUC to support the public campaign to allow Soviet Jews to emigrate to Israel. Yet behind the scenes the TUC worked for the release of individual Russian Jews.

The Histadrut were in regular contact with Jones as chairman of the international committee and saw him as a friend of Israel, which he was. Jones said that his friendly attitude and sympathy towards the Jews and Israel was conditioned by his mother who had a high regard for Jewish people.[3] Jones nevertheless opposed all moves for the TUC to support the campaign to allow Jews from the USSR to emigrate to Israel. He also opposed Arab attempts to bring Middle East politics to the international trade union movement. Although he was personally horrified at the politicisation of the ILO, the TUC supported the compromise regarding the recognition of the PLO. Behind the scenes however the TUC worked with the ICFTU to build up relations between the Histadrut and the Palestinian unions.[4]

Although Cousins, Hayday and Jones had held the line against the Left who were becoming anti-Israel, when they retired they were replaced by a new cadre, who had been ignored by the Histadrut, and saw Israel in a different light. This move to the Left both within the Labour party and the unions meant that by 1972, Labour's traditional support for Israel was being questioned by grass roots left-wing activists who were beginning to show an active interest in foreign affairs and the Arab-Israeli conflict in particular.

Labour's Support for Israel

The move to the Left amongst the leadership of the larger trade unions at the end of the 1960s committed the Labour Party NEC to socialist economic policies, but the shift did not immediately affect the Party's policy on the Middle East, which remained pro-Israel. The situation started to change around the time of the Yom Kippur War in 1973. Although the Parliamentary Labour Party supported Wilson's pro-Israel stance, many local constituency parties did not, adopting instead a pro-Arab stance. The activists responsible for these changes, where former students who came from the two main Trotskyist groups, Militant and Socialist Organiser, which grew out of the IMG and had infiltrated Labour Party constituency organisations with the aim of influencing Labour policies and the party's attitude towards Israel. As had happened in 1968, it only took a small number of activists to instigate these changes.

The International Socialists (IS) concentrated on infiltrating the unions and in 1977 transformed themselves into a political party, the Socialist Workers Party (SWP) with 4000 members, it was the largest Trotskyist party in Britain. The SWP leader was Tony Cliff aka Yigal Gluckstein, who was born in Palestine in 1917. This in part explains the anti-Israel animus of the SWP which was virulently anti-Zionist, insisting that it was not antisemitic, only anti-Zionist; it denied that the Jews were a nation and characterised them as primarily a religious group.

By the early 1980s Militant supporters were well established within the Labour Party and two unions in particular, the Civil and Public Services Association (CPSA) and The Post Office Engineering Union (POEU). *Socialist Organiser*, a weekly socialist newspaper, associated itself with leading figures on the left of the Party, such as Tony Benn and Ken Livingstone. Many Far Left activists advocated anti-Zionist themes, equating Zionism with racism.

Support for Israel within the Labour Party and the unions had also waned due to the retirement of the generation of MPs, party members and trade unionists who had witnessed the plight of the Jews during the Second World War and sympathised with the establishment of the State of Israel. They had been replaced by a number of MPs and local activists for whom the problems of the Palestinians were more important than Labour's traditional identification with the Jews and Israel. Nor did it help that British Jews who in the 1930s and 1940s had been natural supporters of the Labour Party had by the 1970s also moved away from the Party. The electoral significance of Jewish voters was taken over by the Afro-Caribbean immigrant population who were more receptive to supporting third world movements like the PLO.

The Histadrut's stock along with that of its partner in government, the Israeli Labour Alignment gradually declined throughout the 1970s. Although the Alignment managed to hold onto power until 1977, the Histadrut was by then in need of radical reorganisation having lost influence and prestige. The stunning victory of the right-wing Likud party in Israel's 1977 general election led to Israel's remaining friends in the Labour Party questioning their continuing support for Israel.

The Pro-Arab Lobby in Britain

There was also the emergence of pro-Arab groups in Britain which countered the influence of the pro-Israel lobby. The largest and oldest of these organisations were the Council for the Advancement of Arab-British Understanding (CAABU) established in 1967 and the Labour Middle East Council (LMEC) formed in 1969. CAABU's aim was to foster understanding and sympathy between Britain the Arab world; its General Committee included MPs, former government ministers and former British ambassadors to Arab states. LMEC was a pro-Arab pressure group which operated mainly within Parliament but was not affiliated to the Labour Party. Both groups were instrumental in building connections between the PLO and the Labour Party. The pro-Arab lobby was also successful on university campuses during the 1970s as a result of a coalition between Palestinian, Arab and Left-wing British students. Other than CAABU and LMEC the lobby consisted of a number of small organisations often founded by the same people in order to attract a wide range of supporters including trade unionists, students and politicians. One of these groups, the Trade Union Friends of Palestine (TUFP) operated from the same offices as CAABU, had close links with the PLO and the Palestine Trade Unions Federation (PTUF), who also operated from the same address as the Arab League.

TUC Reaction to the 1973 War

The signs of change were apparent in 1973 with the TUC's response to the Yom Kippur War which was even more muted than their reaction to the 1967 Six-Day War.

The British ambassador to Israel reported in January 1973 that the Israelis were not happy with Britain's approach to the Arab-Israel dispute but they recognised her wide interests in the Arab world which could not be put at risk.[5] Both countries were concerned about the impact of Britain's recent entry into the EEC and how it would affect them. The key domestic issue for the Israeli trade unionists at the start of 1973 was the same as for their counterparts in Britain, the economy and the rising cost of living.

Yagol, the Histadrut's European representative, reported that the TUC's long term aim was to build a strong European organisation of unions (The ETUC) as well as rebuild relations with the Communist bloc. He noted that this change of direction could seriously harm both Israel's and the Histadrut's position in the international labour movement especially as the Histadrut had recently failed to achieve official ETUC recognition. Their application had been refused even though Jones, and Len Murray, the incoming General Secretary of the TUC, had both indicated that they had supported the Histadrut's plans.

On October 6, 1973, Yom Kippur (the Day of Atonement), the holiest day in the Jewish religious calendar, Egypt and Syria simultaneously launched a surprise attack against Israel. Egyptian forces crossed ceasefire lines to enter the Israeli held Sinai Peninsula and the Syrian Army moved into the Golan Heights, which had been occupied by Israel since the 1967 war. Within a week the Israelis had successfully counterattacked and the war ended on 24 October when both sides agreed to a UN brokered truce.

The Histadrut immediately sent telegrams to the ICFTU and its leading affiliates, including the TUC, saying that Israel had been attacked on the holiest Jewish holiday asking them to demand that the aggressors withdraw their forces and resume peaceful negotiations. The same day, Murray received a separate telegram from the Histadrut asking for a '*public expression of solidarity with Israel.*'[6]

On 7 October, Harold Wilson, the leader of the Labour Party who had been contacted by the Israeli ambassador, immediately published an announcement condemning the attack.[7] Once again, as in 1956 and 1967, the Party leaders were briefed on the latest developments by Israeli diplomats. The Party was not concerned about British government policy and condemned Israel's' attackers and the Government's pro-Arab bias. Their statement, which included their correspondence with the Israeli Labour Party, noted that the majority of the Labour MP's had voted against the Government's embargo policy.

The TUC however did nothing until TUC International committee meeting on 23 October. The Histadrut paid the price for moving to Brussels, when Yagol contacted Murray on 19 October he was told that it was unlikely that Murray would be able to get back to him for several days. Yagol left a message for Murray that all ETUC affiliates had been approached asking if they would support the workers in Israel who were victims of the war and asked for a contribution from the TUC. He added that the Dutch, Belgian, Austrian and West German unions had agreed either to make direct financial contributions or donations of medical supplies or equipment.[8] The Committee was divided over the Histadrut's request, as some members thought it committed the Europeans to providing aid to only one side rather than both sides in the conflict. The Committee eventually agreed to make a token donation of £250 to the Red Cross after being told that it had been the long-established policy of the TUC to provide assistance through bodies such as the Red Cross. Feather then wrote to Yagol explaining why they were unable to agree to the Histadrut's request.[9]

The TUC also issued a statement, which appealed to the trade unions of those countries involved to call on their governments to keep the cease-fire. It failed to mention the combatants by name, apportion blame for starting the war, or criticise the Government arms embargo.[10] The Histadrut were concerned that the phrase '*lasting peace*' was linked to a '*realistic solution*' and '*for all the peoples of the region*' meaning the Palestinians. Yagol noted that the TUC's position on the war was the most anti-Israel in Western Europe with the exception of Italy and France. By comparison, the AFL-CIO's statement emphasised its support for Israel and condemned the actions of the Soviet authorities in the Middle East.[11]

In the aftermath of the war Yagol met the TUC twice to discuss the conflict and the TUC's response to the war. As a result of these conversations he recommended to the Histadrut that they should ignore the '*warm and emotional attitude*' shown by '*some of our British friends*' and that they should review their relationship and connections with all the European unions especially the British whose disengagement from Israel, Yagol believed, had come as the result of the TUC's move towards Europe and their desire to work more closely with the USSR.

Yagol had realised that Jones, Scanlon and Feather's friendship with the Histadrut had only made it easier for them to support their conciliatory position towards the Palestinians and the Arab terror. Whilst the impression of Soviet interference and the TUC General Council's anti-American stance had only increased their hostility towards Israel, Murray, Jones and Hargreaves, the Head of the International department, all had claimed that they were not surprised by the Arab attack.[12]

The TUC had failed to answer Yagol's questions about Arab aggression and why they had not mentioned their long-standing friendship with the Histadrut. In order to play down their disagreement, the TUC explained that their statement was limited to one issue, the implementation of the ceasefire and the ending of hostilities. All he was offered was that the General Council would look for an opportunity to publicise their friendship and consider the possibility of Murray visiting Israel.

Yagol understood that the TUC's neutrality in the conflict was due to their belief that they had an active role to play in the Middle East crisis. Hargreaves confirmed this by claiming that '*you shall need us and our intervention. You won't be able to manage without intervention and coercion from outside*'. Hargreaves, he wrote in his report, followed Foreign Office policy and would never do or say anything without first getting 'guidance'. Jones confirmed that the TUC's caution towards Israel was caused by Hargreaves influence and described him as a Foreign Office agent. Yagol noted '*It is noticeable that in the past he was offended by something we did, either real or imagined attitude*'. What was clear was that the TUC lacked strong leadership on this issue and with no consensus on the Council it allowed Hargreaves to present a viable alternative that everyone could support.[13]

Israel Gat, who represented the Israel Labour Party in London, was so concerned by the TUC's lack of solidarity towards Israel both during and after the war that he wrote to the Histadrut saying that it was impossible to deal satisfactorily from Brussels with an organisation the size and importance of the TUC. He urged the Histadrut to take action before it was to late by appointing a Histadrut representative to London as well as a labour attaché at the London embassy.[14]

Since its move to Brussels five years earlier, the Histadrut's priority had been the ICFTU and with Cousins retirement, the TUC's focus was the ETUC and improving links with the Soviet Union; which meant they were no longer playing the lead European role in the ICFTU and had been replaced by the Germans and the Scandinavians who were very supportive of Israel. The Histadrut's change of priority also meant that they no longer attempted to seriously lobby the TUC and were therefore to blame for the TUC's response to the war.

Once the fighting had stopped, the Histadrut and the Arab unions restarted lobbying the ICFTU. The Histadrut were unhappy with what they saw as the ICFTU's lack of support during the recent hostilities. Yagol reported that they had wanted to repair the '*shocking impression their former declarations made, but the general attitude is superficial, evasive and insincere*'.[15] He also referred to both the West German DGB and the TUC when highlighting his concerns that the rise in the anti-Israeli and anti-Histadrut attitudes in Europe had been in some part due to the Europeans strengthening their connections with the Soviet bloc. He was concerned that many European trade unionists, mainly in Belgium, had avoided meetings and discussions with him because they were unwilling to commit support for the Histadrut and the TUC's statement focussing on humanitarian aid was an example of this practice.[16]

British Government Action

In July 1973 the Foreign Office decided that in order to save money Israeli labour issues would be covered in future by the labour attaché based in Athens, who would visit Israel at regular intervals. The problems that had beset the Histadrut when they moved to Brussels were about to be repeated and the Foreign Office would soon discover that long term personal relationships and understanding that had been built up over time could not be maintained by spending a few days in Israel every few months.

After the Yom Kippur war, Britain reassessed its policy towards Israel because of the Arab threat to cut off oil supplies to the UK. This revised policy meant that while Israel's security should not be compromised, Britain's extensive interests in the Arab world meant that they had to be more sensitive to Arab attitudes than Israeli ones. The UK was also aware that the Arab states blamed Britain for the establishment of the State of Israel because of the Balfour declaration and Britain's decision to hand back the mandate. The TUC were encouraged by the Foreign Office to back this strategy by rebuilding relations with the Arab trade unions.

In July 1974, the foreign secretary, told the TUC that the Government had maintained a non-aligned approach to the conflict in order to help both sides. The TUC replied saying that it had taken a similar position in order to re-establish contact with the Arab trade unions whilst maintaining the friendship of the Histadrut. When they met again the following year the TUC suggested that in order to reach a peaceful settlement in the Middle East the Government should try to counteract the impression that Britain was favouring Israel. James Callaghan, the foreign secretary answered by saying that the Labour Party had made no secret of their close friendship with Israel or their desire to maintain those close relationships but also had made it clear that they wanted closer relations with the Arab States.

In March 1974, the Histadrut held its 12th national convention which provided an opportunity for the international trade union movement to show solidarity with the Histadrut. Whilst the French, German, Belgian and Dutch unions immediately accepted, Murray rejected the TUC's invitation citing pressure of work. When Yagol asked him to reconsider, Murray was advised by Hargreaves that '*in the present circumstances given the General Council's strict impartiality with regard to the Middle East conflict it might be wise if we avoided accepting invitations in that area*'.[17] The International committee decided however that although the TUC had not previously attended the convention in order to not to appear to take sides in the conflict, a refusal this time could be misunderstood. They decided to send Hugh Scanlon, a senior member of the General Council, who would be able to explain the TUC's approach to the conflict. After informing the Histadrut that Scanlon would attend, Scanlon withdrew. The General Council were unable to find a replacement and sent fraternal greetings which stated that the very serious political and economic situation in Britain had prevented Scanlon from attending. Although it appeared that the TUC had wanted to do the right thing, it is hardly surprising that no replacement for Scanlon was found so soon after the recent war. Scanlon, a powerful personality who had been to Israel before, knew that it was politically expedient for him to turn down the invitation.[18] Although their decision not to attend the convention could have been calculated not offend their Arab friends, the General Council decided to invite the Histadrut to attend their next Congress and resolved that Murray should visit Israel during the next year. The Histadrut knew of his unfamiliarity with the Arab-Israeli conflict and the urgent need for Murray to visit Israel.[19]

As a reaction to the Ma'alot killing of 22 children by three armed Palestinian terrorists on 15 May 1974, the Histadrut wrote to the TUC insisting that they unequivocally condemned this atrocity and actively supported the Histadrut's demand to immediately convene the ICFTU Executive Board. Hargreaves advised Murray that there was no need for independent TUC action as the ICFTU Executive Board would be meeting at the end of May. He also told him that retaliatory action by the Israelis had resulted in heavy Palestinian casualties in refugee camps in the Lebanon and that '*both sides are at fault and the most constructive and charitable approach*'[20] would be to hope that Kissinger's peace-making attempts succeed. Hargreaves concluded by saying that we should adopt this line at the ICFTU. Although the ICFTU had initially condemned the incident, they took no further action.

The Labour Friends of Israel

The Labour Friends of Israel (LFI) was founded in 1956, after the Suez crisis, to promote support for Israel throughout the British labour movement and to strengthen the links between the British Labour Party, the trade unions and the Israeli Labour Party. In order to try and fill the void left by the Histadrut move to Brussels, the LFI concentrated its efforts on building support amongst the leadership of trade unions by taking many delegations to Israel for both Labour MP's and trade union officials. Union leaders who supported the LFI during the 1970's included Joe Gormley (NUM), Gavin Laird (AEEU), Clive Jenkins (ASTMS) and Geoffrey Drain (NALGO). In 1975, the LFI urged the Histadrut to appoint an UK representative because of the deteriorating relationship with the unions which were not helped by the strenuous efforts of the pro-Arab activists.[21] Their work with the unions was described during the late 1970's and up to the Lebanon war as a holding operation, because, although it had many union leaders on their side, it had by that time lost grassroots union support for Israel.[22] In order to formalise the LFI's work within the trade union movement, the Trade Union Friends of Israel (TUFI) was formed in September 1983.

In January 1975 the LFI reported that six Labour MPs had met with Yasser Arafat, the PLO leader and had made plans for PLO 'trade unionists' to meet with their British counterparts. Both Murray and Hargreaves reassured Yagol that they had no intention of inviting Arafat's 'unions'. Murray also told him he intended to visit Israel and Syria later in the year and hoped his visit would bring the Histadrut and the Arab unions closer together.

The International Labour Organisation (ILO)

Israel's position as the sole representative of the Middle East at the Socialist International ended in the late 1960s when the International built links with third world organisations such as the PLO and Arab socialist groups. This was just one part of PLO's efforts to obtain international diplomatic and political recognition for the Palestinians and in February 1975, they applied to the ILO, which was part of the UN, for observer status at all future meetings. The application was made on the grounds that they had already been given consultative status in other UN organisations and had been recognised as the sole spokesman of the Palestinian people. The TUC International department consulted the German DGB union and advised the General Council that the PLO's application was bound to divide the ILO.[23] Yagol wrote to Murray saying that they were concerned about the application and that regardless of the outcome they expected the TUC to support the Histadrut. He urged the TUC to enforce '*measures aimed at the preservation of the constitution and future of the ILO*'. Murray replied saying that the General Council would take his views into consideration.[24]

As no decision on the application was made at the February 1975 meeting, the PLO was invited to attend the next ILO meeting in June, a move which was supported by the TUC.[25] Yagol was reassured by both Murray and Jones that the TUC would continue by supporting the Histadrut.[26] The debates at the June meeting were at times highly contentious, with an emphasis more on political issues rather than the work of the ILO. Although the TUC supported an unsuccessful Australian amendment, the meeting agreed to allow the PLO to attend general and regional ILO conferences. Later when the PLO delegate addressed the meeting, both the Israeli and American delegations walked out. Consequently, the US House of Representatives decided to suspend US financial contributions to ILO and the American Government gave notice to leave the ILO. As well as contacting the Foreign Office, The TUC issued a statement which emphasised their opposition to attempts to exclude Israeli participation in UN organisations.[27] Jones who was personally horrified at the politicisation of the international trade union movement told the 1975 TUC Congress that the ILO was the only forum where all the trade union movements of the world met and was split, '*not industrially, but politically*' and that the General Council had opposed the move because the PLO was not a country nor an established trade union movement. Both Jones and the TUC had been true to their word and had backed the Histadrut.[28]

Len Murray Visits Israel

Len Murray's long awaited visit to Israel took place in August 1975; the Foreign Office provided him with briefing notes which included the Government's view on the conflict, the PLO, the moves to expel Israel from the UN and the Arab boycott.[29] Murray was also given a special travel document which allowed him to enter Israel without having his passport stamped.[30]

Prior to Murray's departure the International committee recommended that the General Council approve their statement opposing moves to expel Israel from the UN. The declaration, which was issued after Murray's return made it clear that they did not approve of UNESCO's decision taken in December 1974 "to exclude Israel from membership of any of its regional organisations and that they would resist any attempt to exclude Israel from any other member organisation of the United Nations family, including the ILO or to limit Israeli participation."[31]

On his arrival in Israel, Murray said that Britain's unions supported Israel's right to exist and that "the TUC had taken a clear stand on attempts to suspend Israel from the UN which would be a grave error and we have given our opinion to the British government and to any organisations that have asked us about it".[32] Murray's three-day visit included a one-hour meeting with Prime Minister Rabin, in which they discussed both political and economic issues. He returned to London with a much greater understanding of both Israel and its problems. Barnea, the Histadrut European representative, thought that his meeting with Rabin had fundamentally changed how he thought of the conflict and had a profound influence on him which shaped his view of the PLO for years to come.[33]

The *Jerusalem Post* noted that traditional trade union friendship for Israel was threatened as the younger union leaders had very little contact with Israel and that the Histadrut had not devoted enough time to the TUC since moving to Brussels. The TUC, the article warned, continued to be '*a dominant element in British life and its millions of members influence the Labour Government through its bloc votes. The fact of Histadrut neglect in fostering valuable ties here is something that needs immediate rectification*'.[34]

The UN Adopts Its 'Zionism Is Racism' Resolution

On 10 November 1975, the UN General Assembly adopted an Arab backed resolution by 72 votes to 35 with 32 abstentions, which stated that '*Zionism is a form of racism and racial discrimination*'. The Histadrut immediately wrote to the ICFTU and the TUC calling on them to demonstrate solidarity with the Histadrut and to publicise their views. The following day Barnea requested a meeting with Murray. Even though Murray had previously spoken about the TUC's position on Israel and the UN, he did nothing for two weeks until after the next General Council meeting. Murray wrote to the Histadrut saying that they had raised the matter with the foreign secretary and endorsed the ETUC statement which stated that the resolution showed "*an alarming lack of responsibility on the part of the UN.*" The ICFTU statement which was very clear and supportive stated that "*the UN decision will hinder the establishment of peaceful relations in the Middle East and that it is morally and historically wrong to equate Zionism with racism.*"[35]

The TUC Goes to Syria

In September 1975, immediately after the TUC Congress, Murray and Jones went to Syria for a short visit. They told their trade union hosts that the TUC supported the UN resolution 242 and that the TUC was not aligned with either side in the conflict as their only concern was to promote a peaceful negotiated settlement. When they offered to assist in promoting discussions at trade union level the Syrians did not respond positively as their reply reflected the hard-line of their Government, that there could be no solution of the conflict without the total withdrawal of Israeli forces from occupied territory, the creation of a Palestine state, and a ban on further emigration into Israel. Jones and Murray reported that the Syrians '*had shown some willingness to reach agreement on the basis that a secular state should replace the present state of Israel*' which was not acceptable either to Israel or the General Council'. But they did however accept that the issue was about providing guarantees of security to Israel and to the new Palestinian State. The two organisations agreed to develop further contacts in the future.[36]

It was noticeable that while Jones and Murray submitted a report on their visit to the General Council, Murray did not present either a written or verbal report on his visit to Israel. Jones spoke at the 1976 TUC Congress about their visit to Syria and asked delegates to support their aim of developing contact between the trade unions of the Arab countries and Israel. '*You may say that is a dream, he said, but we are still going to work for it. We do not believe that it is beyond the bounds of human ingenuity to find a peaceful and a just solution to problems of the Middle East*'.[37]

The TUC and the Campaign to Allow Soviet Jewry to Emigrate to Israel

Although Stalin had supported the establishment of the State of Israel in 1948, for the next three decades Jews living in the Soviet Union experienced state sponsored antisemitism and discrimination in religion, culture and education. Israel's success in the Six-Day War sparked a revival of Jewish pride and interest in Israel amongst some Jews worldwide and the USSR's support for the Arabs only led to a new crackdown on Soviet Jews which resulted in increased antisemitism.

The Government of Israel which from 1948 had been trying unsuccessfully to persuade the Soviet Union to allow its Jewish community to emigrate to Israel using every opportunity to raise the issue. On the eve of Premier Khrushchev's visit to Britain in 1956, the Israel ambassador to Britain reported that issues that would be raised included Soviet Jewry, Israel and the Middle East. The Labour Party as well as most of the British press had written about these issues and had called for a more liberal attitude to the Jews in the USSR.[38] In 1959 Aneurin Bevan MP, the leader of Left in the Labour Party in post-war Britain who was an early supporter of the cause of Soviet Jewry raised the issue on a visit to Moscow. In the autumn of 1963, Harold Wilson who was very supportive of Israel, told Ne'eman, the London representative of the Histadrut, that after numerous visits to the Soviet Union that he had not been impressed by the authorities' treatment of the Jews, as every time he raised the issue the officials avoided getting into a discussion. Wilson admitted that he had only been able to achieve the confirmation of a few exit visas and thought that the situation would only get better if the Soviet Union ever needed American government support.[39]

International relations between East and West which improved during the 1970s because of the policy of detente between America, Russia and China, culminated in 1975, in the signing, of the Helsinki accords which committed the signatories, including Russia to respect the human rights and fundamental freedoms of their citizens. The improvement in diplomatic relations between London and Moscow during this period had helped Jones and Scanlon rebuild links with the Russian trade unions.

The campaign by Jewish communities in America and Europe, which had started during the 1960s, aimed to persuade the Soviet Union to allow Jews to peacefully practice their religion within the USSR, and to leave the country if they so wished. It was in the autumn of 1972 that the international trade union movement first became involved in the Soviet Jewry campaign when the ICFTU circulated the Histadrut's appeal for support for the campaign to allow Jewish emigration from the USSR. Although many unions throughout Europe sent telegrams to their Soviet counterparts it is not clear if any came from Britain.[40] Yagol reported that Feather had discussed Jewish emigration when he met the leaders of the Soviet All-Union Central Council of Trade Unions (AUCCTU) during his visit to Moscow in December 1972.[41]

Between 1973 and 1978, Frank Chapple, the General Secretary of the Electrical, Electronic, Telecommunication and Plumbing Union (EETPU), who had left the Communist party over Hungary in 1956, regularly raised the issues of Soviet Jewry and human rights in USSR at both the International committee and the General Council. Along with Joe Gormley, president of the NUM, they were the first trade unionists to support the British Women's Campaign for Soviet Jewry (the 35s) who campaigned for the release of Jews who had been imprisoned in the USSR and wished to apply to emigrate to Israel.

In March 1973, in response to Chapple's campaigning, the International department prepared a briefing document entitled 'Minorities in the Soviet Union' which examined the position of all minorities in the USSR focusing mainly on the problems facing Soviet Jewry. Although antisemitism was mentioned it was not discussed in any detail. According to the report, the Soviet authorities had exerted pressure on Jews who they suspected of having dual loyalties to the USSR and Israel. Zionism was seen as an international anti-Soviet movement which supported Israel and American foreign policy. Although it was not against the law to emigrate, various difficulties, which were not seen as discriminatory by the Soviet authorities, had been placed in the way of those Jews who had applied to emigrate to Israel.[42]

When Jones and Feather went to Moscow in July 1973, Jones discussed the question of Soviet Jewry with the president of the AUCCTU. He was told that 97 per cent of applications to emigrate had been granted, but there were difficulties for highly qualified scientists and academics or those with access to state secrets. The USSR, the pair were assured, was not antisemitic and that many Jews held important positions.[43]

Yagol reported that the TUC wanted to achieve international unity amongst the European unions which he felt would lead to more contact with the Soviet and Eastern bloc unions and have implications for Israel and the Jews. When Jones was asked, at the 1973 TUC Congress, about the persecution of Jews, he attempted to justify the persecution by quoting the president of the AUCCTU who had told him that antisemitism was forbidden by law.[44] Yagol's fears were confirmed, in the November, when Murray announced an agreement between TUC and the AUCCTU that emphasised the importance of cooperation between the TUC and AUCCTU and between ICFTU and the Communist unions.[45]

Chapple continued to press the TUC to discuss civil liberties in the USSR. In September 1973, his letter to the General Council was sent directly to the Soviet ambassador in London, whose reply in January 1974 was forwarded to the EETPU.[46] He did not consider this a proper course of action and wrote again to the Council asking why they had not discussed the issue of Soviet dissidents.[47] At their April meeting, the International Committee were told that the General Council would only protest in cases of Soviet dissidents[48] that involved trade unionists or trade union matters and not political cases. Chapple made it clear that '*dissidents in the Soviet Union were either individuals seeking greater freedom of expression or minorities, such as Jews who wanted to go to Israel, but that trade union freedoms were not at issue in these cases*'. This view allowed the TUC to ignore the issue of Soviet emigration to Israel and the committee took no further action on the matter.[49] Undismayed, Chapple wrote again in June asking the committee to reconsider their decision as he had found it '*difficult to understand how individual liberties could be separated from trade union liberties*' *and suggested they recommend to the General Council* '*that they should protest strongly against the continued suppression of liberty in the Soviet Union*'.[50] It was made clear to Chapple that the General Council position '*regarding different regimes might not appear even handed but that situations varied from country to country*' *and* '*that in some cases persuasion was far more effective than public denunciation*'.[51]

At the end of March 1975, a delegation from the AUCCTU, led by Alexander Shelepin, their chairman and Politburo member, arrived in Britain as guests of the TUC. The visit, which was a return visit for the TUC's trip to Moscow two years earlier, was very controversial. Even before Shelepin arrived in London questions were asked in Parliament by MP's on both sides of the house as to why as the former head of the KGB who had been accused of complicity in the West German assassination of two exiled Ukrainian leaders was being allowed to enter Britain.[52] Wherever he went he was met by noisy demonstrations organised by the Women's Campaign for Soviet Jewry (the 35s), as well as by Ukrainians, Lithuanians and other ethnic minorities in Britain whose homelands were, they felt, under Soviet occupation. Many politicians and trade unionists could not understand why the TUC had invited him, nor the TUC's indifference to the plight of the persecuted minorities in the Soviet Union. The Soviets were so embarrassed by the strength of the demonstrations that they cut short the visit from four to two days and left the general impression that the visit was a fiasco, especially for the TUC. Shelepin blamed the 'Zionists' for the demonstrations against him.[53]

Prior to Shelepin's visit both the Histadrut and the 35s arranged for their friends, such as Scanlon and Gormley to ask questions. Yagol reported that Shelepin was '*empathic and supported the international promise of Israel's 1967 borders*' but his answers about Soviet Jewry were '*shorter and standard*', and did not rule out a meeting with the Histadrut in the future.[54]

Chapple asked the General Council, in February 1976, if it would be willing to deliver a petition organised by the 35s campaign, to the Soviet ambassador in London for onward transmission to the AUCCTU, because the Soviet Embassy had refused to accept it. The petition, which had been signed by General Council members and many TUC Congress delegates, called on the AUCCTU to investigate the arbitrary dismissal from work of Soviet trade unionists who had applied to emigrate to Israel. Chapple also asked if the Council would approach the AUCCTU for information about a Soviet Jew, Sender Levinzon, a metalworker, who had been sentenced to six years imprisonment. The General Council decided instead to ask the Soviet ambassador for details of their emigration policy and about the cases to which the EETPU had referred.[55] The Embassy's reply denied that Soviet Jews who had wished to emigrate had been dismissed from work and only those applicants who had access to State secrets or who had been convicted of crimes had been refused permission to leave. Two months later, the General Council told the EEPTU that they would not forward the petition because the TUC should not become involved in campaigns organised by non-trade-union organisations and particularly on sectarian issues when the facts in contention had not been clearly established. They advised the EETPU that it might be better to raise individual cases on an informal basis rather than by making official representations.[56]

At the 1976 TUC Congress the EEPTU once again raised the matter of Soviet dissidents who were being dismissed because they were Jewish.[57] In January 1977, Chapple once again asked the General Council to protest to the Soviet Government about the persecution of individuals and minority groups in the Soviet Union as he '*found it difficult to understand how they could protest in every way possible on matters affecting Spain or South Africa but did not act in a similar way with the Soviet Union*'. The following month, the Council decided to continue with their existing policy of raising such cases informally. Chapple then requested that the General Council publish a statement in support of the Labour Party resolution protesting against unfair trial of Yuri Orlov, a non-Jewish Soviet dissident who founded the Moscow Helsinki Watch Group and was sentenced to 10 years penal detention in 1978. The request was refused on the grounds that it was not a trade union issue and therefore not covered by the TUC's policy on human rights.[58]

The 1977 TUC Congress debated two motions relating to human rights. The first, which was adopted, condemned the gross violations of human rights that continued to take place throughout the world and asked member unions to support campaigns on behalf of imprisoned and tortured trade unionists conducted by Amnesty International. Congress rejected the second motion which criticised the lack of credibility in the TUC's response to the suppression of freedom of speech and human rights in the USSR. Jones argued that although the TUC supported detente between East and West and if adopted this resolution would not help as the TUC looked for "*ways to open doors, to create opportunities to change, not to close doors or create continued division*".[59] The EEPTU successfully moved a human rights motion at the 1978 Congress which allowed the TUC to become more flexible over the next decade in their dealings with Soviet Jewry.[60] The ending of the Cold War in 1991 and the Gorbachov reforms in the Soviet Union led the Jews being allowed to emigrate Israel.

Frank Chapple and his union were very much the flag bearers in the 1970s for human rights and Soviet Jewry, especially at Congress. There was however intense rivalry between Chapple and Jones which was partly due to domestic industrial rivalry between the EEPTU and TGWU, their views on the USSR, as well as a very strong personal animosity between them.[61]

The reluctance of the TUC to become involved can be explained by the strong influence of the Left on the General Council and the leadership skills of Jones who ensured that the TUC did not criticise the USSR over human rights, or officially acknowledge the plight of Jews living in the Soviet Union. Even so this did not stop Jones agreeing to become a spokesman for the Histadrut when dealing with the Soviet Union.

The TUC's drive for detente with the Soviet Union was led by Jones, who used every possible tactic to not become involved with the Soviet Jewry campaign. He believed that trade union leaders should be concerned about international trade union rights but not human rights. Jones argued that the Jews were not members of trade unions, or that the unions did not have the full facts or that they were only following government policy. It is also possible that Jones, although not a Communist, behaved as he did because of the support he had received from the communists when he was elected as General Secretary of the TGWU. Whatever the reason, the TUC were out of step with the Labour Party, who were much more flexible and frequently gave their support to the 35s. The TUC, which had denounced antisemitism and discrimination against the Jews in the 1940s, accepted without question the denial by the Soviet authorities that antisemitism existed in the Soviet Union. Jones in particular seemed to have made no connection between Soviet Jewry and his friendship with the Histadrut; keeping each one separate, and because of his position on human rights and the desire to normalise relations with the USSR, Jones opposed all moves for the TUC to support the public campaign to allow Soviet Jewry to emigrate to Israel.

With the TUC moving closer to Europe and the Soviet Union, the TUC became less of a priority for the Histadrut once Cousins had retired. The Histadrut concentrated instead on building links with the German and Scandinavian unions. This explains why the Histadrut, who were very active in mobilising support for Soviet Jewry with the ICFTU and trade unions in the USA and Europe, only raised the issue of Soviet Jewry with the TUC during the early 1970s. Yagol however had helped the 35s build their own links with several British trade unions.[62]

The Arab Boycott of Israel

In the aftermath of the Yom Kippur war, the Arab boycott caused problems for the British Government's policy of maintaining friendship with both Israel and the Arab states in order to promote trade as well as back international initiatives for a settlement of the Arab-Israeli conflict. While bilateral relations had improved, British companies became increasingly reluctant to trade with Israel fearing that a potential boycott would affect their trade with the Arabs. When, in 1976, Israel urged the British Government to adopt similar anti-boycott measures to those planned by the Americans, the Foreign Office advised the prime minister that they considered trade with the Arab States was worth far more to Britain than trade with Israel and that with the exception of the United States there was no other country whose attitude to the boycott was more helpful to Israel than Britain.

In February 1977 the TUC ignored Gormley's request to discuss the case of the Metal Box Company which had been threatened with the loss of substantial business in the Middle East unless it disposed of a 25-year-old investment in an Israeli canning company. The TGWU did approach Metal Box to discuss the matter as they had been told that any closure of the Israeli company could result in substantial job losses. The Government also expressed its concern, but refused to intervene saying that the decision was a purely commercial one. Metal Box subsequently surrendered to the boycotters demands and sold off its investment. After attending the 1977 TUC Congress, Yeruham Meshel, the Histadrut General Secretary, appealed Murray '*in the name of workers solidarity to do everything in your power to prevent British firms from giving in to the Arab boycott*' which he said had affected unemployment in some sectors in Israel.[63] The issue of the boycott was not raised again with the TUC until 1983.

In 1978 the Government ignored the recommendations of a report of the House of Lords Select Committee on anti-boycott legislation, preferring instead to support what it called 'European Community initiatives' to combat boycotts but continued to discuss the effects of the Arab boycott with the Israel embassy.[64]

Israeli Politics Move to the Right

When the Israel Labour Party lost the May 1977 Israeli general election it was much more than just a change of government, it was a political earthquake. The socialist and Zionist ideals of Ben-Gurion and Mapai had controlled the political scene in Palestine from 1935 until 1948 and had formed every government since independence. They were replaced by the Likud movement led by Menachem Begin, which was a mixture of Revisionist Zionism, the supporters of Jabotinsky and the land of Israel movement. The British government were deeply suspicious of the new prime minister, who they saw as an ex-Irgun terrorist and the natural successor to Jabotinsky who championed a Greater Israel stretching from the Jordan to the Mediterranean. The Labour Left, led by Mapai, had dominated the political scene from 1935 onwards, firstly in the Yishuv, the Jewish community in Palestine, from 1930s until 1948 and had formed every government since independence. Mapai also controlled the Histadrut which had administered the Yishuv. The General Secretary of the Histadrut was a senior party member, a member of the Knesset (Parliament) and frequently a Government Minister, an arrangement which allowed the Histadrut to work very closely on international issues with the Labour Party.

Mike Walsh, the former head of TUC International department, described the special relationship that existed between the Israeli Government and the Histadrut: "*In the first half of the 1970s and the 1980s, Israel was denied diplomatic recognition in large parts of the world and that made the significance of Histadrut very much greater, because it was Histadrut through its trade union credentials that could get a presence for Israel in all sorts of countries in the Middle East and Africa. This was why we supported the work of their Afro-Asian Institute. During the 1980s the Histadrut became diplomatically less significant because as things developed, with greater diplomatic recognition, the Israeli presence through Histadrut became less and less important. It was the face of Israel in many countries. It was really important, not just to Histadrut but to the whole Israeli state to be represented on the governing bodies of the ILO and the ICFTU.*"[65]

Three weeks earlier Mason, the British ambassador to Israel wrote a report on the decline of the Histadrut, which he described as one of the triple pillars of the State. Once a great and powerful institution, it now had little influence and prestige but was the second largest employer in Israel, employing some 70,000 workers and provided medical services for nearly 70 per cent of the population. In order to reverse its decline and restore its authority, Mason wrote, "the Histadrut may need radical reorganisation, including electoral reform, and perhaps to hive off some of its activities to the Government or the private sector." He concluded that the Histadrut's future depends on future Government policies and the Israeli economy. "*It will survive, but in what form and with what influence is uncertain*".[66]

Mason reported that Meshel had been invited to attend the TUC Congress in September. He recommended that a meeting be arranged between Meshel and Judd, the Minister of State at the Foreign Office because he considered Meshel to be the most powerful Labour Party figure in Israel. In their discussions Judd told Meshel that although the PLO had said and done some quite unacceptable things there could be no lasting settlement which did not take account of their views. He confirmed that the government's position of not recognising the PLO had not changed. Meshel invited the TUC to attend the Histadrut Convention in

November; once again they declined the invitation on grounds of '*unavoidable domestic commitments*' for all their senior General Council members.[67]

After the 1973 Yom Kippur war most of the African States which had received Israeli agricultural and technical aid packages during the 1950s and 1960s broke off relations with Israel in order to show solidarity with the Arab states which had instituted an oil embargo against the Western nations. Finding itself politically isolated in Africa and the Middle East Israel was forced to look elsewhere for new trade and arms deals. Even though Israel had been openly critical of South Africa's apartheid policies in the past and continued to do so, in November 1974 Israel established an economic alliance with South Africa secretly negotiated by Shimon Peres, Israel's Foreign Minister.[68] By 1977 South Africa had emerged as Israel's single largest customer of military weapons. The new Begin government in Israel ignored the UN embargo and continued to supply arms to South Africa.

In November 1977 as supporters of the anti-apartheid movement in South Africa, the TUC asked the Secretary of State at the Foreign Office in about reports of Israeli military cooperation with South Africa. The Minister replied saying that Israeli military cooperation with South Africa was a matter of international concern and that an approach at trade union level might be helpful. The TUC then contacted the Histadrut who said that the Israeli Foreign Ministry had told them that Israel fully abided by the UN resolution banning arms sales to South Africa. There is no record of the TUC taking any further action on this matter.

Between the 1973 war and Israel's invasion of Lebanon in 1982, the ICFTU kept a watching brief on the situation in the Middle East and only discussed matters or issued statements when tension in the region rose or when serious incidents justified a response. Both the Israelis and the Arabs used ICFTU meetings to defend themselves or attack each other, but although the Histadrut continued to be an active participant in ICFTU from 1977 onwards its actions were limited as the Labour Alignment, of which it was part, no longer governed Israel. During this period there was also limited contact between the Histadrut and the TUC with very little discussion of Israel-Arab conflict by the General Council. There is no record for example, of any discussion of the 1978 Camp David accords which were welcomed by a resolution adopted by the 1979 ICFTU Congress.

The settlements were never a key issue for the General Council which never differentiated between the settlements in the West Bank and Gaza. Both Len Murray and Tom Jackson, who had succeeded Len Jones as chairman of the International Committee, knew that the Histadrut was opposed to the building of Israeli settlements as well as direct contact with the PLO. The two men ensured that there was little public criticism of Israel's actions by the TUC and worked behind the scenes with the ICFTU with the result that in 1978 the TUC made very few interventions with the Histadrut over the PLO terror attacks on Northern Israel or Israel's response, preferring instead to support ICFTU actions.

The TUC Starts to Move Away from Israel and Towards Support for the Palestinians

A series of events took place around the time of the 1979 TUC Congress which appears to be the beginning of a serious effort by grassroots activists to gain TUC support for the Palestinian cause.

In August 1979 the TUC received an unsolicited letter from the Beirut based Palestine Trade Unions Federation (PTUF), the trade union wing of the PLO which drew attention to the problems of the Israeli occupation and called for TUC support.[69] A few weeks later, a petition calling for the recognition of Arab trade unions in the West Bank and Gaza was circulated at Congress by the UK Palestine Coordination (UKPC) committee. The petition, which had been signed by 250 trade unionists was sent to the Israeli Minister of Defence, who was responsible for the administration of the West Bank and Gaza.[70] The signing of this petition by such a large number of delegates is significant as it shows that by 1979 there was a groundswell of support at grassroots level for Palestinian rights. The UKPC which worked under the LMEC umbrella and had PLO support, was to play a pivotal role in promoting the UK campaign for Palestinian rights, as well as coordinating and supporting Palestinian solidarity groups and activists on campus and in the trade unions.

The UKPC then approached Moss Evans, the General Secretary of the TGWU who wrote to Murray asking for information about TUC and ICFTU policy towards the UKPC. Murray replied saying that they had no information about UKPC but had made inquiries with the ICFTU.[71] The UKPC also wrote to the TUC saying that they were arranging for a PTUF delegation to visit to the Britain in November and asked for a meeting with the TUC. In order to hear the views of the PTUF, Murray arranged for the PTUF to meet with a member of the International department. The ICFTU then told the TUC that they had no contact with the PTUF and that the PTUF was considered to be an affiliate of the PLO which promoted the Palestinian cause at international level rather than a real trade union body. Shortly after receiving this reply the PTUF's visit to London was cancelled due to '*visa difficulties*'.[72]

Murray had not arranged to meet with the PTUF himself because at the time he was against opening up any contact with the Palestinian Trade Unions. Aaron Barnea, the Histadrut European representative, thought that this was because Murray had '*fundamentally changed how he thought of the conflict*' after his discussions with Israeli Prime Minister Yitzhak Rabin in August 1975. Murray had only been persuaded to arrange a meeting with the PTUF after reading a very detailed memo prepared by Hargreaves, the Head of the International department, who had very close links with the Foreign Office.[73] Informal contact with the PLO was permitted by the Foreign Office even though the official Government's policy forbade any formal contacts until the PLO had renounced violence.

Over the next 12 months the Histadrut became increasingly concerned about the growing support for the PLO within the European trade unions. It noted the increasing support for the pro-Palestinian activists within the Labour Party, although they had not yet made an impact on the TUC. However, in February 1981 the Histadrut highlighted their concerns in a report to the Israel Foreign Ministry which outlined their plans to send delegations to six European countries including Britain in order to challenge PLO propaganda. These plans do not appear to have come to fruition.[74]

TUC Visit to Israel and Egypt

Cousins and Hayday who believed that the trade union movement had a role to play in any settlement of the Arab-Israeli conflict, failed to bring together the Arabs and the Histadrut. To their credit they never gave up, even though they found it difficult playing the role of honest broker when the TUC was perceived by the Arabs as a pro-Israel organisation. It was the Americans, the AFL-CIO, at their 1977 annual convention who succeeded, when they brought together the Histadrut General Secretary and the president of the Egyptian Federation of Labour (EFL), who shook hands on the platform in the manner of Sadat and Begin.

Following the meeting the Histadrut issued a formal invitation to the Egyptians to visit Israel telling the ICFTU that '*any settlement should be with all Arab countries*' and that they would be willing to host delegations from other Arab counties.[75] The next year, Aaron Barnea, asked Britain's union leaders who had contacts with Arab trade unions to tell them of the Histadrut's desire to establish links with the Arab unions.[76]

As a result of this initiative and improving contacts between Israel and Egypt, a TUC delegation went to both countries` in November 1980. The report of their visit made it clear that the Histadrut was critical of the Israeli Government's settlement policies and was opposed to any dealings with the PLO unless the PLO was willing to accept Israel's right to exist. The delegation told the Egyptians that the Histadrut were committed to Israel's survival and the normalisation of relations with Egypt, and were very anxious to develop cooperative relations at the trade union level. But the EFL, who were reluctant to improve their links with Histadrut in case they caused embarrassment to their Government, told the delegation that although Egypt accepted Israel's right to exist and supported the peace treaty with Israel, any lasting resolution of the Arab-Israel conflict would have to involve the PLO and all the countries of the region, not just Israel and Egypt.[77]

The Israeli Air force's successful strike on Iraq's Osirak nuclear reactor on 7 June 1981 ensured that Menachem Begin was re-elected as Prime Minister in Israel's general election at the end of June. On 10 July the IDF resumed its attacks on Palestinian targets in Southern Lebanon which culminated in the bombing of PLO buildings in downtown Beirut on 17 July which killed as many as 300 people. The international outcry that followed led to worldwide condemnation of Israel's actions, and a temporary embargo on the export of US aircraft to Israel. The ICFTU reacted to events by issuing a statement on 23 July which not only condemned the PLO attacks and the disproportionate response the Israeli army, but also called on affiliates to bring pressure on their governments to bring about a ceasefire.[78] The General Council sent a telegram to the Histadrut expressing their concern and the possible repercussions for world peace.[79] This was an unusual step for the TUC as it normally backed the ICFTU's response and even though a TUC delegation had visited Israel the previous year there had been very little direct contact with the Histadrut on political matters. The Histadrut's reply to the ICFTU, which was also sent to the TUC, noted that a ceasefire was now in place which had put an end to "*the senseless killing of innocent civilians on both sides of the border*" and pointed out that the tension had been caused by the Syrian army's presence in Lebanon and that Israel had "*no dispute with the government or the people of the Lebanon*".[80]

The conflict was discussed again at the next General Council meeting when it was suggested that Arab trade union organisations should also be asked for their views on recent developments. Accordingly, Murray wrote to the Federation of Petroleum Trade Unions (FPTU) in Lebanon in October to ask for their views on how the international trade union movement could help to bring about a peaceful solution to the situation. This was a strange move for the TUC as they had not had any direct contact with the Lebanese unions for several years. However, in view of increasing support for the Palestinians amongst trade unions, both at grass roots and at the TUC, Murray was obviously aware of the need to do something.[81]

The Norwegian Federation of Trade Unions, who had been in contact with both the Palestine General Federation of Workers and the Histadrut, wrote to the TUC in July 1981 saying that they had asked the ICFTU to lead a campaign for a peace settlement in the Middle East. The TUC reply stated that although they supported their efforts they did not yet have any direct contact with the Palestinians. The following January after their meeting with the Foreign Office, the TUC pledged to use their contacts, including those with the Histadrut, to urge negotiations for a lasting and just peace agreement and also invited the Histadrut as an official guest to the 1982 TUC Congress.[82]

The Lebanon War

The 1982 Lebanon War began on 6 June when Israel invaded southern Lebanon to remove the PLO from the area in order to protect northern Israel from terrorist attacks; the invasion was in response to the attempted assassination in London of Shlomo Argov, Israel's ambassador to Britain three days earlier by gunmen belonging to the Abu Nidal group. They had carried out the attempt in order to provoke the Israelis into military action against the PLO. It soon evident that the military operation which had been masterminded by Defence Minister Sharon had more far reaching ambitions to occupy all of Lebanon up to Beirut and the surrounding areas in order to eliminate the PLO rather than just clear a 40 kilometre area on Israel's northern border.

The June meeting of the ETUC, which was held within days of the invasion, was used by the TUC and others to express their concerns although a proposal to issue an ETUC statement was turned down on the grounds that any ETUC action duplicated the work of the ICFTU.[83] The TUC then received a copy of the Histadrut's telegram to the ICFTU which said that the invasion had been carried out in self-defence in order to prevent attacks on Israel from Southern Lebanon. The Histadrut had also endorsed an Israel Labour Party statement calling on the Israeli army to stick to its original plan of only venturing 40 kilometres inside Lebanon, "*supporting the establishment of an effective international force to guarantee peace and stability in the Lebanon and calling for the withdrawal of all foreign forces from the Lebanon*". They also called for negotiations to be started leading to the re-establishment of an independent Lebanon with which Israel would live in peaceful co-existence and that the Israeli army should not occupy Beirut.[84] The ICFTU called for a strict observance of the ceasefire, the withdrawal of both Israeli forces and armed Palestinian groups from Lebanon and for negotiations in which both the Israelis and the Palestinians would recognise the other's right to exist.[85] They also circulated the statement issued by the UGTT, the Tunisian ICFTU affiliate, which reflected the Arab point of view. Although the International Department had prepared a draft statement, the TUC international committee decided against publishing its own statement and supported the ICFTU call instead.[86]

Although the Histadrut had lobbied the TUC in the 1967 and 1973 wars it made no direct contact with the TUC at the start of the Lebanon war. Two months later Murray wrote to both the Histadrut and the FPTU to ask for their views on the situation. Murray made it very clear to the Lebanese that he thought that the Israeli invasion was '*impossible to justify on the grounds that it is necessary to secure Israel against terrorist attacks on Israel by the PLO*' and that the force they had used in Beirut was disproportionate. His letter to the Histadrut was more forthright, saying that '*the prolonged shelling and bombing of Beirut and the killing of Lebanese civilians and the destruction of their homes as a result appears to go far beyond action necessary to protect Israel against terrorist attacks*'. Murray also compared the IRA's terrorist attacks in London to the Israeli armed forces whose actions had been '*on a scale which is not justified on the grounds that it is aimed at combating terrorism.* He concluded by asking if the Histadrut had condemned the destruction of Beirut and the killing of Lebanese civilians and whether it had taken the issue up with the Government.[87]

The Trade Union Friends of Palestine (TUFP)

The Scottish Trades Union Congress (STUC), which was formed in 1897, is an independent trade union centre for Scotland which has no connection with the TUC, that first became interested in the Arab-Israeli conflict in the early 1970s. In October 1975 the STUC adopted a resolution which described the situation in the Middle East as a threat to world peace, but also recognised Israel's right to exist as well as the rights of the Palestinian people.[88] Benny Shiloh, the labour attaché at the Israeli embassy, met with the STUC General Secretary to discuss the resolution. He was told that founding of the State of Israel had been a mistake and that the Histadrut had declined a visit by the STUC because they had wanted to visit neighbouring Arab countries. Shiloh concluded after several meetings with the STUC that they were dominated by communists which explained their unfavourable position towards Israel. He recommended that the STUC General Secretary should be invited to visit Israel in order to prevent future STUC anti-Israeli actions.[89]

Dundee became from 1969 onwards a centre of grassroots support amongst the local Labour Party, trade unions, activists and students at Dundee University for the Palestinian cause. The Trade Union Friends of Palestine (TUFP) was established in Dundee in June 1980 to gather support for a Palestinian homeland within the trade union movement; its founders included George Galloway, then a local Labour Party activist, Yousef Allan, a Palestinian postgraduate student at Dundee University and Dundee MP, Ernie Ross. They all understood that in order to gain Labour Party support for the Palestinian cause, they first needed to gain the backing of the trade unions and the TUC because the block voting system used at Labour Party conferences gave the trade unions disproportionate power and influence over Labour Party policy decisions. By September 1982 the TUFP, which had been backed by Allan's links with the PLO, could count on support from activists from both wings of the Labour Party. Support from the Left included the General Secretaries of the Fire Brigades union (FBU), the Engineers (AUEW) and the Railway union (ASLEF) as well as officers from the General and Municipal Workers union (GMWU), the TGWU and the Scottish Miners. David Warburton, a senior Officer of the GMB Union, who was a member of the LMEC, brought with him the right wing of the trade union movement when he joined the TUFP, which previously had only been supported by the Left.[90]

Israel's invasion of Lebanon provided the TUFP with the opportunity to change TUC policy. In September 1982 at the TUC Congress, Ken Cameron, General Secretary of the FBU and member of TUFP, tabled an emergency motion, written by Galloway, which condemned Israel's invasion of Lebanon and recognised "the national rights of the Palestinian people to self-determination within an independent sovereign state."[91] The TUC International department recommended to the General Council that they should support the emergency motion but with reservations as it differed in certain aspects from existing TUC policy. The TUC had never before dissociated themselves from the call for negotiations based on UN resolution 242. The motion went further than resolution 242 because "*242 does not refer to the Palestinians by name and only affirms the necessity for achieving a just settlement of the refugee problem.*" The Council were warned that if the emergency motion were adopted without any reservations, it would rule out other "*possible ways in which Palestinian aspirations might be satisfied*" and it was thought that the FBU would not want to stand in the way of any settlement that was acceptable to Palestinians. The Council were also advised that if the motion was adopted, any influence the TUC had with the Histadrut might be reduced.[92]

In the three days leading up the debate there were lengthy discussions between the FBU and the General Council. The unions appeared to be divided as the FBU were supported by the TGWU and the GMB and the General Council by NALGO and the AUEW. Cameron was put under a lot of pressure by the General Council who promised that if he withdrew the motion it would be considered by the International Committee. On the advice of colleagues, Cameron refused their requests which gave the General Council no alternative but to oppose the motion.[93]

Opening the debate, on the last day of Congress, Cameron said that "this motion in fact points the real direction for peace and security for all the states, including Israel" and he found it strange that the General Council were opposed to this motion as he had not been trying to be divisive in any way. He told delegates that they could not let the crisis in Lebanon pass without making a statement on the matter and made the point that "If the General Council cannot go along with the policy of the British Labour Party, then there is something wrong with the General Council in their attitude towards this motion." Opposing the motion, Tom Jackson, the Chairman of the International Committee, speaking on behalf of the General Council informed delegates that they did not have to pass the motion in order to record their dislike of what had happened in Lebanon or ensure that UN resolution 242 was upheld because the TUC had already endorsed the ICFTU statement on the matter. He then told the Congress that "You do not need to pass this motion because of your understandable feeling for the need to have a homeland for the Palestinian people. That too is the policy of the General Council." This was technically not true as this was not General Council policy. TUC policy was to support the ICFTU statement which only referred to the rights of the Palestinian people but not that the only way that their rights could be secured was through an independent state. Jackson told delegates that the General Council had asked Cameron to withdraw the motion, saying "let us not divide ourselves. Let us see what will be the result of the discussions that are taking place. We are in an extremely important and delicate stage of Middle Eastern politics and this is not the moment for us in Brighton, with all the troubles that we have got, to go muddying the waters still further." His appeal to Congress to oppose the motion was in vain, as it was carried, on a show of hands, by a very substantial majority with no need for a card vote.[94] Jackson who was pro-Israel and due to retire after Congress took the defeat personally as he believed it reflected on his chairmanship of the International Committee. Cameron's main purpose had been to debate the subject and he had been surprised by the overwhelming support he received for the motion. Galloway, on the other hand, who had been lobbying at Congress, had always felt confident of success.[95]

The TUFP, rather than one of the more established groups, had succeeded, not only because they were in the right place at the right time, but because the TUFP had brought together young ambitious Left-wing Labour Party politicians and union activists as well as having a direct connection with Palestinians and the PLO. Their connection with Dundee and the local university also contributed to their success because of the city's identification with the Palestinian cause during the 1970s had been driven by the many Arab students that had been studying there.

Ken Cameron, the General Secretary of the FBU, said that Israel's invasion of Lebanon and the intense media coverage on TV news bulletins every night of the bombing of Beirut had helped change opinions and brought about increased support for the Palestinians in both the unions and the Labour Party. The TUC had received many letters from all over the world as well as local Trades Councils and union branches calling on them to condemn the Israeli invasion, give recognition to the PLO and endorse the creation of a Palestinian state. Only once before had the TUC received so many letters regarding the Arab-Israel conflict and that was in 1948, when American unions wrote to the TUC calling on them to support the newly declared State of Israel.

During the 1960s Bert Ramelson, the CPGB's industrial organiser, abandoned his previous strategy of working for change primarily at grass-roots level and instituted a new approach which was to put his own people in leading positions in the unions in order influence union policy. This had been necessary because the Party had been in a gradual decline since the late 1940s because of the Cold War and the refusal by the Labour Party to allow the CPGB to affiliate. By the late 1970s, the CPGB had considerable power and influence within the trade union movement, as many leading unions had either communist or communist supporting members on their executive committees. At the end of each year Ramelson would send a list of policies to his members within the unions which the CPGB wanted the trade unions to take up. This ensured that the most important of these polices would appear on the agenda of the TUC Congress the following September. All communist delegates would meet before Congress and discuss tactics to ensure success for their policies and election of their candidates. Along with the three communists who sat on the TUC General Council in 1982, Ken Gill, General Secretary of TASS, George Guy, General Secretary of the Sheet Metal Workers union and Mick McGahey, vice-president of the National Union of Mineworkers, there were other Left wingers who frequently voted with them, whilst not communists themselves, they felt comfortable with communist policies and were also members of the caucus that Ramelson had organised. The result was that the CPGB was able to influence decisions made by the General Council and TUC and Labour Party policy. Even though the CPGB were supportive of the Soviet Union's pro-Arab policy on the Middle East and the Palestinian right to their own homeland, they were not involved in any way with the FBU motion. Their support for the FBU motion had been both coincidental and advantageous as it ensured that a resolution condemning Israel had been adopted, something which had never previously been achieved.[96]

A week after the TUC Congress, the National Union of Mineworkers (NUM) which had been very supportive of Israel and the Histadrut in the past, adopted an emergency resolution on Lebanon which condemned 'the brutal attack by Israel on the Lebanon in pursuit of what appears to be their "final solution" of the Palestinian problem.'[97]

Copies of the Congress resolution were sent to the Foreign Secretary, the Labour Party, the ICFTU, the Histadrut, the FPTU, the Israeli and Lebanese Ambassadors, and the UN. They only received replies from the Labour Party, the Foreign Secretary and the Israel Embassy.[98] The Labour Party said that they supported a peaceful permanent settlement which guaranteed national self-determination for everyone within secure and internationally recognised borders and called on the both the PLO and the State of Israel to recognise each other's legitimate claims to statehood.[99] The Israeli response was that "Israeli military operations against terrorists in the Lebanon had been designed to bring an end to the death, destruction, and terrorism initiated by the PLO against Israel and its citizens and that they constituted a legitimate exercise of the right to self-defence." The International committee report to the 1983 Congress omitted the words "and that they constituted a legitimate exercise of the right to self-defence" which had been Israel's justification for her invasion of Lebanon. This omission indicated bias against Israel, which reflected the attitude to Israel within the unions and the General Council.[100]

The International Committee considered the Foreign Secretary's general comments were not sympathetic to those of the TUC, but noted that he had said that the Congress resolution was close to the view taken by the European Community and the British Government. The TUC then asked him for his comments on their call for independent inquiry into the killings. He replied saying that he doubted "whether a further investigation at this stage would serve much purpose".[101]

Meshel, the Histadrut General Secretary told the TUC that they were disappointed that their Congress resolution had only demanded the withdrawal of the Israeli armed forces and not the withdrawal of all foreign forces from Lebanon. He reminded the TUC of the death and destruction caused by the eight-year-old Lebanon civil war which had involved the PLO and the Syrian army and that "as far as the establishment of an independent, sovereign state for the Palestinian people, which your resolution advocates, I am sure that far from bringing peace and security, such a separate state is a certain recipe for constant tension and more war and bloodshed." Meshel added that the Histadrut supported the position of the Israel Labour Party; that a just solution to the Palestinian problem can only be found "on the basis of territorial compromise with Jordan whose Palestinian citizens account for over 60% of the Jordanian population."[102]

The PTUF which was based in Syria thanked the TUC for their support and asked for a meeting with them. Murray was advised that the PTUF were affiliated to the communist WFTU and replied that they were only interested in making contact with unions that were independent and representative of their members. The TUC also received letters from local Trades Councils detailing resolutions that had been adopted regarding the recognition of the PLO, the establishment of a Palestinian homeland, a boycott of Israel and one which compared Israeli actions in Beirut with the Nazis extermination of the Jews.[103]

Support for the Palestinians within the Labour Party at constituency level, especially in London and Scotland, illustrated the successful infiltration of the Trotskyist activists and the influence of the Left. Their opposition and anger against Israel's invasion of Lebanon played an important part in changing the Party's position on Israel. In August, the *Jewish Chronicle* reported that the Labour Party conference scheduled for the end of September had received only two resolutions on the Middle East, both of which were anti-Israel, one condemning the Israeli invasion of Lebanon, the other advocating support for an independent Palestinian State. Yet by the beginning of September, 46 emergency motions had been submitted to the Labour Party's conference. The FBU's motion urged that "Her Majesty's Government should insist in the strongest possible terms that America cease to support the Zionist fascists in the present Israeli Government".[104]

The Killings at the Sabra and Shatila Palestinian Refugee Camps

If the invasion of Lebanon harmed Israel's support and international reputation, the killing of 600–800 Palestinian and Lebanese civilians in the Sabra and Shatila Palestinian refugee camps[105] in Beirut by Lebanese Phalangist militia caused anger and outrage throughout the world and no more so than at the TUC and the ICFTU. The killings which took place between 16–18 September were blamed on the Israelis as they had controlled access to the camps.

These events marked a profound shift in the attitude of the TUC and the unions to the problems of the Middle East. The TUC issued a statement which expressed their horror and outrage at the brutal murder of civilian refugees in Beirut. It was followed by a call for an independent international inquiry into the killings. The ICFTU sent affiliates copies of their statement as well as those from the Histadrut and the UGTT. The ICFTU, as well as being "shocked and disgusted by the barbaric massacres" once again repeated the call for the fundamental rights both of Israel and the Palestinians to be recognised on the basis of UN resolution 242. The UGTT blamed the "blood thirsty Zionists and their allies," comparing the killings to the acts of the Nazis saying that Israel was "a colonialist and racist state and an aggressor." The Histadrut expressed their "revulsion and profound shock at the massacres" and called for the resignation of the Prime Minister and the Defence Minister, the immediate withdrawal of Israeli forces from Beirut and for a judicial enquiry into the killings.[106]

The TGWU called on the TUC to impose a boycott on all Israeli ships and aircraft until they withdrew their troops from Lebanon. The International department advised that for a boycott to be effective, international agreement and support would be needed, which had not been forthcoming when they had canvassed the ICFTU and other national trade union bodies. Their memo revealed that "It would be unprecedented for the General Council to boycott another country's vessels and aircraft to force political decisions by it" and that the TUC stood a much better chance of influencing Israel through the Histadrut even though there was strong support within unions for a boycott. The proposal for a boycott was not adopted by the General Council.[107]

Following a successful TUC Congress motion, the Labour Party conference unanimously adopted the NEC's resolution which condemned the killings in the Beirut refugee camps, the complicity of the Begin government as well as calling for the establishment of a Palestinian State, with the PLO *to be* involved in negotiations.[108] The conference also adopted very two "hostile" anti-Israel motions, which were narrowly approved due to trade union support.

These resolutions marked the final collapse of the pro-Israel consensus within the labour movement and provided the opportunity for Labour Party grassroots condemnation of Israeli policy. It *showed* how far TUC and Labour Party activists had moved towards the Palestinian nationalist cause since 1967.[109]

Meshel, the Histadrut General Secretary told the TUC that they were disappointed that their Congress resolution had only demanded the withdrawal of the Israeli armed forces and not the withdrawal of all foreign forces from Lebanon. He reminded the TUC of the death and destruction caused by the eight year old Lebanon civil war which had involved the PLO and the Syrian army and that '*as far as the establishment of an independent, sovereign state for the Palestinian people, which your resolution advocates, I am sure that far from bringing peace and security, such a separate state is a certain recipe for constant tension and more war and bloodshed*'. Meshel added that the Histadrut supported the position of the Israel Labour Party; that a just solution to the Palestinian problem can only be found '*on the basis of territorial compromise with Jordan whose Palestinian citizens account for over 60% of the Jordanian population*'.[110]

The PTUF which was based in Syria thanked the TUC for their support and asked for a meeting with them. Murray was advised that the PTUF were affiliated to the communist WFTU and replied that they were only interested in making contact with unions that were independent and representative of their members. The TUC also received letters from local Trades Councils detailing resolutions that had been adopted regarding the recognition of the PLO, the establishment of a Palestinian homeland, a boycott of Israel and one which compared Israeli actions in Beirut with the Nazis extermination of the Jews.[111]

A Histadrut delegation led by Nawf Mashala, an Arab member of the Histadrut Executive Bureau, which had been invited to the UK by the TGWU met with members of the General Council on 11 January 1983 to discuss the situation in the Middle East and how to achieve an agreed, lasting and peaceful settlement. Michael Walsh, the Head of the International department had prepared a briefing note for the General Council which set out clearly the TUC's view on the political situation in the Middle East; that the TUC has had long-established friendly relations with Histadrut and that the recent Congress resolution had reaffirmed TUC support for the recognition of Israel and her security. Although the General Council had no intention of moving from that position, the Congress resolution had marked '*a development in TUC policy, of which the Histadrut should take account, relating to the dependence of any just lasting, agreed political settlement in the Middle East on a satisfactory resolution of the rights of the Palestinian people*'. Walsh advised that the Histadrut should also be made aware of the TUC's condemnation of the inhuman and sustained bombardment of Beirut which could not be justified on grounds of combatting terrorist attacks on Northern Israel, and of the Israeli authorities gross negligence in permitting the brutal killing of Palestinians in the two refugee camps, especially as they claimed that they were to keep order and protect civilians. The note concluded that Israel was no longer seen as a just and beleaguered society because of the crimes of the Israeli Government who seemed bent on ensuring Israeli security through aggression and the force of arms, a policy which in the long run would fail Israel. The General Council was advised firstly that the Histadrut could justify the call, which was supported by the TUC, for the removal of all foreign armies including Israel's from the Lebanon by referring to the Syrian and PLO forces that were already in Lebanon. And secondly that the TUC had taken the view that the only viable group to represent the Palestinians was the PLO, it therefore followed that they should ask the

Histadrut representatives, whom they saw as the representatives of the Palestinians.[112]

In their opening remarks, the TUC made it clear that even though there was a long history of friendly relations between Britain and Israel, many Britons had reassessed their attitude to Israel as a result of Israel's invasion of Lebanon, their "*brutal, protracted, bombardment of Beirut*" and the massacres at the Sabra and Shatila refugee camps. The Histadrut responded by making clear that they had opposed the Lebanon invasion, the bombing of Beirut, and had advocated the withdrawal of Israeli forces from Lebanon. But in their opinion, the PLO had been liable for much of the suffering in Lebanon and most Israelis believed that the PLO would refuse to recognise and negotiate with Israel.

The Histadrut also said that they opposed the policy of settlements in the territories and supported discussions with the Palestinian people, but would not accept the PLO as their representatives. The delegation were told then that if a peaceful solution were to be found, Israel would have to reach an understanding with representatives of the Palestinian people and it seemed to them that the majority Palestinians accepted the PLO as their representatives. The Histadrut were also asked if they had any contact with the Palestinians or any of the Arab trade unions in the Middle East. They confirmed that they did not have any contact with the PLO as they controlled the General Federation of Palestinian Trade Unions (GFPTU) which they did not regard as a proper trade union organisation. They added that, although, that they were prepared to meet without any preconditions representatives of any Arab trade unions, which would not happen unless their governments' had given them permission to do so. When asked '*if the TUC could be an intermediary*', the Histadrut replied that they already had links with Egyptian trade unions and the TUC should understand that a precondition of any contact with the Arab trade unions was that the unions should first recognise Israel and at present dialogue was not possible as they unreservedly supported the PLO. The Histadrut added that it was difficult to see how the TUC could help in the circumstances. In conclusion, the Histadrut asked for the understanding of the TUC with '*the obstacles which other countries in the region put in the way of peace*' as well as the political constraints on its position as '*many Israeli working people supported the aggressive nationalistic policies of the Begin Government and had criticised the Histadrut for its condemnation of the invasion of Lebanon, the bombardment of Beirut, and for its call for an inquiry into the massacres*'. The meeting closed with a TUC representative reminding everyone that as tensions had been rising in the occupied territories '*it was essential that there should be negotiations between the Israeli authorities and genuine representatives of the Palestinians*'. and that the '*TUC hoped that the Histadrut, would in turn understand the concerns of working people outside the Middle East region and take any opportunity to contribute to a dialogue which could lead to a just and lasting peace*'.[113]

The Histadrut's feelings about the meeting are not recorded. Apart from the comprehensive report of the meeting, the International committee minutes indicate very little as regards to future TUC thinking. The committee noted the Histadrut's rejection of the TUC's offer to help and suggested that the TUC should continue to build links with Arab trade unions in the hope that trade union involvement in any future peace settlement might be useful.

The committee also discussed a letter from the National Union of Teachers (NUT), who were concerned about the living and working conditions of the Palestinian people in Lebanon and the occupied territories and suggested that a General Council delegation should visit these areas. The Histadrut supported the idea but made it clear that such a delegation would not have the access they would need in the West Bank and in Beirut and that the Israeli authorities would not permit the delegation to have contact with Palestinian representatives. Under the circumstances the committee agreed not to go ahead with the visit.[114]

Conclusion

The TUC's approval of the FBU resolution had marked the final collapse of the pro-Israel consensus within the labour movement and had a dramatic effect on the TUC-Histadrut relations marking the end of twenty years of support for Israel and the Histadrut. The key element which determined the TUC's attitude towards Israel and the Histadrut, and certainly after 1945, were the views of six biggest unions, especially the TGWU, and the attitude of their leaders, Bevin, Deakin, Cousins and Evans. The smaller unions were only able to promote successful motions at Congress if they had the support of the large unions as had happened in 1982.

The culmination of grassroots support for the Palestinian cause came in 1982 with Israel's invasion of Lebanon. It provided the Left with the opportunity to change both TUC and Labour Party policy with both organisations adopting resolutions which criticised Israel's military action as well as recognising the Palestinian right to their own homeland. The

Left's main concern was never about the settlements but building support for the recognition of the PLO and a Palestinian homeland. Even without the opportunity presented by Israel's invasion of Lebanon it was more than likely that a motion critical of Israel and supportive of the Palestinians would have been adopted by Congress within the next few years. The vote by the 1982 Congress changed everything, it signalled a move away from Israel and the Histadrut to support for the Palestinians and although nobody realised it at the time the TUC had effectively changed sides which would lead to a near total breakdown in the TUC's relations with the Histadrut.

Notes

1. Minkin, The Labour Party Conference: a study in the politics of intra-party democracy, pp. 175–176.
2. Christopher Andrew, *The defence of the realm: the authorized history of MI5* (London: Allen Lane, 2009), pp. 535–536.
3. Author's interview with Jack Jones, London, 11 January 2005.
4. Author's interviews with John Vanderveken, ICFTU General Secretary 1982–92, Brussels, 7 April 2011 and Mike Walsh, Head of TUC International Department, 1980–99.
5. The British Ambassador to Israel, Annual review for 1972, 1 January 1973, TNA: PRO, LAB13/2728.
6. Yagol to TUC, 8 October 1973, MRC, MSS.292D/956/511/1.
7. Comay to the Israeli Foreign Office (Hebrew original), 7 October 1973, ISA, HZ6738/1.
8. TUC briefing on the Middle East, 22 October 1973, MRC, MSS.292D/956/511/1.
9. TUC International Committee minutes, 23 October 1973, MRC, MSS.292D/901/6.
10. TUC statement on the Middle East, 23 October 1973, MRC, MSS.292D/956/511/1.
11. Yagol to Ben-Aharon 6 November 1973 (Hebrew original), PLILMR, IV-219A-5-17.
12. Yagol to Meshel, 26 December 1973 (Hebrew original), ISA, HZ6740/5.
13. Yagol to Ben-Aharon 6 November 1973 (Hebrew original), PLILMR, IV-219A-5-17.
14. Israel Gat to Bahat, 3 December 1973, PLILMR, IV-219A-4-7B.
15. Yagol to Meshel, 26 December 1973 (Hebrew original), ISA, HZ6740/5.
16. Yagol to Ben-Aharon, 6, 9 and 30 November 1973 (Hebrew original), PLILMR, IV-219A-5-17.
17. TUC memo to Walsh, 1 February 1974, MRC, MSS.292D/901/6.

18. International Committee minutes, 4 February 1974, MRC, MSS.292D/901/6.
19. TUC General Council minutes, 1 April 1974, MRC, MSS.292D/901/6 and Yagol to Meshel, 24 April 1974 (Hebrew original), PLILMR, IV-219A-4-149B.
20. Histadrut to the ICFTU 14 April 1974, ISSH:ICFTU, 1452, item 62EB/2, and TUC General Council minutes, 1 June 1974, MRC, MSS.292D/901/6.
21. Cohen to Meshel, 31 January 1975, PLILMR, IV-219A-7-132.
22. Author's interview with Lady Valerie Cocks, Executive Director of TUFI, 1983–90, London, 6 October 2005.
23. TUC memos to Murray, 15 and 19 August 1975, both MRC, MSS.292D/956.9/1.
24. Israel Embassy to Israeli Foreign Ministry, 13 August 1975 (Hebrew original), ISA, HZ6739/3.
25. The TUC sent a copy of their statement to the Foreign Office who replied saying that the Government "will oppose any attempt to deny Israel representation in UN organisations or to exclude Israel from participation in UN activities". Murray to the Foreign Secretary, 28 August 1975, General Council Statement, 29 August 1975, MRC, both MSS.292D/956.9/1, FCO to TUC, 8 September 1975, MRC, MSS.292D/956.9/2.
26. "TUC Secretary-General meets Rabin and "Murray supports Israel's existence," *Haaretz* (Hebrew original), 22 August 1975, MRC, MSS.292D/956.9/2.
27. Author's interview with Aaron Barnea, European Histadrut representative, 1975–78, 28 October 2004, Israel.
28. Mark Segal, "The need to make friends in Britain," *Jerusalem Post*, 29 August 1975.
29. TUC memo to Murray, 13 November 1975, MRC, MSS.292D/956.9/2, TUC memo to Murray, 1 December 1975 and Murray to Meshel, 15 December 1975, MRC, MSS.292B/956.9/1.
30. Report of the visit of the TUC delegation to Syria, TUC International Committee minutes, 6 October 1975, MRC, MSS.292D/901/9.
31. MRC, TUC Congress report 1976, p. 556.
32. Gershon Avner, London Embassy to the Israel Foreign Office, 27 April 1956 (Hebrew original), ISA, HZ329/8.
33. Ne'eman to Simchoni, 11 November 1963 (Hebrew original), PLILMR, IV-219A-1-106.
34. Unions contacted in Britain included, the National Union of General and Municipal Workers, the National Union of Railwaymen and the National Union of Vehicle Builders. Histadrut International Department report, 5 October 1972 (Hebrew original), PLILMR, IV-219-7-97.

35. Feather offered to raise the matter again when the TUC went to Moscow in 1973, Yagol to Ben Aharon, 10 January 1973 (Hebrew original), PLILMR, IV-219A-4-149 and TUC International Committee minutes, 27 March 1973, MRC, MSS.292D/901/4.
36. Report no: IC6/2, "Minorities in the Soviet Union," TUC International Committee minutes, 23 January 1973, MRC, MSS.292D/901/4 and, MRC, TUC Congress proceedings 1973, pp. 235–236.
37. Jack Jones, *Union man: the autobiography of Jack Jones* (London: Collins, 1986), pp. 270–272 and Report IC11/3, "Visit to the Soviet Union", TUC International Committee minutes, 21 August 1973, MRC, MSS.292D/901/5.
38. Yagol to Ben Aharon, 10 September 1973 (Hebrew original), PLILMR, IV-219A-4-7B.
39. Yagol to Ben Aharon, 6 November 1973 (Hebrew original), PLILMR, IV-219A-4-149.
40. TUC International Committee minutes, 23 January 1974, MRC, MSS.292D/901/6.
41. Robert Taylor, *The fifth estate: Britain's unions in the modern world* (London: Routledge, 1978), pp. 149–150.
42. The TUC and the EETPU both described Soviet Jews who wished to leave for Israel as 'Soviet dissidents'.
43. Item 70, Soviet Dissidents; letter from the EETPU, TUC International Committee minutes, 1 April 1974, MRC, MSS.292D/901/6.
44. TUC International Committee minutes, 17 July 1974, MRC, MSS.292D/901/6.
45. TUC International Committee minutes, 5 August 1974, MRC, MSS.292D/901/6.
46. Shelepin visa called an "affront to people", *The Guardian*, 18 March 1975.
47. Zionists, "hired protesters", *The Guardian*, 3 April 1975.
48. Yagol to Meshel, 20 March and 10 April 1975 (Hebrew original), PLILMR, both IV-219A-4-149B.
49. TUC International Committee minutes, 2 February 1976, MRC, MSS.292D/901/9.
50. Paragraph 298, "Soviet Dissents," International Committee report, MRC, TUC Congress proceedings 1976 and TUC International Committee minutes, 5 April 1976, MRC, MSS.292D/901/10.
51. MRC, TUC Congress proceedings 1976, pp. 561–562.
52. Paragraph 278, "Soviet Minorities," MRC, TUC Congress proceedings 1976.
53. MRC, TUC Congress proceedings 1977, pp. 507–510.
54. Author's Interview with Mike Walsh, Head of TUC International Department, 1980–99.

55. Daphne Gerlis, *Those Wonderful Women in Black* (London: Minerva Press, 1996), pp. 121–129.
56. The TUC had abstained in June 1974 at the ILO meeting which had adopted a resolution condemning the Israeli policy of discrimination, racism, and violation of trade union freedoms against the Arab workers in the occupied territories. Memo for TUC/DGB Meeting, 14 December 1974, MRC, MSS.292D/956/511/1, TUC General Council minutes, 5 August 1974, MRC, MSS.292D/901/6 and MRC, ILO conference, TUC Congress report 1974, p. 196.
57. Yagol to Murray, 23 January 1975 and Murray to Yagol, 29 January 1975, both MRC, MSS.292D/956.9/1.
58. TUC International Committee minutes 7, April 1975, MRC, MSS.292D/901/8.
59. Yagol to Meshel, 20 March 1975 (Hebrew original), PLILMR, IV-219A-4-149B and Meshel to Murray, 15 April 1975, MRC, MSS.292D/956.9/2.
60. LMU, TUC Congress proceedings 1978, pp. 591–592.
61. The TUC wrote to the foreign secretary who agreed with the TUC's opinion on the matter. TUC International Committee minutes, 4 August 1975, TUC General Council Statement, 29 August 1975, Murray to Foreign Office, 28 August 1975, Foreign Office reply, 8 September 1975, all MRC, MSS.292D/956.9/1.
62. MRC, International debate, TUC Congress report 1975, p. 490.
63. Murray to Gormley, 15 February 1977, MRC, MSS.292D/956/511/2, Israeli metalworkers to TGWU, 22 February 1977 and TGWU reply, 24 February 1977, PLILMR, IV-208-1-18965 and Malcolm Brown, 'Arab blacklist warning forces Metal Box to look at Israel holdings', *The Times*, 1 September 1977.
64. In March 1979 the Department of Trade issued new guidelines on the Arab boycott which set out the Government's policy in order to "help remove misunderstandings and unnecessary anxieties among British businessmen about the operation of the Arab Boycott of Israel as it affects British firms". The guidance given did "not imply any recognition of the boycott by HM Government nor any willingness on the part of the Government to further its objectives by giving publicity to it". Department of Trade guidelines, "the Arab boycott of Israel", March 1979, TNA:PRO, FCO93/2365.
65. Author's interview with Mike Walsh, TUC International Department, 1966–99, 6 November 2007, London.
66. Memorandum on the history and functions of the Histadrut "The Israeli trade union federation; decline of a triple pillar of the State," from the British Ambassador to the foreign secretary, 25 April 1977, TNA: PRO, FCO 93/1178.

67. Memo to FCO, 25 August 1977, FCO to British Embassy in Israel, 13 September 1977, and Overseas labour advisor to the labour attaché, Athens, 14 November 1977, all TNA: PRO, FCO93/1178.
68. S. Polakow-Suransky, *the Unspoken alliance* (New York: Vintage Books, 2010), p. 80.
69. The Lebanon branch of the PTUF to Murray, 20 August 1979, MRC, MSS.292D/956/9/2.
70. UKPC to TUC, 24 September 1979, MRC, MSS.292D/956/9/2.
71. Evans to Murray, 21 October 1979, Murray reply, 24 October 1979, Murray to Kersten, 24 October 1979, all MRC, MSS292D/956.9/2.
72. UKPC to Murray, 22 October 1979, TUC Memo to Murray, 26 October 1979, Murray to the UKPC, 30 October 1979, ICFTU to Murray, 6 November 1979 and UKPC to TUC, 20 November 1979, all MRC, MSS292D/956.9/2.
73. Author's interview with Mike Walsh, TUC International Department, 1966–99, 6 November 2007, London and Authors Interview with Aaron Barnea, Histadrut European representative in Brussels 1975–80, 23 March 2005, Hod Hasharon.
74. Alon to the Israel Foreign Office, 1 February 1981 (Hebrew Original), PLILMR, IV-219A-7-326.
75. Overseas labour advisor to the TUC, 29 December 1977, MRC,/956/511/2, Meshel letter to Murray, 27 March 1978, MRC, MSS.292D/956.9/2 and TUC International Committee minutes, 9 January 1977, MRC, MSS.292D/901/12.
76. "TUC asked to be mediator", *Jewish Chronicle*, 15 September 1978.
77. Report IC4/4 "visit to Israel and Egypt," TUC International Committee minutes, 12 January 1981, MRC, MSS.292D/901/18.
78. ICFTU press release, 23 July 1981, MRC, MSS.292D/956/511/2.
79. Murray to Meshel, 23 July 1981, TUC memo to Murray, 3 August 1981, both MRC, MSS.292D/956/51.
80. Histadrut to the ICFTU, 26 July 1981, MRC, MSS.292D/956/511/2.
81. Murray to the Federation of Petroleum Trade Unions in Lebanon, 14 October 1981, MRC, MSS.292D/956/511/2.
82. Norwegian Federation of Trade Unions to the TUC, 24 July 1981, TUC reply, 5 August 1981, both MRC, MSS.292D/956/511/2. TUC press release, 5 January 1982, MRC, MSS.292D/956/511/3.
83. Report of the June 1982 ETUC meeting, International Committee minutes, 5 July 1982, MRC, MSS.292D/956/511/2.
84. TUC memo to Murray from Walsh 5 July 1982, MRC, MSS292D/956/511/2.
85. ICFTU Press release, 14 June 1982 and ICFTU Circular No.32 (1982), 11 August 1982, all MRC, MSS.292D/956/511/2.
86. TUC memo to Murray, 5 July 1982, MRC, MSS.292D/956/511/2.

87. Murray to the Federation of Petroleum Trade Unions, 16 August 1982 and Murray to Meshel, 16 August 1982, MRC, MSS.292D/956/511/2.
88. Copies of the resolution were sent to the Egyptian and Israeli ambassadors. STUC to the Israel Embassy, 25 October 1975, PLILMR, IV-277-4.
89. The allegation turned out to be groundless as there had been no evidence that Yagol had refused the visit on those grounds. Shiloh to Barnea, 14 February 1976, Barnea to Shiloh, 24 February 1976, Shiloh to Barnea, 10 March 1976, all (Hebrew original), PLILMR, IV-219A-7-132.
90. Author's interviews with George Galloway, Secretary of the TUFP 1980–83, London, 19 October 2011 and Mike Walsh, TUC International Department, 1966–99, 6 November 2007.
91. International Committee debate, MRC, TUC Congress proceedings 1982, and author's interview with George Galloway.
92. Memo to the General Council "Emergency resolution on the Middle East," 6 September 1982, MRC,MSS.292D/956/511/2.
93. Author's interviews with Ken Cameron, General Secretary of the FBU, 1980–2000, Edinburgh April 2005 and David Warburton, Senior Officer for the GMB Union, 1970–95, Amersham, May 2005.
94. MRC, TUC Congress proceedings 1982, International Committee debate and author's interviews with Ken Cameron, David Warburton and George Galloway.
95. Author's interviews with Ken Cameron, General Secretary of the FBU, 1980–2000, David Warburton, Senior Officer for the GMB Union, 1970–95 and George Galloway, Secretary of the TUFP 1980–83.
96. Francis Beckett, *Enemy Within: The Rise and Fall of the British Communist Party*, p. 158, p. 176 and p. 182, Robert Taylor, *The TUC from the General Strike to New Unionism* (Basingstoke: Palgrave, 2000), p. 231 and author's interview with George Galloway.
97. NUM letter to TUC, 16 September 1982, MSS292D/956/511/2.
98. TUC International Committee minutes, 10 January 1983, MRC,MSS.292D/901/2.
99. Labour Party to the TUC, 3 December 1982, MRC,MSS.292D/956/511/3.
100. TUC to Israel Embassy, 30 September 1982, Israel Embassy to the TUC, 5 October 1982.

     The words in italics were omitted from the International Committee report, MRC, TUC Congress proceedings 1983, p. 216, but were reported in full in the TUC International Committee minutes, 1 November 1982, all MRC, MSS.292D/901/2.
101. TUC International Committee minutes, 1 November 1982, MRC, MSS.292D/901/23, Foreign Secretary to Murray, 4 October 1982, Murray to Foreign Secretary, 29 October 1982 and Foreign Office reply, 12 November 1982, all MRC, MSS.292D/956/511/2.

102. Meshel to Murray, 21 December 1982, MRC, MSS.292D/956/511/3.
103. PTUF to the TUC, 3 October 1982, Walsh memo to Murray, 15 October 1982, TUC reply to PTUF, 28 October 1982. Runcorn, Portsmouth, Harwich and Southampton Trades Councils to the TUC, 15 October – I November 1982, all MRC, MSS.292D/956/511/3.
104. "TUC congress calls for a Palestinian State," *Jewish Chronicle*, 17 September 1982.
105. The numbers of those killed is disputed; the Red Cross estimated 460 had been killed. The IDF intelligence believed the figure was 600–800 whereas some Palestinians believe the figure was 2000. Colin Shindler, *A History of Modern Israel* (Cambridge: Cambridge University Press, 2008), p. 179.
106. Histadrut statement, 20 September 1982, TUC Finance and General Purposes Committee statement, 20 September 1982, TUC General Council minutes, 22 September 1982, ICFTU Press release, 21 September 1982, ICFTU letter to Murray, 22 September 1982, all MRC, MSS.292D/956/511/2 and TUC International Committee report, IC1/8, 4 October 1982, MRC, MSS.292D/901/23.
107. TGWU letter to TUC, 20 September 1982, Walsh memo to Murray and International Department paper IC1/8 on the Middle East, International Committee minutes, all 4 October 1982, MRC,MSS.292D/956/511/2, General Council minutes, 4 October 1982, MRC,MSS.292D/956/511/3.
108. "Labour to unravel Middle East Policy Jumble", *Jewish Chronicle*, 8 October 1982, p. 4 and Labour Party NEC resolution, 29th September 1982, ISA, HZ 8977/6.
109. Telex to Shimon Peres from Haim Zadok, 30 September 1982, ISA, HZ 8977/6.
110. Meshel to Murray, 21 December 1982, MRC, MSS.292D/956/511/3.
111. PTUF to the TUC, 3 October 1982, Walsh memo to Murray, 15 October 1982, TUC reply to PTUF, 28 October 1982. Runcorn, Portsmouth, Harwich and Southampton Trades Councils to the TUC, 15 October – I November 1982, all MRC, MSS.292D/956/511/3.
112. International Committee memo from MW, 4 January 1983, MSS292E/956.9/920.2.
113. TUC report of the meeting with representatives of the Histadrut, report, IC5/2, 11 January 1983, MRC, 292D/956/511/3.
114. International Committee minutes, 7 February 1983, MRC, MSS.292D/956/511/3.

CHAPTER 6

Changing Sides

The final period from 1983 until 2021 examines the TUC's move away from support for Israel and the Histadrut, to its support for the Palestinian Arabs and the international BDS campaign directed against Israel, which, since 2015 has led to the increase in antisemitism in Britain. The two key issues that have dominated since 2002, are the academic boycott of Israel promoted by the University and College lecturers Union (UCU) and the antisemitism crisis in the Labour Party. Both involve the Far Left and have been very divisive in the British labour movement in relation to its view of Israel and Anglo-Jewry. This has spread out into the wider community.

The 1980s—The TUC Moves to Change Sides

From 1982 onwards the TUC and its member unions regularly adopted resolutions containing anti-Israeli and pro-Palestinian rhetoric, with only limited disapproval of Palestinian terrorist activities. These resolutions sometimes crossed the line into antisemitism with the result that a generation of British left-wing trade union activists have been raised on a diet of political conference motions whose only mention of Israel was in connection with its alleged 'brutality' in response to Palestinian terrorism and their 'oppression' of the Palestinian people.

The 1982 TUC Congress was the defining moment for TUC-Histadrut relations as each side from then on had their own set of priorities, for the TUC it was Europe and globalisation and for the Histadrut it was

R. Fraser, *British Trade Unions, the Labour Party, and Israel's Histadrut*, https://doi.org/10.1007/978-3-030-86814-7_6

maintaining relations with more friendly union centres such as Germany. Israel and the Histadrut were still represented in the UK but with a more limited and much less effective presence. The TUC and the Histadrut both continued to refer to each other as friends with a history of good relations stretching back to the 1920s. By the 1980s, the ability of both organisations to influence the political policies of their respective governments had diminished.

Whereas before 1982 there was only limited support for the Palestinian cause within the unions and the TUC, the Left's defeat of the TUC leadership resulted in a breakthrough for the TUFP as more and more unions at both local and national level began to support the Palestinian cause.[1] The TUFP became a very effective lobby group within the British labour movement during the 1980s until its demise in early 1990s, campaigning for Palestinian rights, the disaffiliation of the Histadrut from the ILO, and a boycott of Israeli goods and services.

Neil Kinnock, who became leader of the Labour Party in 1983, was sympathetic towards Israel and keen to rebuild bridges with the Jewish community. As a reaction to the turmoil caused by the calls to recognise the PLO from within the Labour Party, the NEC, withdrew all resolutions on the Israel-Palestine conflict at the Party's 1983 annual conference and replaced it with a statement on the Middle East that did not include a reference to the conflict.

The TUC took a similar stance at their 1983 Congress but did allow discussion of a motion proposed by the right-wing EETPU which acknowledged the legitimate rights of the Palestinian people, and called for the recognition of the Histadrut's achievements as well an increase in bilateral contacts with them. It was an attempt by friends of Israel to regain some of the support lost the previous year. Even though several unions had previously pledged to support the motion including the TGWU, the AUEW and the GMWU, a move which would have guaranteed the motion a majority, the motion was lost. A card vote was not called for as this would have been extremely divisive within the unions.[2]

Not only was support for Israel and the Palestinians very divisive it was also split along a right-wing, left-wing divide in the unions with the AEU and EETPU as the main supporters of Israel with the backing of TUFI whilst the TUFP could now rely on regular support from the major unions on the Left which included the GMB, the FBU, the NUM, SOGAT 82, NALGO and NUPE. As the 1980s progressed the TUFP arranged for many of the major unions to send delegations to the West Bank and Gaza,[3] whereas a decade earlier it had been TUFI which had been organising similar trips to Israel. In order to counter this increasing pro-Palestinian support within the unions and the Labour Party, the Histadrut appointed Ben Sella as its first UK representative for 15 years. His role was to support to the work of the Histadrut's European representative in Brussels and to build on the efforts of TUFI.

The TUC continued to follow Government and Labour Party policy by not having any official contact with the PLO and whenever Yousef Allan of the TUFP contacted the TUC during 1983 he was rebuffed. The Head of the international department, Mike Walsh was in no doubt that Allan had been encouraged to do so by his supporters on the General Council. He told Murray that '*we could expose ourselves to the charge of being willing to listen to one side only in the Middle East conflict if we refused to see him but I feel that we should say that we will not see him because he has no trade union credentials and because the Labour Party is the more appropriate British counterpart*'.[4]

In March 1984 the TUC received letters from two organisations both calling themselves the PTUF, one was based in Tunis which invited the TUC to attend its Congress and the other in Damascus which was looking forward to strengthening relations with them. Walsh concluded after speaking with Allan, who had denied that there were two organisations, that there were two distinct groups split on the same political lines as the PLO and Allan appeared to represent the Tunis group led by Yasser Arafat. Walsh asked Murray for permission to see him in the department with a view to gaining clearer information.[5] A meeting with the TUFP was allowable as it was not an official meeting with the PLO.

Walsh set out the post-1982 attitude of the TUC towards the Arab-Israel conflict in a letter to the Salford Trades Union Council which had been approached by the Palestine Solidarity Campaign (PSC) to support the rights of Palestinian workers. He wrote that the TUC did not formally recognise or associate with single cause organisations such as the PSC which were supported mainly by individual members of the public, regardless of the merits of the cause because their aims were outside the trade union and employment fields in which trade union organisations have influence and some control. Walsh concluded by saying that the TUC had sought to promote a comprehensive peace agreement through its trade union contacts including the ICFTU which recognised of the rights of the Palestinian people to self-determination within an independent state.[6] However this was not totally true since the adoption of the 1975 Helsinki protocol on human rights, the TUC had dropped its longstanding requirement for decisions on international issues to have a trade union connection and therefore its support for self-determination for the Palestinian people was now considered to be a human rights issue.

The July 1985 meeting of the TUC International Committee discussed the TUC's training and assistance programmes for trade unions in developing countries. Given the TUC's standing and influence in the international trade union arena, the TUC was a minor player when compared with the work of the American, German and the Soviet unions. TUC assistance, which had been provided mainly to Commonwealth states, was modest because they did not have the financial resources as compared to the major providers. It was funded either through the ICFTU or occasionally by the TUC. However the meeting was not told that since the 1960s the Histadrut had been a major provider of international support programmes for the third world. This was not surprising as the TUC was moving away from the Histadrut in favour of the Palestinians and had never been totally supportive of the Histadrut's programmes even though they were backed by the ICFTU and were far superior to anything offered by the TUC. The Histadrut delivered its training through the Afro-Asian Institute for several hundred participants each year from trade unions in developing nations in Africa Asia and Central America. Their programmes had been developed to improve the understanding of the character and workings of the State of Israel in response to the never-ending attempts by Israel's enemies to misrepresent Israel's image and Zionism amongst trade unions and international organisations throughout the world.

In response to the Israeli raid on the PLO headquarters in Tunis In October 1985 the TUC followed the ICFTU's lead and wrote to the Histadrut condemning the attack as a '*most brutal violation of the territorial integrity of an independent country and the killing of at least some civilians*' which had seriously set back prospects for peace.[7] A few days later the TUC received an invitation to send a representative to the Histadrut Convention the following month. Mike Walsh suggested to Norman Willis, the general secretary that accepting the invitation would provide the TUC with the opportunity to remind Histadrut of their deep concern about the raid. The General Council agreed and Moss Evans of the TGWU attended the convention as the TUC and ICFTU representative. It is not known how Evans comments were received by the Histadrut but five days later the TUC received a letter from the Histadrut which pointed out that the map on the PTUF letterhead showed a map of Israel and the West Bank with an Arab inscription claiming the entire territory for the Arabs.

They asked the TUC '*Do you consider this to be the proper letterhead for a bona fide trade union, and does this not prove what kind of 'trade union activity' the PTUF engages in?*'[8] At the same time as Evans was in Israel, NALGO asked Willis to meet with a PTUF delegation that they had invited to Britain. As it was not politically acceptable to meet with the PLO, NALGO were told he was busy and they met instead with a member of the International department.[9]

When the Israeli prime minister Shimon Peres came to London in January 1986 Willis was invited to attend a private meeting with him. As well providing Willis with the usual information that the TUC had a long-standing relationship with the Histadrut and that the TUC took up with the Histadrut any enquiries and complaints they received about the action of the Israeli authorities in the West Bank; Walsh was very honest and told him that in his opinion '*British trade unions tend to take up positions rigidly for or against Israel and its policies and there is little attempt to find a reasonable consensus. The insensitivity which the Israelis frequently show to world opinion, in particular the attack on PLO headquarters in Tunis on 1 October, as well as the Palestinian terrorist attacks, not usually committed by the Arafat faction within the PLO, made it almost impossible to gain acceptance of a balanced view of the issues*'. He added that there was no question about the TUC's regard for Histadrut as an independent trade union organisation and wanted to maintain good relations with them. Israel wanted Britain to take strong action to break the Arab boycott as the Arabs were insisting British companies should not deal with Israeli businesses or those with predominantly Jewish interests. Walsh ended the briefing by saying that TUC had been told by the British Government that they had tried to protect British companies against Arab pressure but British business could not afford to break the boycott because trade with the Arab nations was worth much more than trade with Israel.[10]

Walsh's view that the British trade unions were either for or against Israel was borne out a few months later when the AUEW suggested that a joint TUC-Labour Party delegation visit Israel in order to assist the efforts of the Israeli Government to advance the peace process. Walsh told Willis that he doubted that the proposal would be acceptable to some of the unions especially as the issues concerned are so contentious and arouse strong passions on both sides. His view was that there would also be pressure for the delegation to meet with the PTUF and possibly to visit Arab countries in the region. Walsh was proved right when the International

Committee decided that it would not be appropriate, for the TUC to propose or take part in a joint delegation with the Labour Party.[11]

By 1987 the political landscape within the major unions had changed as one by one the unions had withdrawn their support for Israel and the Histadrut, replacing it with a pro-Palestinian position which made it a lot harder for pro-Israel voices to be heard. Lady Valerie Cocks, the Director of the Labour Friends of Israel and TUFI, told the *Jewish Chronicle* that '*A lot of unions which were friendly with us are not so friendly anymore*' and '*there is a well-orchestrated anti-Israel campaign. Militants take over positions of power and put out the propaganda. The Palestinians do their job very well. They are very well organised and well financed*'.[12] The police had to be called to protect Lady Cocks at the annual conference of NALGO, as she was subjected to severe intimidation and harassment whilst handing out leaflets at the TUFI stall, while inside the conference hall delegates voted by a large majority to sever NALGO's links with both the Histadrut and TUFI.[13]

The 1987 TUC Congress once again adopted by a large majority an FBU motion which condemned Israeli harassment of the Palestine trade unions in the territories; Ken Cameron, the general secretary of the FBU, told delegates that the Arab-Israeli conflict was a threat to world peace and could not be solved without the involvement of the Palestinians and the PLO. A pro-Israel amendment from the electricians' union, the EETPU was withdrawn and a second amendment from the Northern Carpet Trades Union which would have eliminated the reference to alleged Israeli harassment was heavily defeated. The AUEW which had been expected to speak in support of Israel did not do so.[14] In December 1987, the first Palestinian intifada, a series of demonstrations and violent riots, started in the West Bank and the Gaza Strip protesting against Israel's occupation of those territories. The response of the ICFTU and ETUC Congresses in which the TUC played a leading role, was to issue statements deploring the increase in violence in the West Bank and Gaza as well as calling for an international peace conference.[15]

In February 1989 after a meeting between the TUC and the Foreign Office, the PLO wrote to the TUC in order to clarify their relationship with the Palestinian organisations represented in London which included the PTUF, which they said, took their political guidelines from the PLO's policies. This confirmed what the ICFTU had told the TUC 9 years earlier that the PTUF was a political organisation and not a proper trade union. The TUC replied saying that they attached great value to their links with the PTUF and its representative Yousef Allan.[16]

On 7 March 1988 a TUC delegation met with the Israeli ambassador to discuss their concerns about the unrest in the Palestinian territories. The General Council had previously voiced '*its grave concern at the acts of brutality perpetrated by Israeli troops on Palestinian civilians in the occupied West Bank and the Gaza Strip*'. In their view '*the mounting death-toll, detentions without trial, and acts of brutality, as witnessed on our television screens are indefensible*' and '*the deportation of Palestinians from the territories was against international law*'. Although the TUC continued to recognise and support Israel's need for secure and defensible borders, that support, in their view, had become more difficult with the lack of a progress towards a political solution. The General Council had also been told that the Histadrut had condemned extremists on both sides that were seeking to undermine Jewish-Arab coexistence, and had pledged to protect the right of Israeli Arab workers to strike in protest at events.[17] In order to see the situation at first hand the TUC accepted an invitation from the Histadrut to send a delegation to Israel and the West Bank and Gaza.[18]

The Palestinian intifada had been in existence for nearly two years by the time of the 1989 TUC Congress and although the TUC still considered the Histadrut a friend, the General Council and International committee had, as Walsh had predicted taken sides, and their report to the Congress that year was biased in favour of the Palestinians. Although the General Council, at their meeting in December 1989 had welcomed the Palestinian National Congress declaration which recognised the right of Israel to exist alongside a Palestinian state they condemned Israeli policies in the West Bank and Gaza. The General Council sent a copy of their conclusions of their discussions to the Foreign and Commonwealth secretary which included details of deportations and detentions of trade unionists and other restrictions on trade unions in the territories by the Israeli military authorities. The Minister replied saying that he shared the concerns of the General Council and that the Government was supporting attempts to bring about a peaceful settlement.[19]

Since the TUC had been unable to arrange to send its own delegation to the region because of other commitments Ada Maddocks and Mike Walsh represented the TUC in an ICFTU delegation which went to Israel, the West Bank and Gaza in July 1989 to examine the economic and working conditions of Palestinian workers. Although most of their report described their extensive discussions with the leaders of the Palestinian General Federation of Trade Unions of the West Bank and the Federation of Trade Unions of the Gaza Strip in East Jerusalem, Nablus, and Gaza it only briefly mentioned their discussions with the Israeli prime minister, his senior Ministers and the Histadrut. The delegation were told by Histadrut that they were dissatisfied not only with their Government's failure to promote a peaceful negotiated settlement regarding the territories but also with the military methods used in those areas which they considered had undermined Israel's commitment to democracy and human rights. They also indicated that they would be willing to meet representatives of the Palestinian trade unions even if they were connected with the PLO.[20]

The 1989 TUC Congress which debated Middle East situation was notable for the fact that Mr W. Morgan of the AUEW told Congress that the one-sided criticism of Israel was not was not good enough and he urged the TUC to adopt an even-handed approach as well as using its influence and prestige to bring together moderates on both sides. Morgan was then heckled and interrupted when he said that the report made no reference to the fact that the cause of unrest and the detention of Palestinians in the territories was not due to the legitimate trade union activity but solely because of their involvement in subversive activities.[21]

Over the following twelve months TUC became more openly critical of Israel government actions believing that as friends of Israel they should speak out against what they saw as their friend's outrageous behaviour towards the Palestinian intifada. The General Council issued a statement in May 1990 which left one in no doubt as to their views by condemning the '*murders*' of Palestinians by '*the Israeli occupation forces*' in the '*occupied*' West Bank and Gaza. They also called upon Israel to negotiate with the PLO, to recognise the right of the Palestinian people to statehood and self-determination as well as urging the British Government to recall its ambassador from Tel Aviv until Israel implemented their demands.[22] However at trade union level, relations continued as normal as the TUC was represented at the Histadrut Congress in April, several British trade unions went on missions to Israel and a Histadrut delegation came to the UK as guests of the TGWU. However the MSF union annual conference adopted a resolution which called for a labour and trade union campaign to put pressure on the British government to implement economic sanctions against Israel and a boycott of Israeli products.[23] When the delegation from North-West region of the TUC returned from their visit to the West Bank as guests of the PTUF, they recommended that their region should sever its links with the Histadrut and campaign for affiliates to do the same.[24]

The four years between 1989 and 1993 were a significant period in the politics of the Middle East and the Israeli-Palestinian conflict. Not only was there the continuing Palestinian intifada, but also the Gulf war and the 1991 Madrid peace conference which was co-sponsored by the United States and the Soviet Union, in an attempt by the international community in the wake of the Gulf war to revive through negotiation the Israeli-Palestinian peace process. The Israeli-Palestinian negotiations eventually led signing of the Oslo Accords, at the White House in September 1993.

During this period the TUC took it upon itself to become involved with and act as the spokesman for the Palestinian trade union movement at the ICFTU, the ILO and with the British and Israeli governments. The TUC Congress reports record the efforts of the Palestinian trade union organisations to amalgamate into one unified body with the aim of joining the ICFTU as well as the problems their leaders faced when wanting to travel abroad which the TUC saw as discrimination against the Palestinians by the Israeli authorities.

During the Gulf War, Iraq fired 42 Scud missiles at Israel with the aim of trying to bring Israel into the war and therefore endangering the US-led coalition which included several Arab countries. At the request of the Americans, Israel did not retaliate and as a result the Histadrut received many messages of solidarity and support from unions and the labour movement from around the world. The British unions were no exception with personal messages sent by the GMB, the CWU and TGWU. The TUC did not send a message of solidarity but instead issued a press release which did not mention Israel or solidarity with the Histadrut but called instead for the UN charter and the resolutions, '*including resolution 242 in the Middle East context, to be applied in future both justly and consistently*'.[25] Once again just as they had in 1967 and 1973 when Israel was under attack, the TUC had failed to prove itself to be a true friend by not issuing a statement of solidarity.

The TUC Congress in September 1991 adopted a resolution proposed by the FBU which called for a UN-backed Middle East Peace Conference which would include the PLO saying that there could be no lasting peace without the resolution of the Palestinian question. The NALGO delegate said that his union felt so strongly about what he described as the '*brutal occupation*' and '*repression*' of Palestinian trade unions that their conference in June had unanimously voted for a motion for a boycott of Israeli goods and sanctions against Israel. The question of TUC bias towards Palestinians was raised once again by the AUEW delegate who noted that written report on the Middle East focused exclusively on the question of Palestinian trade union rights in the territories and asked why the TUC always blamed Israel for the situation.[26] The reality was that the TUC was no longer the honest broker it claimed to be as it was pursuing an agenda which focussed more on one side than the other.

During 1992 the General Council continued to encourage dialogue between Histadrut and the recently formed Palestinian General Confederation of Trade Unions (PGFTU) whom they hoped would join the ICFTU. The General Council whilst encouraging the Histadrut to accept all UN resolutions on the conflict continued to call for a halt to the building of Israeli settlements in the West Bank and Gaza which they believed were a hindrance to any future peace agreement.

The Oslo Accords[27] were warmly welcomed by the General Council who hoped that it would lead to a lasting peace in the region. The 1994 TUC Congress report noted that they had offered to help the ICFTU with trade union training for the Palestinians and that the Histadrut had played an active role in the ICFTU committee by assisting Palestinians working in Israel with legal services as well as building co-operation with Palestinian trade union organisations.[28]

One outcome of the Oslo Accords was that the Histadrut and the PGFTU signed a framework agreement for cooperation in March 1995 which indicated that both organisations supported the peace process. Between 1995 and 2000 the Histadrut and PGFTU carried out many joint seminars, courses and workshops which were held jointly with international organisations including the ICFTU, the ILO and the TUC.[29] As well as backing these international trade union efforts, the General Council continued to monitor the situation of workers in West Bank and Gaza as well as the expansion of Israeli settlements.

The Histadrut collected the union dues of the Palestinian workers' working in Israel which resulted in the PGFTU receiving 3,642,610 NIS in 2000. In November 1999 representatives from both the Histadrut and the PGFTU came to Britain for a seminar 'Bridging the Divide' organised by the TUC which discussed how to attract investment to the region. Cooperation between the two organisations was brought to a halt by the second intifada which started in September 2000.

The 1996 TUC Congress adopted a FBU resolution which called for reaffirmation of the international status of Jerusalem, an end to the construction of new Israeli settlements in occupied territories, as well as Syrian and Lebanon involvement in negotiations about land for peace. The ongoing goodwill generated by the Oslo Accords combined with optimism for the future ensured that the TUC Congress did not discuss any motions about Israel or peace process between 1997 and 2000, something which had not happened since the 1970s. The Labour Friends of Israel took a delegation of General Council members to Israel in January 1997 where they met with the Histadrut, Israeli politicians and government officials as well as the PGFTU. The delegation concluded that developments in the Israeli-Palestinian peace process were reflected in the developing cooperation between the Histadrut and the PGFTU but the difficulties in reaching an agreement about Hebron as well as the construction of a Jewish settlement at Har Homa posed a real threat to the peace process. When in April 1997, the General Council raised these concerns with the British Government the foreign secretary replied saying said that the Government shared their concerns and would take a firm line on the issue in the UN Security Council.[30]

When the Labour Party was in power it was very important for the TUC to have contact with the Party and the government. The TUC had previously worked closely with the Attlee government and more recently had regular meetings with the Foreign Office during the Wilson and Callaghan administrations in the 1970s. But in the 1980s, when the Left had a big influence on the Labour Party during Michael Foot's leadership, there was very little contact between them as Walsh, the Head of the TUC International department, did not trust his opposite number at the Labour Party or their advisors which resulted in very little input from the Party on international issues.[31]

The Second Millennium a Period of Direct Action by the Unions

Once the General Council disbanded the international committee during the 1990s, the TUC only became involved with the Arab-Israel conflict either at times of conflict or to support pro-Palestinian campaigns. They did however continue to meet with Government Ministers and support ICFTU initiatives. Even though former General Secretaries Woodcock, Feather and Murray were supportive of Israel, they all preferred to work, whenever possible, behind the scenes especially at the ICFTU. Those who succeeded them, Norman Willis, John Monks, Brendan Barber and Frances O'Grady all tried and not always succeeded, in steering a neutral course within the constraints of Congress and General Executive policy decisions which, after 2000, became more anti-Israel and pro-Palestinian.

In the 1990s Tony Blair, the Labour leader, had moved the Labour Party away from its socialist roots to the political centre ground whilst at the same time curbing the unions' power and influence within the labour movement. This resulted in a change in status for the unions who were forced to look elsewhere for issues where they could make a difference. The two issues that they and especially those union activists on the Left, focused their energies on were globalisation and the conflict in the Middle East.

The political left, especially the hard Left which had been instrumental in persuading the TUC to adopt pro-Palestinian policies from 1982 onwards formed what is known as the red-green alliance between UK-based Islamists and radical left activists whose common goal is Israel's demonisation and delegitimisation. The result of this collaboration has been that London became, by 2010, one of the centres calling for Israel's delegitimisation with the result that the Palestinian Boycotts, Divestment and Sanctions (BDS) movement have probably found more support in Britain than in any other Western democratic society. For their part in the Red-Green alliance, the radical Left has been able to operate and promote their anti-Israel policies within the unions because of their political and historical connection with the labour movement. This enabled anti-Zionist groups such as the Socialist Workers Party (SWP) to flourish within the unions in the 1980s and 1990s. The structure and operating procedures of the trade unions have also lent themselves to small numbers of activists setting the agenda and promoting anti-Israel policies. All the major unions supported the demonstration in September 2002 organised by the Stop the War Coalition which opposed the allied invasion of Iraq. The Muslim Association of Britain (MAB) was a key partner for the coalition as it could mobilise large numbers of British Muslims for the protests. The demonstration was the first-time anti-Israel banners and placards featured identifying Israel with the United States.[32]

The new millennium ushered in changes to the way in which the Israel-Palestine conflict was perceived by politicians, the media, the unions, academia and the general public. This change was driven partly by the need for 24 hour news gathering by the media but mainly by the internet which provided the opportunity for any organisation or individual to influence events by posting information or photos on social media. The old ways of campaigning and reacting to events with control firmly in the hands of the few, such as politicians or organisations who gave consideration to their responses, were replaced by instant reaction and comment regardless of whether they were true or false. The result has been media manipulation by interested parties using the internet and social media to provide publicity for their cause.

In a similar way to how 1982 was a game changer in TUC attitudes and policies towards Israel, 2002 was a key year for pro-Palestinian, anti-Israel activism which saw a new form of activism, direct action by activists and unions which bypassed the unions' traditional methods of protest. The use of the internet by both sides in the conflict transformed perceptions. The key components necessary for this revolution were the change in status and influence of the trade unions in TUC and the Labour Party, the second intifada which started in September 2000, the United Nations World Conference against Racism in Durban in 2001, the anti-Iraq war campaign and Israel's intervention in Jenin.

When all these different elements came together in London in April 2002 at the time of the Israeli operation 'Defensive Shield', the narrative relating to the conflict was no longer decided by the TUC; but was driven instead by individual unions controlled by the Left. Direct action by the unions themselves bypassed but did not totally replace the long accepted practice of working through the TUC. As a result of British academics calling for an academic boycott of Israel in 2002, Great Britain has been at the forefront of calls for academic, trade union, media, medical, architectural, and cultural boycotts of Israel. In addition to attracting the support of the left-wing of the trade union movement, the BDS movement also appealed to people with liberal and progressive values by defining the goals of the BDS movement by using universally appealing language regarding international law, human rights and universal justice.

The Second Intifada

The second intifada was a period of intense Israeli-Palestinian violence which began in September 2000 after the Camp David Summit had failed to reach a final agreement on the Israeli-Palestinian peace process. As there was no significant barrier between the West Bank and Israel, Palestinian suicide bombers were able to cross easily into Israeli towns and communities where they carried out deadly suicide bombings against civilians. The Palestinians also engaged in rock throwing, gunfire and rocket attacks. The Israelis responded with gunfire, tank and air attacks, and targeted killings. There were large numbers of casualties amongst civilians as well as combatants. When the second intifada ended in February 2005, over 1000 Israelis had been killed along with 2000 Palestinians.

The two trade unions on the Left that had been at the forefront of the campaign for Palestinian rights during the 1980s and 1990s, the FBU and the College lecturers union, NATFHE, were key players in the unions in response to the increased violence of the intifada.

The FBU motion submitted to the 2001 TUC Congress included statements which were to be repeated many times at future union conferences; firstly, they deplored what they considered to be the use of excessive force by the Israel Defence Forces (IDF), secondly, a call for the withdrawal of Israeli forces from Palestinian territory and thirdly, an end to the building of Jewish settlements in the territories and supporting the creation of a Palestinian state alongside Israel. John Monks, the TUC General Secretary, told leaders of Britain's Jewish community that the TUC leadership would not support the resolution unless it incorporated a condemnation of attacks on Israeli civilians and called for the cessation of terrorist outrages.[33] The motion was lost and a crisis was averted as Congress closed a day early due to the 9-11, Al Qaeda terrorist attack in New York.

The General Council however continued to regularly discuss the conflict and in December 2001 they sent an ICFTU statement to the Foreign Secretary along with a note that the PGFTU were concerned because he had refused to condemn Israeli actions while stressing the need for Palestinians to avoid violence. The intifada however ended TUC plans to send a delegation to Israel and the Palestinian Authority as a follow up to their 1999 seminar 'Bridging the Divide'. In February 2002 The General Council discussed the TUC's approach to the conflict which they felt had always been even-handed, and decided they should tell their friends, meaning the Histadrut, when they thought they were in the wrong. The Council then endorsed the ICFTU's condemnation of the bombing by Israeli aircraft of the PGFTU headquarters in Nablus.[34]

The United Nations World Conference Against Racism

Set against the background of the second Palestinian intifada, the NGO Forum at the United Nations World Conference against Racism in Durban, South Africa in August 2001 promoted a virulent anti-Israel agenda and their final declaration which had been submitted by SANGOCO, a South African NGO which had close links with the PLO, was based on the South African anti-apartheid campaign of the 1980s. The declaration, which was to form the basis for the 2005 Palestinian Boycotts, Divestment and Sanctions (BDS) campaign directed at the State of Israel, called for "a policy of complete and total isolation of Israel as an apartheid state ... the imposition of mandatory and comprehensive sanctions and embargoes, the full cessation of all links (diplomatic, economic, social, aid, military cooperation, and training) between all states and Israel."[35]

The Boycotts, Divestment and Sanctions (BDS) Movement

When the call for an academic boycott of Israel failed in 2003 it became clear that to succeed any future campaigns would need support from the Palestinians. This came in July 2005 with the launch of the Boycotts, Divestment and Sanctions (BDS) campaign, which they believe will lead to Israel's isolation and the acceptance of their demands to end the Israeli occupation of Palestinian land, to end discrimination against Palestinian citizens in Israel, and to allow 'the right of return' for several millions of first-generation Palestinian Arab refugees and their descendants. The ultimate aim of BDS is the destruction of the State of Israel by non-violent means through this campaign[36] which was not only directed at supporters of the Palestinian people, but also targeted human rights campaigners and the liberal intelligentsia throughout the Western world. It appealed to them because the call for a Palestinian homeland and the conflict was portrayed as a human rights cause; with Israel depicted as the aggressor and the Palestinian people as the victims.

The Palestinian Solidarity Campaign (PSC), which is the largest Palestinian advocacy organisation in Britain was a marginal advocacy organisation, but was able to make a significant impact once it started working with Britain's trade union movement. This in turn gave it credibility by allowing it to work with established NGOs such as Amnesty International. Although the unions and the TUC are able to make policy and pass resolutions calling for a boycott of Israel or Israeli goods, they can only ask their members for support as they have no power to force them to boycott Israel. Convincing their members or the general public to join them depends on the ability of the union activists to garner publicity for their campaigns. The trade union movement which has always been involved with political and social issues both at home and abroad is the only democratically organised movement in the world whose principal concern has always been conditions of employment and the workplace. Since all these activities involve basic human rights there is extensive co-operation between trade union movement and human rights NGOs in Britain such as the PSC, Oxfam, Christian Aid and War on Want, all of whom support BDS in one way or another. It is the unions rather than the TUC that are the driving forces for BDS; what the TUC brings to the BDS campaigns is their prestige and international standing even though it has continued to call for a two state solution to the conflict. The unions' support for BDS is intended to improve the status of the Palestinians, but frequently overlook BDS calls for demonisation and delegitimisation of the State of Israel.

TUC Reaction to Israel's Military Operation 'Defensive Shield'

In April 2002 as part of their operation 'Defensive Shield' the IDF entered the Jenin refugee camp in the West Bank, which was administered by the Palestinian Authority. The Jenin camp was targeted after Israel had stated that the town had served as a launch site for numerous terrorist attacks against both Israeli civilians and Israeli towns and villages in the area.

The TUC General Council reacted to events by issuing a statement reiterating their deep concern at the continuing violence in the Middle East by calling for a ceasefire, the immediate withdrawal of Israeli troops from Palestinian territories as well as the ending of terror bombings against Israeli civilians.[37] The General Council also discussed a proposal calling for the UK and EU to instigate economic and trade sanctions against Israel, including a boycott of Israeli goods, to ensure compliance with UN Security Council resolutions. After a lengthy discussion, it was decided to consult with several interested parties including the foreign secretary, the Israel ambassador in London and the ICFTU. The foreign secretary told the TUC that the UK arms trade with Israel constituted only 0.1% of Israel's total arms import and embargoes were only effective when imposed on a multilateral basis, and there was no consensus within the EU for an arms embargo; adding that the Government did not believe that the suspension of the EU/Israel Association Agreement would bring the parties any nearer to a peaceful resolution.[38]

In June however, the situation worsened when Palestinian suicide bombers killed 44 Israelis, the reaction of the General Council was once again to discuss the question of economic sanctions against Israel and its effect on Palestinian workers. Strong feelings were expressed comparing the situation of the Palestinians to apartheid South Africa. The difference this time, however, was that the call for sanctions against South Africa had come from the South African people themselves, but this was not the position with the Palestinians. The General Council also rejected the call for the removal of Yasser Arafat by President Bush whom they considered had undermined the cause of peace, supporting the right of the Palestinian people to elect their own leaders. John Monks reported that he had met the general secretary of the PGFTU who had asked him for practical assistance and support.[39]

The General Council discussed the situation again in July and issued a critical statement which censured Israeli Premier Ariel Sharon for a '*total absence of any remorse*' for the deaths of fifteen people including nine children after the IDF had bombed an apartment block in Gaza. They described the action of the IDF as totally unjustified and disproportionate and were '*the latest in a series of atrocities in the area, including some committed by Hamas and other Palestinian groups*'. The Council were told that the General Secretaries of the PGFTU and the Histadrut had agreed to attend the forthcoming Congress in September and that the Executive would be discussing with them how to advance the cause of peace.[40]

Anglo-Jewry's response to the anticipated hostility to Israel at the September's TUC Congress was to arrange for Israel's ambassador in London to put Israel's case in a meeting with John Monks and other union leaders at a dinner organised by TUFI a few days before the Congress opened. Monks turned down a separate meeting with the Board of Deputies of British Jews (BOD) saying that since he would be discussing matters '*in depth*' at a private dinner with the ambassador, he saw no useful purpose in having a meeting with them.[41]

Several months earlier the PGFTU had sent an open letter signed by Shaher Saed, their general secretary to the TUC and British trade unions urging them to distance themselves from the British Government's military, economic and political complicity in what they described as Israeli '*crimes against humanity*;' which the PGFTU argued, included the occupation of Palestinian land, an economic blockade and the arbitrary arrest of '*thousands*' of Palestinians and their torture in '*concentration camps*' and jails.[42] In response to the letter several unions including the two University lecturers unions, NATFHE and the Association of University Teachers (AUT), the National Union of Teachers (NUT) and the Public Services Union (UNISON) all adopted resolutions condemning Israeli actions at their annual conferences.

Speaking just before the TUC Congress debate on the Middle East, Saed, addressed delegates and was rewarded with a five-minute standing ovation after accusing Israel of killing 5000 Palestinians and demolishing 10,000 homes and factories since the start of the intifada. He did however condemn suicide bombings but labelled the Israeli settlements as 'illegal'. The Histadrut general secretary, Amir Peretz, who had also been scheduled to speak at the Congress, cancelled his trip because of '*industrial problems*' in Israel.

The TUC Congress debate was opened by Monks who told delegates that '*we will consider all options... That includes the issue of sanctions, economic as well as in relation to the arms trade*' and that the TUC also intended to send a fact-finding delegation to the region. In the debate, speaker after speaker from a wide range of unions condemned Israel and spoke of their support for the Palestinians. The hostile atmosphere at Congress shocked the many pro-Israeli observers and activists who had expected a more balanced debate especially after their meeting with TUC leaders before Congress. The TWGU General Secretary Bill Morris referred to the unequal conflict between Israel and the Palestinians by saying '*blame cannot be evenly divided*', adding it is '*the occupation against stateless existence...it is helicopter gunships against rocks*'. A speaker for the TSSA union called Israel the Middle East's '*nuclear policeman*', while a UNISON delegate said that while his union supported a secure Israel alongside an independent Palestine, it wanted a '*right of return*' for all Palestinians, until then, '*we should boycott Israeli goods and cease selling it arms*'. CWU general secretary, Billy Hayes said that Israeli prime minister '*Ariel Sharon should get out of the West Bank now — that is the kind of deadline we want*'. He was backed by National Union of Journalists leader Jeremy Dear, who suggested sending British troops to the West Bank '*to stop the occupation*'.

Congress approved the NEC's policy statement which stated that the TUC would keep '*all possible measures*' under review, including a possible call for sanctions to '*assist in advancing the cause of peace*'. Although it urged the Palestinian Authority to stop '*terror bombings*' against Israeli civilians, it also called for an '*immediate termination of Israeli occupation of Palestinian territories and of the settlements policy*'. Even though the statement was critical of Israel's actions, the TUC continued to support a two-state solution.[43]

Over the next 12 months, the General Council's international work was dominated by the Allied invasion of Iraq and the continuing violence in Israel and in the West Bank and Gaza. The foreign secretary, Jack Straw told the General Council in December 2002 that the British Government was seeking the implementation of UN resolutions and that the international Quartet, the UN, the United States, Russia and the European Union, were working on a roadmap towards final status discussions. He added that that the Government and Israel had discussed issues relating to the application of the Geneva Convention relating to Israel's behaviour in the West Bank and Gaza.[44]

Shortly before the invasion of Iraq the General Council met with the prime minister who agreed with their demand that progress in the Middle East peace process was '*absolutely critical*'. Following the meeting the TUC issued a statement on the invasion which also drew attention to their concerns about the situation in Israel, the West Bank and Gaza urging the Government to keep up the pressure to ensure that this led to the full implementation of UN Security Council Resolutions. In July this was followed by a meeting with the foreign secretary which resulted in the General Council welcoming the positive contribution of the British Government to the advances made in the peace process. The TUC also supported the joint statement made by the ICFTU, the Histadrut and the PGFTU which '*called on the leaders on both sides to take the bold steps necessary to achieve the peace that (was) desired by their peoples*'. In September the TUC Congress discussed the Iraq war and adopted a resolution on peace in the Middle East which called on the General Council to continue campaigning for justice for the Palestinian people.[45]

The General Council delegation to Israel and the Palestinian territories eventually went ahead in November 2003 after being postponed because of the Israeli General Election and then the Iraq war. The mission's aim was to identify how the TUC could make a positive contribution to the situation in which the Histadrut and the PGFTU found themselves, rather than being able to develop policies on how the conflict could be resolved, but they soon realised that it was not possible to resolve the trade union and employment issues without addressing the peace process. The delegation concluded that the TUC should make every effort to promote dialogue and contacts between Palestinian and Israeli trade unionists, and encourage UK unions and the global union federations to do the same, as isolating the Histadrut internationally would not be helpful as it failed to recognise the problems they faced. They recommended that the TUC should aim to facilitate contacts between the two trade union movements, ensuring that both the Histadrut and the PGFTU could play as full a part as possible in international events.[46]

For the TUC, 2004 was very much a year of continuing their discussions about the conflict. The previous Congress had not only called for the end of Israeli occupation and the renunciation of all acts of state and terrorist violence but also for an immediate halt to the construction of Israel's separation barrier which they believed was incompatible with a Palestinian State. Whenever the occasion arose the General Council made these views known to the British Government, the Government of Israel, the Palestinian Authority, and International labour and trade union organisations. Although the General Secretaries of both the Histadrut and the PGFTU addressed the 2004 TUC Congress, several of Britain's trade unions had by then adopted anti-Israel, pro-Palestinian resolutions. Most of these unions with the exception of the NUT had little or no contact with their Israeli counterparts; and UNISON, the largest union in Britain was now actively campaigning for the PSC.

The Academic Boycott of Israel

The 2002 Israeli military intervention in Jenin was used by the Far Left and their supporters as the starting point for their direct action in support of the Palestinians with the call for an academic boycott of Israel. The campaign was launched when 125 academics wrote a letter to *the Guardian* newspaper, calling for a European Union moratorium on funding for grants and research contracts for Israeli Universities. Originally this was seen as a spontaneous reaction to what was happening in Israel and the Territories, but subsequent events proved that it was part of a well thought out campaign linking the enemies of Israel, the political left, Jewish anti-Zionists and the Palestinians. It was almost as though they had been waiting for an opportunity to use the Durban BDS protocols to launch the call for a boycott at a time when the world was condemning Israel. This was the start of the new activism and was entirely separate to the mainstream reaction by the TUC. The letter was published on Saturday 6 April 2002 and within days academics from all over the world had signed their petition. Although the letter called for an EU moratorium, it became known within a few weeks as the Academic boycott of Israel. A counter petition condemning the boycott call was published nine days later which ultimately had more signatories than the boycott petition. The *Guardian* boycott letter however caught everyone unprepared as the Israeli and diaspora response was uncoordinated and even condemnations from official sources were slow, with the EU taking two weeks to release a statement opposing the boycott.[47]

NATFHE, the college lecturers union, which had supported Palestinian higher education since the 1980s, immediately backed the boycott call by calling for Britain's universities to sever all their links with Israeli universities and the AUT called for the ending of European Union funding of cultural and research links with Israel. Both unions justified their actions by citing the disruption caused by the violence which had affected the running of Palestinian Universities.[48]

A consequence of the continuing violence throughout 2002 was that the call for an academic boycott of Israel remained in the public domain. The main responses to the boycott call came from individual academics in both Israel and the UK, who saw the issue as an attack on academic freedom, and not as part of a campaign calling for the destruction of the State of Israel as envisaged by the Durban protocols. Surprisingly in view of all the publicity, the boycott call was not discussed or mentioned at the 2002 TUC Congress.

In October 2002 the Board of Deputies of British Jews (BOD) met with NATFHE to discuss the union's support for an academic boycott of Israel and the impact that their hostility towards Israel had on British Jews and students on campus. The BOD pointed out that there had been a rise in antisemitic incidents since the start of the intifada and that anyone '*who engages in anti-Israel rhetoric should have regard to the antisemitic consequences*'. NATFHE responded by condemning racism and antisemitism and that every effort was made '*to ensure that college campuses provide a safe environment for all students free from violence and intimidation*'. As a result the meeting was deemed by both parties to be a success.[49]

The following year pro-Palestinian members of the AUT failed in their first attempt to pass a boycott motion at the AUT council meeting in Scarborough.[50] The 'Wilkie' affair surfaced shortly afterwards in June 2003, when an Oxford Professor, Andrew Wilkie, rejected an application from an Israeli PhD student Amit Duvshani because he had served in the Israeli army and Wilkie told him he had a '*huge problem*' with Israel's treatment of Palestinians. Two days after Wilkie had sent his email, Ronnie Fraser contacted the Sunday Telegraph who published the story. As a result of the worldwide publicity Wilkie was suspended for two months from his post at Oxford University without pay and made to take equal opportunities training.[51]

The 2005 AUT Council meeting in Eastbourne passed motions, by sizeable majorities, to boycott Haifa and Bar Ilan Universities in Israel and distribute pro-boycott literature to its members.[52] The idea of a boycott was roundly condemned by the UK government, the International Council for Science, international petitions, Nobel Prize winners, the scientific journal *Nature* and the *Independent* newspaper but not by the TUC. Just over a month later a special meeting of the AUT Council resoundingly revoked the motions.[53] The boycott attempt had failed because the debate exposed the boycotters aim to delegitimise and demonise Israel rather than building unity to support the Palestinians. The boycotters support for resolutions that excluded from the threat of a boycott '*conscientious Israeli academics and intellectuals opposed to their state's colonial and racist policies*' fell into the trap of holding all Israeli academics collectively responsible. By targeting only Jews and Israelis, the boycotters were being discriminatory and whether intentional or not, antisemitic.[54]

Unfortunately very few voices within the trade union movement spoke out against the discrimination which targeted those who identified with Zionism. Help should have come from the trade unions, yet all too often they helped compound the situation by failing to recognise and often actively denied the existence of a problem. Privately the TUC were fully aware of the situation but refused to be publicly drawn on the issue.

The following month, NATFHE adopted a resolution which related to the failed AUT boycott of Israeli Universities also stated '*that to criticise Israel policy or institutions is not antisemitic*'. The phrase '*anti-Zionism is not antisemitism*' was deleted from the motion on legal advice; and there is little doubt that had the phrase been included the motion would have passed with overwhelming support. That it was prevented on a technicality, legal advice, raised serious concerns about the sensitivity and understanding in future of discrimination and antisemitism in the union.[55]

A year later at the end of May 2007 the AUT and NATFHE merged to form the UCU, and at their inaugural congress in Bournemouth delegates approved motion 30 on the boycott of Israeli academic institutions[56] which instructed the UCU to circulate a Palestinian boycott call to its local branches, arrange a speaking tour by pro-boycott Palestinian academics to encourage members to '*consider the moral implications of links with Israeli academic institutions*' and to campaign for a '*moratorium on research and cultural collaborations with Israel via EU and European Science Foundation funding*'. The motion also stated that '*criticism of Israel cannot be construed as antisemitic*'. By distributing details of the Palestinian Campaign for an Academic and Cultural Boycott of Israel (PACBI), the UCU would have been promoting the PACBI call for the delegitimisation of the State of Israel which clearly stated that Israel created the Palestinian refugee problem and demanded the refugees right to return to their homes as well as claiming Israel was an apartheid state.[57]

The response from the media both in Britain and abroad was to denounce this boycott call. It was condemned by the Russell Group of leading UK universities, several presidents of US and Canadian Universities as well as leading members of the British Government.[58]

Even though the boycotters had won the vote, the UCU were unable to implement the resolution as the legal advice they received made it clear that making a call to boycott Israeli institutions would run a serious risk of infringing UK discrimination legislation. The call to boycott was also considered to be outside the aims and objects of the UCU.[59] Although the TUC had been aware of the call for an academic boycott and the legal opinions, it did not intervene even behind the scenes or issue any statements on the matter.

Britain's academic trade unions had been used by the boycott movement to further their political aims; their success was due to the fact that the issue was in the public domain and had gained worldwide publicity for the BDS movement rather than number of actions which had succeeded.

The Status of the Israel-Palestine Debate in the Trade Unions

Throughout 2006 the TUC leadership maintained regular contact with the PGFTU and in June, Brendan Barber, the TUC general secretary, wrote to the ETUC and the Foreign Office, stating that in the TUC's view the Palestinian people were being collectively punished because of the EU's policy on funding the Palestinian Authority and the Israeli government's decision to withhold monies belonging to the PA were seriously affecting the Palestine economy.[60]

The second Lebanon War in July and August 2006 was a military conflict between Israel and Hezbollah in Lebanon, Northern Israel and the Golan Heights. The TUC General Council wrote to the foreign secretary asking for a meeting, their statement on the war echoed the ICFTU's call for a ceasefire and a return as soon as possible to the road map for peace in the region. The TUC Congress adopted the General Council statement which included once again the right of the Palestinian people to self-determination, the right of Palestinian refugees to return to their homeland, the withdrawal of Israeli troops from all occupied territories and the removal of the '*apartheid wall*'.[61]

Over the next year the TUC continued to press the UK Government and others to secure peace in the Middle East as well as encouraging unions to affiliate to the PSC. A TUC delegation which travelled to Israel and the Palestinian territories concluded that whilst the TUC's position on the Middle East peace process and their relations with the Histadrut and PGFTU remained unchanged, they believed in justice for the Palestinian people and a two-state solution, the removal of restrictions on Palestinian movement such as the wall and roadblocks; as well as friendly relations with Histadrut and the PGFTU which would benefit Palestinian working people.

The report however confirmed that a significant change in TUC policy had taken place, namely that whilst retaining a dialogue with both the PGFTU and the Histadrut, its relationship with each organisation was to be different. Thus although the TUC continued as it always had to raise its concerns with Histadrut regarding Israel's attitude and behaviour towards the Palestinians in the hope that Histadrut might be able to influence the Israeli Government. The delegation proposed that the TUC and the unions support solidarity programmes suggested by the PGFTU, as well as raising with the ETUC and the UK government the issue of goods from the occupied territories, and restrictions on movement of perishable goods from Gaza.[62] Sally Hunt, speaking on behalf of the General Council at the TUC Congress confirmed that the situation in the Middle East was one of the most important areas of work for the TUC particularly building solidarity with the Palestinian trades unions.[63]

By 2007 the political alignment of many trade union leaderships, like the UCU, as well as activists had clearly moved further to the Left. The effect of the Iraq war had resulted in an increased awareness of international issues as well as an 'anti-imperialist' agenda which cited Israel as one of the worst offenders and ally of the USA. The result was that for many on the Left of the trade union movement the Israel-Palestine debate had become the sole international issue.

The BDS campaign against Israel had also become a major issue within the trade union movement, driven in the main by PSC activists and members of the Socialist Workers Party (SWP). Their aim was to get boycott motions onto the conference agenda of as many trade unions as possible and demonise Israel as an apartheid state. The result of the Hamas victory in 2006 in the Palestinian elections had little effect on the BDS campaign and the deteriorating economic situation in Gaza and the West Bank concerned many trade unionists including the TUC.

The real significance of the boycott campaign against Israel was that it had spread to other trade unions. In 2006, parts of a motion at the NUT Teachers Conference calling for a boycott of Israel and comparing it to apartheid were removed by their Executive committee; whilst at UNISON an attempt to boycott the Histadrut was ruled out on a technicality even though the National Executive had pledged to oppose the motion had it been put to conference. Two of the largest unions in the UK, UNISON and the TGWU, now had policies in favour of arms embargoes against Israel as well as calling for a review of the EU-Israel association agreement, whilst UNISON had policy in favour of a goods boycott which they had not yet implemented. In April 2007 the British Journalists trade union (NUJ) voted to boycott Israeli goods but this decision was overturned by the NUJ's national executive committee which '*resolved to take no further action*' over the boycott call.[64] UNISON, voted at its annual conference in Brighton by a majority of roughly 4–1, to support the campaign to boycott Israel. The following week the TGWU voted at its conference to boycott Israeli goods.[65] Throughout this period TUFI's policy was to target 'middle' ground unions both by engaging with the leadership and developing links with grassroots activists, which resulted in a number of motions that were either defeated or withdrawn.

Other Union Protests

There was a concerted effort in the summer of 2007 by Far Left activists to persuade British trade union conferences to adopt BDS policies directed at Israel as the NUJ, UNISON, the UCU, and the TGWU all adopted resolutions aimed at boycotting Israeli institutions, goods and services.[66] None were implemented but by imitating the UCU's unsuccessful call for an academic boycott, they all succeeded in obtaining valuable media coverage. In the light of the TGWU call, the Histadrut decided not to cooperate with the British unions, whilst the British embassy in Israel issued a statement saying '*the British government opposes boycotts of any kind*' and that '*the boycott declared by the TGWU will not harm growing commercial relations between the two countries*'.[67] The British unions support for a boycott of Israel was condemned by several American unions including the AFL-CIO and the American Federation of Teachers[68] as well as the German DGB confederation.[69]

Operation 'Cast Lead'

When Hamas took control of the Gaza Strip in June 2007, the sanctions Israel had put in place on Gaza after Hamas's victory in the 2006 Palestinian elections were increased by limiting the import of goods into Gaza mainly to humanitarian supplies. The response from Hamas was to step up its rocket and mortar attacks on Israel.

In February 2008 the TUC called upon Israel to lift the blockade of Gaza which it said amounted to collective punishment. Although the TUC said it deplored the rocket attacks launched from Gaza against Israeli citizens it felt that the rocket attacks did not justify the blockade.[70] The following month the TUC issued another statement on Gaza after the PGFTU's office had been destroyed by the IDF. While calling for restraint on both sides and condemning the rocket attacks into Israel it labelled the IDF's response as '*disproportionate*'.[71] The Transport Salaried Staffs' Association (TSSA) Conference that summer passed a motion calling '*on the TUC to organise and support a boycott of Israeli goods*'.[72]

On 27 December 2008 Israel launched operation '*Cast Lead*' which lasted three weeks whose aim was to protect the citizens of southern Israel who had been subjected to daily Hamas rocket and mortar fire. Over the previous eight years more than 8000 missiles and mortars had been fired from Gaza at Israeli cities, kibbutzim, villages and towns. The Community Security Trust (CST), whose role is to protect British Jews from antisemitism and related threats, reported that January 2009 was the worst month, since records began being kept in 1984, for antisemitic incidents in Britain, with an upsurge of over 250 incidents linked to Israel's Gaza incursion which was almost half the total number of antisemitic incidents in 2008.[73] The UCU supported 21 student occupations at Britain's universities.[74] The evidence suggests that the rise in antisemitism was because British Jews were being held responsible for the actions of the State of Israel and the rhetoric used often failed to distinguish between Jews and Israelis. A common theme of the anti-Israel rhetoric used was to equate Israel with Nazi Germany and Gaza with the Warsaw Ghetto.

The National Union of Teachers was the first union to hold its annual conference after the conflict, which adopted a resolution calling on the British Government to ban all imports from Israeli settlements as well encouraging its members to boycott settlement goods, especially agricultural produce. This motion appeared to contradict union advice to its members on how to deal with discrimination and racism arising from the Gaza conflict which stated that teachers have a duty, when discussing the conflict, to seek to promote dialogue and analyse sources for bias and balance. Schools have long been bound by the law not to promote partisan political views.[75]

The Scottish Trades Union Congress (STUC) which had been very critical of Israeli actions towards the Palestinians in 2001 and 2002 followed the NUT by adopting a resolution to boycott Israeli goods as well as to 'review' its relationship with the Histadrut. The vote came after the General Council had presented a report calling for BDS action against Israel '*until it complies with international laws and agreed principles of human rights*'. The STUC envisaged '*a targeted consumer led boycott, where trade union members should not put their own jobs at risk by refusing to deal with Israeli products, or work with organisations that are involved in the Israeli occupation of Palestine*'. Israeli goods used for Jewish religious observance were to be exempted from the boycott.[76] In the light of the UCU's legal advice this report appeared to be carefully crafted to ensure it would not attract any legal challenges.

The UCU's 2009 Congress considered five motions on Israel and Gaza including two calling for an academic boycott of Israel. After an overwhelming vote in favour, one motion was declared void as lawyers had advised that any kind of boycott call could prompt legal action against the union. Another motion was amended after legal advice had advised that to pass it without amending it would be unlawful. Congress also agreed for union branches to discuss the Palestinian BDS call and supported plans for a conference to investigate the lawful implementation of the Palestinian BDS campaign.[77]

UNISON's 2007 conference, which had adopted a motion referring to boycotts as a tactic to put pressure on the Israeli government; adopted in 2009 a motion calling for a ban on imports from Israeli settlements. Other unions that passed boycott or divestment motions that year were the FBU,

CWU, the Public Commercial Services Union (PCS), and the Union of Shop, Distributive and Allied Workers (USDAW), which for many years had been opposed to boycotts. The newly formed UNITE union, a merger of the TGWU and Amicus, which had no official unified policy, voted to support the STUC boycott call. The response of the British foreign secretary David Miliband was to express '*dismay*' that the trade unions were discussing motions calling for boycotts of Israel. He said the Foreign Office would be meeting with the union leaders to discuss the issue and that boycotts obstruct cooperation and dialogue, polarise debate and make it harder to achieve the peace.[78] In response the STUC immediately issued a statement saying that the Government's position was wrong and said they would be calling on the Government to support BDS against Israel.

The anti-Israel atmosphere at the union conferences that summer was a preamble to the TUC Congress in September. Brendan Barber, who personally opposed a boycott of Israel, feared that that there would be a BDS motion on the Congress agenda. He was right because the news headlines after the TUC had debated BDS included '*British trade unions to boycott Israeli goods*'[79] and '*TUC backs off from Israel consumer boycott*'.[80] Apart from the usual condemnations of Israel's Gaza operation and the call for a ban on arms sales to Israel the key points in the General Council's statement were support for a boycott of goods and agricultural products from the West Bank settlements, and the need to work closely with the PSC in order to build an effective boycott campaign. It also pledged to campaign for disinvestment by companies associated with '*the occupation*' and those engaged in building '*the separation wall*'. Even though the General Council had condemned the Histadrut's backing of the attacks on Gaza it promised to raise their concerns with them and report next year on future relationships.

How Congress had arrived at its decision was far from straightforward. The FBU had submitted a motion which called for a complete BDS campaign against Israel as well as a '*review*' of the TUC's relationship with the Histadrut including severing links with them. There were two amendments, one from UCU and another from the GMB which overturned the boycott call, named Hamas as a belligerent and changed nature of the review. A vote for a full BDS campaign would have put TUC in direct opposition to the policy of the Labour Government.

Although the GMB amendment was unacceptable to many delegates there would not have been a majority in favour. The TUC leadership preferred a statement which would accommodate everyone's concerns and highlighted the Histadrut's recent statement that had been written at the request of the TUC's International department. The statement took a week to broker as in order to get a majority it needed the support of the GMB, and was finally agreed by the General Council by a one vote margin. This vote had defused a potentially damaging situation which meant that although the FBU motion and UCU amendment were moved but were not debated in favour of the General Council Statement. Barber told Congress that the statement was not a call for a general boycott of Israeli goods and services which would hit ordinary Palestinian and Israeli workers, but sanctions against goods from the 'illegal' settlements. He added that each union could interpret within its own aims and objectives and within the law, how to implement the boycott.[81]

The TUC's decision to support the boycott of goods from the settlements was highly significant on both a political and campaigning level because the TUC had now joined other high profile names including NGO's such as War on Want and some sections of the media which supported a boycott of settlement goods. The British Government could also be considered a party to this campaign as they supported the labelling of goods from the settlements. On a consumer level it was not so significant because unions did not have the power to stop their members buying Israeli goods, nor were most union members aware of the TUC's boycott decision. As the oldest trade union movement in the world, the TUC is well-respected organisation that has played a major part in the International trade union movement but its decision to support a boycott was at odds with that of the International Trade Union Confederation (ITUC), which had a good working relationship with the Histadrut and the PGFTU and actively supported joint projects. In August 2008, the PGFTU and the Histadrut had signed a landmark agreement, negotiated under the auspices of the ITUC and supported by the TUC, which based future relations on negotiation, dialogue and joint initiatives and to advance '*fraternity and co-existence*'.[82] The following year the TUC and the PGFTU signed an agreement to run training throughout factories and workplaces in the West Bank.[83]

Although TUC had regularly said it worked with both sides there had been very little contact with the Histadrut during this period. By deciding to endorse a boycott of goods from the West Bank, the international BDS campaign was now free to use the TUC's name in their campaigns. The implication of their decision was, despite what TUC might say to the contrary, that by encouraging cooperation and affiliation with the PSC, the

TUC had firmly aligned itself with the PSC and all that it stood for including BDS and the Palestinian right of return.

Why then were the largest and most powerful British trade unions calling for a boycott when cooperation between the PGFTU and the Histadrut was increasing? What then was the attraction for them of the BDS campaign, especially as neither the PGFTU nor the Palestinian Authority had called for a boycott, Egypt and Jordan both had direct trading links with Israel and the international roadmap peace plan called for the normalisation of trade relations?

The answer has to be the ideology of the Far Left activists who promoted a boycott by comparing South African apartheid with Israel and its treatment of the Palestinians. This is a false comparison because unlike South Africa under apartheid, Israeli Arabs and other minorities are guaranteed full equal rights under Israeli law which allows them to vote in elections with no legal restrictions on either their movement or employment. The Histadrut is a democratic trade union movement, representing Jews, Muslims and Christians which regularly criticises the actions of the Israeli Government, whilst supporting both the peace process and a two-state solution. This frequently used equivalence with South African apartheid is a fabrication of the facts which has no relevance to the Israeli-Palestinian situation. However the apartheid comparison appealed to Liberal Left and ignored the real aim of BDS which is the delegitimisation and demonisation Israel. The split in the unions over BDS was also reflected in the unions support for the UK Labour government and the policies of the prime minister, Gordon Brown. The GMB and UNITE supported the government whereas those sympathetic to the hard Left were opposed to government policies.

There was also evidence of politically motivated criticism of the Histadrut and the PGFTU by certain elements in the UK trade union movement whenever there was positive work between Israelis and Palestinians or any kind of conciliation or peace process. When the PGFTU signed a positive agreement with the Histadrut, the PGFTU was criticised for giving the 'Zionists' a weapon with which to attack the boycott campaign and a similar attack was made on the PGFTU when they supported the Oslo Agreement. Those groups that showed support and solidarity with persecuted trade unionists elsewhere in the world could be considered hypocritical when they condemned Israel, the one country in the Middle East with a free trade union movement.

In December 2009 the TUC hosted a meeting with those unions which either spoke in the Congress debate or were affiliated to the PSC.[84] They agreed plans for a UK consumer boycott campaign directed at goods from the Jewish settlements in the West Bank. Within days the Government had issued voluntary guidance stating that settlement goods should be clearly labelled as such, as consumers had a right to know the origin of the goods. The TUC whilst welcoming the Government's statement, called for all such goods to be banned from sale in the EU and for the mandatory labelling as settlement goods.[85]

The UCU was heavily criticised by the Anglo-Jewry's leadership for inviting Bongani Masuku, the international secretary of the Congress of South African Trade Unions (COSATU), to take part in a speaking tour of UK universities. Before arriving in the UK, Masuku had been found guilty of hate speech by the South African Human Rights Commission following threats to Jews in a speech he made in March 2009. The UCU ignored the complaints and said that '*Our understanding is that Mr Masuku is seeking a proper hearing in relation to complaints around comments he made back in March. Until that process is properly complete it is not really appropriate for the UCU to comment*'.[86]

Four months later the TUC and the PSC launched their campaign '*Would You Buy Stolen Goods?*' leading with the accusation that the Israeli settlements were built on stolen Palestinian land, and were illegal under international law.[87] Barber made it clear that this was '*not a call for a general boycott of Israeli goods and services, which would hit ordinary Palestinian and Israeli workers. Nor should workers in Britain put their own jobs at risk by refusing to deal with goods from the settlements*' but targeted consumer sanctions which sent a clear message against the settlements.[88] Hugh Lanning, PCS deputy general secretary and chairman of the PSC, said that '*the PSC is committed to not only to build an effective campaign for boycotting settlement goods with the TUC but also to work to take TUC policy further, to support a policy of full boycott, divestment and sanctions*'.[89] Although the TUC has no constituency of its own, any trade union boycott campaign with access to six million union members could have become an effective economic weapon against Israel but it failed to gain widespread support for several reasons; unions are notoriously bad at communicating directly with their members, very few union members apart from the activists were aware of the TUC's campaign and even fewer willing to implement it. More significantly, the TUC and the unions cannot force their members to stop buying Israeli products; so success can only be achieved by the strength of their arguments and in 2010, BDS was not a widely circulated news story in the media which was not helped by the academic unions' continuing failure to institute an academic boycott of Israel. What this campaign did show was that the TUC was now being used by the unions and activists to promote BDS.

In June 2010 the TUC described Israel's military interception of the Gaza aid flotilla[90] as disproportionate and called for Israel's blockade of Gaza to be immediately lifted. The TUC also worked with the Muslim Council of Britain to place an open letter in *The Guardian* calling on the British prime minister to do all he could to end the blockade which was signed by 14 trade union General Secretaries. The TUC also supported the demonstration against the flotilla incident which was held in London in early June, which was addressed by Sally Hunt on behalf of the TUC.[91]

The flotilla incident led to more attacks on the Histadrut for condoning Israel's actions in an attempt to further delegitimise Israel within the trade union movement. UNISON's annual conference passed a motion calling for the suspension of its relations with the Histadrut pending a review. These attacks on the Histadrut were also aimed at preventing PGFTU-Histadrut co-operation which was seen as a threat to the UK trade union boycott campaign.

The TUC then used its Congress to strengthen ties with the PSC and reinforce its BDS campaign against Israel. Barber, told Congress that the TUC's current plans now included divesting from and boycotting the goods of companies which profited from the 'illegal' settlements, the occupation and the construction of the wall, while continuing to demand that the Government and the EU prohibited the import of such goods. The supporters of the PSC however failed to persuade the TUC to support a full boycott of Israel and the Congress resolution was a compromise between the pro-Hamas, PSC affiliated unions and the more moderate ones. The resolution also condemned the Histadrut for its backing of the Israeli government during the Gaza flotilla incident but endorsed the PGFTU's statement. However the Histadrut issued a statement which called on the Israeli government to ease the blockade of Gaza which it did ten days later.[92] The TUC's endorsement of the BDS campaign and the PSC was a major change in TUC policy which had replaced its previous strategy of engagement and reconciliation. PGFTU support for a boycott of settlement goods but not a general boycott of Israel did not seem to matter to the PSC and its supporters in British unions even though a successful boycott campaign would affect the 30,000 Palestinians employed in these communities.

The second ITUC Congress in Vancouver, Canada, in June 2010 committed the organisation to continue to support cooperation between the Palestinian and Israeli trade union movements and also called upon the international community to support Palestinian economic reconstruction and development.[93] Just before the Congress, the Histadrut released a statement on the Gaza aid flotilla which called for an easing of Israel's blockade of Gaza, which helped Congress reject calls for boycotts against Israel. A vehemently anti-Israel resolution submitted by the Congress of South African Trade Unions, was not presented to Congress. While the TUC used the Congress to promote its settlement boycott policy, the TUC general secretary chaired a sub-committee which included the Histadrut and the PGFTU, and drafted the Congress resolution on the Middle East. The TUC's involvement with the ITUC resolution showed that it was either being hypocritical or it did not genuinely believe in the aims of the PSC and BDS and was trying to support both sides at the same time.

TUC Congress 2011

In July 2011, the TUC responded to a request from the PGFTU by issuing a statement in support of the Palestinian National Authority's bid for UN recognition as a state based on the 1967 borders; the TUC also wrote to the UK Government urging them to support this position at the UN vote in September.[94]

Two months later the TUC Congress voted to review its relationship with the Histadrut whilst reaffirming its commitment to the boycott movement and the PSC. The UNITE motion, which combined the political aims of the Far Left, called for withdrawal of UK forces from Afghanistan, the immediate cessation of NATO action in Libya and recognition of the state of Palestine.[95] In spite of opposition from the RMT, a PCS amendment was adopted which called on all unions to review their relations with the Histadrut and all other Israeli organisations.[96]

The TUC's decision to work with the PSC was, on the face of it is difficult to understand because the PSC's aims differed from the TUC's over the PSC's opposition to a two-state solution and the call for a full boycott of all Israeli goods. The PSC not only continued its attempts to undermine Israel's right to exist but also opposed TUC and ITUC policy for closer cooperation between the Histadrut and the PGFTU, something which would benefit both Israeli and Palestinian workers. The 2010 Congress resolution compromise arose because only some of the unions on the TUC executive supported the PSC, but in 2011 the TUC finally and openly decided which side it was on. The Far Left anti-war, anti-Israel activists backed by the largest unions chose the PSC over its trade union colleagues the Histadrut and the PGFTU.

The TUC renewed its campaign to boycott Israeli settlement goods in July 2012 when it obtained a legal opinion that concluded that the Israeli settlements were illegal under international law and that on this basis the UK could, under EU and World Trade Organisation law, unilaterally ban the trade that sustained them.[97]

UCU EUMC Resolution

One of the most significant moments in recent British-Israel trade union relations took place in May 2011 at the UCU Congress in Harrogate when delegates overwhelming adopted a resolution dissociating the union from the EUMC working definition of antisemitism with only four votes against.[98] Although it was not realised at the time this resolution set off a chain of events which was to affect how the British trade union movement behaved in future towards Israel and in the long term, the actions of British Labour Party towards Anglo-Jewry and Israel.

The Far Left which had been in control of the UCU since 2006 had adopted an average of four anti-Israel motions each year between 2007 and 2011, many of which had been described as antisemitic by Jewish members of the union. Anti-Israel UCU activists were also vehemently opposed to the EUMC working definition of antisemitism which in their opinion limited their ability to criticise the actions of the State of Israel. The definition which took into account contemporary antisemitism had been written in 2005 to help law enforcement agencies understand modern antisemitism and had no legal status in Britain. Sue Blackwell, a well-known pro-boycott activist had submitted the motion to the UCU NEC committee as a reaction to the actions of the Birmingham University Guild of Students who, after a controversial lecture on campus, passed a motion requiring all societies and speakers in future to work with the EUMC guidelines to ensure incidents on campus would not allow antisemitic language or behaviour.[99]

After nine years of standing up for Israel within the UCU and at Congress, the adoption of this motion dissociating his union from a definition of antisemitism Ronnie Fraser, a UCU member, concluded that the UCU was no longer a place that was hospitable to Jews. As a result he and his lawyers instituted legal action against the UCU which alleged '*institutional antisemitism*' which came to court a year later in November 2012. His claim stated that as an orthodox Jew with a strong attachment to Israel the union had harassed him by '*engaging in unwanted conduct*' relating to his Jewish identity, the purpose and effect of which had been and continued to violate his dignity and had created '*an intimidating, hostile, degrading humiliating and offensive environment*' for him.[100] The complainant lost his action as the forty–nine page written judgment rejected all ten of his complaints ruling them out of time.[101] There were many reasons for the failure of this action not least because the Judge refused to rule on antisemitisim. Although it is not against the law in the UK to be an antisemite, antisemitic incidents are considered as incitement of racial hatred. Because there was no legal definition of antisemitism in the UK, the blood libels and the Holocaust were widely accepted as the standards for antisemitic remarks but not subjecting Israel to double standards or calls for the delgitimisation or demonisation of Israel which were included in the EUMC definition.[102]

In the four years between 2012 and 2015, the UCU Congress adopted only three anti-Israel motions. But it was not only the UCU who were being careful, as most of Britain's leading trade unions also held back from adopting anti-Israel motions during this period. One possible reason was as a consequence of the legal action against the UCU all the unions and the TUC were now aware of their legal responsibilities and as a result unions were thinking carefully before adopting anti-Israel motions.

The 2012 TUC Congress adopted a resolution which called for the ending of the Israeli blockade of Gaza, instructed the General Council to organise a delegation to Gaza, and to work with the PSC to determine how the TUC might most effectively contribute to ending the blockade.[103] Two months later in November 2012 Israel launched 'Operation Pillar of Defence', an eight-day military operation in the Hamas-governed Gaza Strip in response to multiple rocket attacks on Israel. The reaction of the unions such as UNITE,[104] UNISON[105] and the NUJ[106] who had supported the Congress resolution was to condemn what they saw as further Israeli aggression against the Palestinian people while the TUC wrote to the foreign secretary urging him to pursue all avenues to end the conflict in Gaza.[107]

Reaction to Israel's 'Operation Protective Edge'

Israel's military operation 'Operation Protective Edge' which lasted from 8 July 2014 until 26 August 2014 was the third round of fighting between Israel and Hamas since 2008. Israel's aim was to protect its citizens from rockets fired into Israel from Gaza while Hamas's aim was to bring international pressure to bear on Israel to lift its blockade of the Gaza Strip.

For Anglo-Jewry however, 'Operation Protective Edge' was a wakeup call because much of the criticism of Israel's actions was conflated with Jews which resulted in an upsurge in antisemitism which was the longest period of sustained antisemitism in Europe since the Second World War. The coming together of a series of factors such as London being the centre of delegitimisation, the conflation of anti-Jewish and anti-Israel hatred, the increased use of social media[108] and an anti-Israel narrative promoted by the media all combined to produce this upsurge in antisemitism. The figures for antisemitic incidents in the UK recorded by the CST have shown there is a linkage between the increase in incidents and military operations in the Israel-Palestine conflict.

There were at least fifty anti-Israel demonstrations around the UK after the start of the Gaza crisis. A common theme of the anti-Israel rhetoric used was to equate Israel with Nazi Germany and Gaza with the Warsaw Ghetto. While most of the demonstrators voiced their protests in entirely legitimate ways, there were several examples of antisemitic chants such as '*Heil Hitler*' and '*Dirty Jews go to hell*', and '*Kill the Jews*' and the use of Jewish, rather than specifically Israeli, symbols on placards. The CST recorded 302 antisemitic incidents, a rise of over 400% from the previous July.[109]

By the time hostilities had started the trade union conference season had finished with the exception of the TUC Congress. The General Council issued a statement on Gaza which was adopted by Congress that condemned the death toll in Gaza and considered the British government's response to hostilities unacceptable. The TUC also urged the government to end arms sales to Israel as well as the suspension of the EU-Israel Association Agreement. Their statement, which included a short reference to the upsurge in antisemitism, committed the TUC to maintain pressure on companies 'complicit' in arms trading, the settlements and the occupation which was a key aim of the PSC's activism and part of the international BDS campaign.[110]

The TUC and the unions have never had that same close relationship with the Jewish community as the Labour Party or the CPGB. The majority of Britain's Jews, who joined the Labour and Communist Parties in the 1930s, had left their trade union roots behind them after the Second World War when they moved into the middle classes. From then on, Anglo-Jewry's support for Israel in Britain has been directed towards the political parties and Parliament and not the trade unions, which by then no longer had a large number of Jewish members to put pressure on them.

The consequence was that only a handful of Jews became union leaders and the only two Jewish trade unionists regularly spoke at the TUC Congress on behalf of the Jews were Moses Sclare of the Leeds Tailors Union and Solomon Lever of the London Jewish Bakers Union. The move towards the Left within the unions in the late 1960s and 1970s saw three Jewish left-wingers, hold prominent positions, Laurie Sapper, general secretary of the AUT, his brother, Alan Sapper, general secretary of the Association of Cinematograph, Television and Allied Technicians (ACTT) and John Tuchfeld, assistant general secretary of TASS, all of whom were silent on Israel. Both Alan Sapper and Tuchfeld were members of the CPGB and associates of Bert Ramelson, the industrial organiser for the CPGB. There have however been a number of trade union leaders, who have stood up for Israel, the most prominent being Sam Watson, Frank Cousins, Fred Hayday and Jack Jones none of whom had any Jewish connections. The only Jew to have held office in the 2000s was Roger Lyons, the former joint general secretary of Amicus, who served as president of the TUC during 2003–2004 and a long-standing member of TUFI. In 2013, ten years after he had visited Israel on behalf of the TUC, Lyons condemned TUC plans to take a delegation of major union representatives to Gaza alongside the PSC warning that they were being drawn into their '*orbit of extremism*'.[111]

The long-awaited TUC delegation to Israel and the Palestinian National Authority eventually took place in February 2016. As it was no longer possible to visit Gaza the delegation spent most of its time in the Palestinian areas on the West Bank where they met with UN, Palestinian Authority representatives, the PGFTU and other groups. In their meeting with the Histadrut, it was made it clear to the TUC that although the Histadrut still welcomed constructive dialogue; the policies of some of the British trade unions now made this impossible for them. Since 2010 there had been very little contact between Histadrut and the TUC and the British unions outside of the international bodies and forums. The Histadrut had found it more worthwhile to pursue contacts with other EU unions rather than spending time on a virtual non-existent relationship with the TUC.

The TUC and the unions had by 2016 provided the PSC with its greatest success in the UK. Not only was the PSC able to directly influence General Council policy but affiliation by individual unions had provided funding for the PSC as well as access to their activists, union magazines and potential recruits.[112] The adoption of pro-BDS resolutions and policy by the unions were promoted by the BDS movement as 'victories' to indicate increased support in the UK. The political situation in Israel had also made it easier to obtain union support with right wing Israeli governments and a stalled peace process. However the majority of the motions on Palestine submitted to annual union conferences tended not to represent the views of the general membership, but instead the political positions of a minority of their members, the socialist and left-wing activists, who attended the conferences. The effect of all the BDS activity in the unions resulted in many Jewish members resigning, which in turn reduced interaction even further with the Jewish community leaving TUFI as Anglo-Jewry's main conduit for contact the TUC and the unions.

Antisemitism, the Labour Party and the Unions

Between 2012 and 2015 there was a significant decrease in the frequency of anti-Israel resolutions adopted by the major unions including the UCU. It is not clear why this happened but the unions became much more circumspect and cautious before adopting boycott policies. At the time of the 2014 Gaza war, the main unions all supported the anti-Israel demonstrations but the only anti-Israel resolution adopted was at the TUC Congress. It is very easy for unions to adopt a policy but it can be difficult to implement it as the UCU discovered in 2015 when they were unable for legal reasons to implement a BDS policy which had been discussed and adopted by the UCU Congress.[113]

The unions may have been more circumspect but they continued to support the PSC's BDS policy calling for the delegitimisation and destruction of the State of Israel usually at their annual conferences or when the conflict was in the media due to an outbreak of violence. When accused of their rhetoric disguising antisemitism as anti-Zionism, they issued a denial saying that they were opposed to antisemitism. The reality was that the Left, whether members of the unions or the Labour Party were only opposed to antisemitism as defined by their own political goals and not the Government's or Anglo-Jewry's definition of antisemitism. In 2017, ten years after the UCU had been formed, the anti-Israel activists in the union were still trying to implement boycotts and BDS even though they had ignored warnings that these policies would lead to an increase in antisemitism. The Far Left blamed the 'Zionists' for supporting what they call 'Israeli war crimes', that their control of the media limited discussion of the issues and they manufactured and coordinated the crisis surrounding antisemitism in the Labour Party. It was clear that when they used the term 'Zionists' they actually meant Jews.

Antisemitism which had always affected Anglo-Jewry became a major issue for the community when Jeremy Corbyn, a left-wing activist, was elected leader of the Labour Party in 2015. His election was widely welcomed by left-wing trade union leaders and activists because it provided them with the opportunity to demonise Israel and cross the line into antisemitism; by masking it as anti-Zionism. This was exactly what had happened in 2006 when the Far Left took control of the UCU which was seen at the time as a takeover by those on the periphery of Labour politics; their anti-Zionist policies made the union an intimidating, hostile, and offensive environment for Jews. It was in reality, the pattern for what happened in the Labour Party; fringe racist anti-Israel policies had crossed over into mainstream politics which resulted in a rise in antisemitism within the Party.

In the spring of 2016 fifty Labour Party members were suspended for alleged antisemitic and racist comments which resulted in the Labour Party leadership establishing the Chakrabarti inquiry into claims of antisemitism in the Party. Although the lack of understanding of the meaning and effects of the antisemitism were not solely the province of the Labour Party, much of the public discussion turned on whether anti-Zionism was antisemitism or not. While the inquiry report recognised right-wing antisemitism, it ignored the opportunity to investigate modern left wing contemporary antisemitism surrounding the discussion about Israel. The upsurge in anti-Zionist rhetoric and antisemitism in the Labour Party and the unions had its roots in the 2014 Gaza war which had raised Anglo-Jewry's concerns at the time. However the signs of left-wing antisemitism had been there for a long time as the unions had ignored the warnings issued in 2002 by the Board of Deputies of British Jews (BOD) that the extreme anti-Zionist rhetoric used by Far Left union activists had crossed the line into antisemitism and would become commonplace unless firmly dealt with by their leaders which of course it wasn't, as NATFHE denied they were being antisemitic.[114]

The Chakrabarti inquiry forced the anti-Israel movement to make submissions to the inquiry as to what they understood to be antisemitism, as well as their belief that anti-Zionism was not antisemitism. The PSC wrote that they believed that '*If the inquiry finds it necessary to define antisemitism, to adopt the approach that antisemitism is hatred of or discrimination against Jewish people on the basis of their religion or identity*' and that it was not antisemitic to criticise Zionism or the Israeli government's policies and actions.[115] The PSC, along with many other anti-Israel submissions, condemned the use of the EUMC definition of antisemitism, saying it denied their right to challenge what they allege is the racism of the Israeli state.

The PSC wrote that they considered Zionism to be a political ideology whereas Britain's Chief Rabbi Ephraim Mirvis had said that Zionism was '*the right to Jewish self-determination in a land that has been at the centre of the Jewish world for more than 3000 years*'.[116]

Shortly after the Chakrabarti inquiry started its investigation, the Parliamentary Home Affairs Committee decided to investigate the rise of antisemitism in Britain. It became clear that Anglo-Jewry had adopted a definition of antisemitism[117] when the Chief Rabbi told the Parliamentary Committee, '*We would like everybody to follow*' the International Holocaust Remembrance Alliance (IHRA) working definition of antisemitism;[118] the IHRA is an intergovernmental body comprising of thirty-one countries, including the United Kingdom that produced a refined version of the EUMC working definition of antisemitism which labelled as antisemitic calls for the demonisation and delegitimisation of the State of Israel.[119] In December 2016 the UK government announced that it had adopted the IHRA definition of antisemitism in order to counter the increase in antisemitic incidents in Britain and has subsequently been adopted by the Scottish government, the Welsh Assembly and many local authorities in the UK.

The Labour Party's inability and unwillingness to deal quickly and transparently with complaints of antisemitism against party members became a matter of concern for Anglo-Jewry. The problem was that neither Jeremy Corbyn, nor the Labour Party or the unions wanted to accept the IHRA definition of antisemitism because their understanding of antisemitism was different to that of the IHRA definition. The main thrust of the Left's argument against the IHRA definition was that it was not antisemitic to denounce as racist Zionism, Israel or its policies, In their opinion the adoption of the IHRA definition limited their ability to campaign for a Palestinian state, BDS and the Palestinian right of return. At their 2017 Congress, the UCU, the only union to disassociate itself from the EUMC definition of antisemitism voted overwhelmingly, to disassociate itself from the IHRA definition of antisemitism because it '*conflates antisemitism with criticism of Israel*'.[120]

The row over antisemitism in the Labour Party rumbled on and at the beginning of September 2018 the Party finally adopted the IHRA definition but only after four union leaders; Len McCluskey, the UNITE general secretary, an influential member of the Labour Party NEC and a key supporter of Jeremy Corbyn, Paddy Lillis of USDAW, Dave Prentis of UNISON and Tim Roache of GMB all had called for the adoption of the IHRA definition, along with all its examples of antisemitism to be included in Labour's new code of conduct.[121] Prentis had previously said that UNISON had not intervened in the Labour Party's debate on antisemitism, but had made clear and categoric statements speaking out against all forms of racism which included antisemitism.[122] Although he supported the adoption of the definition, McCluskey accused Jewish community leaders of being '*intransigent*' and showed '*truculent hostility*' describing Labour's antisemitism row as '*wildly exaggerated*'.[123] McCuskey's comments were echoed by PCS leader Mark Serwotka, who was president-elect of the TUC. He described Labour's antisemitism row as '*a story that does not exist*' and suggested the allegations were created by Israel to distract from its '*atrocities*'. Both these comments raised once again the question of antisemitism on the Left and their reluctance to recognise and abide by the terms of the IHRA definition. Neither the Labour Party, the TUC nor the PCS condemned Serwotka's comments or distanced themselves from his suggestion that Israel had created allegations of antisemitism in Labour. The TUC spokesman refused to comment specifically on his remarks about Israel and would only say that '*the TUC opposes antisemitism and discrimination of all kinds, as do our member unions. All TUC unions have a commitment to tackling racism and promoting equality in their rules. If anyone experiences antisemitism or any form of discrimination in the union movement, they should be confident that they can raise it with their union, and their union will take their concerns seriously*'[124]

The TUC's comments echoed those made regularly by the Labour Party and the unions whenever they or their members were accused of antisemitic comments or behaviour. It was their usual answer, and was expected of them. They believed that by making the statement it relieved them of all responsibility, but the reality was that the statement was meaningless as more often than not no further action was taken and no one was satisfied especially those who had made the allegation of antisemitic behaviour in the first place.

The adoption of the IHRA definition of antisemitism did little to diminish the row over antisemitism and in April 2019, the *Sunday Times* reported that Labour had received 863 complaints against Party members. The article claimed that more than half of the cases were unresolved while there had been no investigation in 28% of them.[125] One of the founding missions of the TUC was to oppose racism yet the TUC has played no part in the debate over the issue of antisemitism in either the unions or the Labour Party. The TUC which has been in existence for over 150 years has never yet debated antisemitism at Congress. Confirmation that the Labour Party had joined the UCU as a hostile environment for Jewish supporters of Israel took place at the June 2018 Labour Party conference at the start Palestine debate with the waving of Palestinian flags and chanting slogans by hundreds of Labour members including McCluskey.

The 2018 TUC Congress adopted a motion which condemned the American Government announcement that it would stop all funding to the United Nations Relief and Works Agency (UNRWA) and the Israeli Nation State Law which stated that Israel is the nation state of the Jewish people. The motion, which was supported by the General Council, was moved by ASLEF and seconded by UNITE. The teachers union, the NEU, and PCS also spoke to the motion and there were no speakers against. The motion was carried unanimously to a background of cheers and applause with delegates waving Palestinian flags in support of the motion.[126] The resolution was obviously written at the behest of the PSC as all the unions who spoke in the debate including the proposers were affiliated to the PSC.

The UCU Left group, who have influenced the union's policies on boycotts of Israel and their disassociation from both the EUMC and IHRA definitions of antisemitism failed in their attempts to defend the attacks on Jeremy Corbyn at both the 2018 and 2019 UCU Congresses. Both motions which were remitted stated that the attacks on him were based on the '*conflation of antisemitism and anti-Zionism*'.[127] However the 2018 UCU Congress did adopt a resolution regarding free speech about Israel which said that the Government's use of the IHRA working definition of antisemitism was in order to deter campus criticism of Israel as well as the conflation of antisemitism and anti-Zionism.[128] In October 2019 the UCU sent an e-mail to branches encouraging members to observe Holocaust Memorial day in January 2020. However, the UCU was forced to apologise after it had left out Jews from a description of all the different groups murdered in the Holocaust. If this mistake is looked at in the context of the union's past record of creating a hostile environment for Jews as well as dissociating itself from the IHRA definition of antisemitism one can only speculate if it really was what the union described as a genuine '*drafting error*'.[129]

Delegates at both the 2019 TUC Congress and the Labour Party conference overwhelmingly adopted similar resolutions for the application of an '*ethical foreign policy*' which could lead to the implementation of the boycott of Israeli goods. The TUC resolution once again reaffirmed the TUC's existing boycott of Israeli settlement goods but also called on the TUC to '*prioritise Palestinian rights to freedom justice and equality, including by applying these principles based on international law to all UK trade with Israel*'. The policy also committed the TUC to '*raise the pressure on corporations complicit in arms trading and supporting Israel's illegal occupation and settlement building*'. Because of the overwhelming support given to the resolution, the expectation was that the unions would also reaffirm and increase their support for BDS. Although the motion did not change existing TUC policy or their longstanding support for a two-state solution based on peace and security for both the Israelis and Palestinians, it reaffirmed the PSC's close links with the TUC.[130]

The Labour Party resolution called on a future Labour government '*to adhere to an ethical policy on all UK's trade with Israel, in particular by applying international law on settlements in the occupied Palestinian Territories and stopping any arms trade with Israel that is used in violation of the human rights of the Palestinians*' as well as opposing any proposed solution that did not recognise the Palestinians' right to self-determination and the Palestinian right of return. When the debate ended the auditorium was a sea of Palestinian flags, banners and chants of '*Free Palestine*'.[131] With the adoption of these motions, Corbyn supporters and the Far Left made sure that any future Labour government would have the support of the British labour movement for a boycott of the State of Israel as well as the Palestinian right of return.

The PSC built on the success of the latest TUC resolution by holding a conference for trade unionists in October 2019. The aim of the event was to bring together trade unionists and activists in order to plan for future BDS campaigns in the UK, in the belief that the International BDS movement was growing stronger and that the trade union movement was at its centre. Delegates discussed the work of British unions with their Palestinian counterpart and were also were given advice on how to deal with issues such as how to break links with the Histadrut, challenge the IHRA definition of antisemitism and exclude TUFI.[132]

In March 2018 more than 2000 people gathered outside Parliament for a demonstration organised by the leaders of Britain's Jewish community to protest that the Labour Party under Jeremy Corbyn's leadership had lost the trust of the majority of Britain's Jews because he had ignored their concerns about antisemitism within the party. Yet a year later Labour's antisemitism crisis had not improved but got worse as the numbers of unsolved disciplinary cases had increased and several people who stood up to anti-Jewish racism in the Labour party had been vilified and trolled by Corbyn supporters. It had reached the point where some of the Labour Party MPs had resigned from the Party citing Corbyn's leadership and his failure to deal with antisemitism.

Labour's crisis over antisemitism continued to make the headlines when in July 2019, following the screening of a BBC documentary about Labour's ongoing antisemitism crisis in which seven former Labour employees spoke out about their experiences. They alleged that senior advisors and allies had repeatedly intervened in cases of alleged antisemitism; the Labour Party responded by questioning the whistle blowers' motives and threatened some with legal action. UNISON and the GMB, two of Britain's biggest trade unions, took the unusual step of saying publicly that they were concerned by Labour's response as the law protects employees from unfair treatment who speak out about wrongdoing when an issue is raised. This was the second intervention in the crisis by the GMB and UNISON who ten months earlier had urged the party to adopt the IHRA definition of antisemitism.[133]

In November 2019, at the height of the general election campaign, the Chief Rabbi Ephraim Mirvis wrote that in his opinion Jeremy Corbyn was not fit to be prime minister because of his handling of the Labour Party's antisemitism crisis. The Chief Rabbi described the antisemitism in the Labour Party as a '*poison sanctioned from the top*' and alleged that Labour's claims it was doing everything possible to tackle anti-Jewish racism in the party was a '*mendacious fiction*'. Len McCluskey who had previously described Labour's antisemitism crisis as '*wildly exaggerated*' and had accused Jewish community leaders of being '*intransigent*' and of '*truculent hostility*' defended the Labour party and Jeremy Corbyn. McCluskey described the Chief Rabbi's remarks as '*wrong*' and '*quite extraordinary*' and that he '*fundamentally disagreed*' with him. The crisis then intensified when Corbyn refused to apologise to the Jewish community for his repeated failure to tackle the issue.[134] McCluskey went on the offensive a few days later when the Jewish Labour Movement (JLM) published, a 47-page dossier testimony from 70 whistle blowers, which showed that there was '*overwhelming evidence that antisemitism is pervasive at all levels of the Party*'. McCluskey dismissed '*out of hand*' the claims that the Party was antisemitic and accused the JLM, Labour's oldest Jewish affiliate of '*disgraceful*' attacks on the leader.[135]

Labour's antisemitism crisis had deeply affected the morale of Anglo-Jewry who felt let down by Corbyn's failure to deal with it quickly and transparently and they were also worried about the possibility that he could win the forthcoming general election. Yet throughout the crisis the TUC remained silent preferring instead to campaign against racism, the rise of the far Right and fascism, as well as Islamophobia and discrimination against Black and minority ethnic groups but not antisemitism.

The day after the general election McCluskey said '*Labour made mistakes*' and that one of the reasons for Labour's election disaster was Corbyn's '*failure to apologise for antisemitism in the party when pressed to do so, capping years of mishandling of this question*'.[136]

Notes

1. The TUFP's supporters included the General Secretaries of ASLEF, FBU, AUEW-TASS, the Tobacco Workers union and SOGAT, several of whom were members of the TUC General Council. The TUFP was active within many unions and the Scottish TUC.
2. 'Unionists backing Israel', *Jewish Chronicle*, 18 September 1983.
3. These included the TGWU, FBU, GMB, MSF, NGA, NUPE, SOGAT 82, AUT, NALGO, and the NUT, J. Edmunds, *The Evolution of British Labour Party Policy on Israel from 1967 to the Intifada*, pp. 34–35.
4. Walsh to Murray, 9 August 1983, MRC, MSS.292D/956.9/4.
5. Walsh to Murray, 2 March 1984, MRC, MSS.292D/956.9/4.
6. Walsh to Salford Trades Union Council Manchester, 17 April 1984, MRC, GC minutes, TUC/F-1685.
7. TUC to Histadrut, 4 October 1985, MRC, MSS292D/956/511/3.

8. Histadrut to TUC, 12 December 1985 and 17 December 1985, both MRC, MSS.292D/956.9/5.
9. Walsh to Willis, 14 December 1985, MRC, MSS292D/956.9/5.
10. Walsh to Willis, 20 January 1986, MRC, MSS.292D/956.9/5.
11. Walsh to Willis, 28 April 28 1986, TUC to AEU 29 April 1986, both MRC, MSS.292D/956/4.
12. 'Trade unionists intensify campaign against Israel', *Jewish Chronicle*, 4 June 1987.
13. 'NALGO cuts link', *Jewish Chronicle*, 19 June 1987.
14. 'Palestine,' motion, MRC, TUC Congress report 1987.
15. Middle East report, MRC, TUC Congress report 1987, pp. 223–225.
16. Other groups mentioned in the letter under the direction of the PLO included Medical Aid for Palestinians, TUFP, General Union of Palestinian students and the Joint Committee for Palestine. PLO letter to TUC, 27 January 1989, MRC, MSS.292D/956.9/7, TUC letter to PLO, 17 February 1989, MRC, MSS 292D/956/511/4.
17. TUC notes for meeting with Israeli ambassador, 7 March 1988, MRC, MSS292D/956/511/4.
18. Walsh memo Willis, 19 April 1988, MRC, MSS292D/956/511/4.
19. Item 221, The Middle East, MRC, TUC Congress Report 1989, p. 180.
20. TUC report, IC 7/8, the ICFTU mission to Israel and the Occupied Territories, 10 July 1989, MRC, MSS 292D/956/511/4.
21. Middle East debate, MRC, TUC Congress Report 1989, p. 180.
22. General Secretary sent a copy of his statement to the Israeli Government, General Council notes, 23 May 1990, MRC, MSS.292C/956/511/5.
23. MSF to TUC, 23 July 1990, MRC, MSS.292C/956/511/5.
24. TUC NW Regional Council to Walsh, 14 August 1990, MRC, MSS.292C/956/511/5.
25. The Histadrut booklet of solidarity messages from unions from all around the world, LMU, HD6851.
26. 'Middle East', MRC TUC Congress report 1991, pp. 475–477.
27. In September 1993, Israel and the PLO signed the Declaration of Principles on Palestinian Self-Rule, which became known as the Oslo Accords. Israel agreed to limited Palestinian self-rule in Gaza and the West Bank in return for the PLO formally recognising the State of Israel. The signing of the Accords was originally seen as an interim step towards ratification of a formal peace treaty between the two sides.
28. Section (7.8) Middle East, MRC, TUC Congress report 1994.
29. The TUC co-operated with UNISON in a project to assist the development of a trade union of health workers in Gaza, funded by the Department for International Development.
30. 'Middle East', MRC, TUC Congress Report 1997.

31. Author's Interview with Mike Walsh, London, 14 December 2013.
32. The MAB is a front for the Muslim Brotherhood which supports Hamas and Hezbollah and does not recognise the State of Israel. The MAB organised the April 2002 demonstration in London protesting against Israeli military action in the West Bank.
33. 'TUC delegation to meet Israelis and Palestinians' *Jewish Chronicle*, 14 September 2001.
34. Item 7.8 'Middle East', MRC, TUC General Council report 2002.
35. Item 424, World Conference against Racism, NGO Forum declaration, 3 September 2001, https://www.hurights.or.jp/wcar/E/ngofinaldc.htm.
36. Palestinian Civil Society Call for BDS, 9 July, 2005, https://bdsmovement.net/call.
37. TUC Press release, General Council statement on the Middle East, 25 April 2002.
38. Item 7.8 'Middle East', MRC, TUC General Council report 2002.
39. Ibid.
40. Ibid.
41. 'Blair backing Israel at conference fringe meeting', *Jewish Chronicle* 6, September 2002.
42. Brent Trades Council, "Open letter from the PGFTU to British Trade Unions," 2002, http://www.brickman.dircon.co.uk/BTUC.htm [link no longer available].
43. Ibid.
44. Item 6.3 'Middle East', MRC, TUC General Council report 2003.
45. 'The General Council support the joint statement of the Foreign Secretary and the Norwegian Foreign Minister on 21 January that '*the international community must take as much care to address the crisis in Israel and the Occupied Territories as the crisis that results from Iraqi weapons of mass destruction*'. TUC statement on Iraq, 26 Feb 2003, https://www.tuc.org.uk/international-issues/tuc-statement-iraq-26-feb-2003 [link no longer available].
46. The report of the TUC delegation to Israel and Palestine November 2003, https://www.tuc.org.uk/research-analysis/reports/tuc-delegation-israel-and-palestine-november-2003.
47. Open letter published in *The Guardian*, 6 April 2002 and the petition 'Protest against call for European boycott of academic and cultural ties with Israel', 15 April 2002.
48. NATFHE NEC emergency resolution on Palestine, 13 April 2002 and the AUT 2002 Congress motion on the Middle East. https://www.academics-for-israel.org/index.php?page=Documents.
49. 'Lecturers union condemns antisemitism', Board of Deputies of British Jews press release, 21 October 2002.

50. AUT statement 'AUT rejects boycott of Israeli institutions', 9 May 2003, https://www.academics-for-israel.org/index.php?page=daut2.
51. Julie Henry, "Outrage as Oxford bans student for being Israeli," *Sunday Telegraph*, 29 June 2003.
52. The academic boycott of Israel resolutions adopted by the AUT Council, 22 April 2005, https://www.academics-for-israel.org/index.php?page=daut1.
53. Motions carried at the AUT Special Council, 26 May 2005, https://www.academics-for-israel.org/index.php?page=db2.
54. 5. The academic boycott of Israel resolutions adopted by the AUT Council on 22 April 2005, https://www.academics-for-israel.org/index.php?page=daut1.
55. The 2005 NATFHE adopted an amended resolution supporting the AUT's boycott actions after the conference steering committee ruled that three motions supporting the 'boycott' were out of order following the AUT decision to reverse their boycott motion.
56. UCU Circular UCU/31, 4 July 2007, Congress resolution on Israel/Palestine: arrangements for implementation, www.ucu.org.uk/circ/rtf/ucu31.rtf.
57. The Palestinian Civil Society Calls for Boycott, Divestment and Sanctions against Israel Until it Complies with International Law and Universal Principles of Human Rights, 9 July 2005. www.pacbi.org/boycott_news_more.php?id=66_0_1_10_M11.
58. *The Financial Times*, *The Independent*, *The Observer*, *The Sunday Times* and *The Times* all published anti-boycott editorials. An example is from the *Guardian* "Boycott plan puts our reputation at risk," 12 June 2007.

    Prime Minister Blair was quoted in the *Guardian*: "Blair tells lecturers to call off Israeli boycott," 6 June 2007.

    Many academic Institutions and groups declared themselves to be against the UCU boycott including Universities UK, Russell Group, LSE, UCL, Oxford, Open University, University of British Columbia, McGill University, Université de Montreal, NYU, UC Berkeley and Columbia. Other professional bodies that rejected the boycott included the American Association of University Professors, American Association for the Advancement of Science, American Federation of Teachers, British Academy, and the Royal Society.
59. 'Israel boycott illegal and cannot be implemented, UCU tells members', 28 September 2007, https://www.ucu.org.uk/article/2829/Israel-boycott-illegal-and-cannot-be-implemented-UCU-tells-members.
60. 'Palestine' MRC, TUC General Council Report 2006.
61. Composite Motion 16, MRC, TUC Congress debate 2006.
62. Report of a TUC delegation to Israel and Palestine, January 2007, https://www.tuc.org.uk/research-analysis/reports/solidarity-trade-unions-middle-east.

63. MRC, TUC General council report 2007.
64. NUJ statement, 8 July 2006, https://www.nuj.org.uk/inner.php?docid=1790 [link no longer available].
65. Unison conference motion 53, http://cms.unison.co.uk/MotionText.asp?DocumentID=997416 [link no longer available], "T&G urges a ban on Israeli goods," *The Jewish Chronicle*, 29 June 2007.
66. 'National Union of Journalists abandons Israel boycott', *The Guardian*, 10 July 2007.
67. 'Major British workers' union joins moves to boycott Israel', *Haaretz*, 8 July 2007.
68. "U.S. Labor Leaders Blast British Unions' "Boycott Israel"" *Resolutions*, July 2007, http://www.jewishlaborcommittee.org/2007/07/us_labor_leaders_blast_british.htm.
69. "German Unions Follow U.S. Labor to Oppose Boycott Against Israel", September 2009, http://www.jewishlaborcommittee.org/2007/09/german_unions_follow_us_labor.html.
70. TUC statement on the Gaza blockade, 2 February 2008, https://www.tuc.org.uk/international-issues/countries/israelpalestine/human-rights/tuc-statement-gaza-blockade.
71. TUC statement on the Gaza, 4 March 2008, http://www.tuc.org.uk/international/tuc-14396-f0.cfm [link no longer available].
72. 'Palestine', motion 103, TSSA Conference 2008, 11–14 May 2008.
73. The CST protects British Jews from antisemitism and related threats, CST antisemitic Incidents report, Jan–June 2009.
74. The students' demands were all fairly similar: a university statement condemning Israel's invasion, the creation of a scholarship programme for Palestinian students, twinning with the Islamic University of Gaza, the showing of the Gaza appeal, which the BBC had refused to broadcast and the suspension of links with defence companies especially those involved in supplying arms to Israel. The University authorities dealt with the occupations in different ways ranging from reaching a settlement within 24 hours to the forcible eviction of the students. The majority of Universities issued statements which met their students' demands. The universities occupied were SOAS, LSE, Essex, King's College, Birmingham, Sussex, Warwick, Manchester Met, Oxford, Leeds, Cambridge, Sheffield Hallam, Bradford, Nottingham, Queen Mary's, Manchester, Strathclyde, University of East Anglia, Glasgow, Goldsmiths and Bradford.
75. The NUT's advice for teachers on the Gaza conflict, http://www.teachers.org.uk/resources/word/Gaza-6pp-A4-6289.pdf [link no longer available] and The NUT conference 2009 resolution "stop the spread of war" http://www.teachers.org.uk/resources/word/Conference%20Resolutions.doc [link no longer available].

76. 'Top Scottish trade union body supports Israel boycott', *Jerusalem Post*, 23 April 2009 and the STUC Delegation report on Palestine, http://www.stuc.org.uk/files/Palestine/Delegation%20Report%202009.pdf. [link no longer available], 'Palestine and Israel boycott, disinvestments and sanction discussion', STUC Congress 2009, http://spsc.scottishpsc.org.uk/files/STUCbds.pdf [link no longer available].
77. Motions 24–29, UCU Congress, 27–29 May 2009, https://www.ucu.org.uk/article/3888/Business-of-the-strategy-and-finance-committee.
78. 'Britain's Miliband raps Israel boycott efforts', *JTA*, 23 June 2009.
79. 'British trade unions to boycott Israeli goods', *The Jerusalem Post*, 17 September 2009.
80. 'TUC backs off from Israel consumer boycott', *The Times*, 18 September 2009.
81. General Council statement on the Middle East, MRC, TUC Congress Report 2009.
82. The International Trade Union Confederation (ITUC) was formed on 1 November 2006, out of the merger of the International Confederation of Free Trade Unions (ICFTU) and the Soviet led World Confederation of Labour. 'Israeli and Palestinian Trade Unions reach historic agreement', 6 August 2008, https://www.ituc-csi.org/israeli-and-palestinian-trade.
83. TUC Briefing, Building Decent Work in the West Bank, 20 August, 2009, https://www.tuc.org.uk/research-analysis/reports/building-decent-work-west-bank.
84. Present at the meeting were representatives of GMB, UCU, Unison, Unite and USDAW. Representatives of PSC included the Chair, Hugh Lanning. The FBU sent its apologies.
85. TUC statement on Government policy on labelling goods from the illegal West Bank settlements, 10 December 2009.
86. 'Expel this race-row union, says Board', *the Jewish Chronicle*, 10 December 2009.
87. As the West Bank and Gaza are not yet recognised as sovereign states and have no legal status as such therefore calling the settlements illegal under international law is open to question.
88. TUC press release 'Don't buy settlement goods', 8 April 2010, http://www.inminds.co.uk/article.php?id=10353.
89. 'Now is the time to act', *Morning Star*, 10 April 2010.
90. The Gaza flotilla was a convoy of six ships which attempted to deliver aid to Gaza and break the Israeli and Egyptian blockade of the Gaza. On 31 May 2010 the convoy was intercepted by Israeli forces in international waters in the Mediterranean.
91. Press release, 'TUC condemns attack on Gaza aid flotilla', 31 May 2010, https://web.archive.org/web/20100605040749/http://www.tuc.org.uk/international/tuc-18003-f0.cfm.

92. 'Middle East', TUC General Council report 2010, and Histadrut statement on the flotilla, 31 May 2010, https://web.archive.org/web/20100604060247/http://www.tuliponline.org/?p=1828.
93. The resolution also called for a two-state solution and the "*universal recognition of Israel's right to exist, next to an independent viable Palestinian state*" and criticised Israel and Egypt's tight restrictions on the Gaza Strip's border crossings, Israeli settlement building in the West Bank and Hamas's "*extremist policies*". ITUC Congress resolution 'Democracy, peace, security and the role of the United Nations', 25 June 2010, https://www.ituc-csi.org/unions-of-the-world-unite-for,7152.
94. 'TUC backs Palestinian statehood bid', 29 July, 2011, https://www.tuc.org.uk/research-analysis/reports/tuc-backs-palestinian-statehood-bid.
95. The motion which restated the previous year's decision to support BDS was proposed by Andrew Murray, Chief of Staff at Unite, who was also chair of the Stop the War Coalition and was to become an advisor to the Labour party leader Jeremy Corbyn in 2017.
96. 'Palestine' Composite motion 18, TUC Congress Report 2010.
97. 'The UK can lawfully ban goods from the illegal Israeli settlements', TUC, 9 July 2012, https://www.tuc.org.uk/news/uk-government-can-legally-ban-israeli-settlement-goods.
98. The European Monitoring Centre on Racism and Xenophobia (EUMC) first published the EUMC working definition of antisemitism on 28 January 2005, https://www.antisem.eu/eumc-working-definition-of-antisemitism/.
99. During a lecture in February 2010 by US army veteran Mike Prysner to the Birmingham University Friends of Palestine Society, Prysner compared Gaza to a concentration camp which was deemed to be an antisemitic remark according the EUMC working definition of antisemitism.
100. Claimant's Skelton argument, Mr R Fraser-v-University & College Union, p. 4, paragraph 5–6.
101. Reserved Judgment, Mr R Fraser-v-University & College Union, 25 March 2013, Case Numbers: 2203390/201, https://www.judiciary.gov.uk/judgments/fraser-uni-college-union/.
102. Ronnie Fraser, 'Fraser versus the University College Union: A Personal Reflection' in *Anti Zionism on Campus, The University, Free Speech, and BDS*, ed. A. Pessin and D. Ben Attar (Indiana University Press, 2018).
103. Motion 76 'Palestine-blockade of Gaza', TUC General Council report 2012.
104. 'Unite statement of solidarity with the people of Gaza', http://gallery.mailchimp.com/4f205ffabc02c1048c024eebe/files/016_Gaza_Unite_solidarity_statement.pdf.

105. 'UNISON issues statement on Gaza violence', 16 November 2012, https://www.unison.org.uk/news/article/2012/11/gaza-violence-unison-statement/.
106. 'IFJ condemns targeting of journalists in Gaza,' 19 November 2012, https://www.nuj.org.uk/news/ifj-condemns-targeting-journalists-gaza/ [link no longer available].
107. TUC to Foreign Secretary William Hague, 19 November 2012, https://www.tuc.org.uk/research-analysis/reports/pursue-all-avenues-end-gaza-conflict-says-tuc.
108. The All-Party Parliamentary Group Against Antisemitism, commissioned Lancaster University to analyse the explosion of comment on twitter. They downloaded a sample of 22 million tweets from July and August 2014 and carried out a detailed analysis of 38,460 tweets which contained the words "*Israel*" *or* "*Gaza*", *along with the words* "*Jew*", "*Jews*" *or* "*Jewish*". Their report concluded that some of the tweets contained explicit anti-Jewish invective which if shouted out on the streets which would clearly be racially or religiously aggravated public order offences. Others wished violence upon Jews as proxies for Israelis, or simply just as Jews, https://lancslaw.wordpress.com/2015/02/12/the-spectre-of-nazism-haunts-social-media/.
109. CST Antisemitic Incidents Report 2014, p. 4.
110. TUC Council Statement on Gaza, 18 September 2014, TUC Congress report 2014.
111. 'Trade unionists warned over extremism threat', *Jewish Chronicle*, 12 September 2013.
112. The seventeen unions affiliated to the PSC represent more than 80% of trade union members of the TUC.
113. The 2015 UCU Congress debated and approved a BDS resolution which was immediately declared "*void and of null effect*'. The boycotters' intention was that all UCU members would be sent "*a dedicated email, reminding them of [the UCU's] policy on Israel, and with a link to the PACBI guidelines*". If the UCU had gone ahead and sent out such an email, they would have been in breach of the legal advice they had received in 2007. Motion 43, "UCU and BDS Campaign", UCU Congress 2015, https://www.ucu.org.uk/7521#43.
114. In 2002 the BOD met with the academic unions, who had backed the call for an academic boycott of Israel, and warned them that "*those who engage in anti-Israel rhetoric should have regard to the antisemitic consequences.*" BOD Press Release, "Lecturers union condemns antisemitism", 21 October 2012.
115. The PSC Submission to the Chakrabarti inquiry, https://www.palestinecampaign.org/psc-gives-evidence-chakrabarti-inquiry.

116. Chief Rabbi Ephraim Mirvis, 'Ken Livingstone and the hard Left are spreading the insidious virus of anti-Semitism', *The Telegraph*, 3 May 2016.
117. The Jewish Leadership Council (JLC), and the Community Security Trust (CST), in their oral and written submissions to both the House of Commons Home Affairs committee inquiry into Antisemitism in the UK endorsed the IHRA working definition of antisemitism, http://data.parliament.uk/writtenevidence/committeeevidence.svc/evidencedocument/home-affairs-committee/antisemitism/oral/35121.html.
118. Chief Rabbi Mirvis in answer to question 440 to the House of Commons Home Affairs committee inquiry into Antisemitism in the UK, 14 July 2016, http://data.parliament.uk/writtenevidence/committeeevidence.svc/evidencedocument/home-affairs-committee/antisemitism/oral/35121.html.
119. The IHRA working definition of antisemitism was adopted by IHRA on 26 May 2016, https://www.holocaustremembrance.com/resources/working-definitions-charters/working-definition-antisemitism.
120. UCU Congress 2017, Composite motion 57: International Holocaust Remembrance Alliance (IHRA) definition of antisemitism, https://ucu.org.uk/article/8802/Business-of-the-Equality-Committee-2017#5.
121. 'Len McCluskey's explosive intervention means Labour's anti-Semitism row will go on', *The New Statesman*, 16 August 2018 and Justin Cohen, 'Third Union boss urges Labour to adopt full IHRA definition', *Jewish News*, 11 August 2018.
122. Prentis's statement, which was endorsed by the NEC, said that Unison's founding principles made it clear that any racism by union members conflicted with the aims and values in the rule book and brought the union into disrepute, 'UNISON: 25 years strong', 12 April 2018, https://www.unison.org.uk/news/article/2018/04/unison-25-years-strong/.
123. 'Corbyn ally Len McCluskey accuses Jewish leaders of 'intransigent hostility' to Labour', *Jewish Chronicle*, 16 August 2018.
124. 'Labour stands by union boss who claimed Israel 'created' antisemitism row', *Independent*, 15 September 2018.
125. 'Vile antisemitic taunts met with 'a slap on the wrist'', *The Sunday Times*, 7 April 2019.
126. Emergency motion, 'Cuts to UNWRA and the nation state law', MRC, TUC Congress Report 2018.
127. Antisemitism, Anti-Zionism, and the Defence of Jeremy Corbyn, motion 32, UCU Congress 2018, https://www.ucu.org.uk/article/9500/Business-of-the-Equality-Committee#32, and Motion 75 Corbyn, Labour and general election, UCU Congress 2019, https://www.ucu.org.uk/article/10088/Business-of-the-strategy-and-finance-committee#75.

128. "Free speech Israel", motion 37, UCU Congress 2018, https://www.ucu.org.uk/article/9501/Business-of-the-Strategy-and-Finance-Committee#L10.
129. The email described how the Nazis had persecuted groups such as 'trade unions, including social democrats and Communists, Europe's Roma and Sinti people, Black people, disabled people, freemasons, gay and lesbian people, Jehovah's witnesses and asocials, which included beggars, alcoholics, drug addicts, prostitutes and pacifists'. It also specifically mentioned 'non-Jewish Poles and Slavic POWs'. 'University and College Union apologises after failing to include Jews on list of groups of Holocaust victims', *Jewish Chronicle*, 2 October 2019.
130. 'Palestine – supporting rights to self-determination', motion 75, TUC Congress 2019, https://congress.tuc.org.uk/motion-75-palestine-supporting-rights-to-self-determination/.
131. 'Palestine flags flown as Labour conference backs 'ethical foreign policy' motion', *Jewish News*, 24 September 2019.
132. The event was supported by the TUC, Unite, UNISON, GMB, NEU, ASLEF, UCU, RMT, FBU, TSSA, CWU, and PCS. 'Solidarity with Palestine: Next steps for the UK Trade Union movement' PSC conference report, 12 October 2019, https://www.palestinecampaign.org/psc-trade-union-conference-report/.
133. 'Labour antisemitism row: Two of Britain's biggest unions voice concerns over treatment of whistleblowers', *Independent*, 17 July 2019.
134. 'Len McCluskey attacks Chief Rabbi Ephraim Mirvis after he claimed Jeremy Corbyn is not fit to be Prime Minister because of his handling of the Labour Party's antisemitism crisis', *Daily Mail*, 28 November 2019.
135. 'Unite union leader Len McCluskey dismisses dossier accusing Labour of antisemitism', *The Times*, 6 December 2019. The JLM was previously known as Poale Zion.
136. 'Brexit Is The Reason Labour Lost – This Is How It Can Win Again,' *HuffPost*, 13 December 2019, https://www.huffingtonpost.co.uk/entry/mccluskey-corbyn-defeat-blame-antisemitism-metropolitan-manifesto_uk_5df3ba57e4b0ca713e5ee6bb?guce_referrer=aHR0cHM6Ly93d3cuZ29vZ2xlLmNvLnVrLw&guce_referrer_sig=AQAAAF5JSYF6qX_-zz6WVcvSpgvNC2NtqSmrc37k25NMuRRhD1fddji-oxHJqwEQxnll6_WoJVlywixE_QRgYOb5UQv6v5PBpH2NpjFVlnqFLrb2bOOTAC7WwNm0IcflXfMhbwMtXwK0BtD6Ca_j2B44CIgU5huyZx1KbNXXDgIk0ABJ&guccounter=1.

CHAPTER 7

Conclusion

The Lessons of the Last 100 Years

The one thing that stands out above all else over the last 100 years is that for the majority of that time the TUC has not been very supportive of Israel or the Histadrut, neither could they be considered or described as a pro-Zionist organisation. Also discredited is the commonly held belief that because the Labour Party and its leaders have been very friendly towards Jews in Palestine and Israel, it automatically followed that the TUC, their partners in the British labour movement, were also very supportive of Israel.

Similarly the friendship which both the Histadrut and the TUC have frequently referred to that stretched back to the 1920s implying that the TUC was pro-Israel, this is not true. Only twice in the last 100 years can the TUC be justifiably described as pro-Zionist, for the rest of the time it has been thought of as Zionist because of its association with the Labour Party. It is evident that the TUC's ambivalence towards the Jews of Palestine and Israel has been consistent and unlike the Parliamentary Labour Party they can never be considered true Zionists, but only Zionists by default.

The TUC had a longstanding policy of referring political matters raised by the Histadrut to the Labour Party so that the TUC would only discuss an international political matter raised by the Histadrut if it had a trade union connection. It would appear that this policy was more strictly

R. Fraser, *British Trade Unions, the Labour Party, and Israel's Histadrut*, https://doi.org/10.1007/978-3-030-86814-7_7

applied to the Histadrut than to other international issues. A case certainly could be made for a trade union connection with regard to the rise of Hitler in Germany or the Spanish Civil War, but it is much harder to make a trade union connection to justify supporting the UN or rearmament for the defence of peace in 1950s or even the Hungarian revolution.[1] Another contradiction was that the TUC did take political positions because they had to as they were members of the National Council of Labour which regularly issued statements on political matters nor must we forget that the General Council and the International Committee regularly discussed Palestine and other international issues. Ernest Bevin may have supported the Jews of Palestine when he was President of the TUC and when he was responsible for Labour Party Foreign policy but it was Citrine in the 1930s who decided TUC policy which gave rise to the TUC's indifference to the Jews of Palestine. We shall never know Citrine's true feelings but maybe Berl Locker who dealt regularly with Citrine knew the answer when he wrote to his colleagues in Palestine in 1943 that Citrine would never say anything (*publically*) against the Zionists, 'but in his heart there are reservations'.[2] Unfortunately Citrine's legacy was to affect TUC-Histadrut relations for another 30 years.

The roots of the TUC's indifference towards the Jews of Palestine were well established by 1945. The reality was that their focus was habitually domestic and that even the Holocaust had failed to motivate them enough to support the need for a Jewish homeland in Palestine—they just didn't care enough. As a consequence of the TUC's pre-war ambivalence towards the problems of Jewish refugees fleeing from Nazi Germany, the record shows that British trade unionists did virtually nothing on their behalf. Instead the TUC remained silent letting the Labour Party speak on their behalf. The news of the murder of tens of thousands of Jews in Poland in 1942 resulted in the passing of notes of regret by the General Council and the issue was never discussed again.[3] The behaviour of the TUC was like 'the dog that didn't bite', it made a lot of noise but to very little effect.

The TUC's priority in 1945 after the war was to support the Foreign Secretary, Ernest Bevin, whose Middle East policy was to prioritise rebuilding links with the Arab States over those with Israel. He had a loyal lieutenant in Vincent Tewson who always wanted to do the right thing for his country and regardless of any personal feelings towards Jews and the Holocaust; he believed that if he openly gave his support to the Histadrut and Israel it would antagonise the Arab world and damage British interests. Tewson ensured the TUC's continued commitment to the British Government's Middle East policies until his retirement in the 1960s.

The Histadrut was certainly not blameless as they could have done more. Although the Histadrut did its best during the 1940s and 1950s they never took full advantage of the 'golden' period in relations in the 1960s and then squandered most of this goodwill with their decision to move to Brussels which took place at the wrong time, when changes were taking place in Britain within the labour movement including an upsurge in interest in the Palestinian cause. Whilst they concentrated on the leadership of the unions they ignored the changes that were taking place at grassroots level, so that relations were never the same again between the Histadrut and the TUC and the Foreign Office labour advisor. None of the warning signs for the future, the deterioration in Anglo-Israel relations and the move towards the Left at the TUC, could be fully covered by monthly visits to London. As a result the excellent relationship between the TUC and the Histadrut started to unravel.

It is not clear if the Histadrut has ever really understood the motives and priorities of the TUC. The Histadrut's most powerful weapon in the battle for hearts and minds was and still is, to take people to Israel in order to better understand Israel's problems and the political situation. Yet even these efforts ultimately failed because of the Histadrut's inability to convert friends into political allies. By the 1970s the Histadrut realised that the TUC's main focus was Europe and the Eastern Bloc, the Histadrut turned its back on Britain and gave priority instead to its European friends. The Helsinki Accords of 1975 led to Congress passing a resolution which allowed the TUC more flexibility in its interpretation of human rights. From then on the TUC ceased to insist on a trade connection and became much more political which opened the door for them to openly support non-trade union political issues which in turn led the successful landmark vote at the 1982 Congress to support the Palestinian right to their own homeland.

This one act eliminated 60 years of indifference towards the Jews and led to the TUC supporting the Palestinian Arabs. From then on the TUC and its member unions regularly adopted resolutions containing anti-Israeli and pro-Palestinian rhetoric, with only limited disapproval of Palestinian terrorist activities. These resolutions have sometimes crossed the line into antisemitism with the result that almost two generations of British left-wing trade union activists have been raised on a diet of political conference motions whose only mention of Israel was in connection with its 'brutality' and 'oppression' of the Palestinian people.

Since 1980s the TUC has never mentioned or ever considered how the conflict affected Israelis whether they were Jews or Arabs and their emphasis since 1990 has always been about the Palestinian suffering. There was also a subtle change during this period in the title of their discussions from 'the Middle East' to 'the Occupied Territories' which confirmed the TUC's moving towards the Palestinians and away from the Israelis. It was also noticeable that only rarely was there discussion of the problems facing trade unions in Arab countries. One of the hangovers from the 1960s which occasionally appeared 20 years later in the TUC committee minutes was that the TUC seemed to be very patronising when giving advice which frequently took the form of a white colonialist power saying 'we know best.'

The second Palestinian intifada which started in September 2000 acted as the catalyst in bringing about significant changes as to the how the Israel-Palestine conflict was presented by the media. The result was that London became one of Europe's centres for promoting the delegitimisation of the State of Israel. At its heart was and still is the red-green alliance between UK-based Islamists and radical Left activists whose common goal is Israel's demonisation and delegitimisation. The result of this collaboration was that the BDS movement directed at Israel has had more support in Britain than in any other Western democratic society. This alliance also led to more direct action by the unions themselves which bypassed but not totally replaced the long accepted practice of working through the TUC. Support for the Palestinians enabled the PSC to build links with Britain's trade unions and the TUC because the radical Left were able to promote their policies within the unions. This gave rise to the TUC frequently criticising the actions of the Government of Israel towards the Palestinians and especially their military actions directed against Hamas in Gaza. After the Gaza war in 2014, the TUC promised to lobby the international trade union movement on behalf of the international BDS campaign. The result of this obsession with BDS is that almost 100 years after the Histadrut first made contact with the TUC, relations between the two organisations are now almost non-existent.

The 2005 BDS mission statement includes the call for the end of the Israeli occupation and colonisation of Palestinian land as well as the implementation of the right of return for Palestinian refugees. Since 1982 the TUC and the unions have supported the right of Palestinians to a homeland and have been unwilling to acknowledge that the aims of the BDS movement and the PSC, who are opposed to the existence of a Jewish state in any part of Palestine, can be interpreted as antisemitism according to the IHRA definition.

There has never been any discussion by the TUC regarding the fate of the Jewish population if the BDS campaign should achieve its objective of replacing the Jewish state with an Arab state. Their support for BDS while also supporting a two state solution conveniently ignores this fact and one wonders how much longer this contradiction can continue.

There has never been any discussion by the TUC that their support for BDS implies that if the BDS aim to eliminate the Jewish state was implemented and replaced by an Arab state what would happen to the Jews living there? Where would they go? History has shown that since the Second World War many Arab states have ethnically cleansed their population of Jews.

Unlike the Labour Party, the TUC has avoided discussing or acknowledging the issue of antisemitism as well as to whether it should adopt the IHRA definition of antisemitism or how to reconcile TUC support for a two-state solution with support for the PSC. Although the TUC say that they oppose racism in any form which includes antisemitism they have not only avoided discussing antisemitism but have also been unwilling to label, when necessary, remarks directed at Israel and the Jews by union activists as antisemitic. There is a circular discussion which they don't want to have and it offers a possible answer as to why the TUC stayed out of Labour antisemitism crisis. If the TUC were to drop their support for a two-state solution in favour of any solution which replaced the Jewish State with an Arab State then the TUC would be labelled as antisemitic according to the IHRA definition and if they adopted the definition it would be contrary to their attachment to and promotion of the aims of the PSC and the BDS campaign.

This situation is unlikely to change as long as, in Britain, it is not against the law to be an antisemite[4] especially as their support for BDS is unlikely be challenged at either at the TUC Congress or the General Council. Another factor has been the failure of the TUC and the unions to recognise that the rhetoric often used by activists crossed the line into antisemitism and has been compounded by their failure to wholeheartedly apologise for the offence caused. Whilst the British labour movement and the unions over the last 40 years consolidated their support for Palestinian rights and a Palestinian homeland they have created a very divisive situation which ignored warnings from the Jewish community to control their inflammatory anti-Zionist rhetoric in support of BDS which they correctly predicted would result in increased antisemitism.

Those unions, especially those under the control or influence of the Far Left as well as the TUC have not yet adopted the IHRA definition for two reasons, firstly because of their affiliation to the PSC and secondly like Corbyn they believe that it limits their ability to criticise Israel. These constraints have not however seemed to apply to many Labour controlled local Councils in Britain which have adopted the definition.[5] It is also the height of hypocrisy that after four leading trade union leaders urged the Labour Party to adopt the IHRA definition of antisemitism 2018, none of the unions represented on the Labour Party's NEC in 2021 have adopted the IHRA definition; the Community trade union is the only one so far to adopt it and the UCU is the only union to have disassociated themselves from the definition. It is therefore not surprising that the TUC has not adopted the IHRA definition nor said anything about Labour's antisemitism crisis. If the unions were to adopt the definition it is probable that like the Labour Party, they would at best pay lip service to the definition or totally ignore it.

The TUC which has held many Congress debates over the years about the rise of fascism has never held one about antisemitism. It is almost as though there has been a reluctance amongst delegates and even the leadership to openly discuss or mention the problems facing Jews. The 1992 debate on the rise of fascism in Europe was typical, delegates talked about racism, black people, Muslims, Moseley and attacks on immigrants the 1930s but no one mentioned the Jews not even when a delegate talked about what happened at Belsen concentration camp in WW2. Since its inception the TUC has never issued a statement solely dedicated to the rise of antisemitism in the UK nor the problems facing the Jews. Sadly this state of affairs is unlikely to change in the near future.

In theory the TUC and the Histadrut are still 'friends' nearly one hundred years after the first contact was made as they have never officially broken off relations, but in practice they are more like acquaintances than friends, as each organisation has gone their own way with no real contact outside international trade union conferences. Since 2016 the Histadrut has concentrated on building relations with unions in Europe and elsewhere that are willing to work with them. The last time the TUC talked to the Histadrut was in London in October 2019 at a meeting requested by Peter Lerner, the new Director-General of the Histadrut's International Relations Division. The Histadrut emphasised their willingness to meet and work with the TUC but this was something which the TUC found almost impossible because of its unilateral support for a Palestinian state, the PGFTU, BDS and the PSC. The TUC's position was clearly set out by their international spokesman Sally Hunt in 2018 when she called for an independent Palestinian state alongside an independent Israel and rejected the USA's unilateral recognition of Jerusalem as the capital of Israel. She also demanded the ending of Israeli settlements in the West Bank and for settlement goods not be allowed into the EU or other jurisdictions.[6] As long as the Far Left and the largest unions continue to control the direction and policies of the TUC, support for the PSC and BDS will continue a unless a settlement is reached in the Israel-Palestine conflict nothing will change especially their belief that the aims of BDS are not antisemitic. Despite all this, the one inconsistency in TUC support for BDS and the PSC is their continued backing for a two-state solution to conflict. By continuing to press for a two-state solution the TUC would say they cannot be accused of antisemitism as Israelis are still living there. The offer of an independent Palestinian state alongside an Israeli state has been turned down several times by the Palestinian leadership. One wonders how the TUC would react if a final settlement with two independent states was to be agreed by the Israel and the Palestinians.

Between 2000 and 2019 the TUC Congress debated the Israel-Palestine conflict 14 times and adopted nine resolutions critical of Israel's actions with over half of the speakers coming from five unions, PCS, TSSA, UNISON, FBU, CWU and ASLEF all of which are affiliated to the PSC.

Three British trade unions UNITE, the NEU and the UCU appear to focus on the conflict in the Middle East between Israel and Palestine almost to the exclusion of other international issues. Although there had been plenty of anti-Israel rhetoric and talk of solidarity there was very little evidence that any of the unions especially those affiliated to the PSC have done anything to help improve the lives of ordinary Palestinians. Campaigning on behalf of the Palestinians or for BDS may have cost the unions large sums of money and resources, yet they appear to have given very little in terms of aid or towards training programmes for Palestinians. Their support for the PSC appears to be more about the political ideology of the Far Left which wants to destroy Israel rather than providing help for the Palestinian people. One can only wonder what would happen to the TUC if a 2 state solution was achieved.

Antisemitism and the Labour Party became a major concern when Jeremy Corbyn was elected the leader of the Labour Party in 2015. His election was widely welcomed by Left wing trade union leaders and Far Left activists because it provided his acolytes with the opportunity to demonise Israel and use rhetoric which often crossed the line into antisemitism; by masking it as anti-Zionism. This led to a breakdown in relations between the Labour Party and Anglo-Jewry over the issue of antisemitism in the party which was due in part to their support for the PSC and the BDS movement. In June 2019 after nearly three years of complaints of alleged antisemitism in the Labour Party, the Equality and Human Rights Commission (EHRC) launched a formal investigation into whether the Party had 'unlawfully discriminated against, harassed or victimised people because they are Jewish'.[7] In a similar fashion to Ronnie Fraser who brought his legal action against the UCU in 2012 because he believed his union was institutionally racist and antisemitic, Anglo-Jewry believed that the Labour Party under Corbyn was similarly institutionally racist and hoped that their complaints would be upheld.

The Labour Party started the second decade of the twenty-first century with Sir Keir Starmer, Jeremy Corbyn's successor as leader of the Labour Party promising a policy of zero-tolerance towards antisemitism the party, he wrote: 'The principle of what I succeed to achieve is clear: if you are antisemitic, you cannot and should not be in the Labour Party. No ifs, no buts.' One of his first acts as leader was to offer an apology to the Jewish community on behalf of the Party.[8]

In April 2020 an internal Labour Party investigation into its handing of antisemitic complaints was leaked to the press. The 860 page study, which was completed in the last month of Jeremy Corbyn's leadership, concluded that there was 'no evidence of antisemitism complaints being treated any differently to other forms of complaint or of current or former staff being motivated by antisemitic intent'. The report was not submitted to the EHRC on the advice of Party lawyers.[9]

The EHRC report, which was published in October 2020, found that the Labour Party led by Jeremy Corbyn was responsible for three breaches of the Equality Act, political interference in antisemitism complaints and inadequate training for those handling the complaints. The reaction of Anglo-Jewry's leadership was that the EHRC's findings were 'a damning verdict on what Labour did to Jews under Jeremy Corbyn and his allies'.[10] Six weeks later Labour's national executive committee approved a draft action plan which was submitted to the EHRC. A Labour spokesperson said the plan was an important step towards Keir Starmer's 'commitment to rebuilding trust and confidence with our Jewish members and the Jewish community.'[11]

As we have seen the Labour Party's adoption of the IHRA definition has made no difference to the Left wing activists either in the Labour Party or the unions who continue to believe the Jews are the problem and not the victims. They will continue to demonise Israel and believe that Anglo-Jewry used the issue of antisemitism to undermine Corbyn. Even through the EHRC investigation found Labour guilty and Labour's resolve to regain the trust of the Jewish community, trade union support for BDS and the PSC will continue to trump all other concerns.

For the TUC, the new decade meant no change in their attitude towards Israel; they actually increased their anti-Israel rhetoric and have continued to ignore the Histadrut. The 2020 TUC Congress adopted a motion which stated its 'full opposition to the Israeli government's stated intention to officially annex parts of the West Bank in violation of international law, with such a move being another significant step in the creation of a system of apartheid'.[12] This was the first time the TUC had identified Israel as an apartheid state. In November 2020 the TUC issued its clearest statement yet, making Palestinian rights a priority for the TUC; calling for 'respect for all Palestinian rights, including the right to collective self-determination and the right to return.'[13] If the TUC was serious about their support for a two state solution then they would debate the issues with the Histadrut, not just with their friends in the PSC and the BDS movement.

Although the Israeli government's annexation plans were set aside by the 'Abraham Accords',[14] a series of agreements brokered by the United States between August and December 2020 in which the UAE, Sudan, Bahrain and Morocco agreed to normalise their relations with Israel. The accords were opposed by UNISON, UNITE, the GMB and the NEU who co-signed a PSC press release. In their view the accords offer Israel improved diplomatic and trade relations whilst ignoring the rights of the Palestinians.[15]

At the end of March 2021 a group of academics mostly from Israel, Germany and America published a document called the 'Jerusalem Declaration on Antisemitism' (JDA) which stated that; it is not antisemitic to criticise or oppose Zionism as a form of nationalism, to promote BDS, to describe Israel as a settler colonial or an apartheid state, or to support a one-state solution.[16] The Far Left, anti-Zionists and the PSC, who have argued that the IHRA definition shuts down free speech and any discussion of Israel, have welcomed the JDA because it upholds their view that to denounce as racist, Zionism, Israel or its policies is not antisemitic. The Jerusalem Declaration is a however a political document rather than a definition because it protects anti-Zionists from being labelled as antisemites. The British Government insisted in October 2020 that British universities adopt the IHRA definition of antisemitism, because it would allow public bodies such as universities to understand that some criticism of Israel can be antisemitic.[17] The response of the anti-Zionists including the UCU has been to encourage universities to replace the IHRA definition with the JDA definition.

The IHRA definition is a working non-legally binding definition and an analytical tool, which can be used to explain whether a complaint is antisemitic and which category it would fall into. The IHRA definition helped help frame the discussion around Labour and Jeremy Corbyn. It really became the lens in which Labour's record on antisemitism was examined and easily understood. This was an extraordinary use of the working definition of antisemitism in that it forced people to stand up and take positions on it about antisemitism and how they viewed the issue which allowed the general public to react according to how they wanted to react. The definition allowed Corbyn's position on antisemitism to be clarified in people's minds in an easily understandable manner; the result was the vote against Labour in the 2019 general election.

In May 2021 there was a third round of fighting between Israel and Hamas. The violence, which lasted 11 days and was marked by daily barrages of 300–450 Hamas rockets aimed at Israel's towns and cities. The IDF countered the missile threat with its Iron Dome defence system and 1500 attacks on Hamas targets in Gaza. During the conflict, British Jews came under physical and verbal attack with the CST recording 351 antisemitic incidents in May, the majority of which were directly linked to the conflict in Israel and Gaza. This figure exceeded the 317 antisemitic incidents recorded during the July 2014 war.

As antisemitism surged during the conflict, many Labour MPs were called on to show restraint after using social media to declare their solidarity with Palestine. The TUC, STUC, NEU and Unison all issued statements of solidarity with the Palestinian people as well as condemning the Israeli government's violence in Gaza. However only the Unison statement noted concern about the recent upsurge in antisemitism in the UK and condemned 'those who seek to blame Jewish people for the actions of the Israeli government and sow fear, hatred and division in our communities'.[18] The reaction of the unions to the JDA definition and the war seemed to indicate that relations between British Jews and the trade unions are unlikely to improve for the foreseeable future.

Just over 100 years ago after the TUC first endorsed the Labour Party's War Aims memorandum calling for a Jewish homeland in Palestine we find that the TUC still supports that aim albeit in 2020 they are calling now for a Palestinian Arab State alongside the Jewish State of Israel. On the face of it this a very commendable attribute for which the TUC should be very proud; but both the Labour Party and the TUC now have similar policies which are highly critical of actions of the State of Israel towards the Palestinians whilst backing the PSC and the international BDS campaign. In addition Left wing activists in both the Labour Party and the unions are also extremely critical of the IHRA definition of antisemitism. The end result is that the TUC now identifies itself in a much stronger way as pro-Palestinian than one could never have described the TUC, even in the 'golden period' as pro-Zionist.

Notes

1. International policy document submitted to the 1954 TUC Congress, IC 6/5, 22 July 1954, MRC, MSS292/9101/11.
2. Berl Locker statement to Mapai committee, minutes of meeting, MSILP, 2-024-1943-6, 6 October 1943.
3. The Holocaust and the murder of six million Jews by the Nazis was only mentioned once at a TUC Congress either during or after the war when in 1943, Isidore Nagler, the AFL fraternal delegate addressed Congress. MRC, TUC Congress report, 1943, p. 271.
4. 'Antisemitism, as such, is not a criminal offence. The law does not punish people for holding thoughts or beliefs, however unpleasant these may be. The same applies to Holocaust denial and criticism of Israel. It is only when people start to act on those thoughts or beliefs that the law steps in. It punishes actions rather than attitudes.' The Law of Antisemitism, Campaign Against Antisemitism, https://antisemitism.org/law/how-the-law-works/.
5. At the beginning of 2019, 188 local councils in England and Wales had adopted the IHRA definition which included every council in London, Manchester, Merseyside, 87 which were Labour controlled councils and 83 Conservative controlled councils. By September 2020 the figure had increased to over 260 councils.

6. Sally Hunt's speech to the UGTT International Trade Union Forum to support Palestinian people, Tunis, Tunisia, 20 January 2018. She was TUC General Council international spokesperson, ITUC General Council member and General Secretary of the UCU. www.tuc.org.uk/speeches/tuc-president-sally-hunt-solidarity-palestine.
7. EHRC investigation into Labour Party following complaints about antisemitism, 28 May 2019, https://www.equalityhumanrights.com/en/our-work/news/investigation-opened-labour-party-following-complaints-about-antisemitism.
8. 'Keir Starmer: How I'll rid Labour of anti-Semitism', *Evening Standard*, 7 April 2020.
9. 'Labour antisemitism investigation will not be sent to equality commission', *Sky News*, 12 April 2020, https://news.sky.com/story/labour-antisemitism-investigation-will-not-be-sent-to-equality-commission-11972071.
10. 'UK Jewish groups: Anti-Semitism report is 'damning verdict' on Corbyn's Labour', *Times of Israel*, 29 October 2020, https://www.timesofisrael.com/uk-jewish-groups-anti-semitism-report-is-damning-verdict-on-corbyns-labour/.
11. 'Labour NEC approves antisemitism draft action plan', *Jewish Chronicle*, 7 December 2020.
12. 'Solidarity with Palestine and resisting annexation', motion 66, TUC Congress 2020, https://congress.tuc.org.uk/motion-66-solidarity-with-palestine-and-resisting-annexation/.
13. Other demands included, UK recognition of the State of Palestine, and the suspension of UK-Israel trade agreements until Palestinian rights are respected. TUC Report, 'Justice for Palestine', 29 November 2020, https://www.tuc.org.uk/Justiceforpalestinereport.
14. The Abraham Accords Declaration, https://www.state.gov/the-abraham-accords/.
15. PSC Statement on Palestine and Western Sahara, 18 December 2020, https://www.palestinecampaign.org/statement-on-palestine-and-western-sahara/.
16. The Jerusalem Declaration on Antisemitism, https://jerusalemdeclaration.org/.
17. 'Universities may face cuts if they reject definition of antisemitism, says education minister', *Independent*, 9 October 2020, https://www.independent.co.uk/news/education/education-news/antisemitism-universities-gavin-williamson-funding-cuts-b911500.html.
18. UNISON statement: In solidarity with Palestinian workers, 18 May 2021, https://www.unison.org.uk/news/article/2021/05/unison-statement-in-solidarity-with-palestinian-workers/.

Appendix: List of Organisations and Key Personnel

British Legation/British Embassy in Israel—Ambassador

1948–49	No representation	1965–69	Sir Michael Hadow
1949–51	Sir Alexander Knox Helm	1969–72	Sir Ernest Barnes
1951–54	Sir Francis Evans	1972–75	Sir Bernard Ledwidge
1954–57	Sir John Walter Nicholls	1975–76	Thomas Elliott
1957–59	Sir Francis Rundall	1976–80	Sir John Mason
1959–63	Sir Patrick Hancock	1980–81	John Robinson
1963–65	Sir John Beith	1981–84	Sir Patrick Moberly

British Legation/British Embassy in Israel—Labour Attaché

1950–53	Ivor Thomas	1967–70	O. John Skinner
1953–55	William Poulsom	1970–73	T. Spence
1955–57	William Harry Marsh	1973–78	S. Corcoran (Based in Athens)
1958–61	John Parker	1978–80	R.J. Ross (Based in Athens)
1962–67	Cyril Marshall		

R. Fraser, *British Trade Unions, the Labour Party, and Israel's Histadrut*, https://doi.org/10.1007/978-3-030-86814-7

Foreign Office Labour Advisor on International Labour Questions

1949–51	H. Gee	1963–76	G. Foggon
1952–53	J.A. Diack	1977–79	H. Hurst
1954–55	D.C. Barnes	1980–81	H. Hurst
1956–58	G.F. Bulmer	1982–83	E. Toms
1959–63	W.A. Treganowan		

Histadrut—General Secretary

1920–21	David Zakai	1921–35	David Ben-Gurion
1935–44	David Remez	1984–92	Yisrael Kessar
1944–49	Yosef Sprinzak	1992–94	Haim Haberfeld
1949–50	Pinchas Lavon	1994–95	Haim Ramon
1950–56	Mordechai Namir	1995–2006	Amir Peretz
1956–61	Pinchas Lavon	2006–2013	Ofer Eini
1961–69	Aharon Becker	2013–2019	Avi Nissenkorn
1969–73	Yitzhak Ben-Aharon	2019–current	Arnon Bar-David
1973–84	Yeruham Meshel		

Histadrut—International Department

1948–56	Reuven Barkatt, Director
1956–60	Reuven Barkatt, Chairman, Ezra Hayut Director
1960–64	Yehudit Simchoni, Chairman, Ezra Hayut, Director
1964–67	Yehudit Simchoni, Chairman, Zeev Levin, Director
1967–68	Zeev Haring, Chairman, Hugo Morratt, Director
1968–69	Zeev Haring, Chairman, Shmuel Bahat, Director
1969–74	Yitzhak Ben-Aharon, Chairman, Shmuel Bahat, Director.
1974–83	Yeruham Meshel, Chairman, Avraham Alon, Director
2008–current	Avital Shapira-Shabirow, Director
2018–current	Peter Lerner, Director General

Histadrut/Jewish Agency/Palestine Labour Political Committee/Poale Zion—London

1928–32	Dov Hoz
1938–48	Berl Locker
1948–70	Schneier Levenberg

Histadrut Representative Based in London

1960–64	Gideon Ne'eman
1964–68	Eli Marx
1982–85	Ben Sella

Histadrut European Representative Based in Brussels

1968–71	Hanan Lehmann
1971–75	Yonah Yagol
1975–78	Aaron Barnea
1978–81	Yachov Hadassi
1981–86	Michael Ziff

ICFTU—General Secretary

1949–60	J.H. Oldenbroek
1960–67	Omer Becu
1967–72	Harm G. Buiter
1972–82	Otto Kersten
1982–92	John Vanderveken

Israel Legation/Embassy—Ambassador

1948–49	Joseph Linton	1983–88	Yehuda Avner
1949–50	Mordechai Eliash	1988–93	Yoav Biran
1950–50	Mordechai Kidron	1993–98	Moshe Raviv
1950–59	Eliahu Elath	1998–2000	Dror Zeigerman
1959–65	Arthur Lourie	2001–4	Zvi Stauber
1965–70	Aharon Remez	2004–7	Zvi Heifetz
1970–73	Michael Comay	2007–11	Ron Prosor
1974–77	Gideon Rafael	2011–15	Daniel Taub
1977–79	Abraham Kidron	2016–20	Mark Regev
1979–82	Sholmo Argov	2020–present	Tzipi Hotovely

Israel Legation/Embassy—Labour Attaché

1952–53	Moshe Bar-Tal
1974–77	Benny Shiloh

Israel Labour Party Representative in London

1972–74	Israel Gat

Ministry of Labour—Labour Attaché

1950–58	A. Greenhough
1958–63	A. Gordon Wallis DFC
1964–65	A.G. Read
1966–69	J. Oates
1970–73	Miss E.R. Rylands

TUC—General Secretary

1926–45	Sir Walter Citrine
1946–59	Sir Vincent Tewson
1960–68	George Woodcock
1969–72	Vic Feather
1973–83	Len Murray
1984–92	Norman Willis
1993–2003	John Monks
2003–12	Brendan Barber
2013–current	Frances O'Grady

TUC—Head of International Department

1946–52	Ernest Bell
1952–59	Donald Bowers
1960–79	Alan Hargreaves
1980–99	Michael Walsh (seconded to the Foreign Office 1977–79)
2003–18	Owen Tudor
2019–current	Mariella Kohon, Senior International Officer

Bibliography

Unpublished Sources

International Institute of Social History Archives, Amsterdam

ICFTU series files:

18	95	3510
23	192	3511
24	359a	3513
44	288D	3514
46	1452	3516
63	3501	3517
65	3503	3520
66	3504	3522
69	3506	3289
90	3508	Z047449
93	3509	

ETUC series files:

R. Fraser, *British Trade Unions, the Labour Party, and Israel's Histadrut*, https://doi.org/10.1007/978-3-030-86814-7

1452

WFTU series files:

38	75	202
66	92	392a

Israel State Archives, Jerusalem

Foreign Office Records

G series files:

G 2776/9

HZ series files:

HZ 36/7	HZ 336/8	HZ6740/5
HZ 43/14	HZ 1389/28	
HZ 329/8	HZ 6738/1	

Lavon Archives, Tel Aviv

Histadrut Records

IV series files:

4-11-1947-9A
4-11-1952-10B
IV 104-39-3-8
IV 104-49-1-28
IV-104-49-1-40
IV-104-49-2-44
IV-104-49-2-41
IV-104-49-1-43
IV-104-49-1-44LA
IV-104-71-2-20A
IV-104-286-1-320
IV-104-286-367
IV-104-1296-3
IV-104-1296-5
IV-208-1-3309
IV-208-1-3313
IV-208-18965
IV-208-1-5212
IV-208-1-5213
IV-208-1-5217
IV-208-1-10089
IV-208-1-14407
IV-208-1-5220
IV-208-1-6061
IV-208-1-6063
IV-208-1-3313
IV-208-1-8593
IV-209-4-42
IV-209-4-359
IV-209-4-405
IV-219A-1-14A
IV-219A-1-16B
IV-219A-1-18
IV-219A-1-29C
IV-219A-1-32A
IV-219A-1-32B
IV-219A-1-33A
IV-219A-1-44A
IV-219A-1-106
IV-219A-1-129B
IV-219A-1-142C
IV-219A-1-160C
IV-219A-7-352
IV-219A-2-18B
IV-219A-3-32
IV-219A-3-19A
IV-219A-4-7A
IV-219A-4-7B
IV-219A-4-149
IV-219A-4-149B
IV-219A-3-14
IV-219A-3-15
IV-219A-3-30
IV-219A-3-32
IV-219A-3-33
IV-219A-3-41
IV-219A-3-47
IV-219A-5-1
IV-219A-5-17
IV-219A-6-29
IV-219-7-97
IV-219A-7-132
IV-277-4

Histadrut Executive Committee Minutes:
25 June 1947
29 September 1948
11 August 1949
11 May 1950
17 September 1953
4 March 1958
Histadrut Conference Proceedings:
28 May 1949
Council of the Histadrut Proceedings:
28–31 October 1952
21 June 1953

London School of Economics Archives, University of London, London

Levenberg Collection: G/1/2

Modern Record Centre, University of Warwick, Warwick

TUC Collection:
MSS series file:

MSS.159/5/2/124
MSS.292/20/13
MSS.292/20/21
MSS.292/20/27
MSS.292/20/30
MSS.292/20/31
MSS.292/20/32
MSS.292/20/34
MSS.292/24.1/9
MSS.292/900/5
MSS.292/901/1
MSS.292/901/5
MSS292/901/6
MSS.292/901/8
MSS.292/901/12
MSS.292/901/13
MSS.292/901/15
MSS.292B/901/3
MSS.292B/901/4
MSS.292B/901/5
MSS.292B/901/7
MSS.292B/901/9
MSS.292B/901/10
MSS.292B/901/12
MSS.292C/20/31
MSS.292C/918.2/3
MSS.292C/918.2/9
MSS.292C/918.23/2
MSS.292D/901/1
MSS.292D/901/2
MSS.292D/901/3
MSS.292D/901/4
MSS.292D/901/5
MSS.292D/901/6
MSS.292D/901/7
MSS.292D/901/8
MSS.292D/901/9
MSS.292D/901/10
MSS.292D/901/12
MSS.292D/901/15
MSS.292D/901/16
MSS.292D/901/18
MSS.292D/901/21
MSS.292D/901/23
MSS.292/918/2
MSS.292/918/3
MSS.292/956.9/1
MSS.292/956.9/2
MSS.292/956.9/3
MSS.292/956.9/4
MSS.292/956.9/5
MSS.292/956.9/6
MSS.292/956.9/7
MSS.292/956.9/8
MSS.292/956.9/9
MSS.292B/956.9/1
MSS.292B/956.9/2
MSS.292B/956.9/3
MSS.292B/956.9/5
MSS.292D/956/4
MSS.292D/956.9/1
MSS.292D/956.9/2
MSS.292D/956.9/3
MSS.292D/956.9/4
MSS.292D/956.9/5
MSS.292D/956.9/7
MSS.292D/956.9/51
MSS.292D/956/511/1
MSS.292D/956/511/2
MSS.292D/956/511/3
MSS 292D/956/511/4
MSS.292C/956/511/5
MSS.292C/20/31
MSS.292D/20/16
MSS.292C/918/2/9
MSS.292C/918.23/2
MSS.292/156.9/8
MSS.480/4/1/12
MSS.480/4/1/13
TUC/ F-1685

TUC Congress proceedings:
1892–2020

Moshe Sharett Israel Labor Party Archive, Israel

2-024-1943-6
2-024-1945-11

The National Archives: Public Records Office, London

Records of the Foreign Office

FO series files:

FO371/52540
FO371/52541
FO371/64485B
FO371/6761
FO371/67613
FO371/82513
FO371/82526
FO371/82637
FO371/98318
FO371/98785
FO371/98819
FO371/98820
FO371/104733
FO371/104849
FO371/115610
FO371/115610-2
FO371/122384
FO371/158745
FO371/180866
FO921/312
FO1110/199

Records of the Foreign and Commonwealth Office

FCO series files:

FCO17/42
FCO28/1161
FCO95/917
FCO17/343
FCO59/493
FCO59/589
FCO77/20
FCO93/1178
FCO93/704
FCO93/1146
FCO93/1146
FCO93/2365

Records of the Ministry of Labour

LAB13 series files:

LAB13/448
LAB13/449
LAB13/450
LAB13/554
LAB13/1079
LAB13/1080
LAB13/1111
LAB13/1255
LAB13/1129
LAB13/1147
LAB13/1149
LAB13/1181
LAB13/1182
LAB13/1309
LAB13/1352
LAB13/1353
LAB13/1420
LAB13/1503
LAB13/1581
LAB13/1764
LAB13/1852
LAB13/2006
LAB13/2180
LAB13/2215
LAB13/2291
LAB13/2440
LAB13/2445
LAB13/2449
LAB13/2474
LAB13/2559
LAB13/2590
LAB13/2599
LAB13/2625
LAB13/2630
LAB13/2673
LAB13/2680
LAB13/2728
LAB13/2736

Records of the Colonial Office

CO series files:
CO733/438/11
CO859/1512

Records of the Board of Trade

BT series files:
BT 58/1243

Records of the Security Service

KV5 series files:
KV5/16

Records of the Prime Minister's Office

PREM series files:
PREM11/1172
PREM15/1853
PREM16/1815
PREM16/1473
PREM19/295

Records of the Cabinet Office

CAB series files:
CAB 195/15

People' History Museum, Manchester

The Labour Party archive files:

JSM/ZIO/41
JSM/ZIO/42
JSM/ZIO/45
JSM/ZIO/47
JSM/ZIO/48
JSM/ZIO/149
WG/PAL/193
WG/PAL/195
1935-45 Box LP Foreign /defence policy
NCL Minutes Jan 40-Dec 43 (Box 4 136)
International sub-committee of the National Executive, LP-1-110815

TUC Library Records, London Metropolitan University, London

HD series file:
HD 8759
HD 6851
Weizmann Archive, Rehovot
Correspondence

Interviews

Great Britain

Ken Cameron, General Secretary of the FBU, 1980–2000
George Galloway, Secretary of TUFP, 1980–84
Bill Gilby, Vice Chairman of TUFP 1982, Treasurer, 1985–2003
Lady Valerie Cocks, Executive Director of TUFI, 1972–90
Lord Healey, Labour MP 1952–1992 and Government Minister
Tom Jenkin, TUC International Department, 1973–2003
Jack Jones, General Secretary of the TGWU, 1969–78
John Monks, General Secretary of the TUC
Bill Spiers, General Secretary of the Scottish TUC, 1998–2006
Owen Tudor, Head of the TUC International Department, 2003–18
Mike Walsh, Head of TUC International Department, 1980–99
David Warburton, Senior Officer GMB, 1970–95

Europe

Tom Barry Braunthal, Press Secretary for ICFTU, 1957–73
Per Ahlmark, Deputy Prime Minister of Sweden, 1976–78
Tim Noonan, Director Campaigns and Communications, ITUC
John Vanderveken, ICFTU 1951–92, General Secretary, 1982–92

Israel

Areila Andresen, daughter of Reuven Barkatt
Aaron Barnea, Histadrut European representative in Brussels, 1975–80
Avital Shapira, Director of International Relations of the Histadrut, 2000–present

Shmuel Bahat, Deputy Chairman, Histadrut International department, 1974–83
Zipi Divir, International Officer, Israel Teachers Union, 2015–18
Hanan Lehman, Histadrut Labour Attaché in London, 1966–70
Israel Gat, International Secretary of the Israel Labour Party, 1972–2003
Yachov Hadassi, Histadrut European representative in Brussels, 1978–81
Misha Harish, MK 1973–1996, General Secretary of Israel Labour Party, 1989–96
Dolly Gerasi, Histadrut International Department, 1965–95
Nawaf Massalha, MK 1988–2003, Member of the Central Committee of the Histadrut
Meron Medzini, Director, Israel Government Press Office, 1962–78
Benny Shiloh, Labour attaché at Israel Embassy, London, 1974–77
Yehuda Paz, Director 1980–97, Histadrut Afro-Asian Institute
Kobi Sharett, son of Moshe Sharett, second Prime Minister of Israel
Victor Shemtov, MK 1969–1988, General Secretary of Mapam, 1979–85
Aaron Yadlin, MK 1959–81, General Secretary of Israel Labour Party

Published Sources

Diaries and Memoirs

Attlee, Clement, *As it Happened* (London: Heinemann, 1954).
Ben-Gurion, David, *Israel a Personal Story* (London: NEL, 1972).
Benn, Tony, *Years of hope: diaries, papers and letters 1940–62* (London: Arrow Books, 1995).
Crossman, Richard, *Palestine Mission* (London: Harper, 1947).
Crossman, Richard, *The Diaries of a Cabinet Minister Vol. 1 Minister of Housing, 1964–66* (London: Hamilton: Cape, 1975).
Crossman, Richard, *The Diaries of a Cabinet Minister Vol. 2, Lord President of the Council and Leader of the House of Commons, 1966–68* (London: Cape, 1976).
Crossman, Richard, *The Diaries of a Cabinet Minister Vol. 3, Secretary of State for Social Services, 1968–70* (London: Cape, 1977).
Catterall, Peter, ed., *The Macmillan Diaries, 1951–57* (London: Macmillan, 2003).
Citrine, Lord, *Men and Work* (London: Hutchinson, 1964).
Citrine, Lord, *Two Careers* (London: Hutchinson, 1967).
Dalton, Hugh Dalton, Baron, *The political diary of Hugh Dalton, 1918–40, 1945–60* (London: Cape in association with the London School of Economics and Political Science, 1986).
Dalton, Hugh, *Fateful Years* (London: Muller, 1957).
Dalton, Hugh, *High Tide and After* (London: Muller, 1962).
Goren, Z., *Dov Hos – A Pre-State Statesman* (Ramat Efal: Yad Tabenkin, 1999).

Healey, Denis, *The Time of My Life* (London: Michael Joseph, 1989).
Heath, Edward, *Course of my life* (London: Hodder and Stoughton, 1998).
Jones, Jack, *Union man: the autobiography of Jack Jones* (London: Collins, 1986).
Macmillan, Harold, *The Tides of Fortune* (London: Macmillan, 1969).
Macmillan, Harold, *Riding the Storm, 1956–59* (London: Macmillan, 1971).
Manor, Ehud, *Berl Locker: A Zionist Diplomat, Socialist and Optimist* (Jerusalem: Hasifria Hatzionit, 2010).
Morgan, Janet, ed., *The Backbench Diaries of Richard Crossman* (London: Hamilton: Cape, 1981).
Nutting, Anthony, *No End of a Lesson; the story of Suez* (London: Constable, 1967).
Pearce, Robert, ed., *Patrick Gordon Walker: political diaries 1932–1971* (London: Historians' Press, 1991).
Shuckburgh, Evelyn, *Descent to Suez, Diaries 1951–56* (London: Weidenfeld, 1986).
Stewart, Michael, *Life and Labour: an autobiography* (London: Sidgwick & Jackson, 1980).
Williams, Philip, ed., *The Diary of Hugh Gaitskell, 1945–1956* (London: Cape, 1983).
Wilson, Harold, *Chariot of Israel: Britain, America and the State of Israel* (London: Weidenfeld and Nicolson, 1989).

Collections of Documents

Medzini, Meron, ed., *Israel's Foreign Relations: Selected Documents 1947–1974* (Jerusalem: Ministry of Foreign Affairs, 1976). 1946).
McIntosh, John and Ireland S., *Report of the World Trade Union conference, London, February 6th to 17th, 1945* (London: TUC, 1945).
Report of the Anglo American Committee of Enquiry regarding the problems of European Jewry and Palestine (London: HMSO, 1946).
The Labour Party Foundation Conference and Annual Conference Reports 1900–1905 (London: Hammersmith Bookshop, 1967).
TUC Congress reports: 1892–2018.

Newspapers and Periodicals

Daily Herald
Daily Telegraph
The Economist
Haaretz
Jerusalem Post
Jewish Chronicle
Jewish News

Jewish Vanguard
Labour Herald
Labour Weekly
New Statesman
New York Times
Observer
Palestine Post
Palestine Report
The Financial Times
The Guardian
The Independent
The News Line
The New York Times
The Times
The Times of Israel
The Washington Daily News
Tribune

Pamphlets

AFL-CIO news
Free Palestine Journal, 1969–1973
Labour Friends of Israel, 'Israel and the Left' (1970)
Labour Friends of Israel, 'Labour Looks at Israel 1967–1971' (1972)
Labour Friends of Israel, '50 Eventful Years: Poale Zion Affiliation to the Labour Party 1920–1970'
Middle East Research Group and UKPC, 'Palestinian Workers and Trade Unions,' 1980
Bert Ramelson, 'The Middle East, crisis causes, solution', The CPGB, 1967
TUFP Newsletters, No: 1–3 June 1982–March 1983
TUFP 'Facts about the Histadrut,' August 1984

Journal Articles and Book Chapters

Nathan Abrams, 'Jute, Journalism, Jam and Jews: the anomalous survival of the Dundee Hebrew Congregation,' *Northern Scotland*, Vol. 3, No. 1 (May 2012), pp. 86–97.
Anthony Adamthwaite, 'Suez Revisited', *International Affairs*, Vol. 64, No. 3 (Summer, 1988), pp. 449–464.
Anthony Adamthwaite, 'Suez Revisited', in *British Foreign Policy 1945–56*, edited by Michael Dockrill and John Young (London: Macmillan, 1989), pp. 225–245.

Yves Beigbeder, 'The United States' Withdrawal from the International Labor Organization,' *Industrial Relations*, Vol. 34, No. 2 (1979), pp. 223–240.

Cecil Bloom, 'The Politics of Immigration, 1881–1905', *Jewish Historical Studies, Transactions of the Jewish Historical Society Volume 33 (1992–94)* (London: Jewish Historical Society, 1995).

Cecil Bloom, 'The British Labour Party and Palestine 1917–1948,' *Transactions of the Jewish Historical Society of England*, Vol. 36 (2001), pp. 141–172.

Peter Brod, 'Soviet-Israeli Relations 1948–56', in *The Left against Zion*, edited by Robert Wistrich (London: Valentine Mitchell, 1979), pp. 50–70.

Brookshire, Jerry, 'The National Council of Labour, 1921–1946', *Albion: A Quarterly Journal Concerned with British Studies*, Vol. 18, No. 1 (Spring, 1986), pp. 43–69.

Anthony Carew, 'The Schism within the World Federation of Trade Unions: Government and Trade Union Diplomacy', *The International Review of Social History*, Vol. XX1X (1984), pp. 297–335.

Anthony Carew, 'The American Labor Movement in Fizzland: the Free Trade Union Committee and the CIA', *Labour History*, Vol. 39 (1998), pp. 25–42.

Anthony Carew, 'Conflict within the ICFTU: Anti-Communism and Anti-Colonialism in the 1950s', *International Review of Social History*, Vol. 41 (1996), pp. 147–181.

Carew, Anthony, A False Dawn; The WFTU 1945–1949 and Towards a Free Trade Centre: the ICFTU (1949–72) in *The International Confederation of Free Trade Unions* (Berlin: Peter Lang, 2000).

Christine Collette, 'The Utopian Visions of Labour Zionism, British Labour and the Labour and Socialist International in the 1930s', in *Jews, Labour and the Left, 1918–48*, edited by Christine Collette and Stephen Bird (London: Ashgate, 2000), pp. 71–92.

Robert B. Cullen, 'Soviet Jewry', *Foreign Affairs*, Vol. 65, No. 2 (Winter, 1986), pp. 252–266.

June Edmunds, 'The Evolution of British Labour Party Policy on Israel from 1967 to the Intifada', *Twentieth Century British History*, Vol. 11 (2000), pp. 23–41.

Israel Feinstein, 'Jewish Immigration in British Party politics in the 1890s', *Migration and settlement: proceedings of the Anglo-American Jewish Historical Conference* (The Jewish historical Society, 1971).

Ronnie Fraser, 'Fraser versus the University College Union: A Personal Reflection' in *Anti-Zionism on Campus, The University, Free Speech, and BDS*, edited by A. Pessin and D. Ben (Attar: Indiana University Press, 2018).

Johan Franzén, 'Communism versus Zionism: The Comintern, Yishuvism, and the Palestine Communist Party', *Journal of Palestine Studies*, Vol. 36, No. 2 (Winter 2007), pp. 6–24.

Manfred Gerstenfeld, interview with Shimon T. Samuels, 'Antisemitism and Jewish Defense at the United Nations World Summit on Sustainable Development,

2002, Johannesburg, South Africa,' in *Post-Holocaust and Antisemitism*, No. 6, 2 March 2003.

Peter Hahn, 'The influence of organized labor on U.S. policy toward Israel, 1945–1967', in *Empire and revolution: the United States and the Third World since 1945* (Columbus: Ohio State University, 2001), pp. 154–177.

The Institute of Jewish Affairs, 'The Pro-Arab Lobby in Britain', *The Institute of Jewish Affairs Research Reports*, 22 & 23 (1981), 1–18 (pp. 12–13).

Bernard Hennessy, 'Trade Unions and the British Labor Party', *The American Political Science Review*, Vol. 49, No. 4 (Dec., 1955), pp. 1050–1066.

Jason Heppell, 'A Question of 'Jewish Politics'? The Jewish Section of the Communist Party of Great Britain, 1936–45,' in *Jews, Labour and the Left, 1918–48*, edited by Christine Collette and Stephen Bird (London: Ashgate, 2000), pp. 93–121.

Paul Keleman, 'Zionism and the British Labour party 1917–1939', *Social History*, Vol. 21, No. 1 (1990), pp. 71–87.

Jon Kimche, 'British Labour's turnabout on Zionism', *Commentary* (1947), pp. 512–517.

Thomas A. Koelble, 'Trade Unionists, Party Activists, and Politician: The Struggle for Power over Party Rules in the British Labour party and the West German Social Democratic Party', *Comparative Politics*, Vol. 19 (1987), pp. 253–286.

Gerd Koram, 'New Politics for an American Labor leader: Sidney Hillman, 1942–46', *American Jewish History* (1994), pp. 195–213.

Mordechai E. Kreinin, 'Israel and the European Economic Community', *The Quarterly Journal of Economics*, Vol. 82, No. 2 (May, 1968), pp. 297–312.

Tony Kushner, 'Jewish Communists in Twentieth-century Britain: the Zaidman collection,' *Labour History Review*, Vol. 55 (1989), pp. 66–75.

Tony Kushner, Antisemitism and Austerity; the August riots in Britain in Panikos Panayi, ed., *Racial Violence in Britain 1840–1950* (Leicester: Leicester University Press, 1993), pp. 149–168.

Denis MacShane, *British Unions in Europe in Trade Unions in British Politics: the first 250 years* (London: Longman, 1991).

Lewis Minkin, 'The British Labour Party and the Trade Unions: Crisis and Compact', *Industrial and Labor Relations Review*, Vol. 28, No. 1 (Oct., 1974), pp. 7–37.

Obituary: 'Reuven Barkatt (1906–1972)', *Socialist Affairs*, Vol. xxii, No. 5 (May 1972), pp. 103–104.

Ritchie Ovendale, 'The Palestine Policy of the British Labour Government 1945–1946', *International Affairs*, Vol. 55, No. 3 (1979), pp. 409–431.

Ritchie Ovendale, 'The Palestine Policy of the British Labour Government 1947: The Decision to Withdraw', *International Affairs*, Vol. 56, No. 1 (1980), pp. 73–79.

Jill Pellew, 'Communication: the Home Office and the Aliens act 1905', *Historical Journal*, Vol. 32, No. 2 (1989), pp. 369–385.

Yoram Peri, 'The fall from favour: Israel and the Socialist International', *Institute of Jewish Affairs research report*, 21 and 22, 1980.

George Perkovich, 'Soviet Jewry and American Foreign' Policy, *World Policy Journal*, Vol. 5, No. 3 (Summer, 1988), pp. 435–467.

R. Rein, 'Echoes of the Spanish Civil War in Palestine: Zionists, Communists and the Contemporary Press', *Journal of Contemporary History*, Vol. 43, No. 1 (2008), pp. 9–23.

Jonathan Schneer, 'Hopes Deferred or Shattered: The British Labour Left and the Third Force Movement, 1945–49', *The Journal of Modern History*, Vol. 56, No. 2 (June, 1984), pp. 198–226.

Avi Shlaim, 'Britain and the Arab Israeli war of 1948', in *British Foreign Policy 1945–56*, edited by Michael Dockrill and John Young (London: Macmillan, 1989), pp. 77–100.

Gideon Shimoni, 'Poale Zion: A Zionist Transplant in Britain (1905–1945)', in *Studies in Contemporary Jewry* Vol. 2, edited by Peter Y. Medding (Bloomington: Indiana University Press, 1986), pp. 227–268.

Nick Thomas, *University of Nottingham* 'Challenging Myths of the1960s: The Case of Student Protest in Britain', in *Twentieth Century British History*, Vol. 13, No. 3 (2002), pp. 277–297.

Shmuel Tzabag, 'Co-operation in the Shadow of a Power Struggle: Israel: The Likud Governments and the Histadrut 1977–84', *Middle Eastern Studies*, Vol. 31, No. 4, Israel (Oct., 1995), pp. 849–888.

Peter Weiler, 'British Labour and the Cold war: foreign policy of the Labour Government 1945–51', *British Studies*, Vol. 26, No. 1 (1987), pp. 54–82.

John P. Windmuller, 'The Stockholm Congress of the ICFTU', *Industrial and Labor Relations Review*, Vol. 7, No. 3 (Apr., 1954), pp. 434–443.

John P. Windmuller, 'Cohesion and Disunity in the ICFTU: The 1965 Amsterdam Congress', *Industrial and Labor Relations Review*, Vol. 19, No. 3 (Apr., 1966), pp. 348–367.

Chris Wrigley, 'Now you see it now you don't, Wilson's foreign policy' in *The Wilson Governments*, edited by Coopey, Fielding and Tiratsoo (London: Pinter, 1993), pp. 123–135.

Secondary Sources

Alderman, Geoffrey, *The Jewish Community in British Politics* (Oxford: Oxford University Press, 1983).

Alderman, Geoffrey, *London Jews and London Politics, 1889–1986* (London: Routledge, 1984).

Alderman, Geoffrey, *Modern British Jewry* (Oxford: Clarendon Press, 1998).

Allen V.L., *Trade Union Leadership* (London: Longmans, 1957).
Andrew, Christopher, *The defence of the realm: the authorized history of MI5* (London: Allen Lane, 2009).
Aronoff, Myron J., *Power and Ritual in the Israel Labor Party* (Armonk: Sharpe, 1993).
Bailer, Uri, *Between East and West: Israel's foreign policy orientation 1948–1956* (Cambridge: Cambridge University Press, 1990).
Bard, Mitchell G., *Myths and Facts a guide to the Arab – Israeli Conflict* (Chevy Chase: American Israeli Cooperative Enterprise, 2002).
Bar-Zohar, Michael, *Ben Gurion a Biography* (New York: Delacorte Press, 1978).
Beckett, Francis, *Enemy Within: The Rise and Fall of the British Communist Party* (London: John Murray, 1995).
Board of Deputies of British Jews, *The Aliens Bill 1905* (London, 1905).
Bregman, Ahron, *A History of Israel* (Basingstoke: Palgrave Books, 2002).
British Labour Policy on Palestine: a collection of documents, speeches and articles, 1917–1938 (London: Poale Zion, 1938).
Brivati, Brian, *Hugh Gaitskell* (London: Richard Cohen, 1996).
Bullock, Alan, *The life and times of Ernest Bevin 1881–1940* (London: Heinemann, 1983).
Bullock, Alan, *Ernest Bevin Foreign Secretary 1945–1951* (London: Heinemann, 1983).
Buwalda, Petrus, *They did not dwell alone: Jewish emigration from the Soviet Union, 1967–1990* (Washington: Johns Hopkins University Press, 1997).
Burridge, Trevor, *Clement Attlee: a political biography* (London: Cape, 1985).
Campbell, Alan, Fishman, Nina, and McIlroy, John, eds., *British trade unions and industrial politics 64 – Vol. 2. The high tide of trade unionism, 1964–79* (Aldershot: Ashgate, 1999).
Campbell, John, *Edward Heath: a biography* (London: Jonathan Cape, 1993).
Carlton, David, *Britain and the Suez Crisis* (Oxford: Blackwell, 1988).
Castle, Barbara, *The Castle Diaries* (London: Weidenfeld and Nicolson, 1984).
Cesarani, David, ed., *The making of Modern Anglo-Jewry* (Oxford: Basil Blackwell, 1990).
Cesarani, David, *The Jewish Chronicle and Anglo-Jewry, 1841–1991* (Cambridge: Cambridge University Press, 1994).
Cesarani, David, *The Left and the Jews The Jews and the Left* (London: Profile Books, 2004).
Chan, Stephen, *The Commonwealth in World Politics 1965–1985* (London: Lester Crook, 1988).
Clegg, H., *A History of Trade Unions since 1889, Vol. 3, 1939–1951* (Oxford: OUP, 1994).
Chill, Dan, *The Arab boycott of Israel* (New York: Praeger, 1976).
Citrine, Lord, *Two Careers* (London: Hutchinson, 1967).

Cohen, Michael J., *Palestine and the Great Powers 1945–1948* (Princeton: Princeton University Press, 1982).

Cohen, Michael J., *Palestine to Israel from mandate to independence* (London: Frank Cass, 1988).

Corthorn, Paul and Davis, Jonathan, eds., *The British Labour Party and the wider world: domestic politics, internationalism and foreign policy* (London: Tauris Academic Studies, 2008).

Crossman, Richard, *A Nation Reborn* (London: Hamish Hamilton, 1960).

Daniel, A., *Labor Enterprises in Israel: The Institutional Economy, Volume 2* (New Jersey: Transaction, 1976).

Defries, Harry, *Conservative Party Attitudes to Jews 1900–1950* (London: Frank Cass, 2001).

Dockrill, Michael and Young, John, eds., *British Foreign Policy 1945–56* (London: Macmillan, 1989).

Donoughue, Bernard, *Herbert Morrison: portrait of a politician* (London: Weidenfeld and Nicolson, 1973).

Eban, Abba, *Personal Witness Israel through My Eyes* (New York: Putnam, 1992).

Edmunds, June, *The Left and Israel, party policy change and internal democracy* (London: Macmillan, 2000).

Epstein, Leon, D., *British Politics in the Suez crisis* (Urbana: University of Illinois, 1964).

Emanuel, Charles Herbert Lewis, *A century and a half of Jewish history extracted from the minute books of the London Committee of Deputies of the British Jews* (London: Routledge, 1910).

Endelman, Todd M., *The Jews of Britain, 1656 to 2000* (Berkeley, Calif.: University of California Press, 2002).

Feiler, Gil, *From Boycott to economic Cooperation: the political economy of the Arab boycott of Israel* (London: Frank Cass, 1998).

Feldman, David, *Englishmen and Jews social relations and political culture 1840–1914* (New Haven: Yale University Press, 1994).

Foot, Michael, *Aneurin Bevan Vol. 2 (1945–1960)* (London: Granada, 1975).

Foote, Geoffrey, *The Labour Party's Political Thought: A History* (Basingstoke: Macmillan Press, 1997).

Fraser, Ronald, *1968: a student generation in revolt* (London: Chatto & Windus, 1988).

Frankel, Joseph, *British Foreign Policy 1945–73* (London: Oxford University Press, 1975).

Freidman, Isaiah, *The Question of Palestine British Jewish-Arab relations: 1914–1918* (New Jersey: Transaction Publishers, 1992).

Friso, Enzo, *Occupation: international trade unionist: struggling for justice in a global world* (Brussels: ETUI, 2001).

Gartner, Lloyd, *The Jewish immigrant in England 1870–1914* (London: Simon Publications, 1973).

Gerlis, Daphne, *Those Wonderful Women in Black* (London: Minerva Press, 1996).

Goodman, Geoffrey, *The Awkward Warrior; Frank Cousins: His Life and Times* (London: Davis–Poynter, 1979).

Gordon, Michael R., *Conflict and Consensus in Britain's Foreign Policy 1914–65* (Stanford: Stanford University Press, 1969).

Gorny, Joseph, *The British labour movement and Zionism 1917–1948* (London: Frank Cass, 1983).

Gupta, Partha, Sarathi, *Imperialism and the British labour movement 1914–64* (London: Macmillan, 1975).

Harris, Kenneth, *Attlee* (London: Weidenfeld and Nicolson, 1982).

Harrison, Martin, *Trade Unions and the Labour Party since 1945* (London: George Allen, 1960).

Heinlein, Frank, *British government policy and decolonisation 1945–63* (London: Frank Cass, 2002).

Hertzberg, Arthur, *The Zionist Idea: A Historical Analysis and Reader* (Philadelphia: The Jewish Publication Society, 1997).

Hinton, James, *Labour and Socialism: a history of the British labour movement 1867–1974* (Brighton: Wheatsheaf Books, 1983).

Holmes, Colin, *Antisemitism in British Society 1876–1939* (London: Edward Arnold, 1979).

Holmes, Colin, *John Bull's island immigration and British society, 1871–1971* (Basingstoke: Macmillan, 1988).

Horne, Alistair, *Macmillan* (London: Macmillan, 2008).

Howard, Adam, *Sewing the Fabric of Statehood* (Urbana: University of Illinois, 2017).

Howard, Anthony, *RAB: the life of R A Butler* (London: Cape, 1987).

Howe, Stephen, *Anticolonialism in British politics* (Oxford: Clarendon, 1993).

Hyam, Ronald, *Britain's Declining Empire: The Road to Decolonisation, 1918–1968* (Cambridge; Cambridge University Press, 2006).

Judt, Tony, *Postwar: a history of Europe since 1945* (London: William Heinemann, 2005).

Kavanagh, Dennis, ed., *The Politics of the Labour Party* (London: Allen & Unwin, 1982).

Kelemen, Paul, *The British Left and Zionism History of a divorce* (Manchester: Manchester University, 2012).

Kelly, Saul, ed., *Whitehall and the Suez Crisis* (London: Frank Cass, 2000).

Kochan, Lionel, ed., *The Jews in Soviet Russia since 1917* (London: Oxford University Press, 1972).

Kurland, Samuel, *Cooperative Palestine; the story of the Histadrut* (New York: Sharon Books, 1947).

Kushner, Tony, *The Holocaust and the Liberal Imagination* (Oxford: Blackwell, 1994).
Kyle, Keith, *Suez* (London: Weidenfeld, 1991).
Lamb, Richard, *The failure of the Eden government* (London: Sedgwick and Jackson, 1987).
Lamb, Richard, *The Macmillan Years 1957–1963* (London: John Murray, 1995).
Laqueur, Walter, *A History of Zionism* (New York: Schocken Books, 1972).
Laybourn, Keith, *The rise of socialism in Britain c. 1881–1951* (Stroud: Sutton, 1997).
Laybourn, Keith and Murphy, Dylan, *Under the red flag: the history of communism in Britain, c. 1849–1991* (Stroud: Sutton, 1999).
Levenberg, S., *The Jews and Palestine: a Study in Labour Zionism* (London: Poale Zion, 1945).
Lipman V.D., *Social History of the Jews in England 1850–1950* (London: Watts and Co, 1954).
Lloyd, Selwyn, *Suez 1956* (London: Cape, 1978).
Lochery, Neill, *Loaded Dice; The Foreign Office and Israel* (Continuum: London, 2007).
Lockman, Zachary, *Comrades and Enemies Arab and Jewish workers in Palestine 1906–1948* (London: University of California, 1996).
Louis, William Roger, *The British Empire in the Middle East 1945–1951* (Oxford: Clarendon Press, 1984).
Lovell, John and Roberts B.C., *A Short History of the TUC* (London: Macmillan, 1980).
Lucas, Noah, *The Modern History of Israel* (New York: Praeger Publishers, 1975).
Peretz Merhav, *The Israeli Left* (San Diego: Barnes and Co, 1980).
J. MacDonald, *Socialist in Palestine* (London: Jewish Socialist Labour Confederation Poale-Zion, 1922).
Martin, Ross M., *TUC: The Growth of a Pressure Group, 1868–1976* (Oxford: OUP, 1980).
Martin, Ross, *Trade Unionism* (Oxford: Clarendon Press, 1989).
Medding, Peter, Y., *Mupai in Israel: Political Organisation and Government in a New Society* (London: Cambridge University Press, 1972).
Mendes-Flohr, Paul and Reinharz, Jehuda, *The Jew in the Modern World* (New York: OUP, 1995).
Miller, Rory, *Divided against Zion: anti-Zionist opposition in Britain to a Jewish state in Palestine, 1945–1948* (London: Frank Cass, 2000).
Milligan, Stephen, *The new barons: union power in the 1970s* (London: Temple Smith, 1976).
Minkin, Lewis, *The Labour Party Conference: a study in the politics of intra-party democracy* (London: Allen Lane, 1978).

Monroe, Elizabeth, *Britain's Moment in the Middle East* (London: Chatto and Windus, 1981).

Morgan, Kenneth O., *Labour in power: 1945–1951* (Oxford: OUP, 1984).

Morgan, Kenneth O., *Labour people: leaders and lieutenants, Hardie to Kinnock* (Oxford: Oxford University Press, 1992).

Morgan, Kenneth O., *Callaghan: a life* (New York: Oxford University Press, 1997).

Morris, Benny, *Righteous Victims a History of the Zionist-Arab Conflict 1881–2000* (New York: Vintage Books, 2001).

Morris, Benny, *1948; a History of the first Arab-Israeli war* (New Haven: Yale University Press, 2008).

Muenzner Gerhard, *Jewish Labour Economy in Palestine* (London: Victor Gollancz, 1945).

Nicholson, Marjorie, *The TUC Overseas, the Roots of Policy* (London: Allen and Unwin, 1986).

Ovendale, Ritchie, *The Middle East since 1914* (Harlow: Longman, 1992).

Ovendale, Ritchie, *The origins of the Arab-Israeli wars* (London: Pearson, 2004).

Ovendale, Ritchie, *Britain, the United States and the end of the Palestine Mandate, Governments* (Woodbridge: The Royal Historical Society, 1989).

Ovendale, Ritchie, *The Foreign Policy of the British Labour Governments 1945–51* (Leicester: Leicester University Press, 1961).

Pappe, Ilan, *The making of the Arab-Israeli Conflict 1947–51* (London: Tauris, 2001).

Pearce, Edward, *Denis Healey: a life in our times* (London: Little, Brown, 2002).

Pelling, Henry, *A History of British Trade Unionism* (London: Macmillan, 1976).

Pelling, Henry, *The British Communist Party: A Historical Profile* (London: A. and C. Black, 1975).

Pelling, Henry, *The Labour Governments 1945–51* (London: Macmillan, 1984).

Pimlott, Ben, *Hugh Dalton* (London: Cape, 1985).

Pimlott, Ben, *Harold Wilson* (London: Harper Collins, 1993).

Pimlott, Ben, ed., *Trade Unions in British Politics: the first 250 years* (London: Longman, 1991).

Pinkus, Benjamin, *The Jews of the Soviet Union: the history of a national minority* (Cambridge: Cambridge University Press, 1987).

Pomfret, Richard W.T. and Toren, Benjamin, *Israel and the European Common Market: an appraisal of the 1975 free trade agreement* (Tübingen: Mohr, 1980).

Polakow-Suransky, Sasha, *The unspoken alliance: Israel's secret relationship with apartheid South Africa* (New York: Pantheon Books, 2010).

Prittie, Terence and Nelson, Walter Henry, *The economic war against the Jews* (New York: Random House, 1977).

Revusky, Abraham, *Jews in Palestine* (New York: Vanguard Press, 1945).

Rolef, Susan, Hattis, *Israel's Anti-Boycott Policy* (Jerusalem: The Leonard Davis Institute for International relations, 1989).

Rubinstein, W.D., *The Left the Right and the Jews* (Beckenham: Croom Helm, 1982).
Sachar, Howard, *A History of Israel: from the Rise of Zionism to our time* (New York: Knopf, 2008).
Sandbrook, Dominic, *Never had it so good: a history of Britain from Suez to the Beatles* (London: Little, Brown, 2005).
Sandbrook, Dominic, *White Heat: a history of Britain in the swinging sixties* (London: Little, Brown, 2006).
Saville, John, *The Politics of Continuity: British Foreign Policy and the Labour Government, 1945–46* (London: Verso, 1993).
Segev, Tom, 1967, *Israel, the war and the year that transformed the Middle East* (London: Little, Brown, 2007).
Seyd, Patrick, *The Rise and Fall of the Labour Left* (Basingstoke: Macmillan Education, 1987).
Shlaim, Avi, *The Iron Wall Israel and the Arab world* (London: Penguin Books, 2000).
Sheffer, Gabriel, *Moshe Sharett: biography of a political moderate* (Oxford: Clarendon Press, 1996).
Shimoni, Gideon. 'Poale Zion: A Zionist Transplant in Britain (1905–1945)', in *Studies in Contemporary Jewry*, edited by Peter Y. Medding, Vol. 2 (Bloomington: Indiana University Press, 1986), pp. 227–268.
Shindler, Colin, *The Land Beyond Promise, Israel, Likud and the Zionist dream* (London: Tauris, 2002).
Shindler, Colin, *A History of Modern Israel* (Cambridge: Cambridge University Press, 2008).
Shindler, Colin, *Israel and the European Left between Solidarity and Delegitimisation* (New York: Continuum, 2012).
Seifert, Roger and Sibley, Tom, *Revolutionary communist at work: a political biography of Bert Ramelson* (London: Lawrence & Wishart, 2012).
Slowe, Peter, *Manny Shinwell* (London: Pluto Press, 1993).
Srebrnik, Henry, *London Jews and British communism, 1935–1945* (Or: Valentine Mitchell, 1995).
Taylor, Robert, *The fifth estate: Britain's unions in the modern world* (London: Routledge and Kegan Paul, 1978).
Taylor, Robert, *The Trade Union Question in British Politics; Government and the Unions since 1945* (Oxford: Blackwell, 1993).
Taylor, Robert, *The TUC from the General Strike to New Unionism* (Basingstoke: Palgrave, 2000).
Tessler, Mark, *A History of the Israeli-Palestinian Conflict* (Bloomington: Indiana University Press, 1994).
Teveth, Shabtai, *Ben Gurion: The Burning Ground 1886–1948* (London: Robert Hale, 1987).

The report of the First British Commonwealth Labour Conference, 1925 (London, Trades Union Congress and the Labour Party, 1925).

Vickers, Rhiannon, *The Labour Party and the world Vol. 1 The evolution of Labour's foreign policy, 1900–51* (Manchester: Manchester University Press, 2003).

Vickers, Rhiannon, *The Labour Party and the world Vol. 2 Labour's foreign policy since1951* (Manchester: Manchester University Press, 2011).

Vital, David, *A People Apart; A Political History of the Jews in Europe 1789–1939* (Oxford: OUP, 1999).

Wedin, Ake, *International Trade Union Solidarity, ICFTU 1957–1965* (Stockholm: Prisma, 1974).

Wendehorst, Stephan E.C., *British Jewry, Zionism, and the Jewish State, 1936–1956* (Oxford: Oxford University Press, 2012).

Williams, Francis, *Twilight of Empire: memoirs of Prime Minister Clement Attlee* (Westport, Conn: Greenwood Press, 1978).

Williams, Francis, *Ernest Bevin* (London: Hutchinson, 1952).

Williams, Philip M., *Hugh Gaitskell: a political biography* (London: Cape, 1979).

Windmuller, John, *American Labor and the International Labor Movement 1940 to 1953* (Ithaca New York: Cornell University, 1954).

Windmuller, John, *The International Trade Union Movement* (Deventer: Kluwer, 1980).

Young, John W., *The Labour Governments 1964–70, Volume 2: International Policy* (Manchester: Manchester University Press, 2003).

Theses

Portner, Z.D., 'The British Labour Party and Israel 1945–1995' (unpublished LLB (Hons) thesis, University of Greenwich, 1995).

Sargent, A., 'The British Labour Party and Palestine 1917–1949' (unpublished Doctor of Philosophy thesis, University of Nottingham, 1980).

Index[1]

[1] Note: Page numbers followed by 'n' refer to notes.

R. Fraser, *British Trade Unions, the Labour Party, and Israel's Histadrut*, https://doi.org/10.1007/978-3-030-86814-7

D

E

J

K

L

The manufacturer's authorised representative in the EU is Springer Nature Customer Service Centre GmbH, Europaplatz 3, 69115 Heidelberg, Germany. If you have any concerns regarding our products, please contact ProductSafety@springernature.com

Printed and bound by CPI Group (UK) Ltd, Croydon, CR0 4YY

22/09/2026

02221066-0011